FLIGHT

VOLUME ONE

Villard • New York

2007 Villard Books Trade Paperback Edition

Compilation copyright © 2004 by Image Comics, Inc.
All contents and characters contained within are ™ and © 2004 by their respective creators.

Published in the United States by Villard Books, an imprint of The Random House Publishing Group, a division of Random House, Inc., New York.

VILLARD and "V" CIRCLED Design are registered trademarks of Random House, Inc.

Grateful acknowledgment is made to Scott McCloud for permission to reprint his essay "The Year that Comics Took Flight." Reprinted by permission of the author.

ISBN 978-0-345-49636-2

Originally published in 2004 by Image Comics, Inc., Berkeley, California. This edition published by arrangement with Flight LLC.

Printed in the United States of America

www.villard.com

9 8 7 6 5 4 3 2

Editor/Art Director: Kazu Kibuishi
Assistant Editors: Kean Soo and Phil Craven
Our Editor at Villard: Chris Schluep

CONTENTS

Air and WAter

by
Enrico
Casarosa

poem
by
Kean
Soo

inspired
by
Antoine
de
Saint-
Exupéry

This quiet stillness
broken by a thundering storm
the roar of the engine
drowns everything out

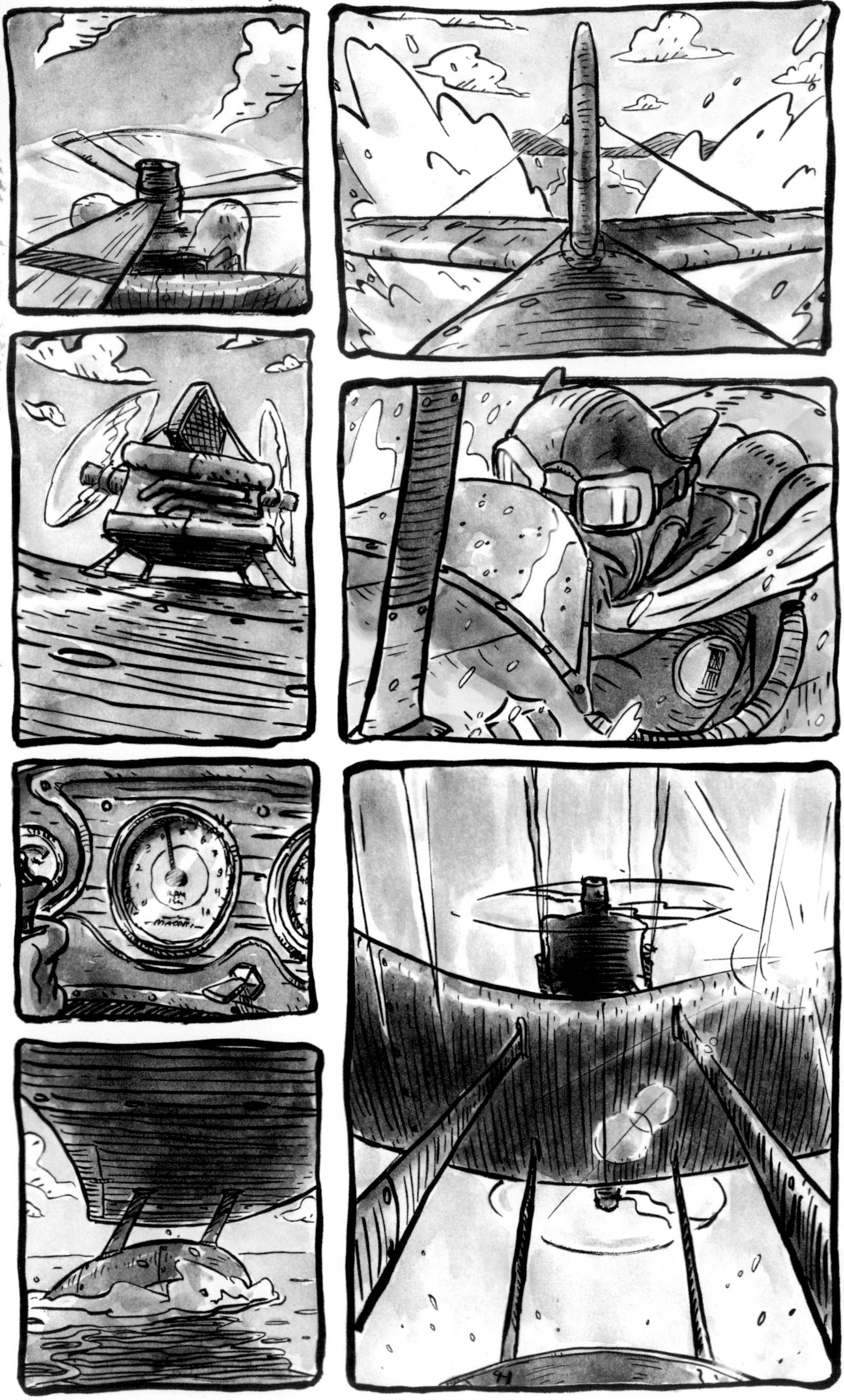

Slicing through the calm surface
the wind cuts into my skin
water arching across my vision

Heart in my throat
watching the needles rise
a shudder runs through me
the moment is ripe

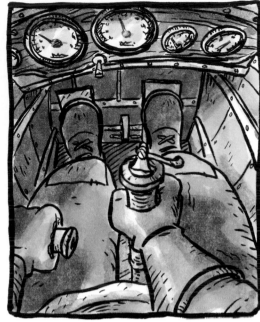

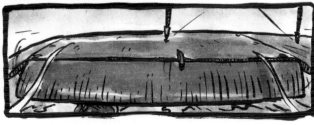

My grip tightens
steel feathers respond

and the sound fades
the world falls away ...

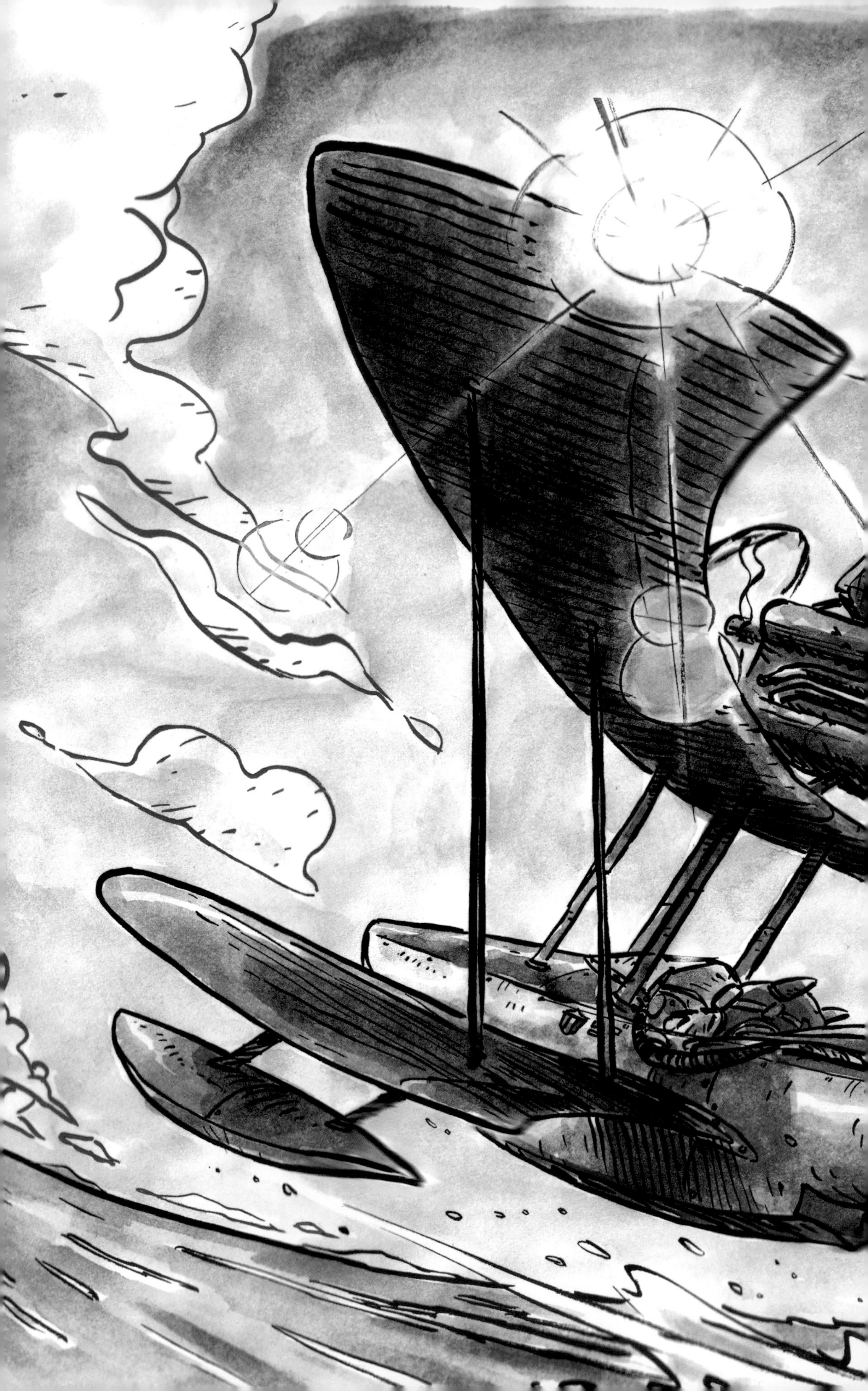

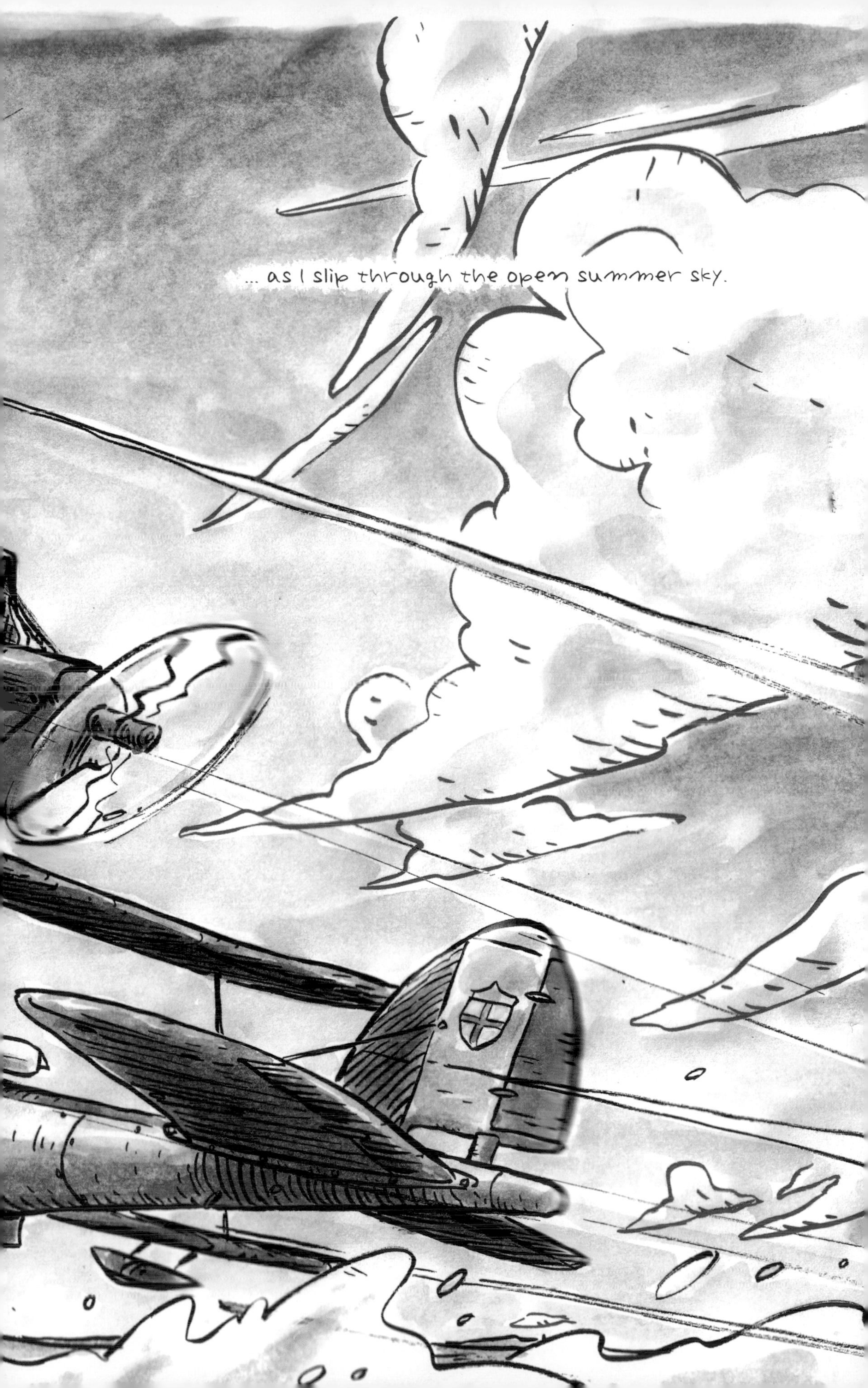
... as I slip through the open summer sky.

"Maiden Voyage," by Kazu Kibuishi

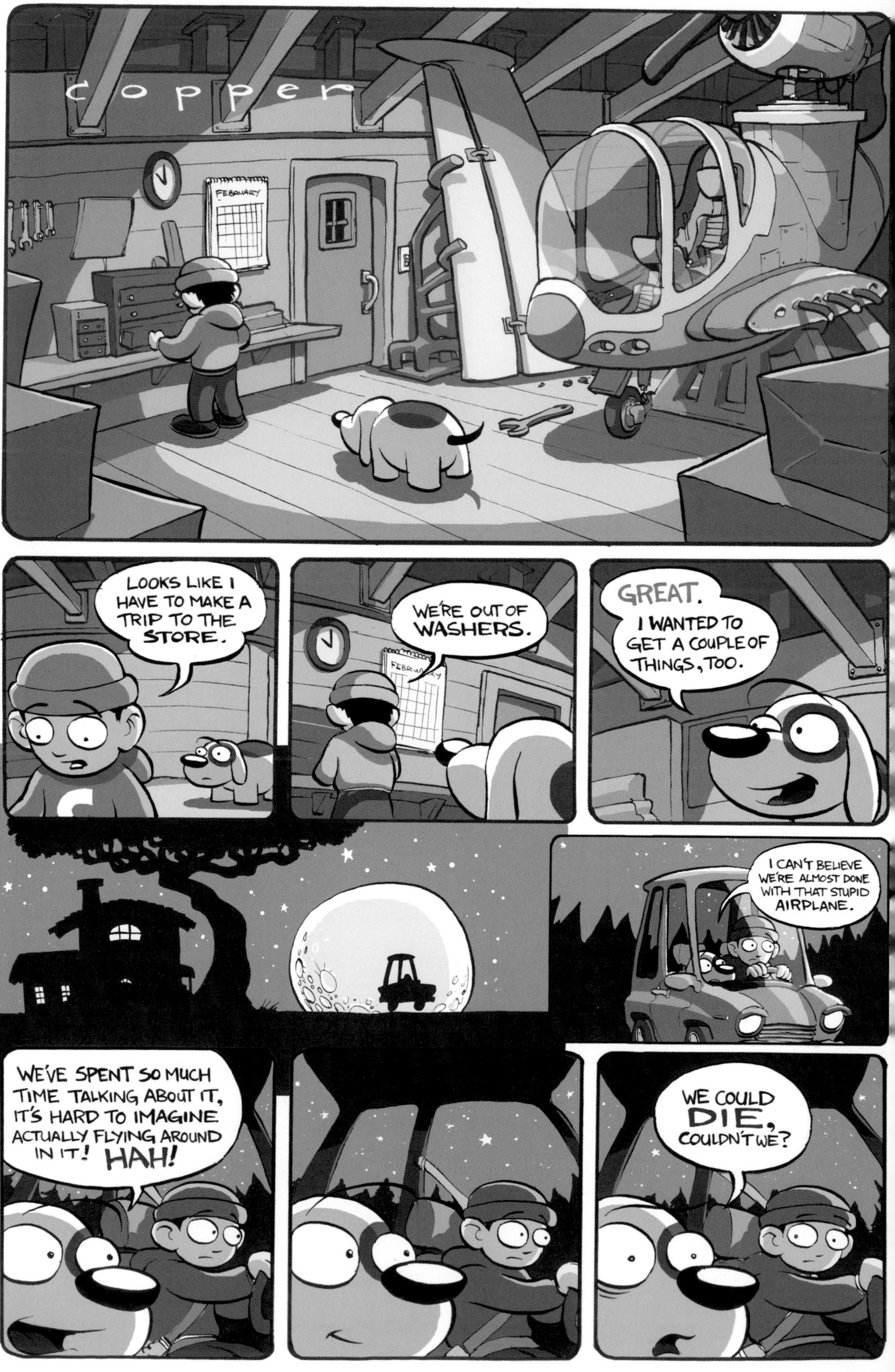
copper
FEBRUARY
LOOKS LIKE I HAVE TO MAKE A TRIP TO THE STORE.
WE'RE OUT OF WASHERS.
FEBRUARY
GREAT. I WANTED TO GET A COUPLE OF THINGS, TOO.
I CAN'T BELIEVE WE'RE ALMOST DONE WITH THAT STUPID AIRPLANE.
WE'VE SPENT SO MUCH TIME TALKING ABOUT IT, IT'S HARD TO IMAGINE ACTUALLY FLYING AROUND IN IT! HAH!
WE COULD DIE, COULDN'T WE?

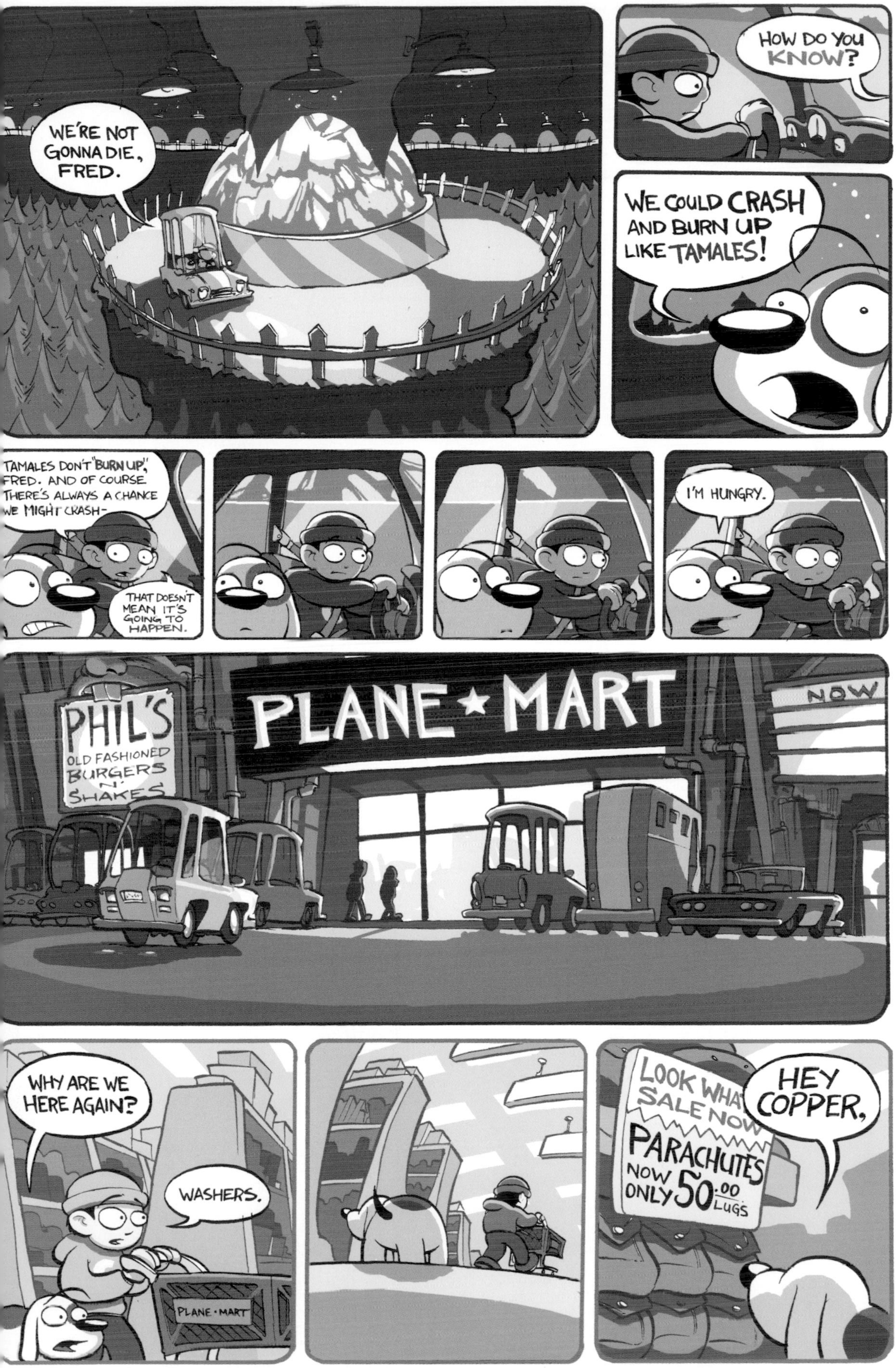
WE'RE NOT GONNA DIE, FRED.
HOW DO YOU KNOW?
WE COULD CRASH AND BURN UP LIKE TAMALES!
TAMALES DON'T "BURN UP," FRED. AND OF COURSE THERE'S ALWAYS A CHANCE WE MIGHT CRASH-
THAT DOESN'T MEAN IT'S GOING TO HAPPEN.
I'M HUNGRY.
PLANE★MART
PHIL'S
OLD FASHIONED
BURGERS N' SHAKES
NOW
WHY ARE WE HERE AGAIN?
WASHERS.
PLANE • MART
LOOK WHAT'S ON SALE NOW
PARACHUTES
NOW ONLY 50.00 LUGS
HEY COPPER,

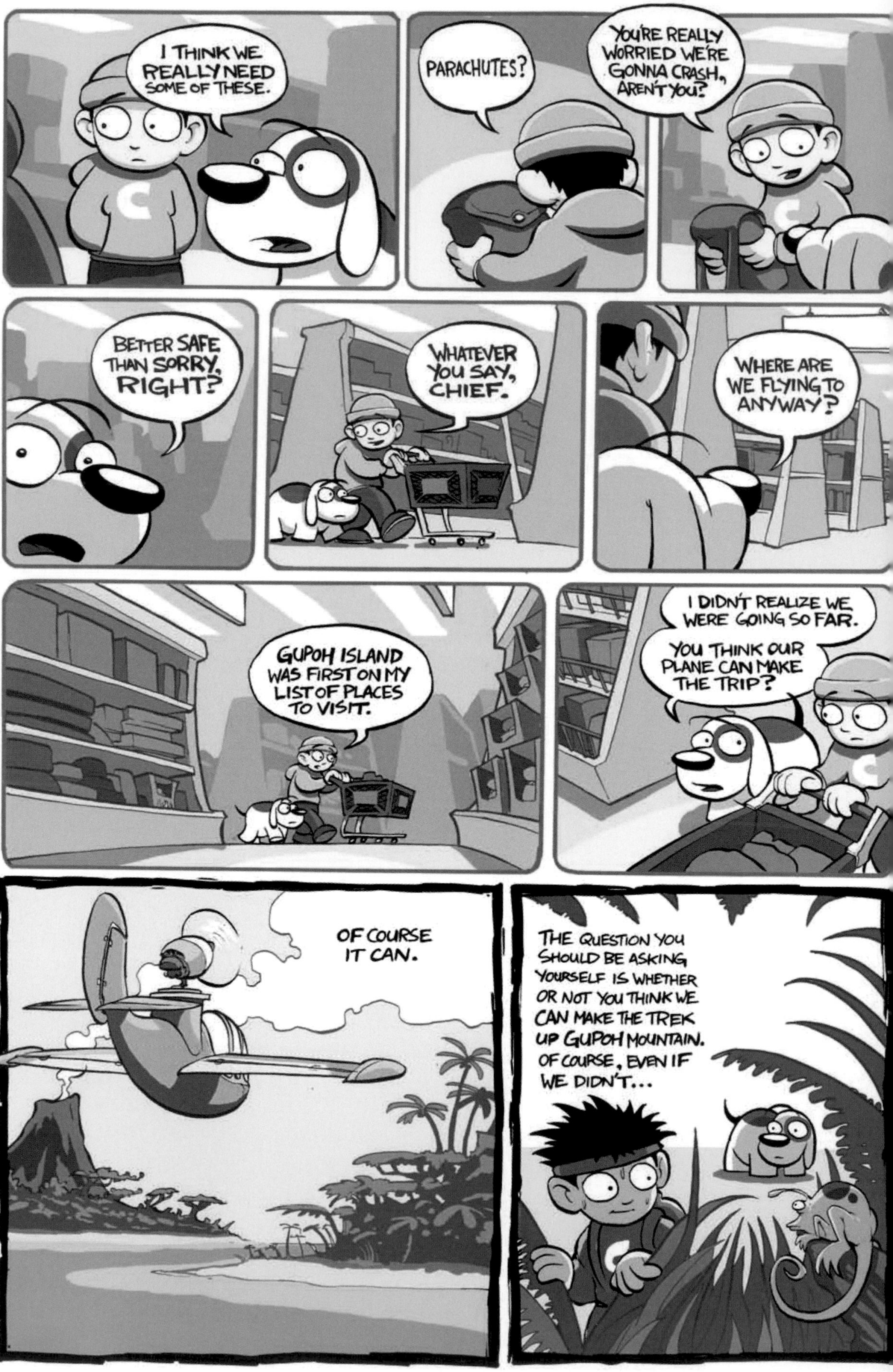
I THINK WE REALLY NEED SOME OF THESE.
PARACHUTES?
YOU'RE REALLY WORRIED WE'RE GONNA CRASH, AREN'T YOU?
BETTER SAFE THAN SORRY, RIGHT?
WHATEVER YOU SAY, CHIEF.
WHERE ARE WE FLYING TO ANYWAY?
GUPOH ISLAND WAS FIRST ON MY LIST OF PLACES TO VISIT.
I DIDN'T REALIZE WE WERE GOING SO FAR.
YOU THINK OUR PLANE CAN MAKE THE TRIP?
OF COURSE IT CAN.
THE QUESTION YOU SHOULD BE ASKING YOURSELF IS WHETHER OR NOT YOU THINK WE CAN MAKE THE TREK UP GUPOH MOUNTAIN. OF COURSE, EVEN IF WE DIDN'T...

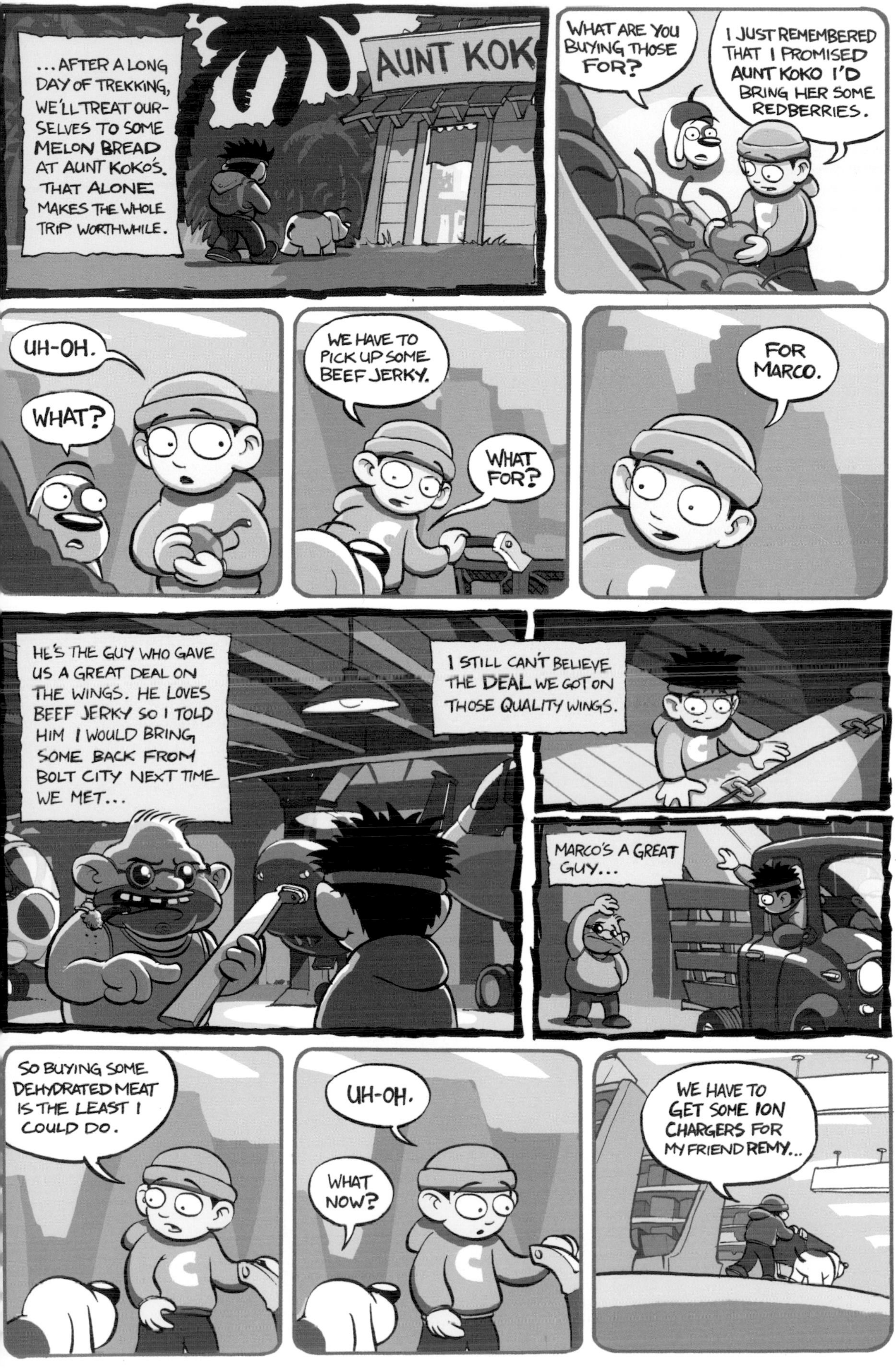
...AFTER A LONG DAY OF TREKKING, WE'LL TREAT OURSELVES TO SOME MELON BREAD AT AUNT KOKO'S. THAT ALONE MAKES THE WHOLE TRIP WORTHWHILE.
AUNT KOK
WHAT ARE YOU BUYING THOSE FOR?
I JUST REMEMBERED THAT I PROMISED AUNT KOKO I'D BRING HER SOME REDBERRIES.
UH-OH.
WHAT?
WE HAVE TO PICK UP SOME BEEF JERKY.
WHAT FOR?
FOR MARCO.
HE'S THE GUY WHO GAVE US A GREAT DEAL ON THE WINGS. HE LOVES BEEF JERKY SO I TOLD HIM I WOULD BRING SOME BACK FROM BOLT CITY NEXT TIME WE MET...
I STILL CAN'T BELIEVE THE DEAL WE GOT ON THOSE QUALITY WINGS.
MARCO'S A GREAT GUY...
SO BUYING SOME DEHYDRATED MEAT IS THE LEAST I COULD DO.
UH-OH.
WHAT NOW?
WE HAVE TO GET SOME ION CHARGERS FOR MY FRIEND REMY...

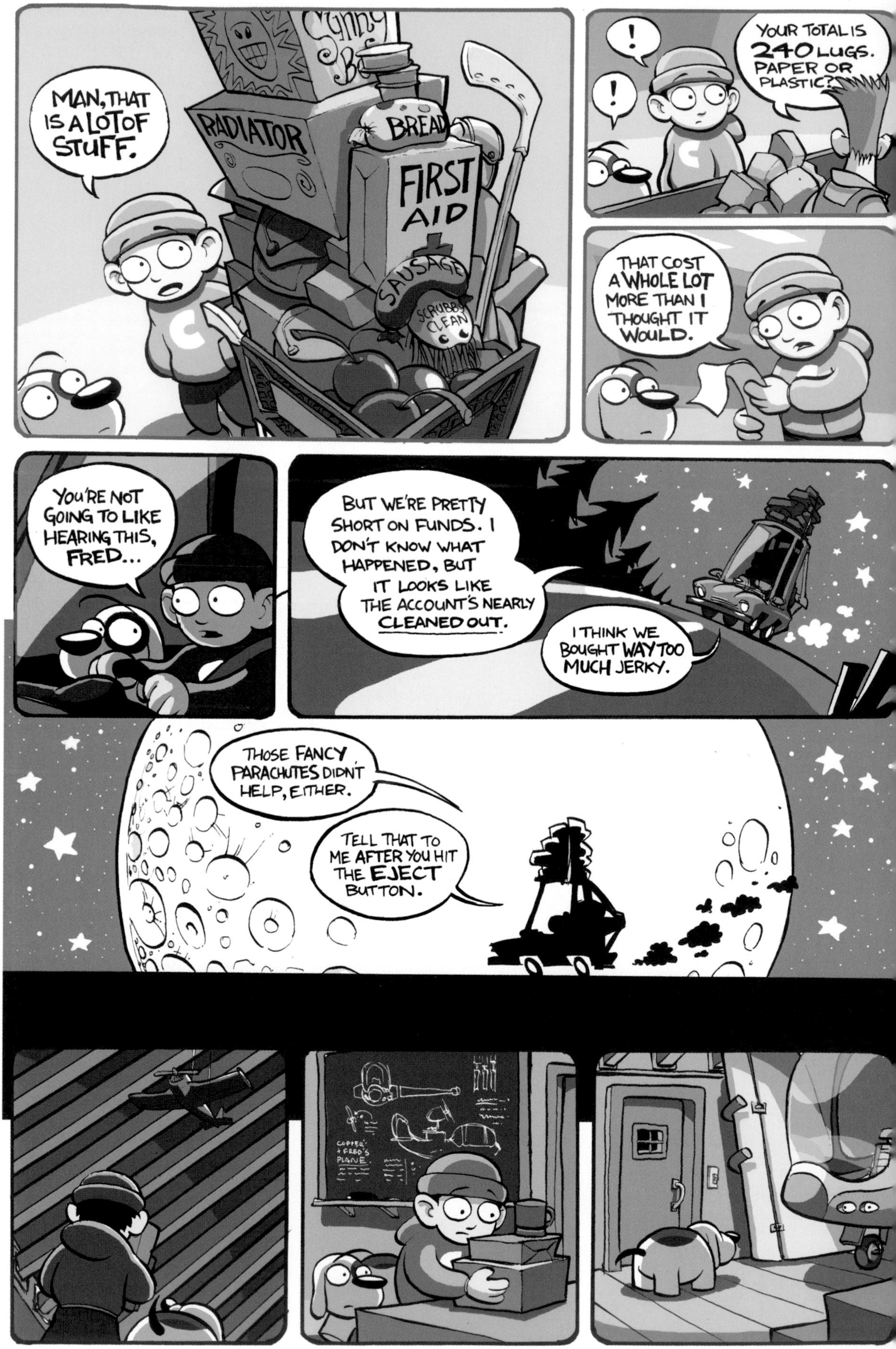
MAN, THAT IS A LOT OF STUFF.
RADIATOR
BREAD
FIRST AID
SAUSAGE
SCRUBBY CLEAN
!
!
YOUR TOTAL IS 240 LUGS. PAPER OR PLASTIC?
THAT COST A WHOLE LOT MORE THAN I THOUGHT IT WOULD.
YOU'RE NOT GOING TO LIKE HEARING THIS, FRED...
BUT WE'RE PRETTY SHORT ON FUNDS. I DON'T KNOW WHAT HAPPENED, BUT IT LOOKS LIKE THE ACCOUNT'S NEARLY CLEANED OUT.
I THINK WE BOUGHT WAY TOO MUCH JERKY.
THOSE FANCY PARACHUTES DIDN'T HELP, EITHER.
TELL THAT TO ME AFTER YOU HIT THE EJECT BUTTON.

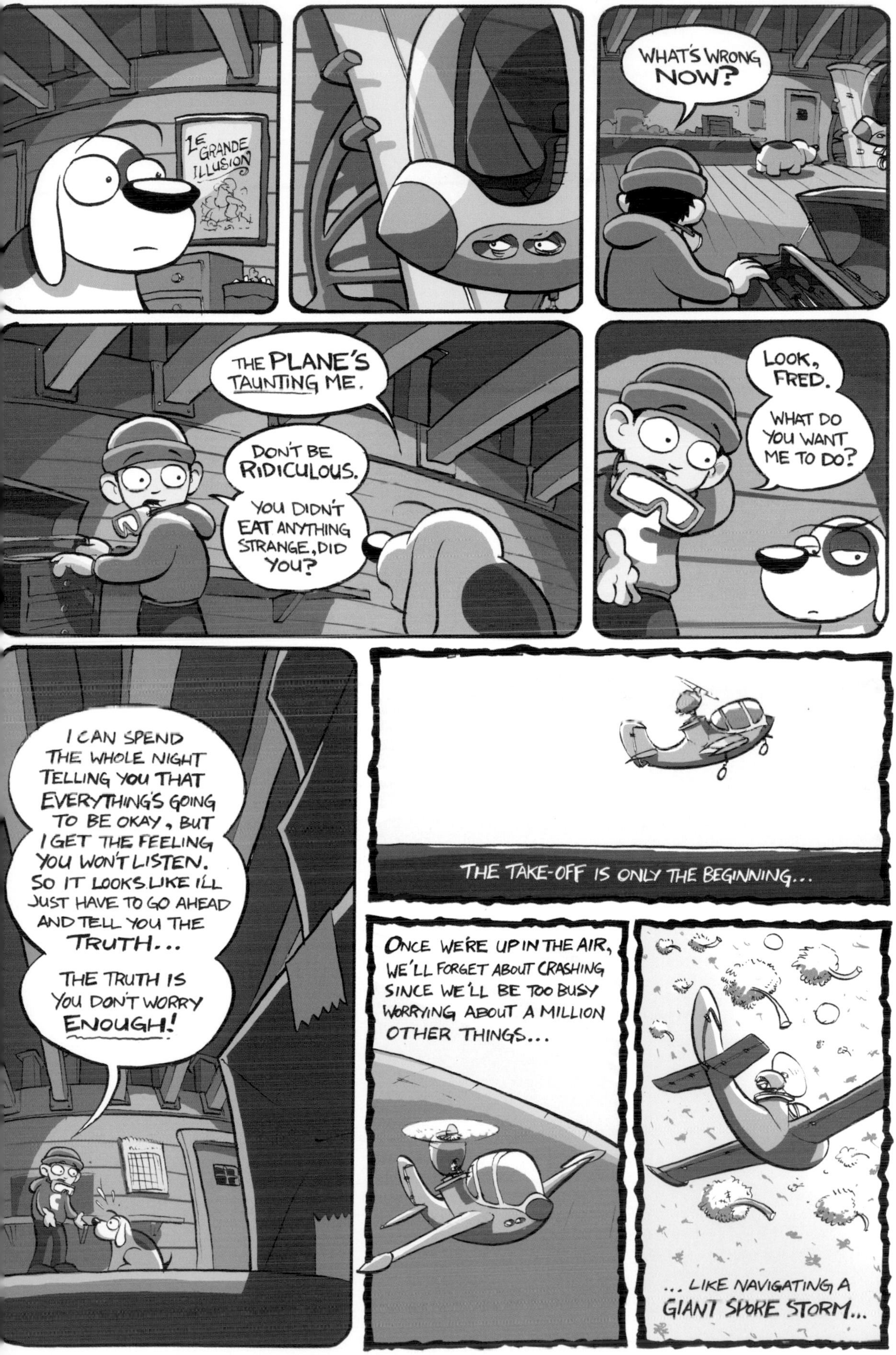
LE GRANDE ILLUSION
WHAT'S WRONG NOW?
THE PLANE'S TAUNTING ME.
DON'T BE RIDICULOUS.
YOU DIDN'T EAT ANYTHING STRANGE, DID YOU?
LOOK, FRED.
WHAT DO YOU WANT ME TO DO?
I CAN SPEND THE WHOLE NIGHT TELLING YOU THAT EVERYTHING'S GOING TO BE OKAY, BUT I GET THE FEELING YOU WON'T LISTEN. SO IT LOOKS LIKE I'LL JUST HAVE TO GO AHEAD AND TELL YOU THE TRUTH...
THE TRUTH IS YOU DON'T WORRY ENOUGH!
THE TAKE-OFF IS ONLY THE BEGINNING...
ONCE WE'RE UP IN THE AIR, WE'LL FORGET ABOUT CRASHING SINCE WE'LL BE TOO BUSY WORRYING ABOUT A MILLION OTHER THINGS...
... LIKE NAVIGATING A GIANT SPORE STORM...

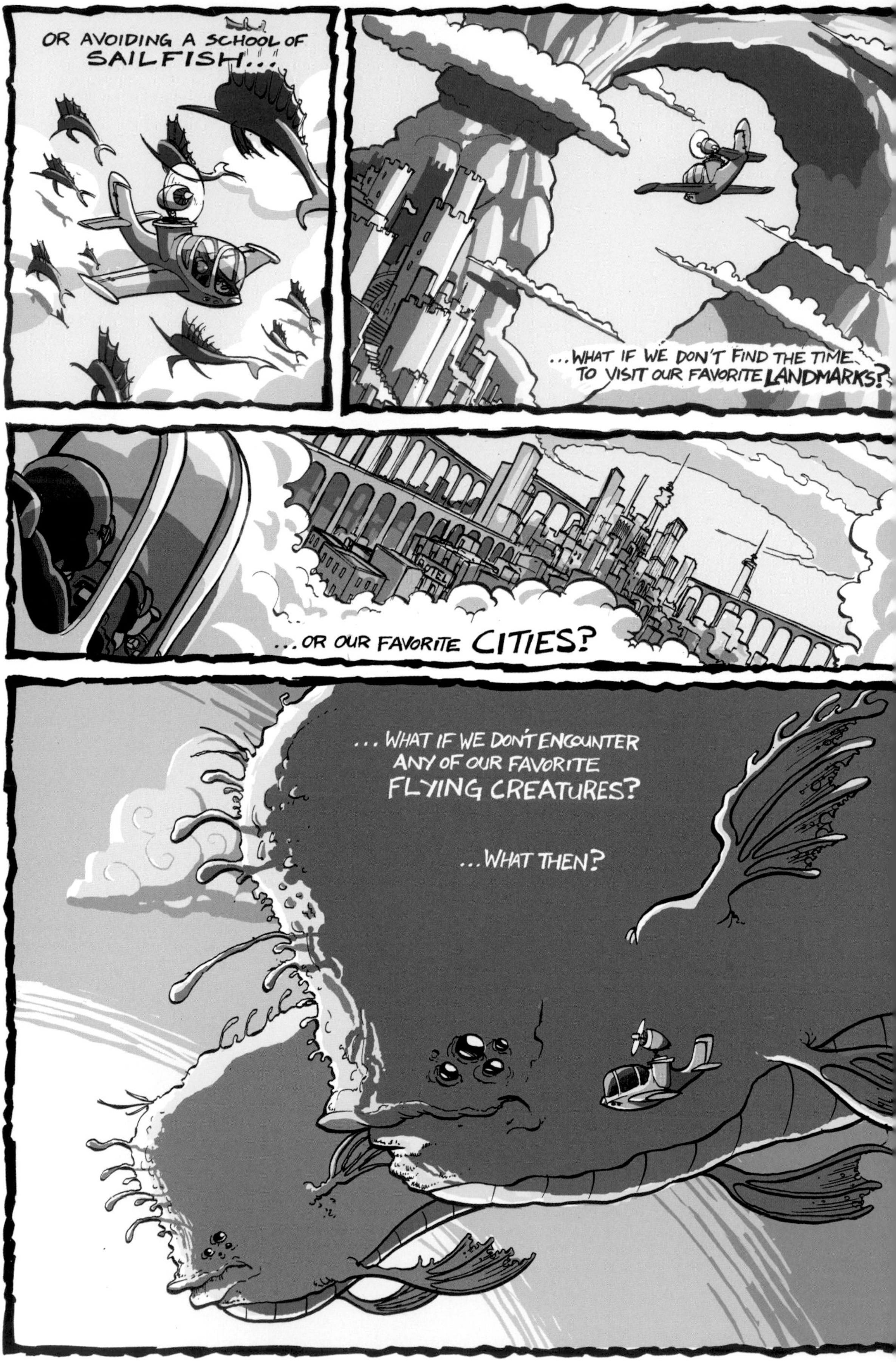
OR AVOIDING A SCHOOL OF SAILFISH...
...WHAT IF WE DON'T FIND THE TIME TO VISIT OUR FAVORITE LANDMARKS?
HOTEL
...OR OUR FAVORITE CITIES?
...WHAT IF WE DON'T ENCOUNTER ANY OF OUR FAVORITE FLYING CREATURES?
...WHAT THEN?

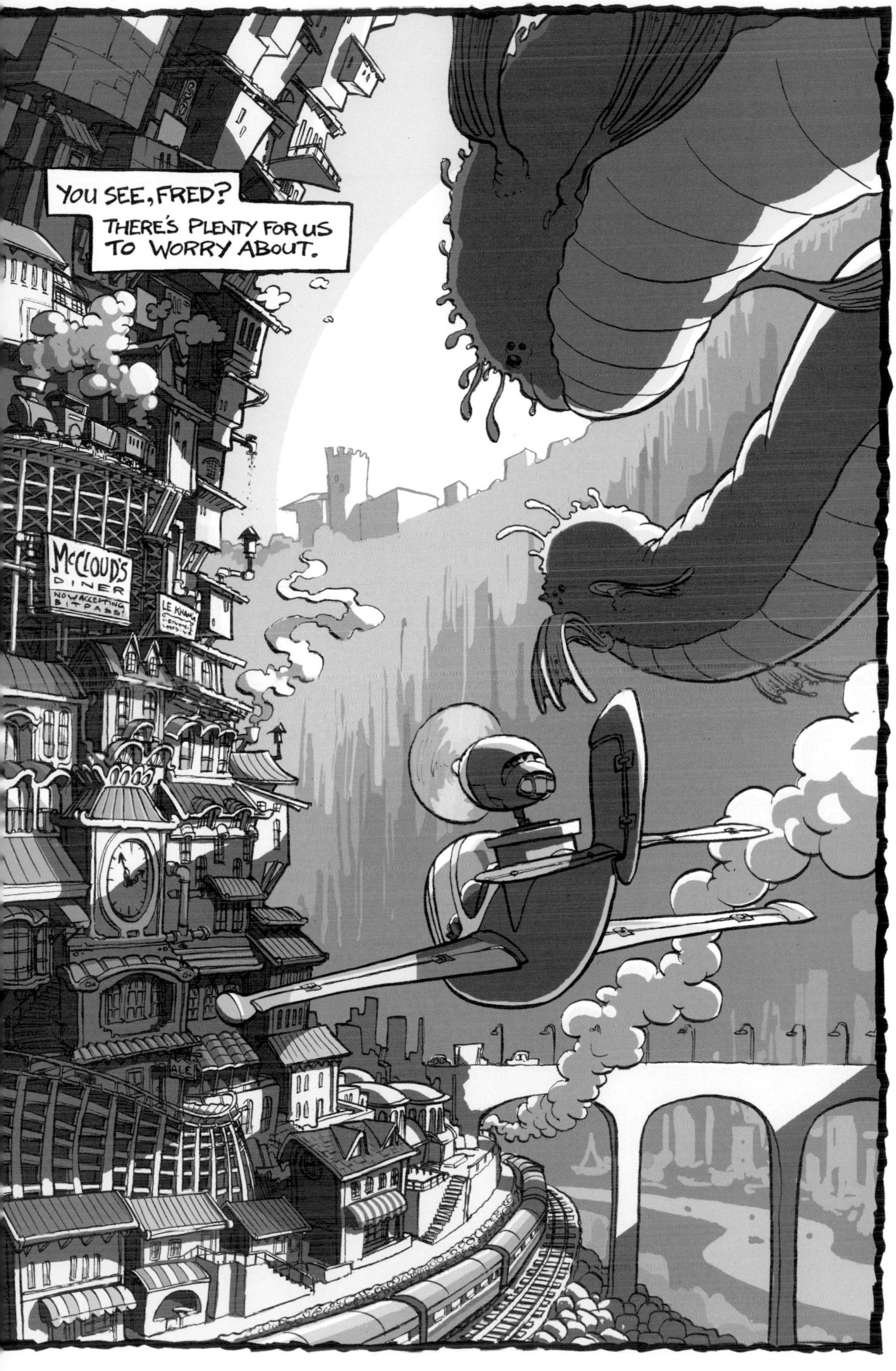
YOU SEE, FRED?
THERE'S PLENTY FOR US TO WORRY ABOUT.
McCLOUD'S DINER
NOW ACCEPTING BITPASS!
LE KHANH
ALE

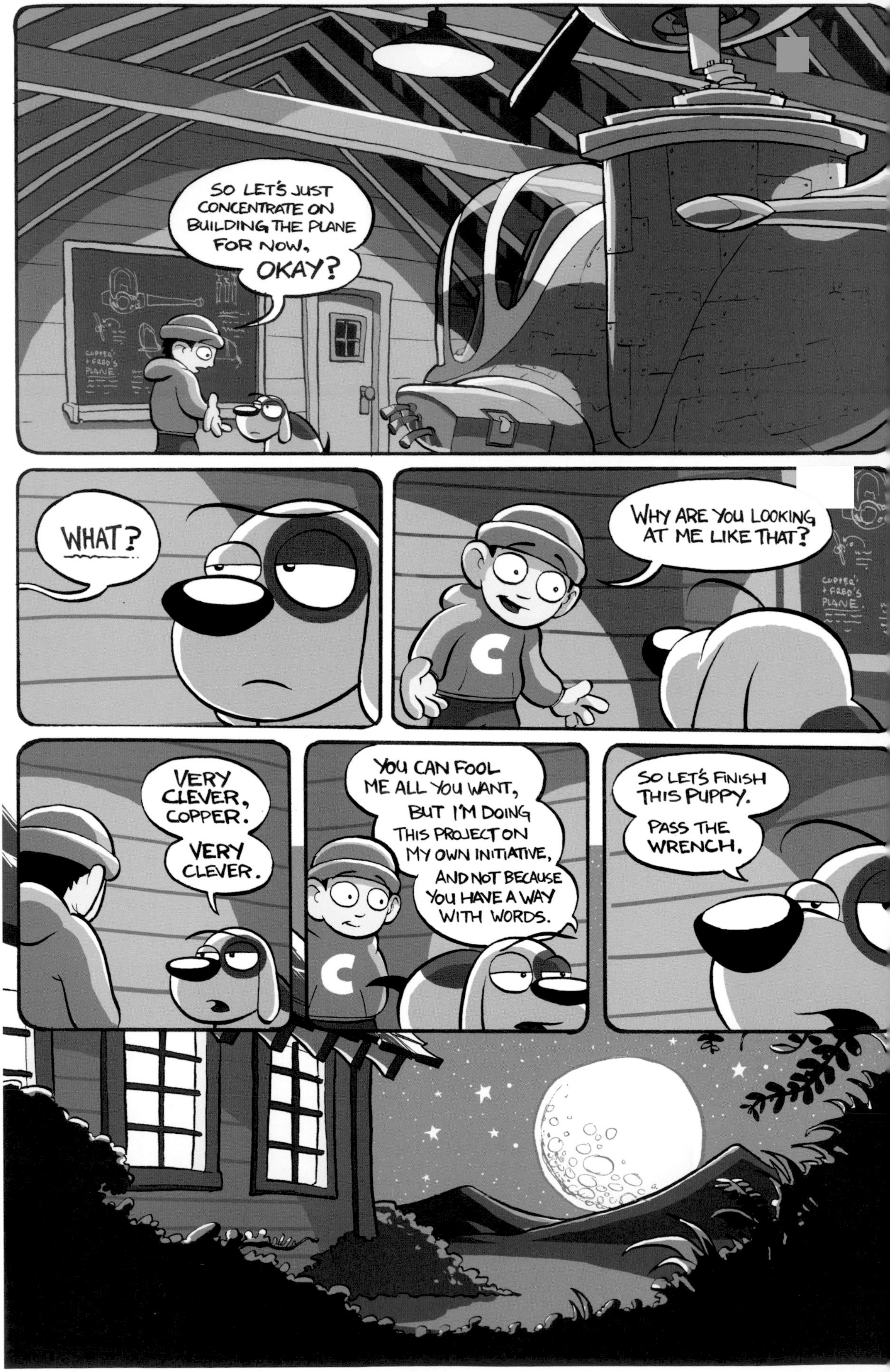
COPPER + FRED'S PLANE
SO LET'S JUST CONCENTRATE ON BUILDING THE PLANE FOR NOW, OKAY?
WHAT?
WHY ARE YOU LOOKING AT ME LIKE THAT?
VERY CLEVER, COPPER.
VERY CLEVER.
YOU CAN FOOL ME ALL YOU WANT,
BUT I'M DOING THIS PROJECT ON MY OWN INITIATIVE,
AND NOT BECAUSE YOU HAVE A WAY WITH WORDS.
SO LET'S FINISH THIS PUPPY.
PASS THE WRENCH.

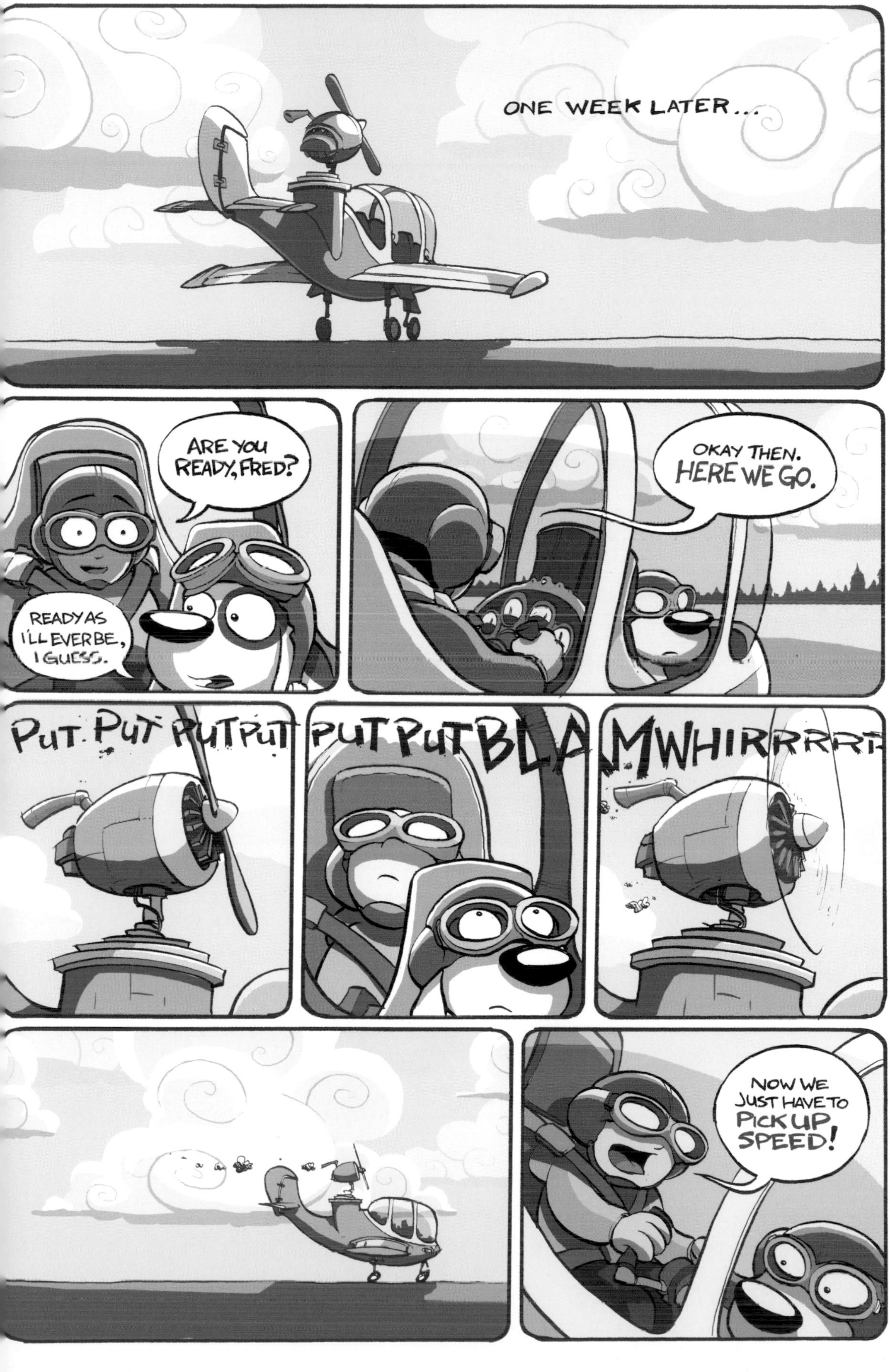
ONE WEEK LATER...
ARE YOU READY, FRED?
READY AS I'LL EVER BE, I GUESS.
OKAY THEN. HERE WE GO.
PUT. PUT PUTPUT PUT PUT BLAM WHIRRRRR
NOW WE JUST HAVE TO PICK UP SPEED!

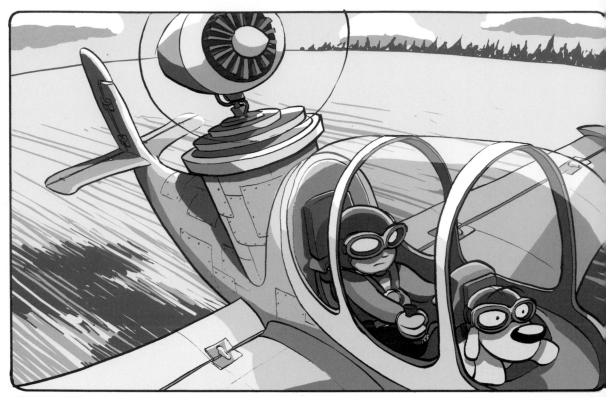

EVERYTHING'S LOOKIN' GOOD!

WE'LL REACH FLIGHT VELOCITY SOON!!

COPPER?! HOW MUCH RUNWAY WE GOT?!

AT LEAST A MILE! THAT'S MORE THAN ENOUGH!

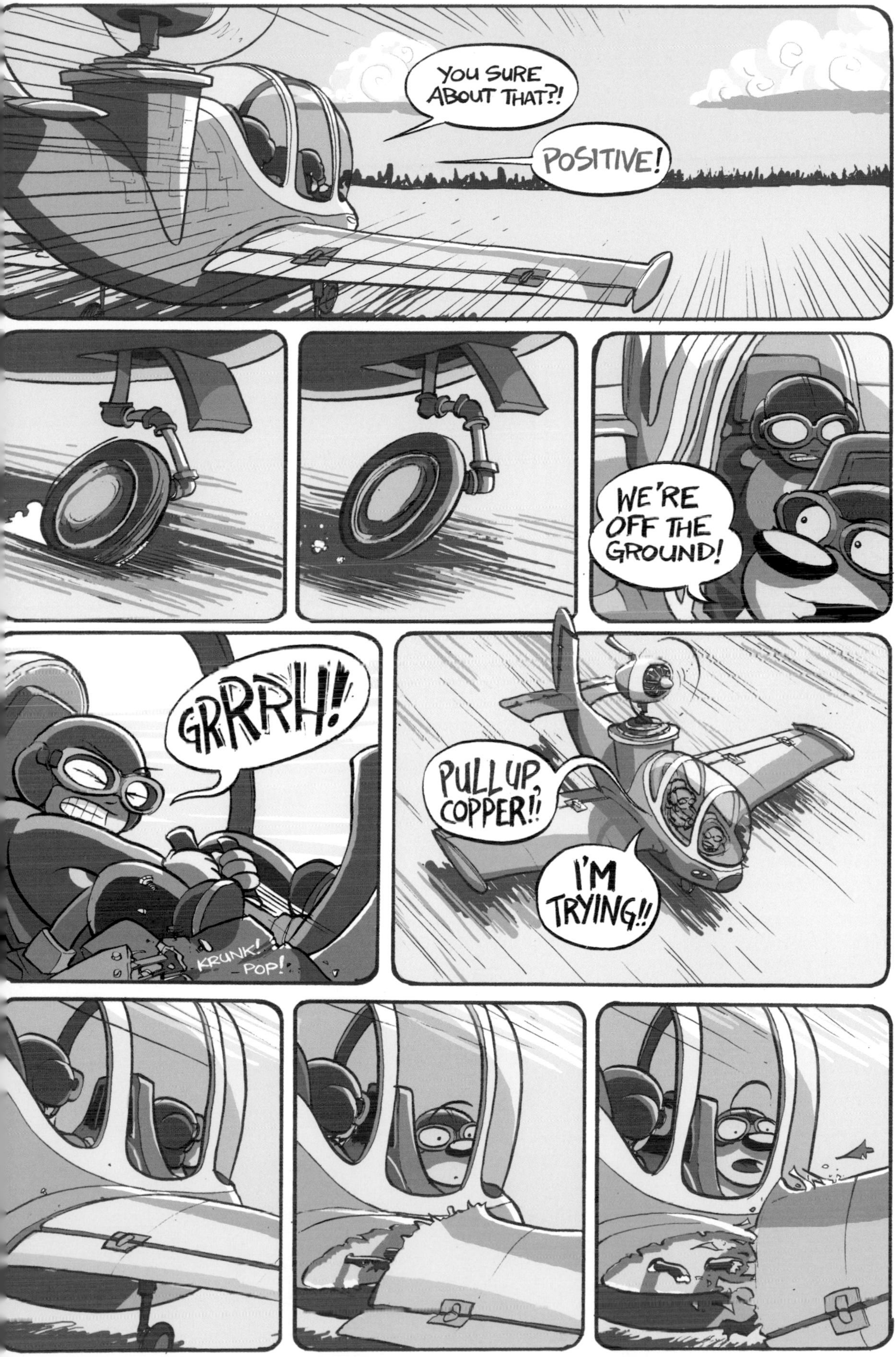
YOU SURE ABOUT THAT?!
POSITIVE!
WE'RE OFF THE GROUND!
GRRRH!
KRUNK!
POP!
PULL UP, COPPER!!
I'M TRYING!!

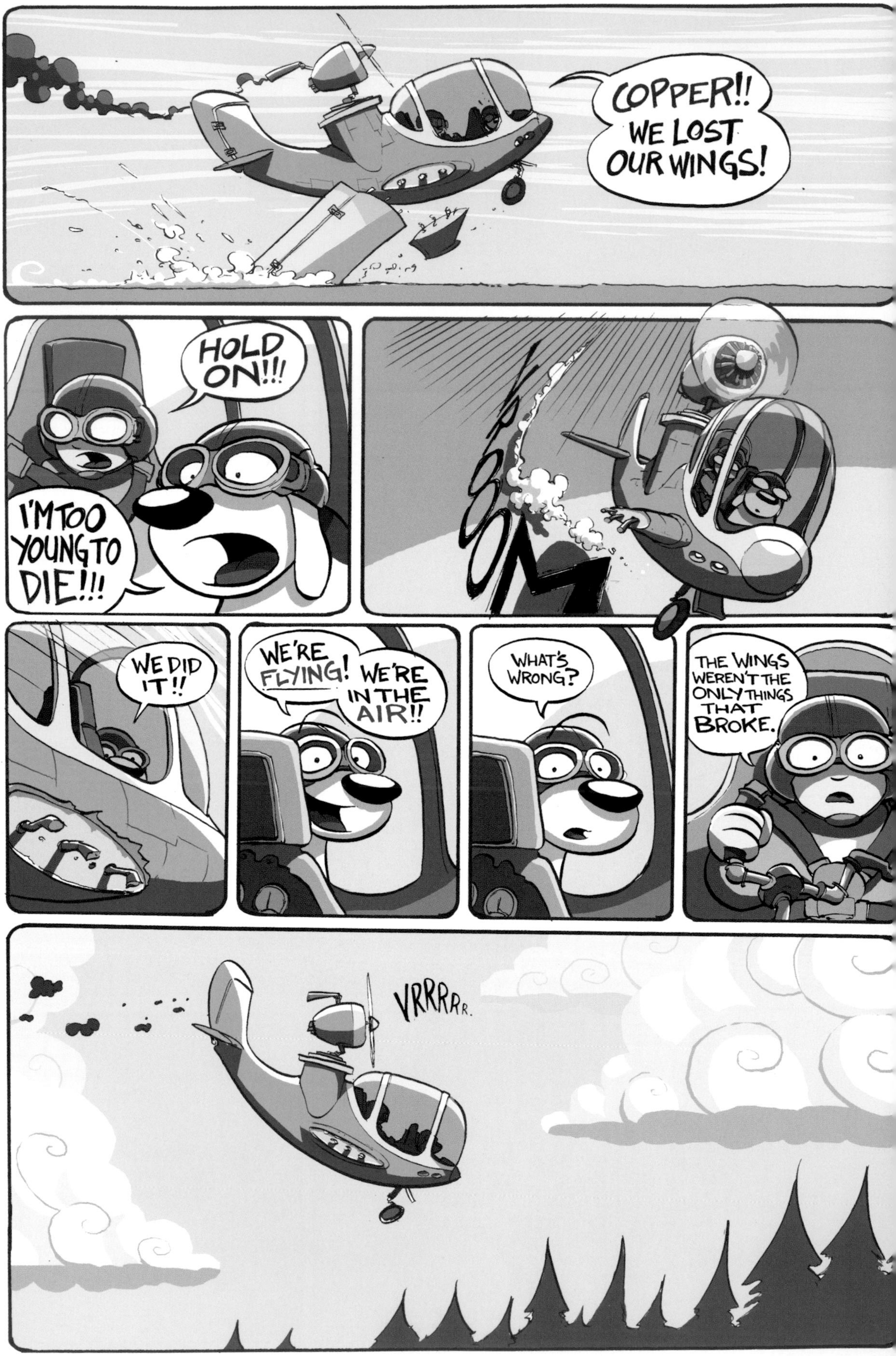
COPPER!! WE LOST OUR WINGS!
HOLD ON!!!
I'M TOO YOUNG TO DIE!!!
VROOOM
WE DID IT!!
WE'RE FLYING!
WE'RE IN THE AIR!!
WHAT'S WRONG?
THE WINGS WEREN'T THE ONLY THINGS THAT BROKE.
VRRRRR.

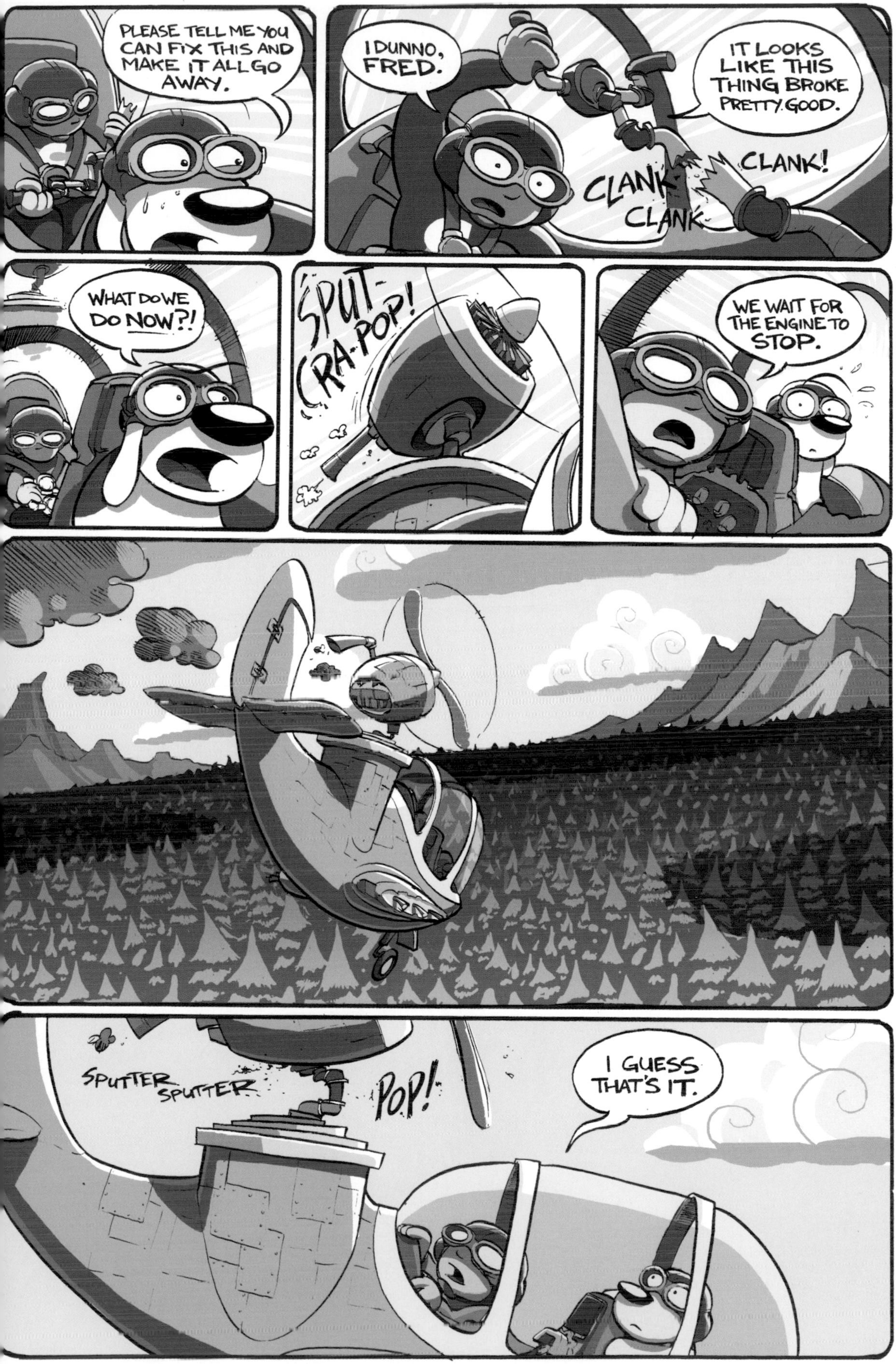
PLEASE TELL ME YOU CAN FIX THIS AND MAKE IT ALL GO AWAY.
I DUNNO, FRED.
IT LOOKS LIKE THIS THING BROKE PRETTY GOOD.
CLANK
CLANK
CLANK!
WHAT DO WE DO NOW?!
SPUT-
CRA-POP!
WE WAIT FOR THE ENGINE TO STOP.
SPUTTER SPUTTER
POP!
I GUESS THAT'S IT.

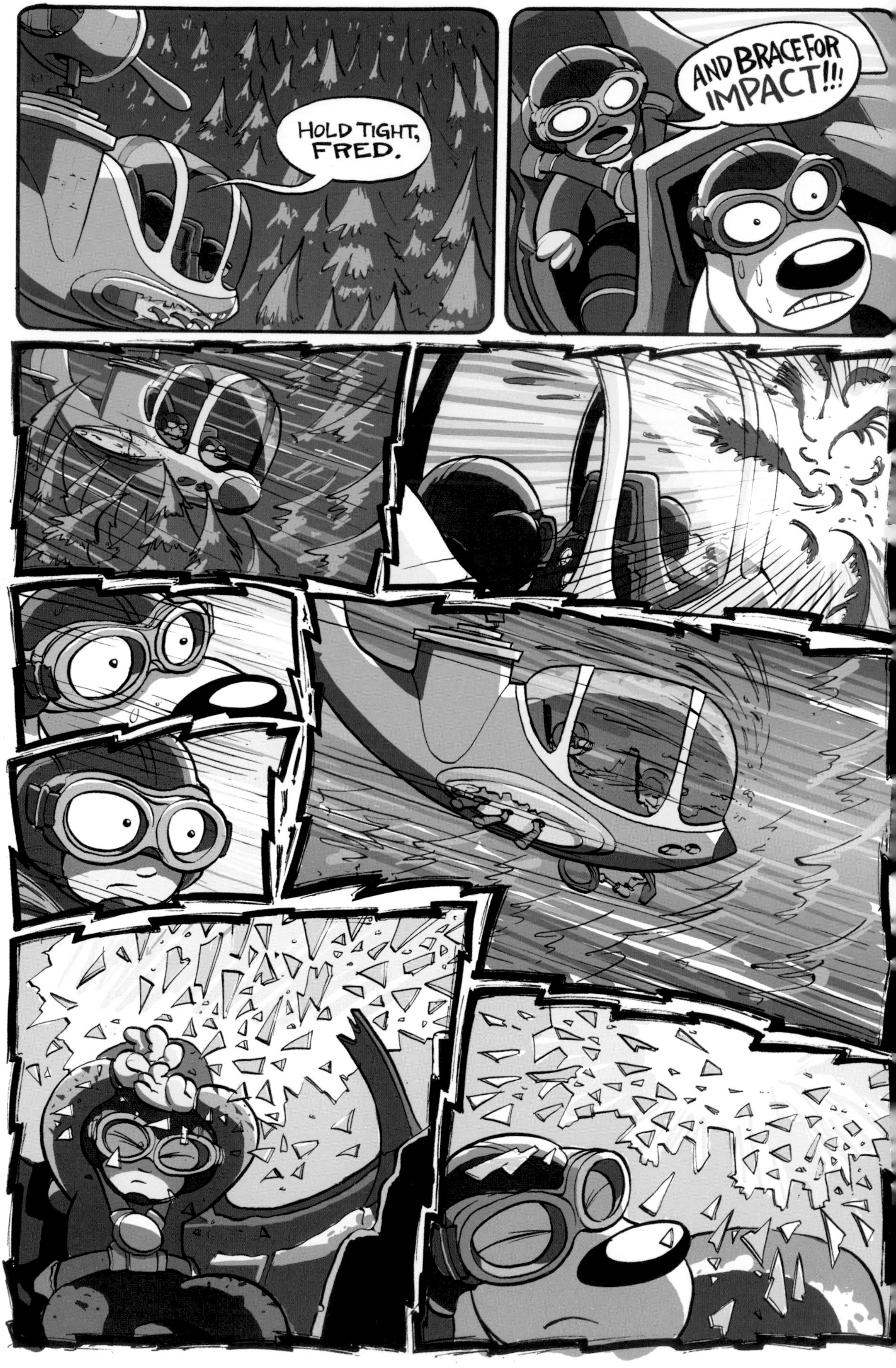
HOLD TIGHT, FRED.
AND BRACE FOR IMPACT!!!

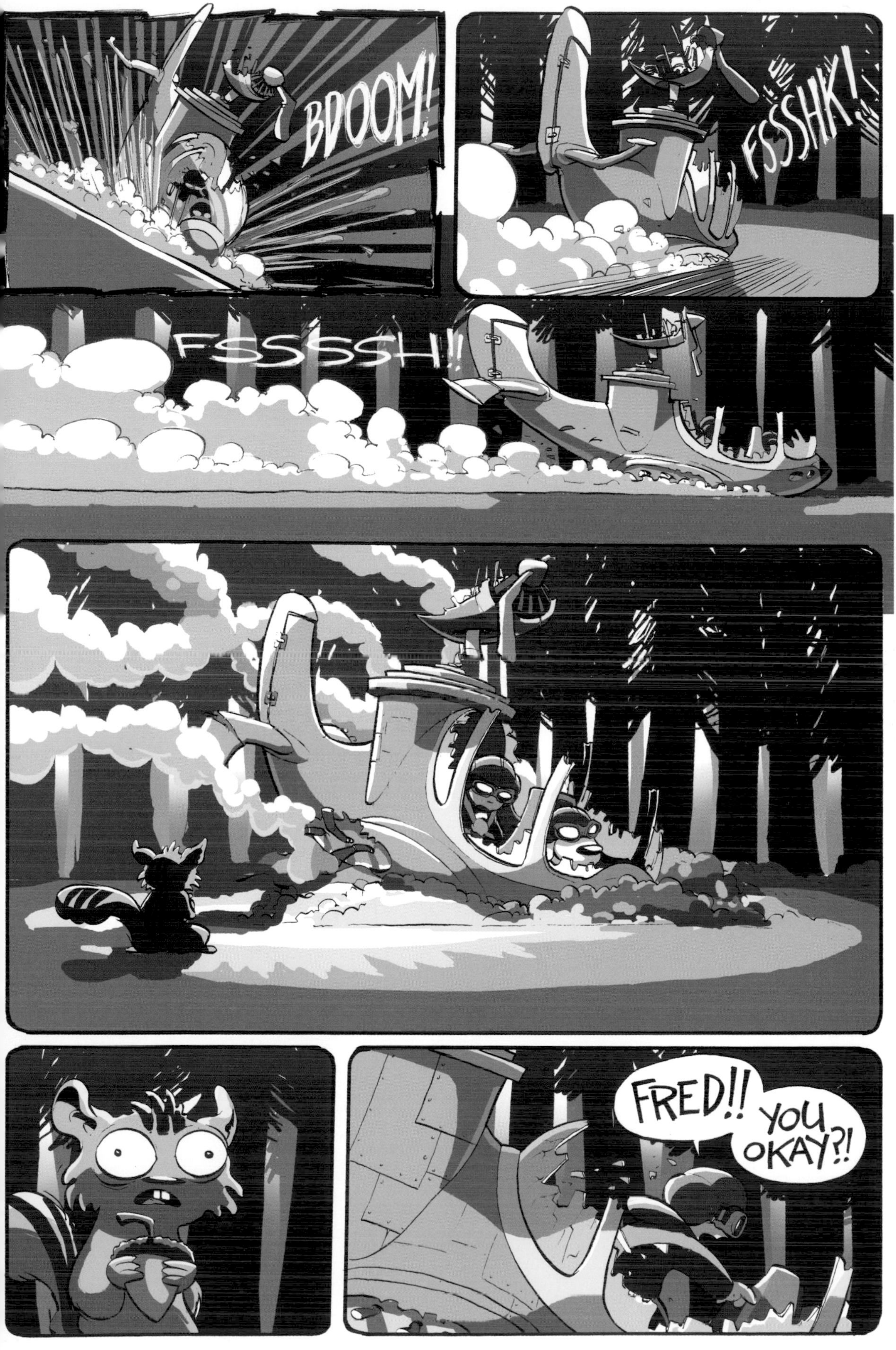
BDOOM!
FSSSHK!
FSSSSH!!
FRED!! YOU OKAY?!

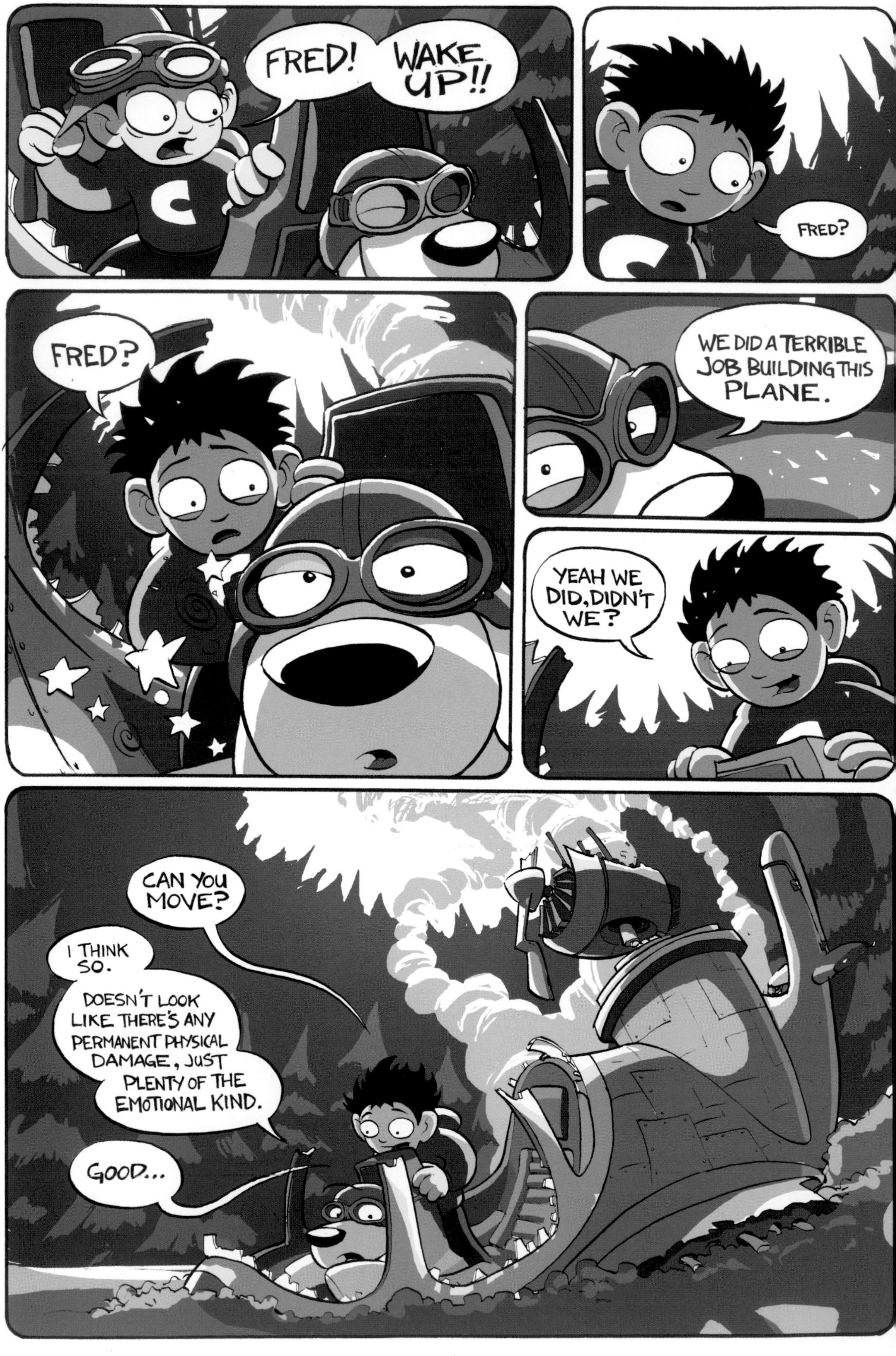
FRED!
WAKE UP!!
FRED?
FRED?
WE DID A TERRIBLE JOB BUILDING THIS PLANE.
YEAH WE DID, DIDN'T WE?
CAN YOU MOVE?
I THINK SO.
DOESN'T LOOK LIKE THERE'S ANY PERMANENT PHYSICAL DAMAGE, JUST PLENTY OF THE EMOTIONAL KIND.
GOOD...

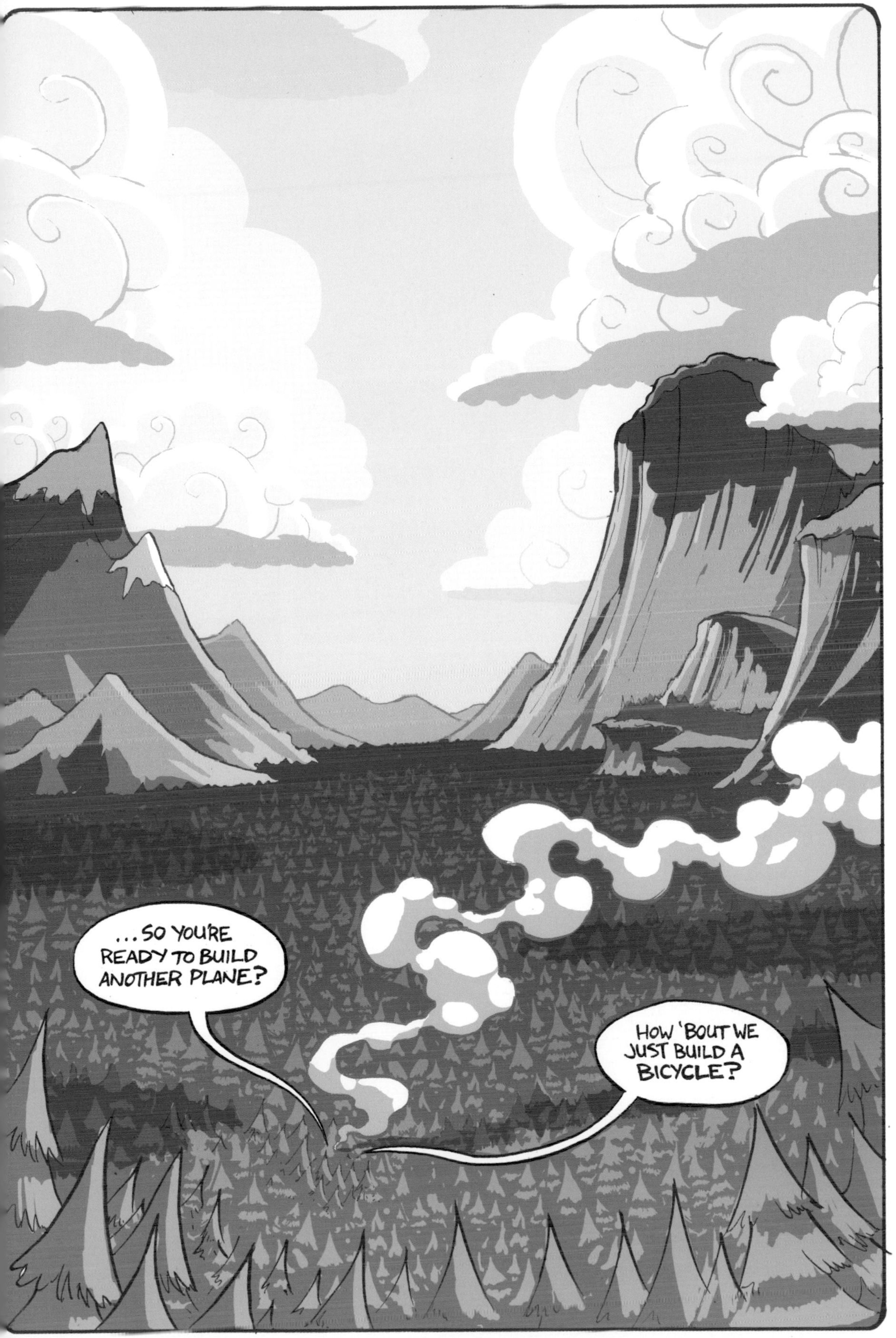
...SO YOU'RE READY TO BUILD ANOTHER PLANE?
HOW 'BOUT WE JUST BUILD A BICYCLE?

"Hugo Earheart," by Jake Parker

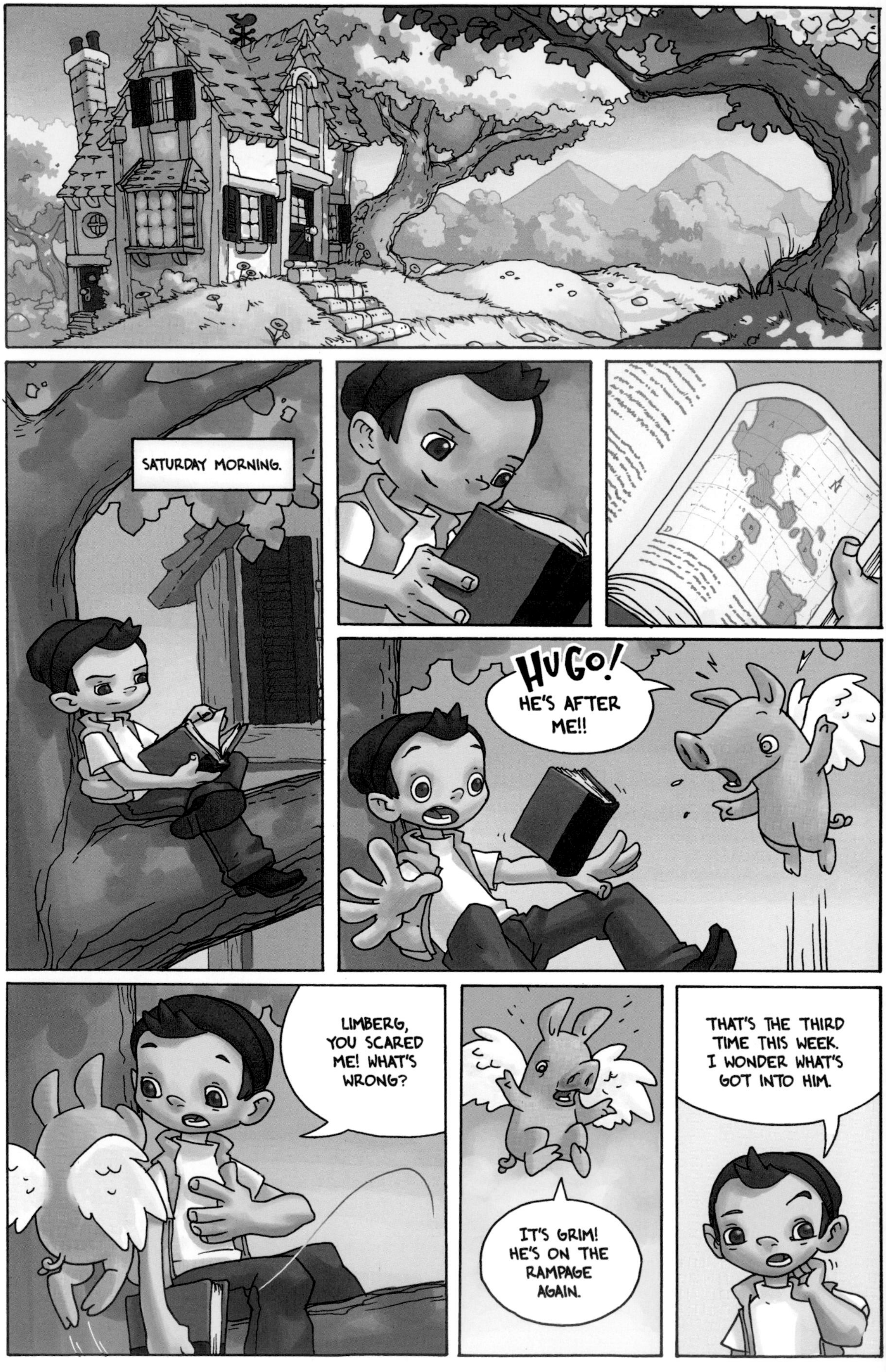
SATURDAY MORNING.
HUGO!
HE'S AFTER ME!!
LIMBERG, YOU SCARED ME! WHAT'S WRONG?
IT'S GRIM! HE'S ON THE RAMPAGE AGAIN.
THAT'S THE THIRD TIME THIS WEEK. I WONDER WHAT'S GOT INTO HIM.

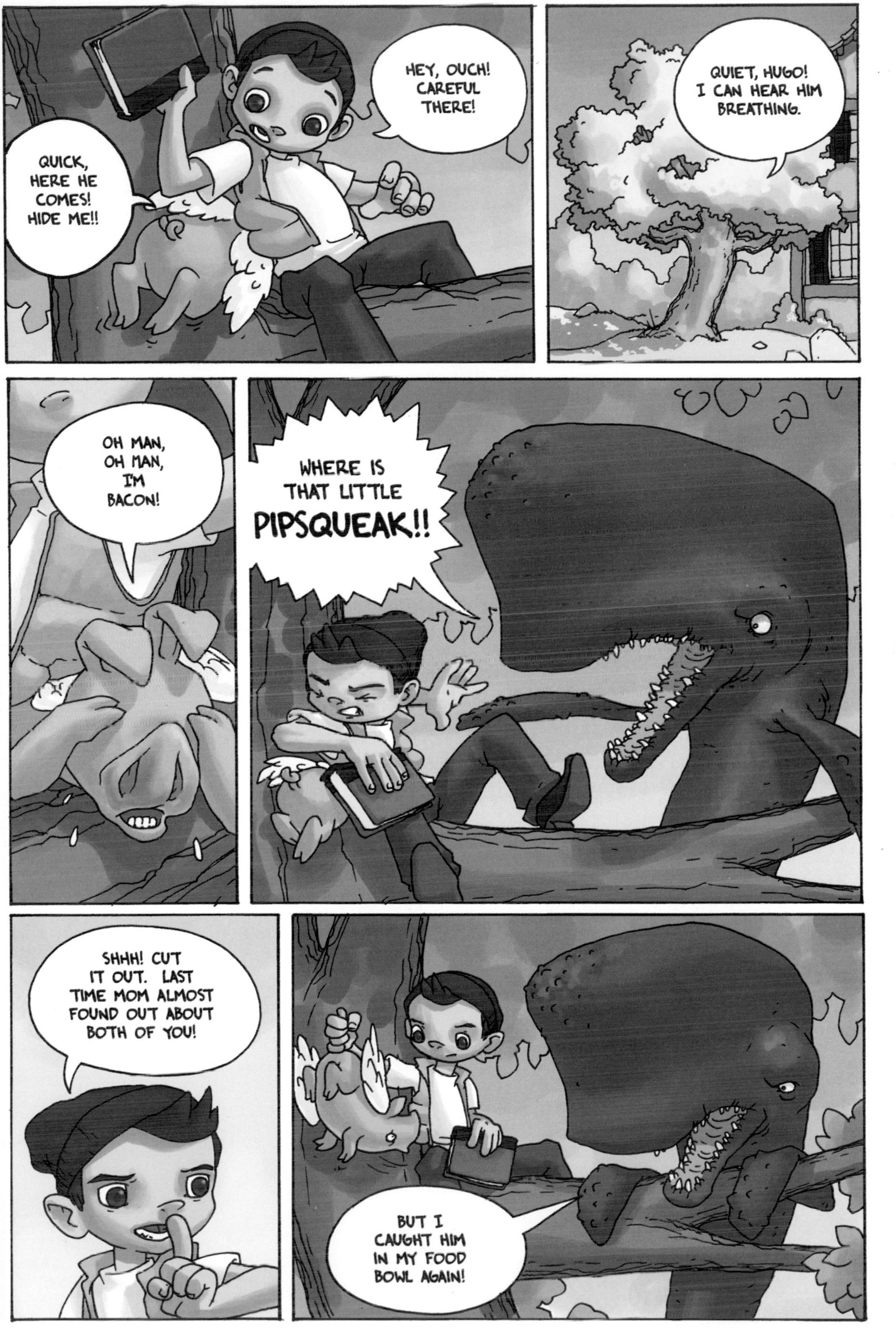
QUICK, HERE HE COMES! HIDE ME!!
HEY, OUCH! CAREFUL THERE!
QUIET, HUGO! I CAN HEAR HIM BREATHING.
OH MAN, OH MAN, I'M BACON!
WHERE IS THAT LITTLE PIPSQUEAK!!
SHHH! CUT IT OUT. LAST TIME MOM ALMOST FOUND OUT ABOUT BOTH OF YOU!
BUT I CAUGHT HIM IN MY FOOD BOWL AGAIN!

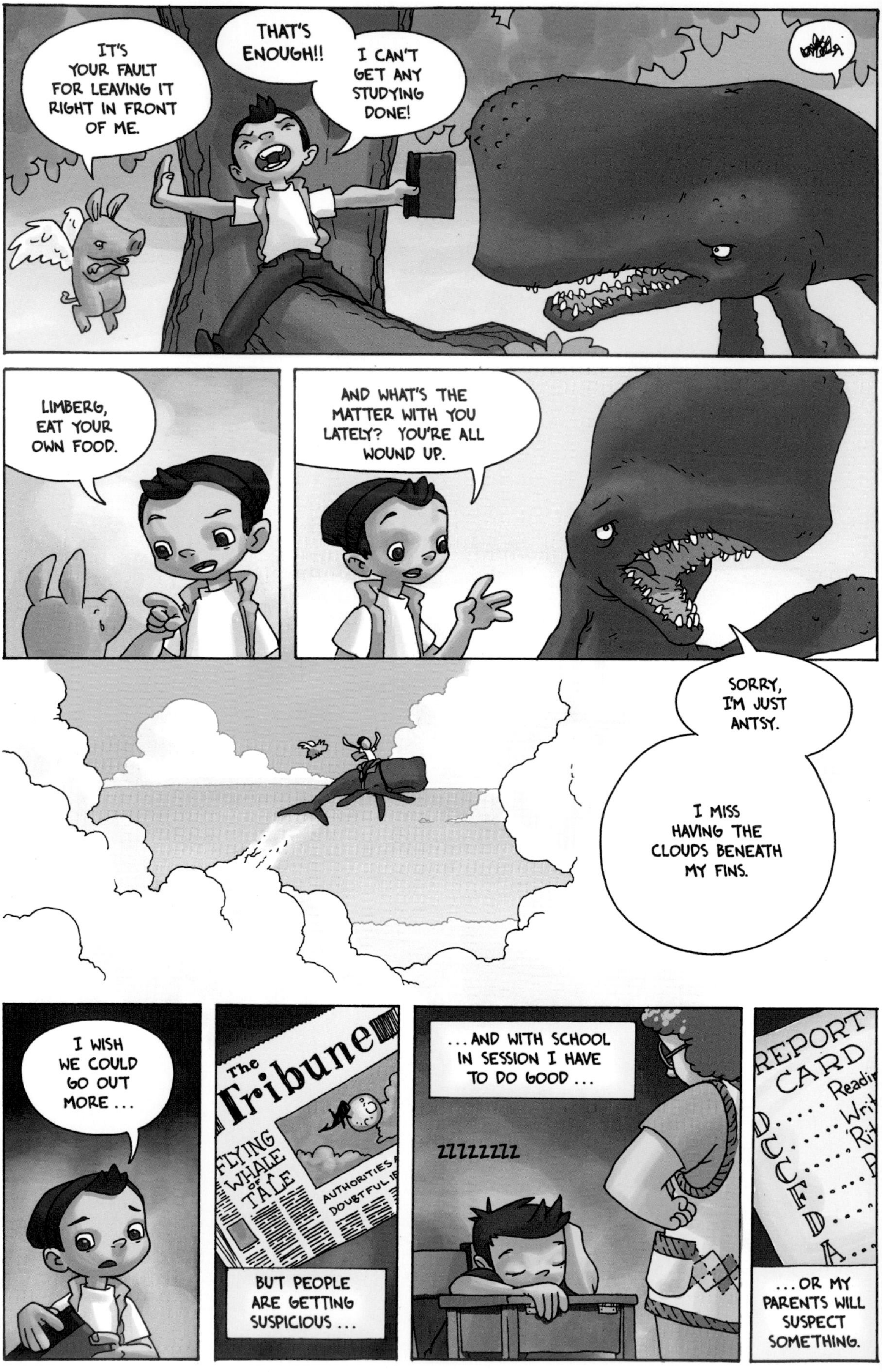
IT'S YOUR FAULT FOR LEAVING IT RIGHT IN FRONT OF ME.
THAT'S ENOUGH!!
I CAN'T GET ANY STUDYING DONE!
LIMBERG, EAT YOUR OWN FOOD.
AND WHAT'S THE MATTER WITH YOU LATELY? YOU'RE ALL WOUND UP.
SORRY, I'M JUST ANTSY.
I MISS HAVING THE CLOUDS BENEATH MY FINS.
I WISH WE COULD GO OUT MORE...
The Tribune
FLYING WHALE of a TALE
BUT PEOPLE ARE GETTING SUSPICIOUS...
...AND WITH SCHOOL IN SESSION I HAVE TO DO GOOD...
ZZZZZZZ
REPORT CARD
...OR MY PARENTS WILL SUSPECT SOMETHING.

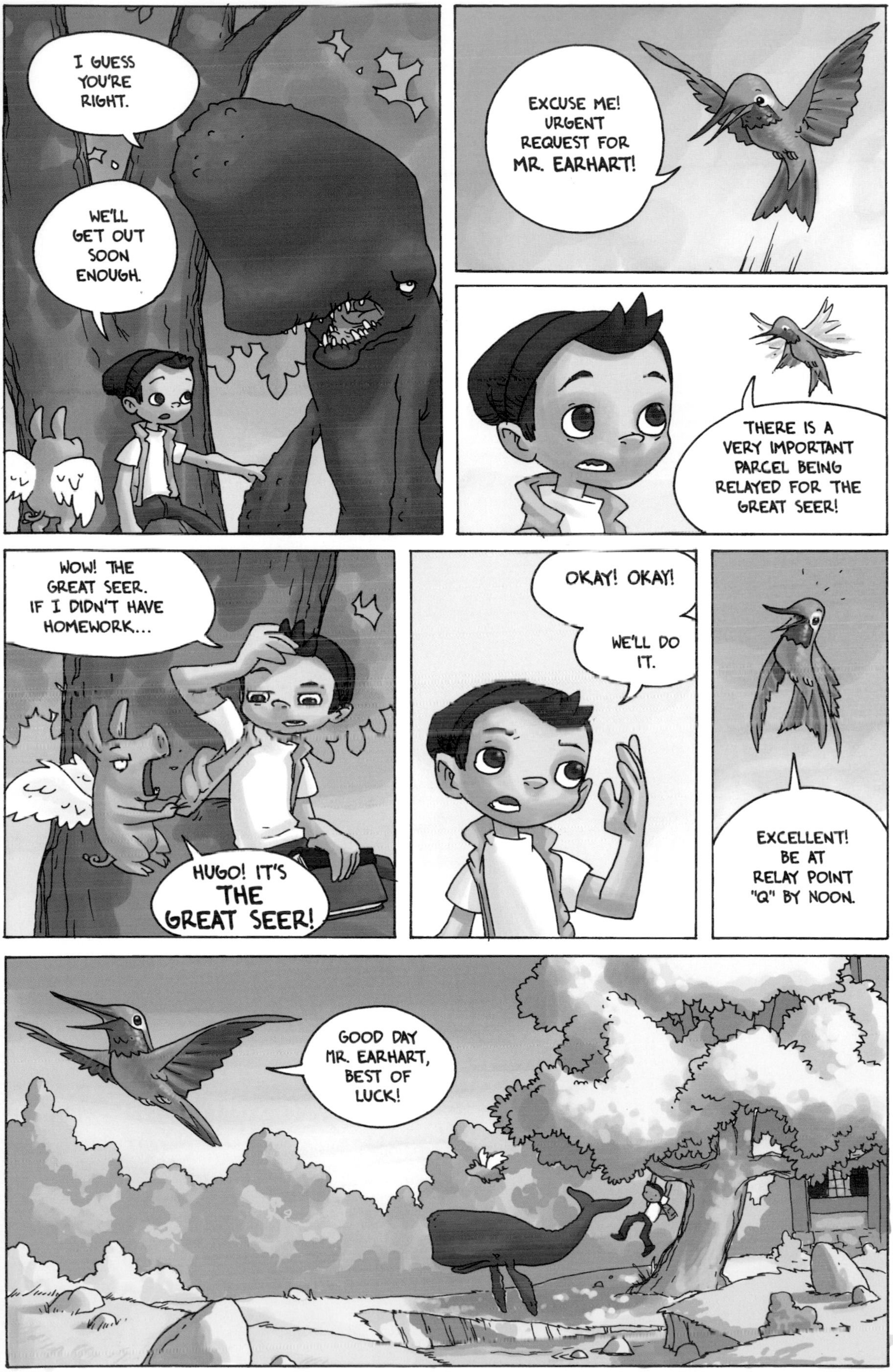
I GUESS YOU'RE RIGHT.
WE'LL GET OUT SOON ENOUGH.
EXCUSE ME! URGENT REQUEST FOR MR. EARHART!
THERE IS A VERY IMPORTANT PARCEL BEING RELAYED FOR THE GREAT SEER!
WOW! THE GREAT SEER. IF I DIDN'T HAVE HOMEWORK...
HUGO! IT'S THE GREAT SEER!
OKAY! OKAY!
WE'LL DO IT.
EXCELLENT! BE AT RELAY POINT "Q" BY NOON.
GOOD DAY MR. EARHART, BEST OF LUCK!

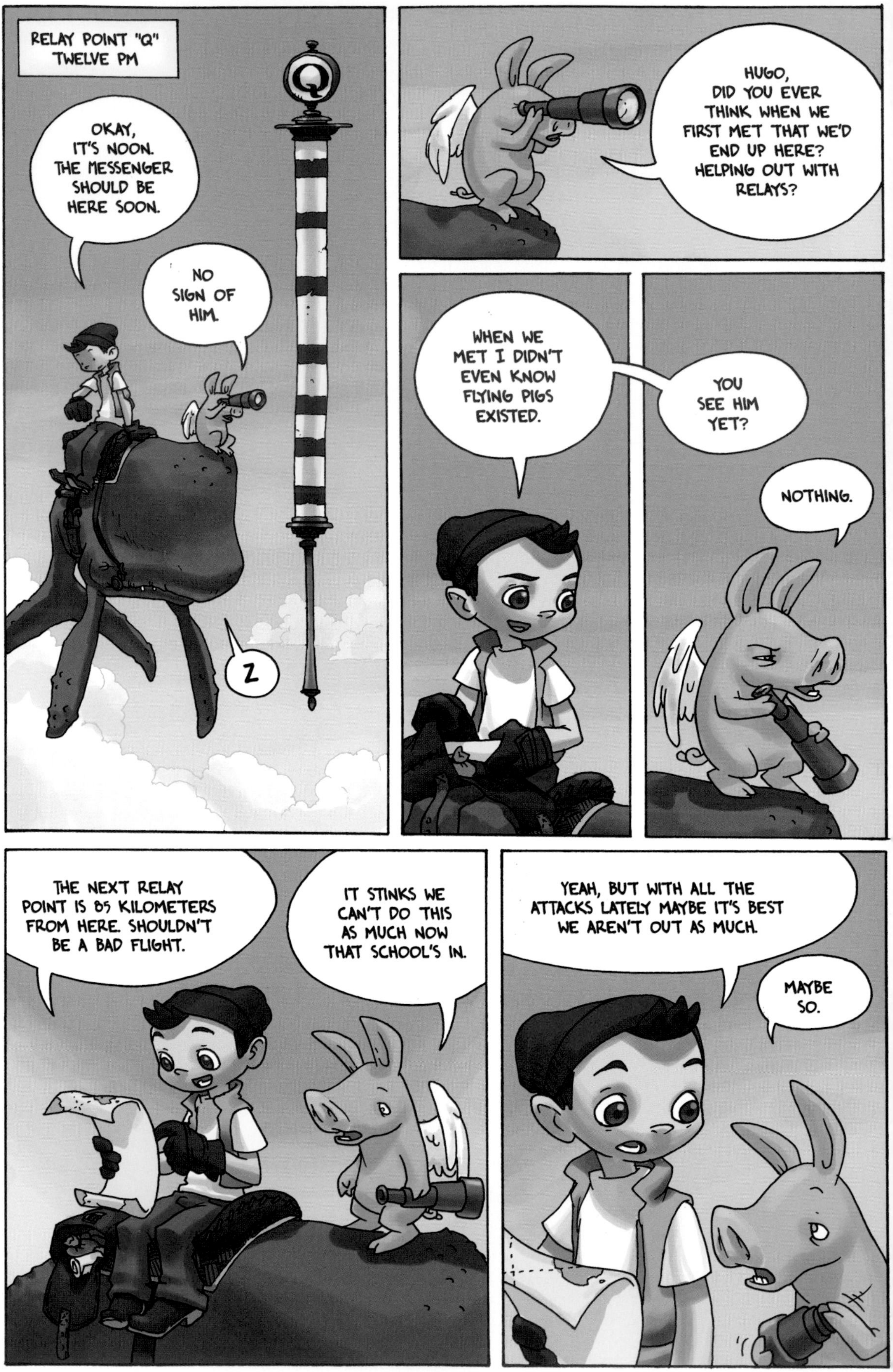
RELAY POINT "Q" TWELVE PM
OKAY, IT'S NOON. THE MESSENGER SHOULD BE HERE SOON.
NO SIGN OF HIM.
Z
HUGO, DID YOU EVER THINK WHEN WE FIRST MET THAT WE'D END UP HERE? HELPING OUT WITH RELAYS?
WHEN WE MET I DIDN'T EVEN KNOW FLYING PIGS EXISTED.
YOU SEE HIM YET?
NOTHING.
THE NEXT RELAY POINT IS 85 KILOMETERS FROM HERE. SHOULDN'T BE A BAD FLIGHT.
IT STINKS WE CAN'T DO THIS AS MUCH NOW THAT SCHOOL'S IN.
YEAH, BUT WITH ALL THE ATTACKS LATELY MAYBE IT'S BEST WE AREN'T OUT AS MUCH.
MAYBE SO.

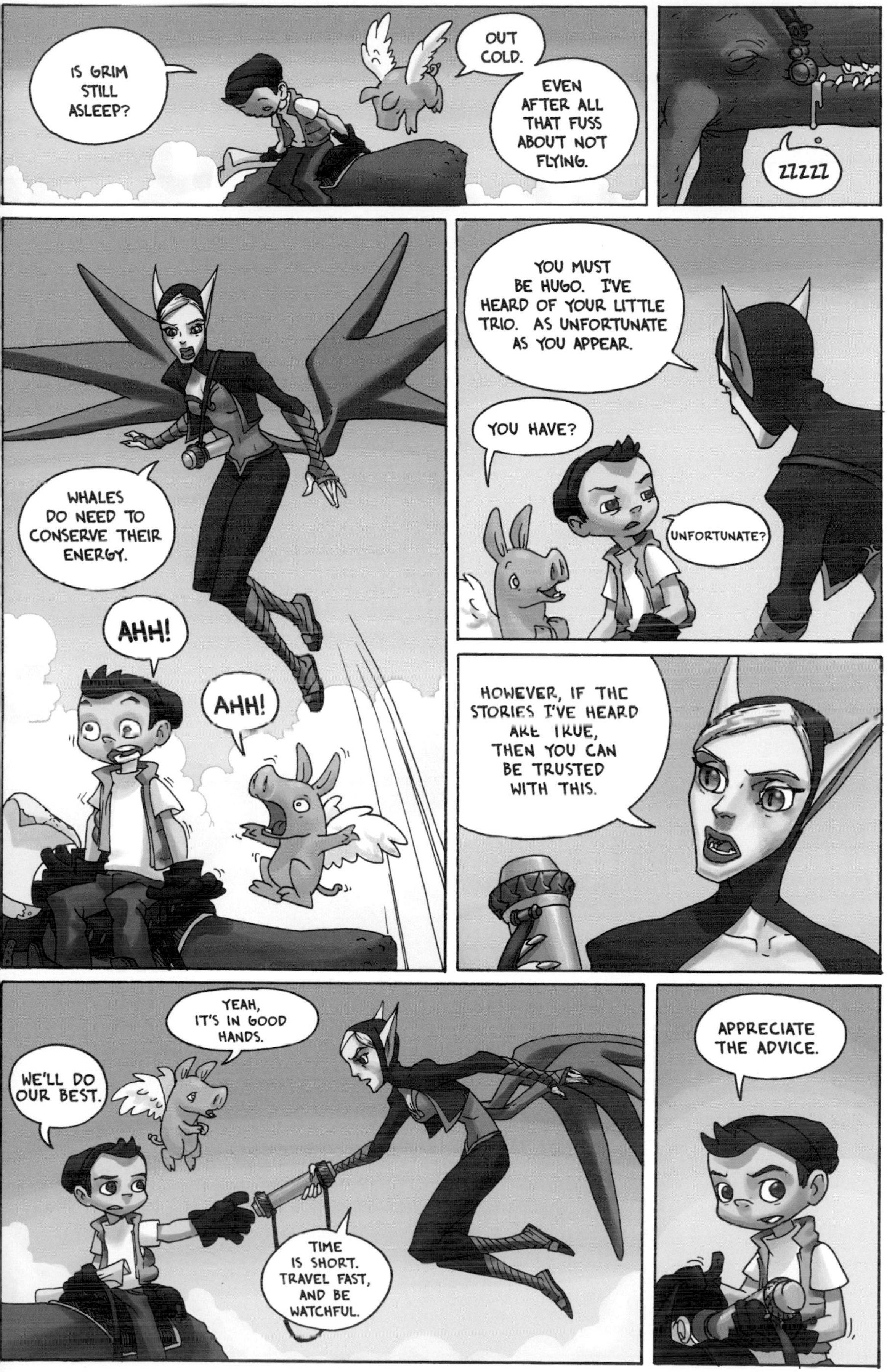
IS GRIM STILL ASLEEP?
OUT COLD.
EVEN AFTER ALL THAT FUSS ABOUT NOT FLYING.
ZZZZZ
WHALES DO NEED TO CONSERVE THEIR ENERGY.
AHH!
AHH!
YOU MUST BE HUGO. I'VE HEARD OF YOUR LITTLE TRIO. AS UNFORTUNATE AS YOU APPEAR.
YOU HAVE?
UNFORTUNATE?
HOWEVER, IF THE STORIES I'VE HEARD ARE TRUE, THEN YOU CAN BE TRUSTED WITH THIS.
WE'LL DO OUR BEST.
YEAH, IT'S IN GOOD HANDS.
TIME IS SHORT. TRAVEL FAST, AND BE WATCHFUL.
APPRECIATE THE ADVICE.

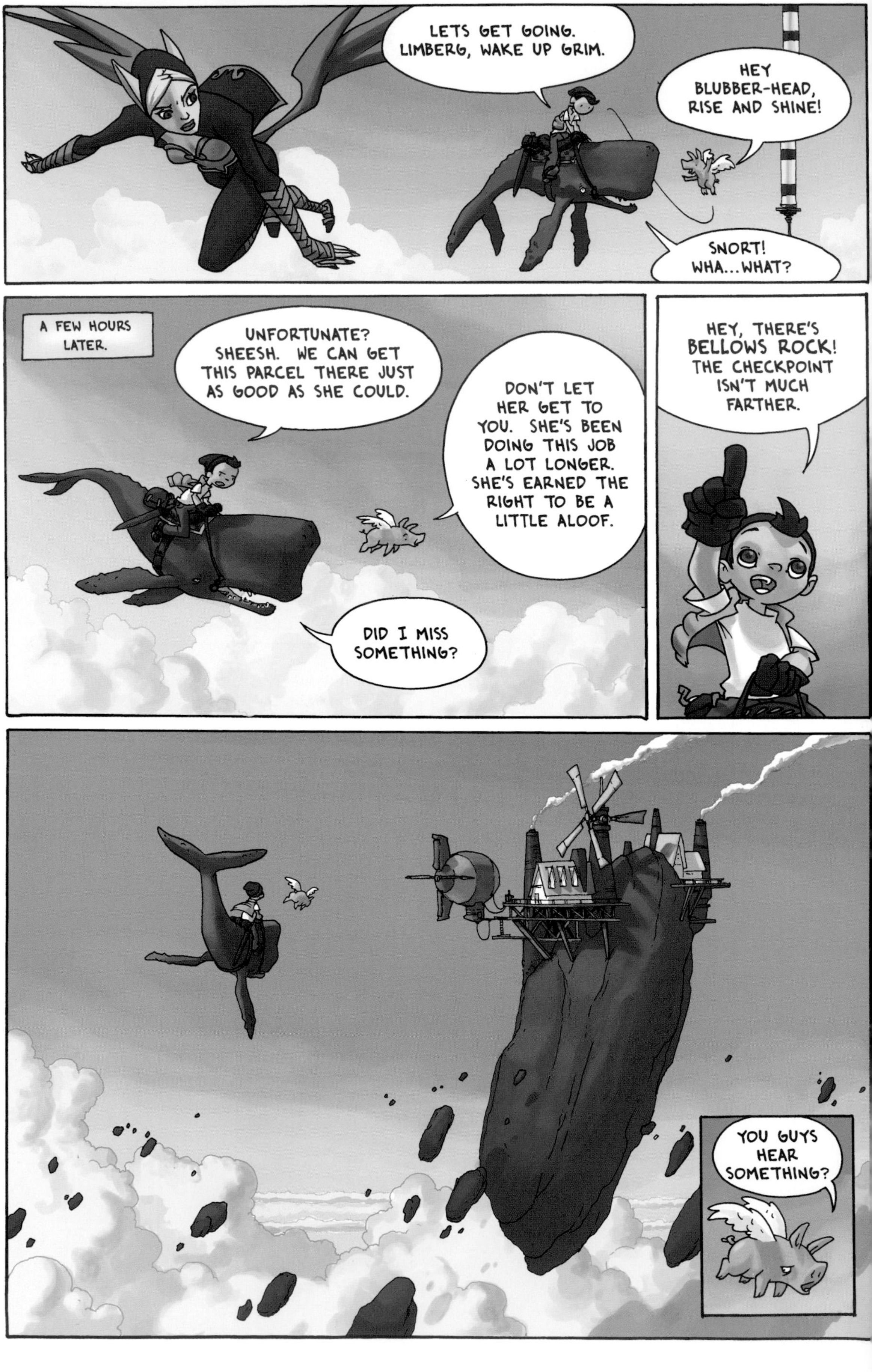
LETS GET GOING.
LIMBERG, WAKE UP GRIM.
HEY BLUBBER-HEAD, RISE AND SHINE!
SNORT! WHA...WHAT?
A FEW HOURS LATER.
UNFORTUNATE? SHEESH. WE CAN GET THIS PARCEL THERE JUST AS GOOD AS SHE COULD.
DON'T LET HER GET TO YOU. SHE'S BEEN DOING THIS JOB A LOT LONGER. SHE'S EARNED THE RIGHT TO BE A LITTLE ALOOF.
DID I MISS SOMETHING?
HEY, THERE'S BELLOWS ROCK! THE CHECKPOINT ISN'T MUCH FARTHER.
YOU GUYS HEAR SOMETHING?

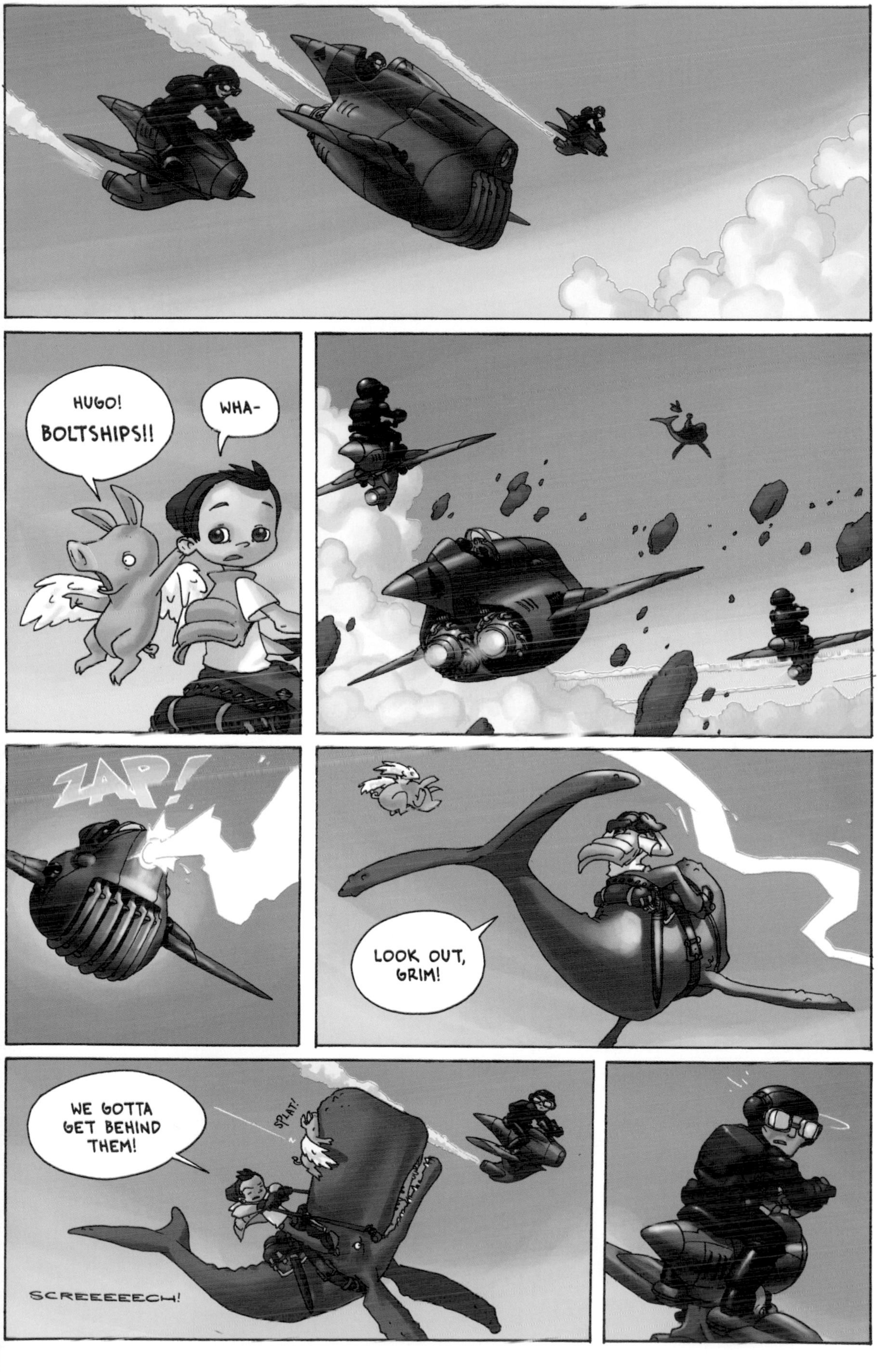
HUGO! BOLTSHIPS!!
WHA-
ZAP!
LOOK OUT, GRIM!
WE GOTTA GET BEHIND THEM!
SPLAT!
SCREEEEEECH!

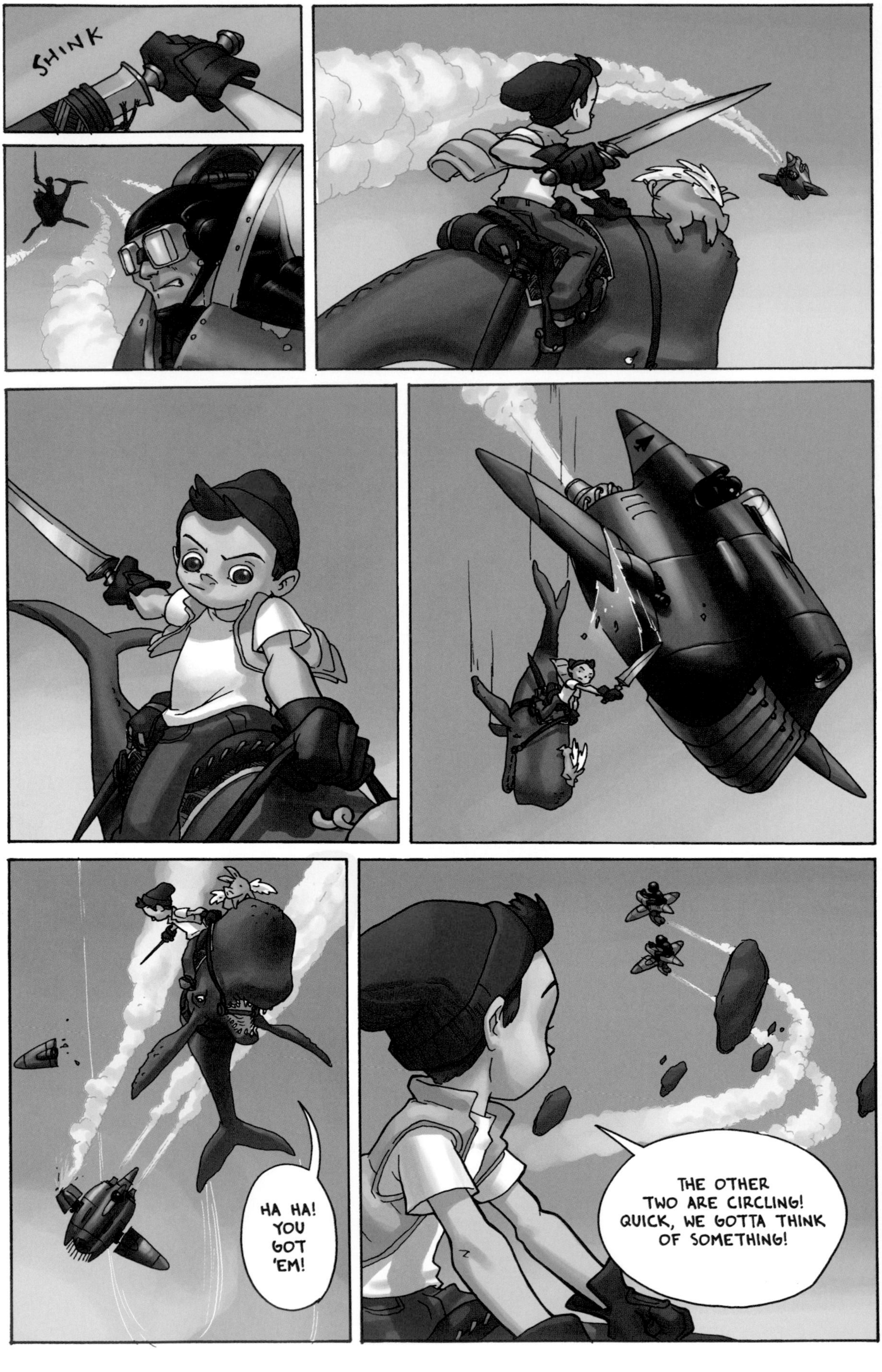
SHINK
HA HA! YOU GOT 'EM!
THE OTHER TWO ARE CIRCLING! QUICK, WE GOTTA THINK OF SOMETHING!

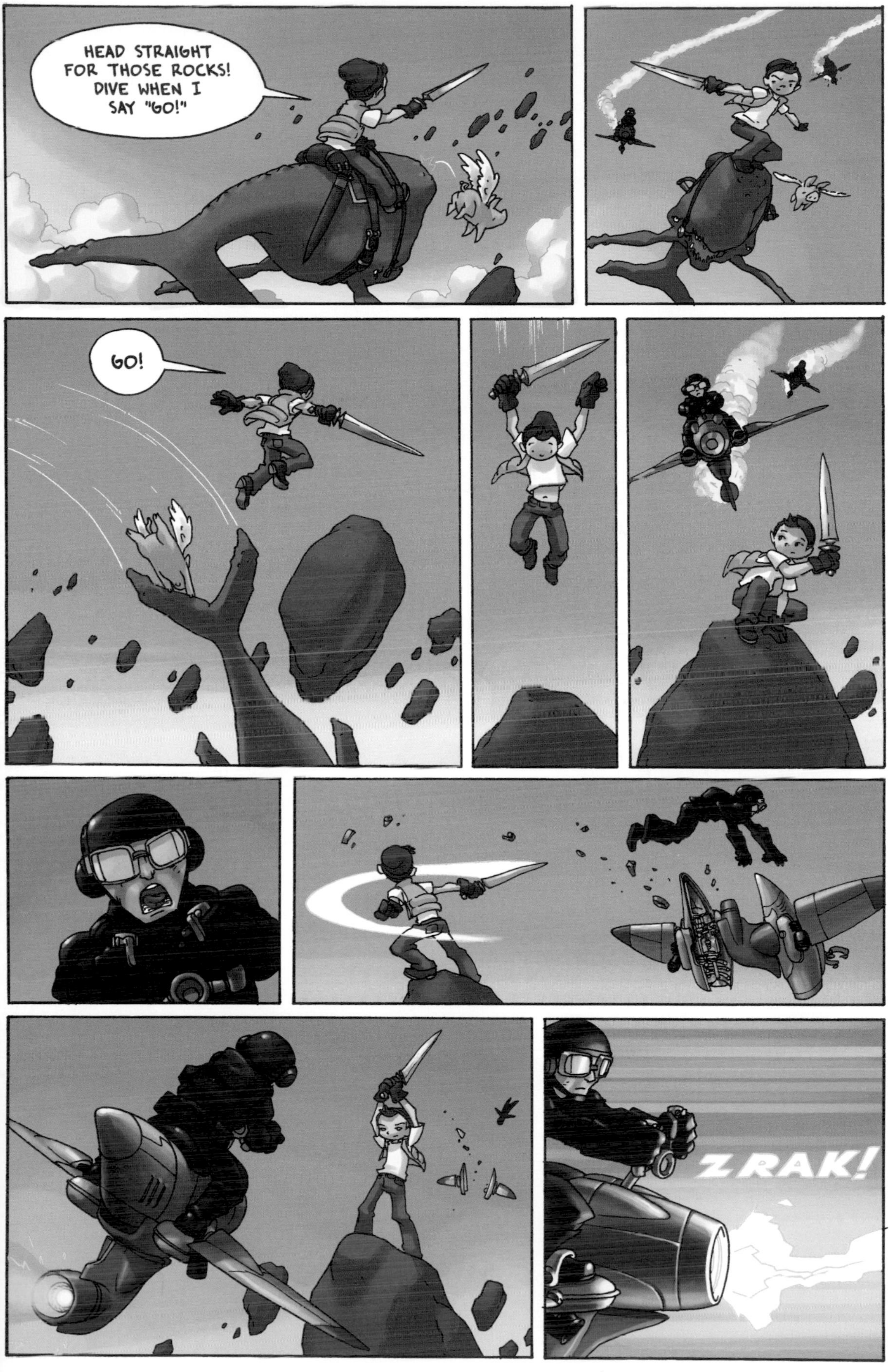
HEAD STRAIGHT FOR THOSE ROCKS! DIVE WHEN I SAY "GO!"
GO!
ZRAK!

CRACK!

WHAT WAS THAT?

FEELS LIKE I'M FALLING.

WE GOTTA CATCH HIM!

OH MY GOSH! HUGO FELL!

THERE'S NO WAY WE CAN REACH HIM!

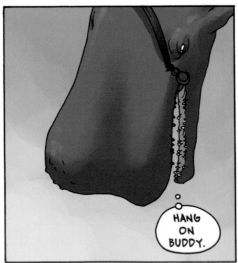

HANG ON BUDDY.

WAIT! WHO'S THAT?!!

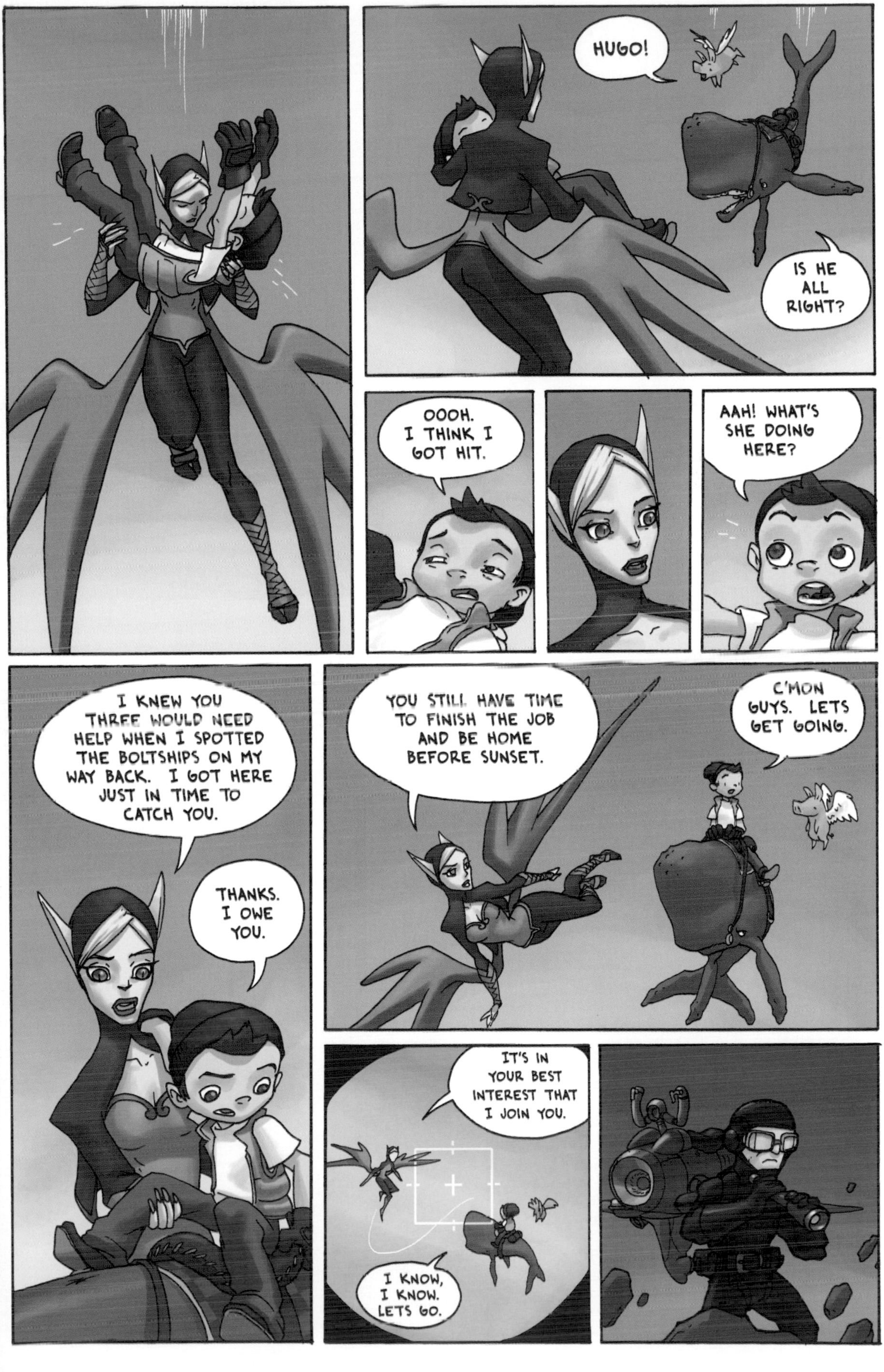
HUGO!
IS HE ALL RIGHT?
OOOH. I THINK I GOT HIT.
AAH! WHAT'S SHE DOING HERE?
I KNEW YOU THREE WOULD NEED HELP WHEN I SPOTTED THE BOLTSHIPS ON MY WAY BACK. I GOT HERE JUST IN TIME TO CATCH YOU.
THANKS. I OWE YOU.
YOU STILL HAVE TIME TO FINISH THE JOB AND BE HOME BEFORE SUNSET.
C'MON GUYS. LETS GET GOING.
IT'S IN YOUR BEST INTEREST THAT I JOIN YOU.
I KNOW, I KNOW. LETS GO.

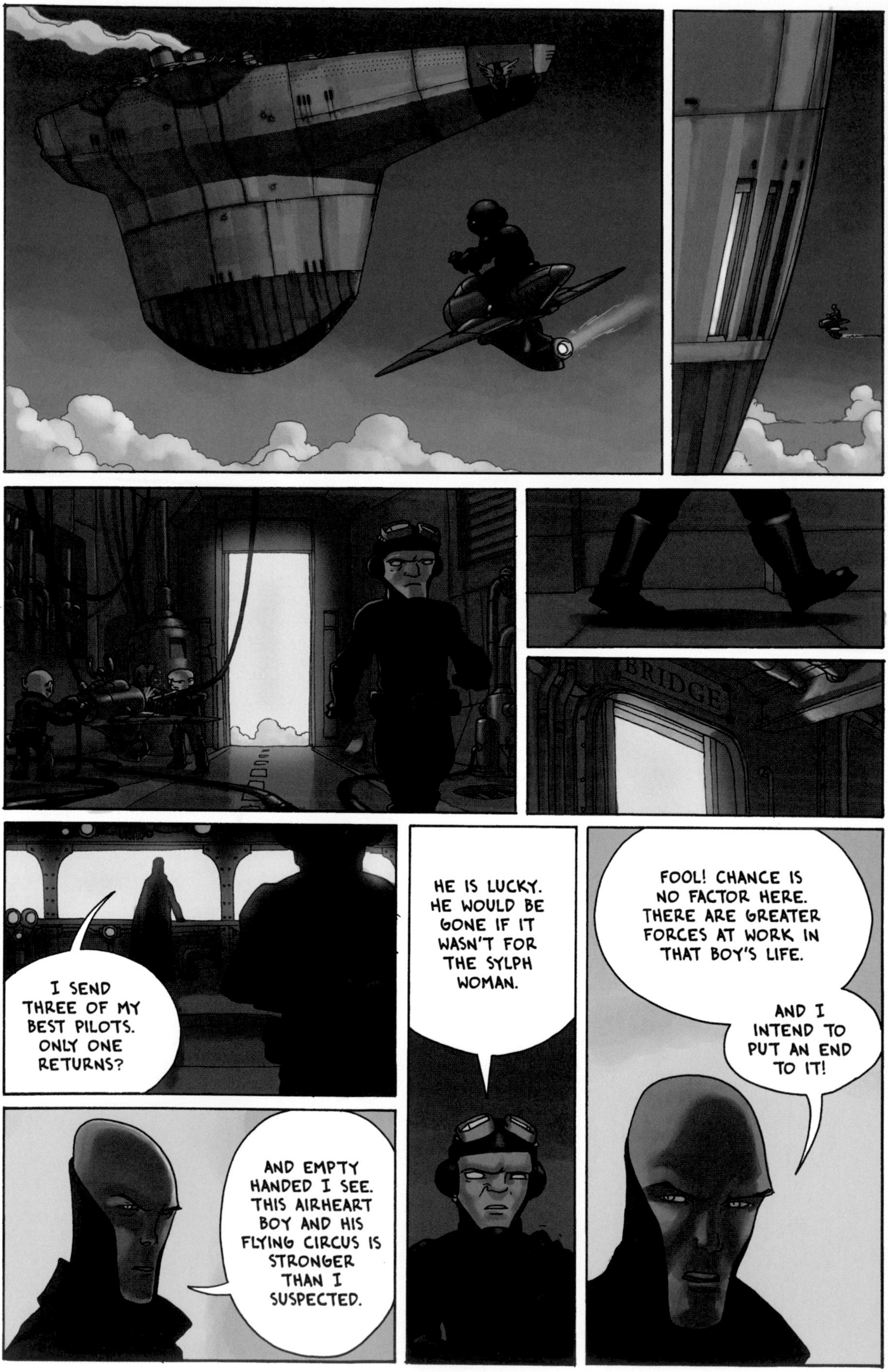
BRIDGE
I SEND THREE OF MY BEST PILOTS. ONLY ONE RETURNS?
AND EMPTY HANDED I SEE. THIS AIRHEART BOY AND HIS FLYING CIRCUS IS STRONGER THAN I SUSPECTED.
HE IS LUCKY. HE WOULD BE GONE IF IT WASN'T FOR THE SYLPH WOMAN.
FOOL! CHANCE IS NO FACTOR HERE. THERE ARE GREATER FORCES AT WORK IN THAT BOY'S LIFE.
AND I INTEND TO PUT AN END TO IT!

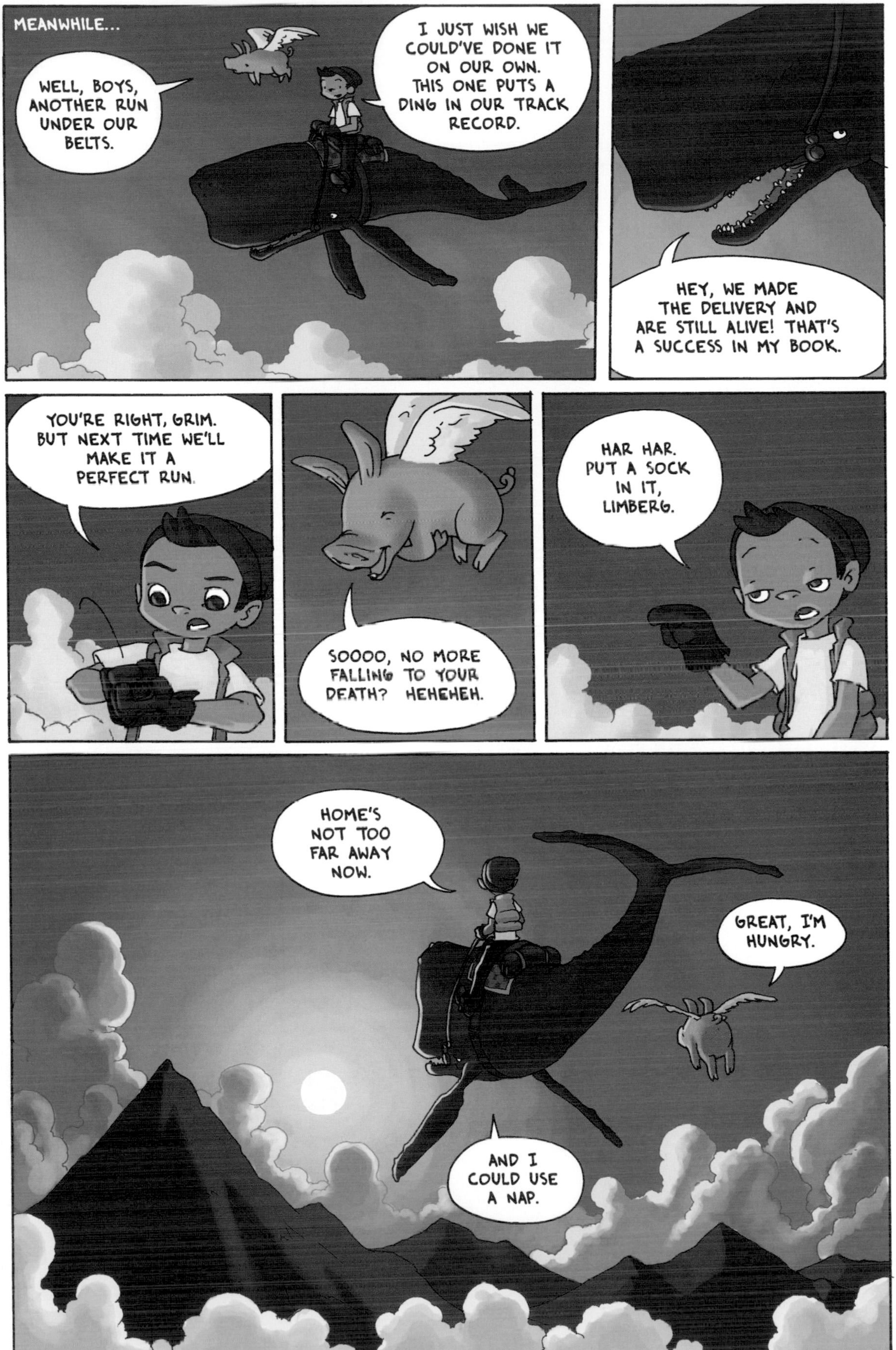
MEANWHILE...
WELL, BOYS, ANOTHER RUN UNDER OUR BELTS.
I JUST WISH WE COULD'VE DONE IT ON OUR OWN. THIS ONE PUTS A DING IN OUR TRACK RECORD.
HEY, WE MADE THE DELIVERY AND ARE STILL ALIVE! THAT'S A SUCCESS IN MY BOOK.
YOU'RE RIGHT, GRIM. BUT NEXT TIME WE'LL MAKE IT A PERFECT RUN.
SOOOO, NO MORE FALLING TO YOUR DEATH? HEHEHEH.
HAR HAR. PUT A SOCK IN IT, LIMBERG.
HOME'S NOT TOO FAR AWAY NOW.
GREAT, I'M HUNGRY.
AND I COULD USE A NAP.

I wish...

by vera brosgol

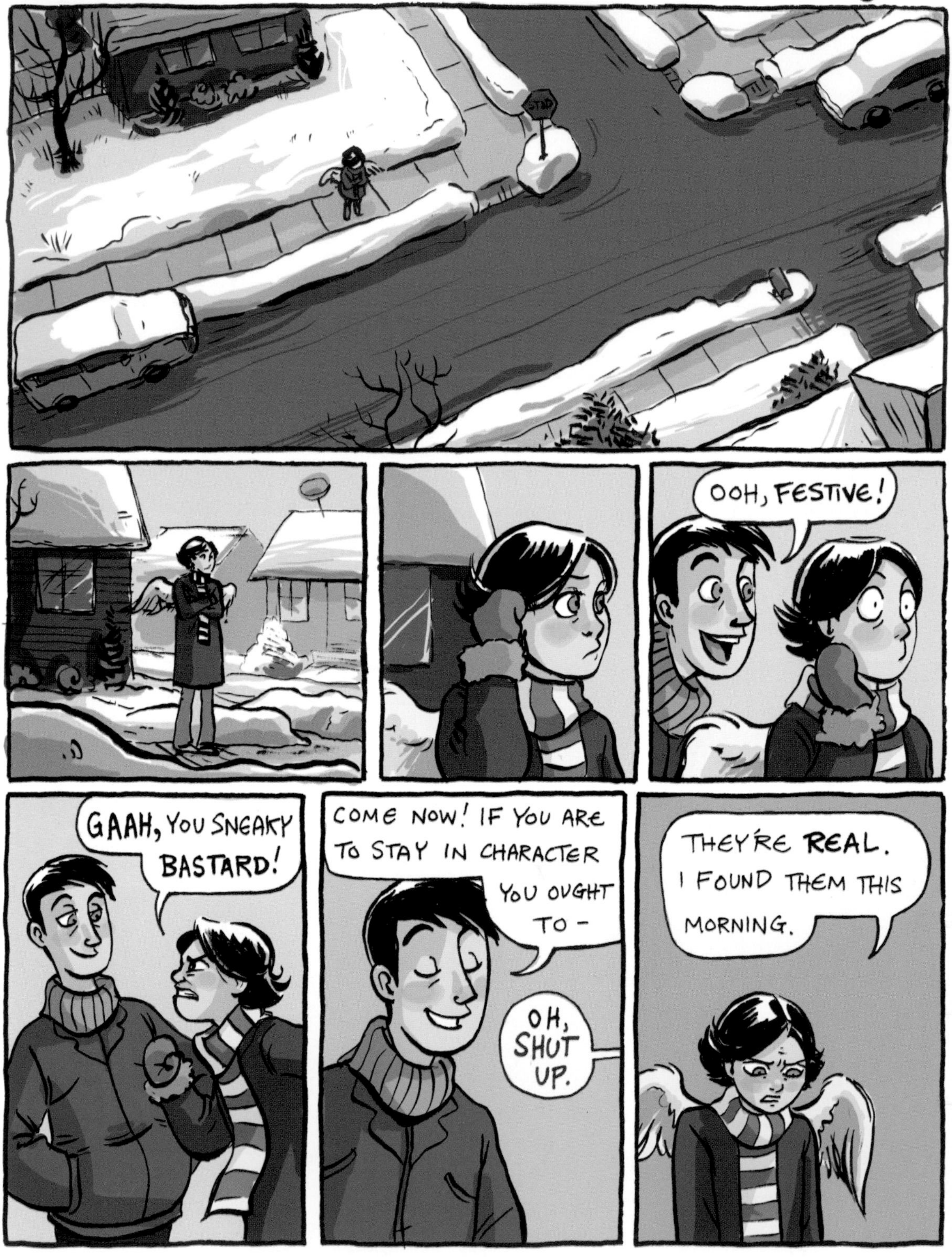
STOP
OOH, FESTIVE!
GAAH, YOU SNEAKY BASTARD!
COME NOW! IF YOU ARE TO STAY IN CHARACTER YOU OUGHT TO -
OH, SHUT UP.
THEY'RE **REAL**. I FOUND THEM THIS MORNING.

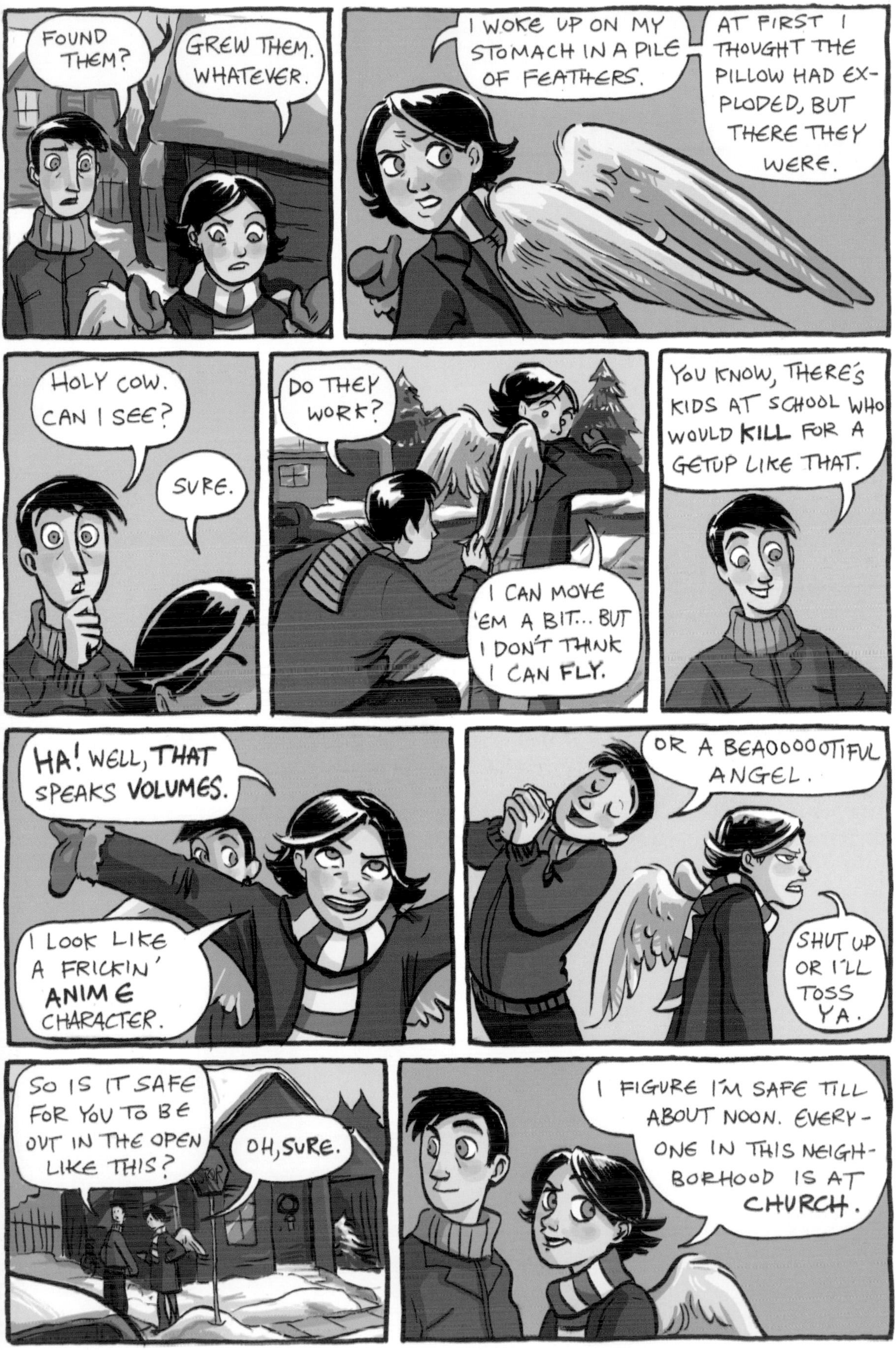
FOUND THEM?
GREW THEM. WHATEVER.
I WOKE UP ON MY STOMACH IN A PILE OF FEATHERS.
AT FIRST I THOUGHT THE PILLOW HAD EXPLODED, BUT THERE THEY WERE.
HOLY COW. CAN I SEE?
SURE.
DO THEY WORK?
I CAN MOVE 'EM A BIT... BUT I DON'T THINK I CAN FLY.
YOU KNOW, THERE'S KIDS AT SCHOOL WHO WOULD KILL FOR A GETUP LIKE THAT.
HA! WELL, THAT SPEAKS VOLUMES.
I LOOK LIKE A FRICKIN' ANIME CHARACTER.
OR A BEAOOOOOTIFUL ANGEL.
SHUT UP OR I'LL TOSS YA.
SO IS IT SAFE FOR YOU TO BE OUT IN THE OPEN LIKE THIS?
OH, SURE.
I FIGURE I'M SAFE TILL ABOUT NOON. EVERYONE IN THIS NEIGHBORHOOD IS AT CHURCH.

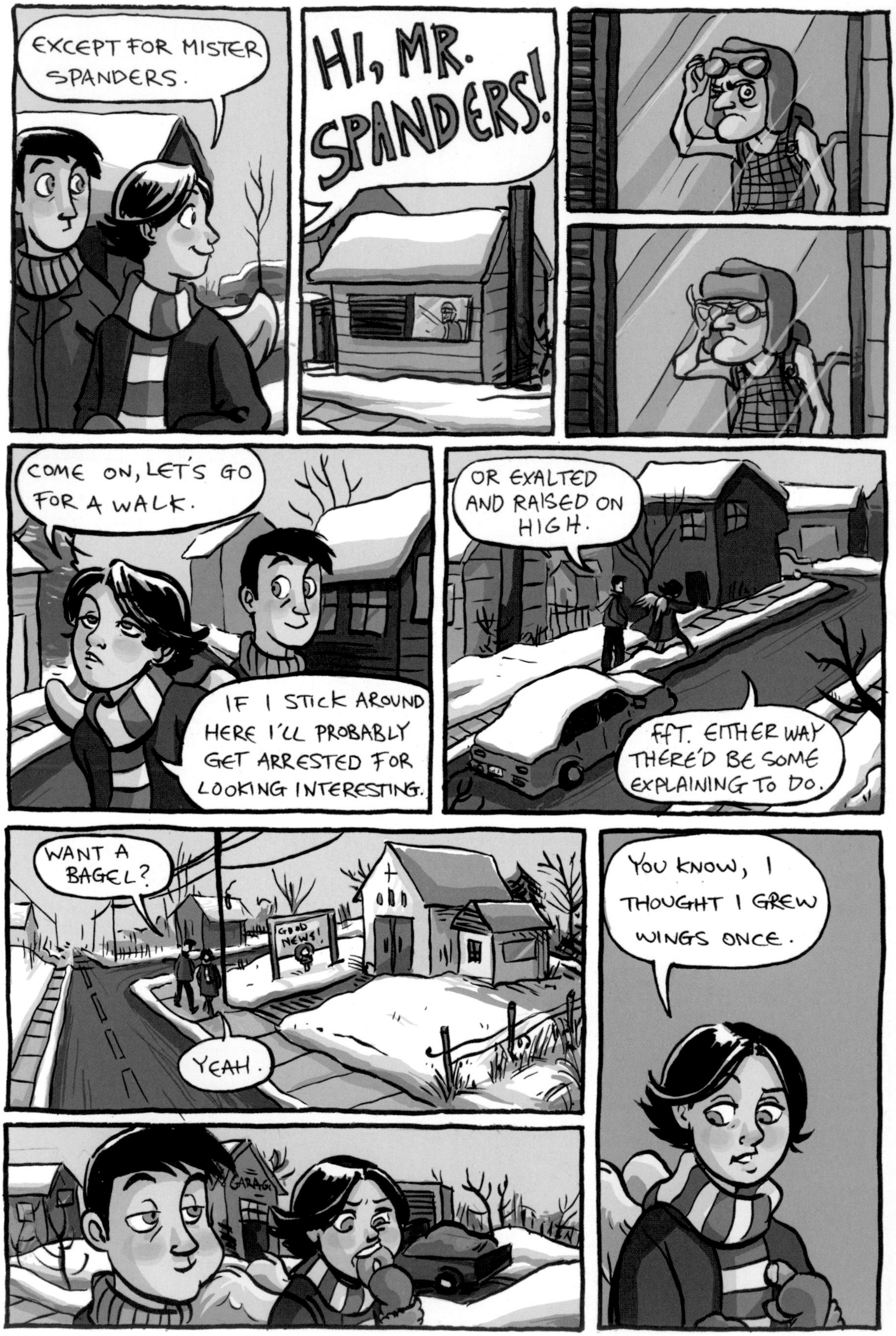
EXCEPT FOR MISTER SPANDERS.
HI, MR. SPANDERS!
COME ON, LET'S GO FOR A WALK.
IF I STICK AROUND HERE I'LL PROBABLY GET ARRESTED FOR LOOKING INTERESTING.
OR EXALTED AND RAISED ON HIGH.
FFT. EITHER WAY THERE'D BE SOME EXPLAINING TO DO.
WANT A BAGEL?
GOOD NEWS!
YEAH.
YOU KNOW, I THOUGHT I GREW WINGS ONCE.
GARAGE

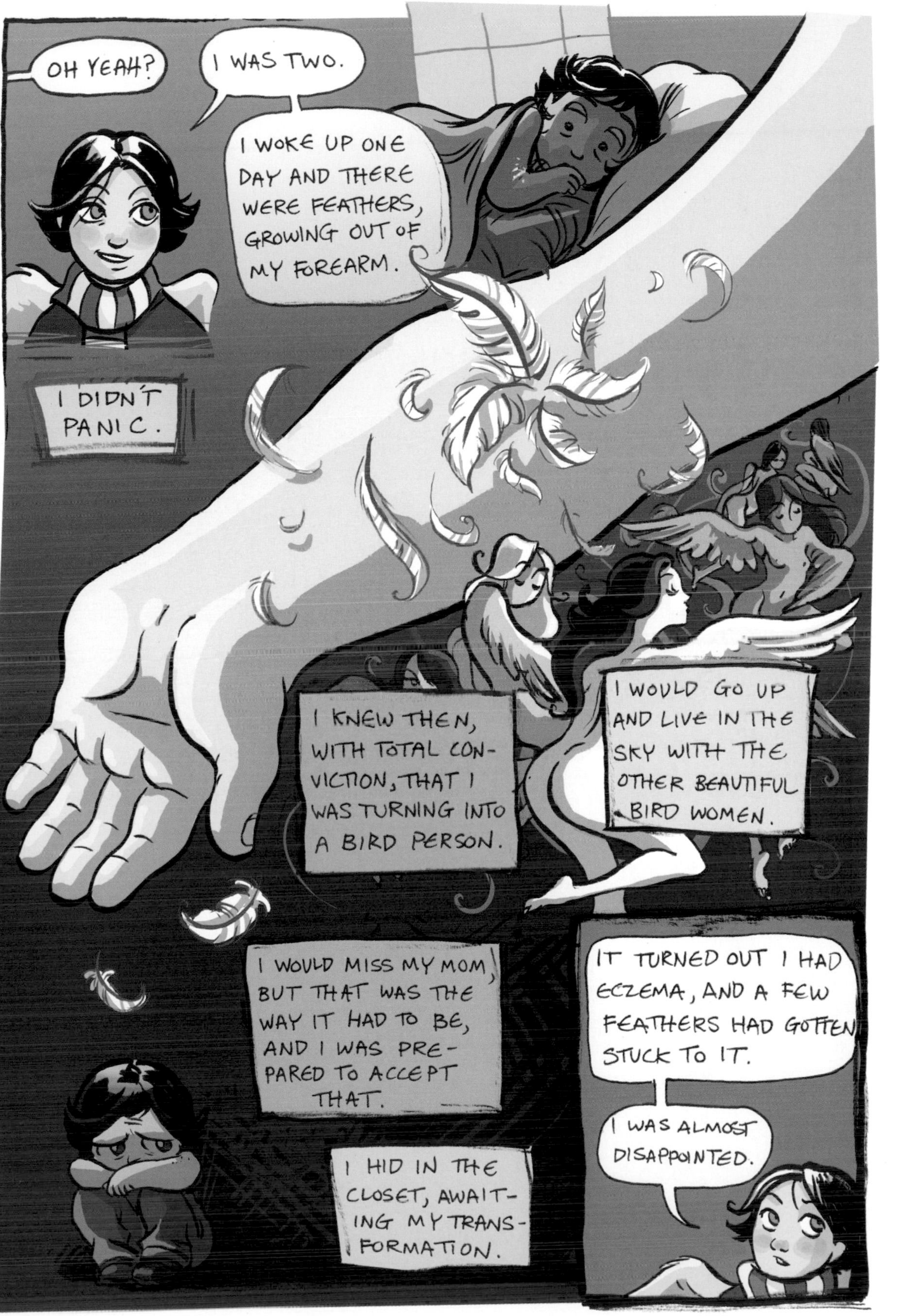

OH YEAH?
I WAS TWO.
I WOKE UP ONE DAY AND THERE WERE FEATHERS, GROWING OUT OF MY FOREARM.
I DIDN'T PANIC.
I KNEW THEN, WITH TOTAL CONVICTION, THAT I WAS TURNING INTO A BIRD PERSON.
I WOULD GO UP AND LIVE IN THE SKY WITH THE OTHER BEAUTIFUL BIRD WOMEN.
I WOULD MISS MY MOM, BUT THAT WAS THE WAY IT HAD TO BE, AND I WAS PREPARED TO ACCEPT THAT.
I HID IN THE CLOSET, AWAITING MY TRANSFORMATION.
IT TURNED OUT I HAD ECZEMA, AND A FEW FEATHERS HAD GOTTEN STUCK TO IT.
I WAS ALMOST DISAPPOINTED.

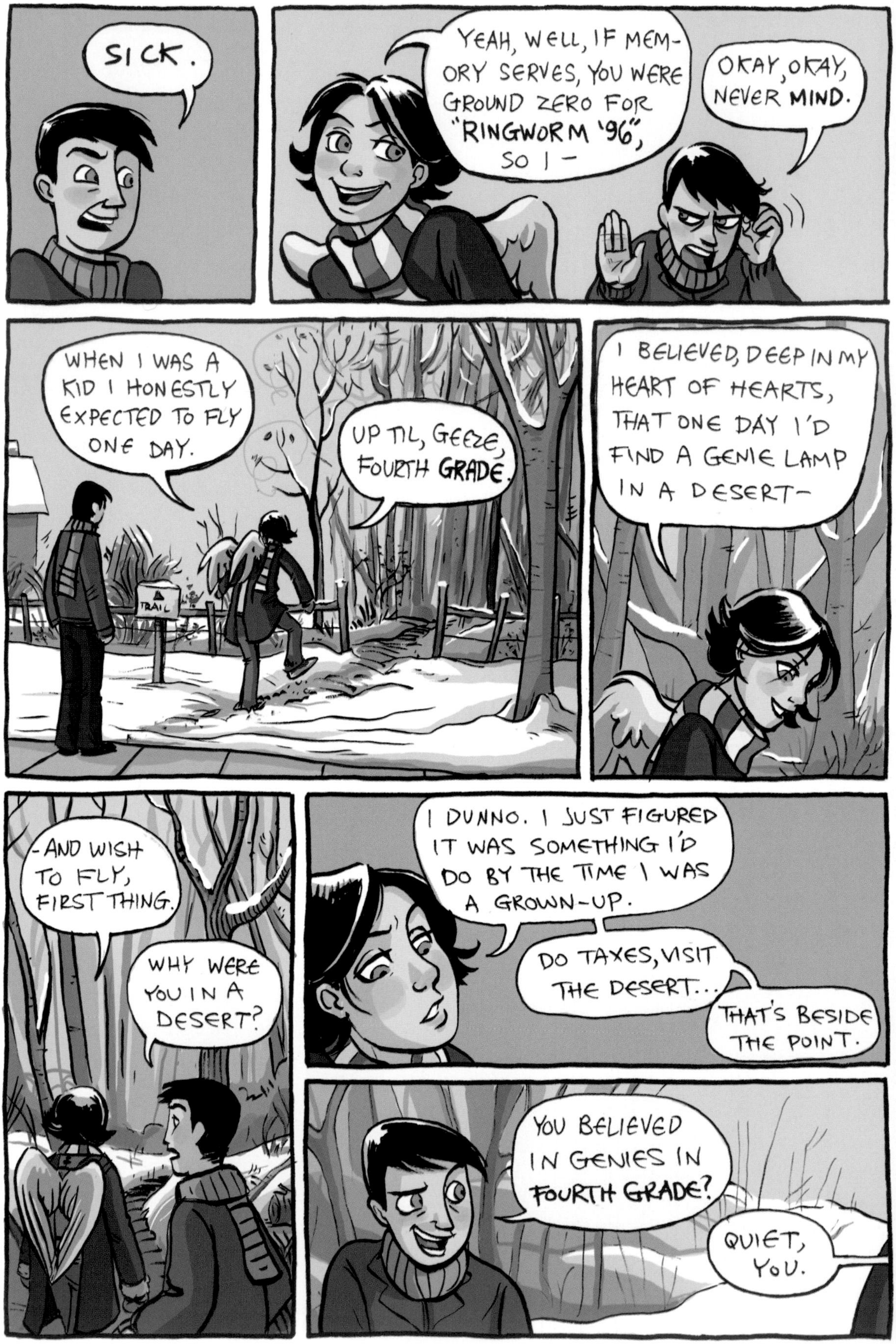
SICK.
YEAH, WELL, IF MEMORY SERVES, YOU WERE GROUND ZERO FOR "RINGWORM '96", SO I –
OKAY, OKAY, NEVER MIND.
WHEN I WAS A KID I HONESTLY EXPECTED TO FLY ONE DAY.
UP TIL, GEEZE, FOURTH GRADE.
TRAIL
I BELIEVED, DEEP IN MY HEART OF HEARTS, THAT ONE DAY I'D FIND A GENIE LAMP IN A DESERT–
–AND WISH TO FLY, FIRST THING.
WHY WERE YOU IN A DESERT?
I DUNNO. I JUST FIGURED IT WAS SOMETHING I'D DO BY THE TIME I WAS A GROWN-UP.
DO TAXES, VISIT THE DESERT...
THAT'S BESIDE THE POINT.
YOU BELIEVED IN GENIES IN FOURTH GRADE?
QUIET, YOU.

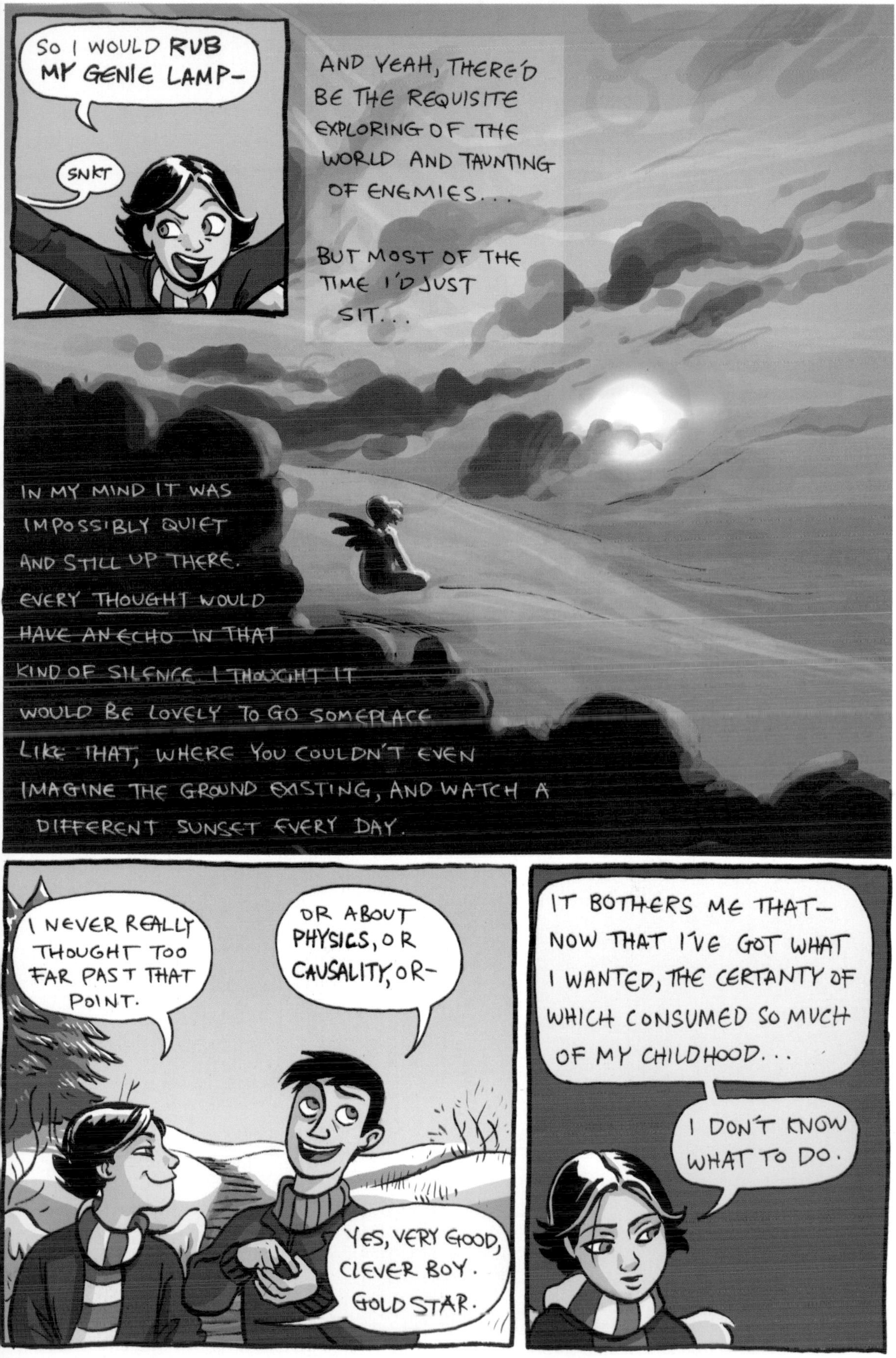

So I would RUB MY GENIE LAMP—
SNKT
AND YEAH, THERE'D BE THE REQUISITE EXPLORING OF THE WORLD AND TAUNTING OF ENEMIES...
BUT MOST OF THE TIME I'D JUST SIT...
IN MY MIND IT WAS IMPOSSIBLY QUIET AND STILL UP THERE. EVERY THOUGHT WOULD HAVE AN ECHO IN THAT KIND OF SILENCE. I THOUGHT IT WOULD BE LOVELY TO GO SOMEPLACE LIKE THAT, WHERE YOU COULDN'T EVEN IMAGINE THE GROUND EXISTING, AND WATCH A DIFFERENT SUNSET EVERY DAY.
I NEVER REALLY THOUGHT TOO FAR PAST THAT POINT.
OR ABOUT PHYSICS, OR CAUSALITY, OR—
YES, VERY GOOD, CLEVER BOY. GOLD STAR.
IT BOTHERS ME THAT— NOW THAT I'VE GOT WHAT I WANTED, THE CERTANTY OF WHICH CONSUMED SO MUCH OF MY CHILDHOOD...
I DON'T KNOW WHAT TO DO.

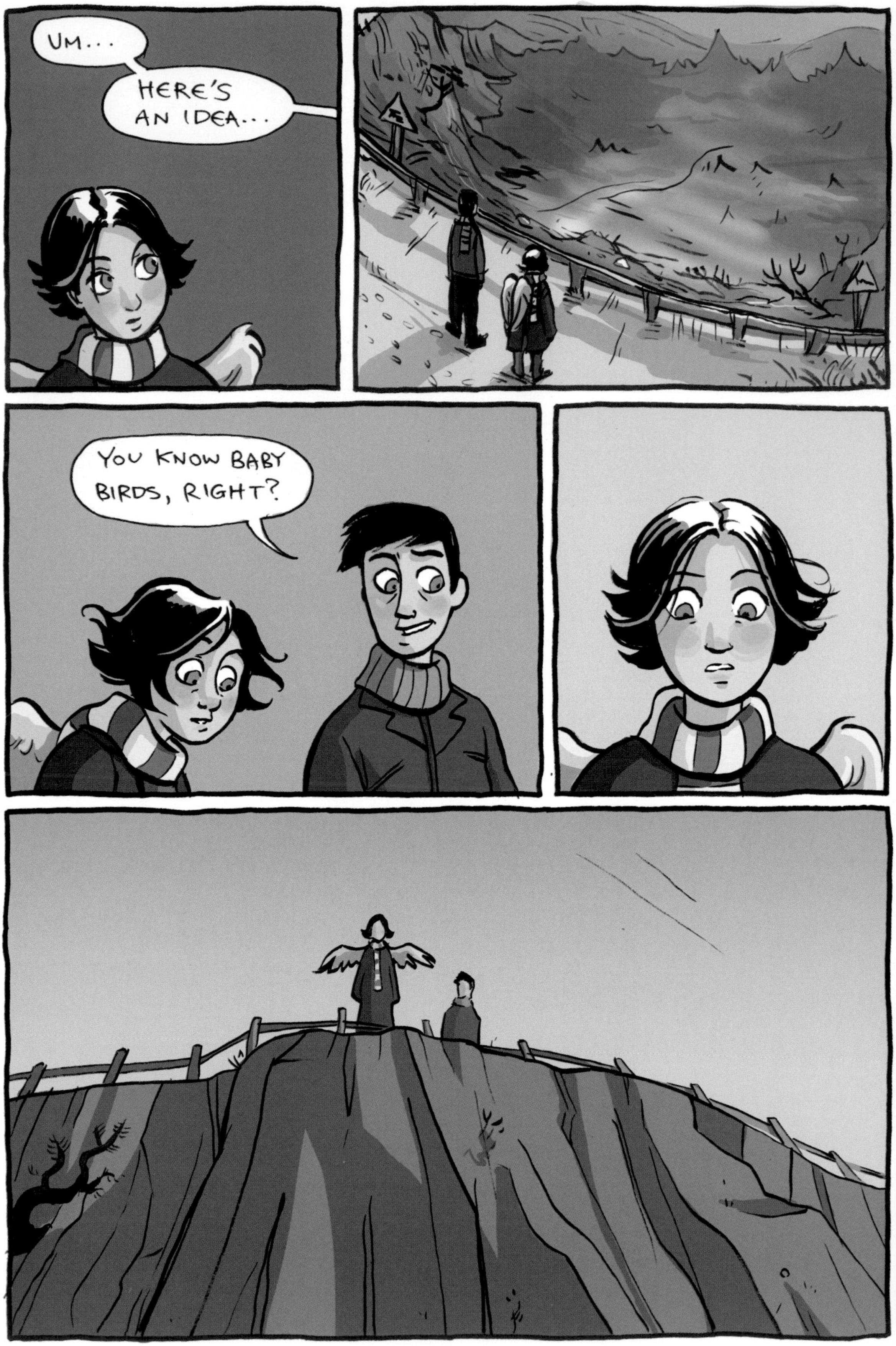
UM...
HERE'S AN IDEA...
YOU KNOW BABY BIRDS, RIGHT?

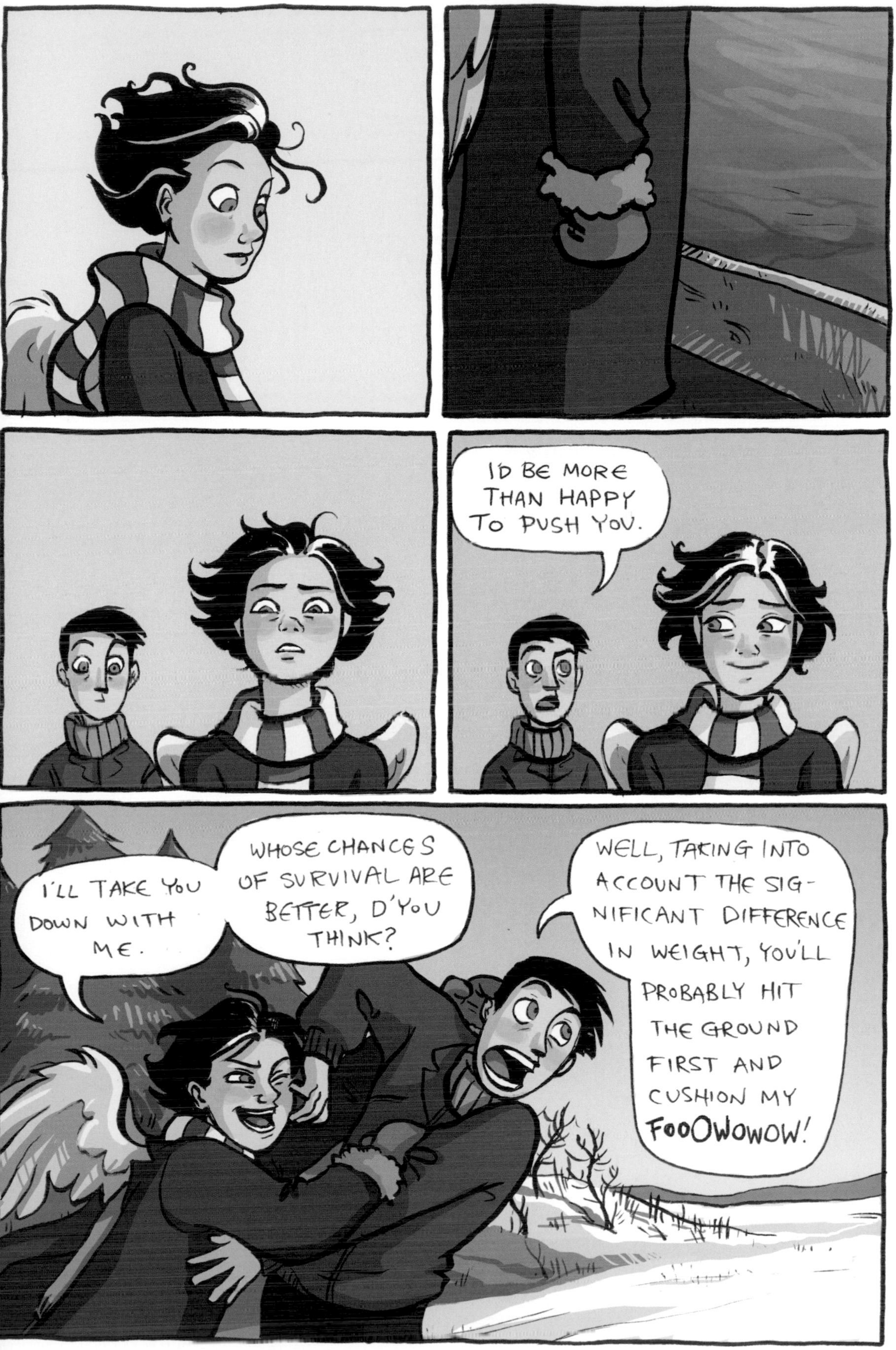

I'D BE MORE THAN HAPPY TO PUSH YOU.
I'LL TAKE YOU DOWN WITH ME.
WHOSE CHANCES OF SURVIVAL ARE BETTER, D'YOU THINK?
WELL, TAKING INTO ACCOUNT THE SIG-NIFICANT DIFFERENCE IN WEIGHT, YOU'LL PROBABLY HIT THE GROUND FIRST AND CUSHION MY FOOOWOWOW!

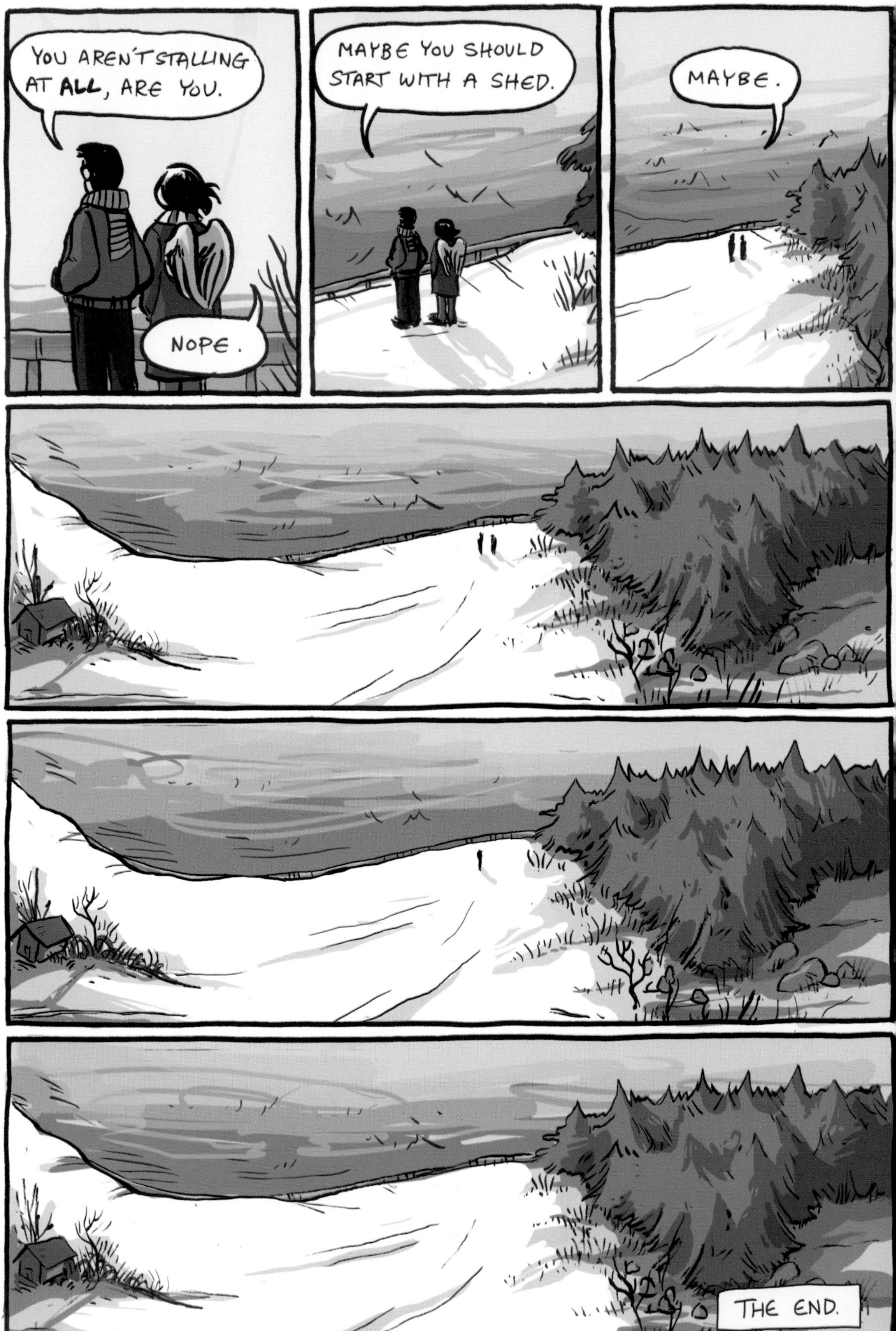
YOU AREN'T STALLING AT ALL, ARE YOU.
NOPE.
MAYBE YOU SHOULD START WITH A SHED.
MAYBE.
THE END.

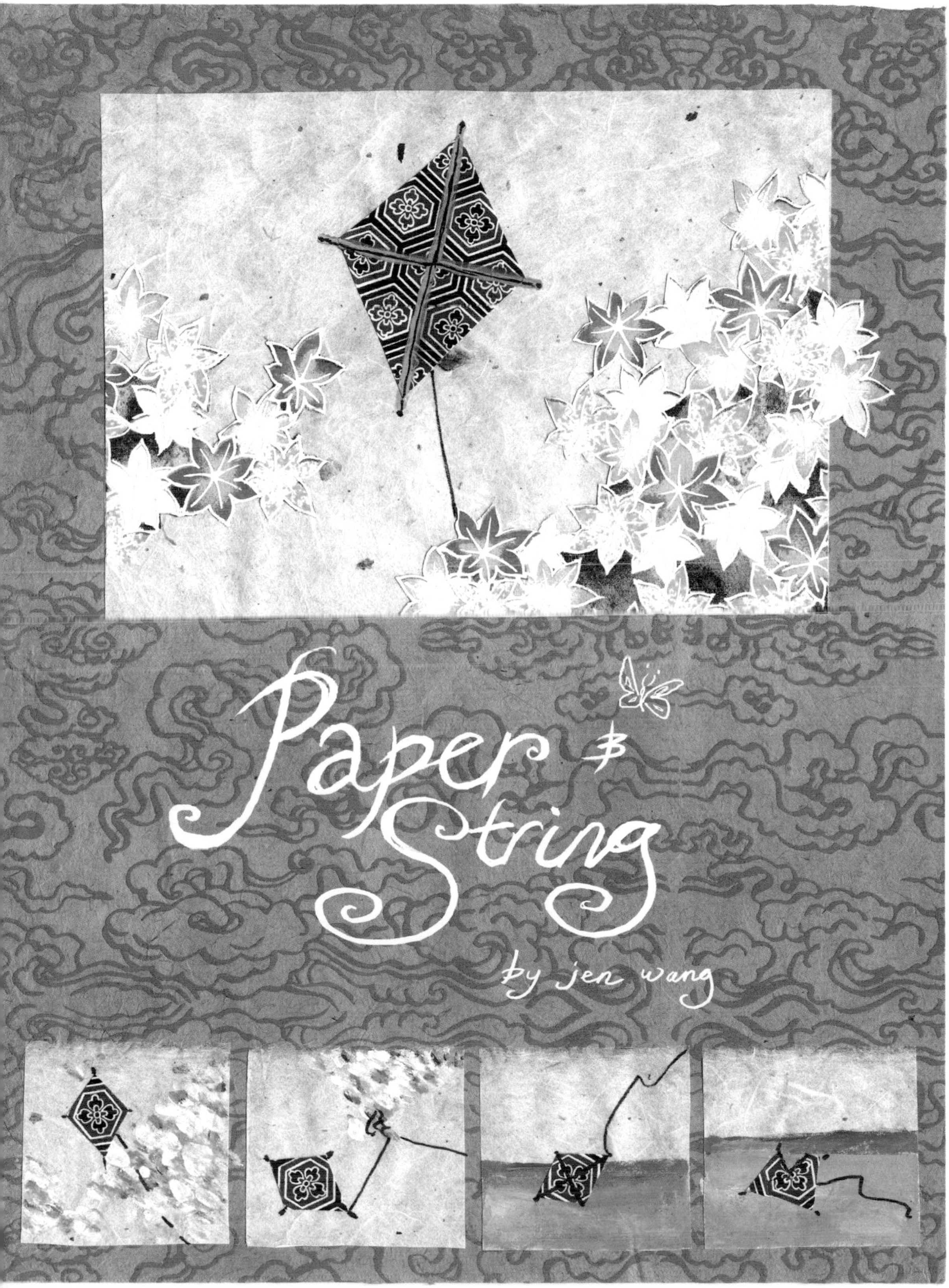
Paper & String
by jen wang

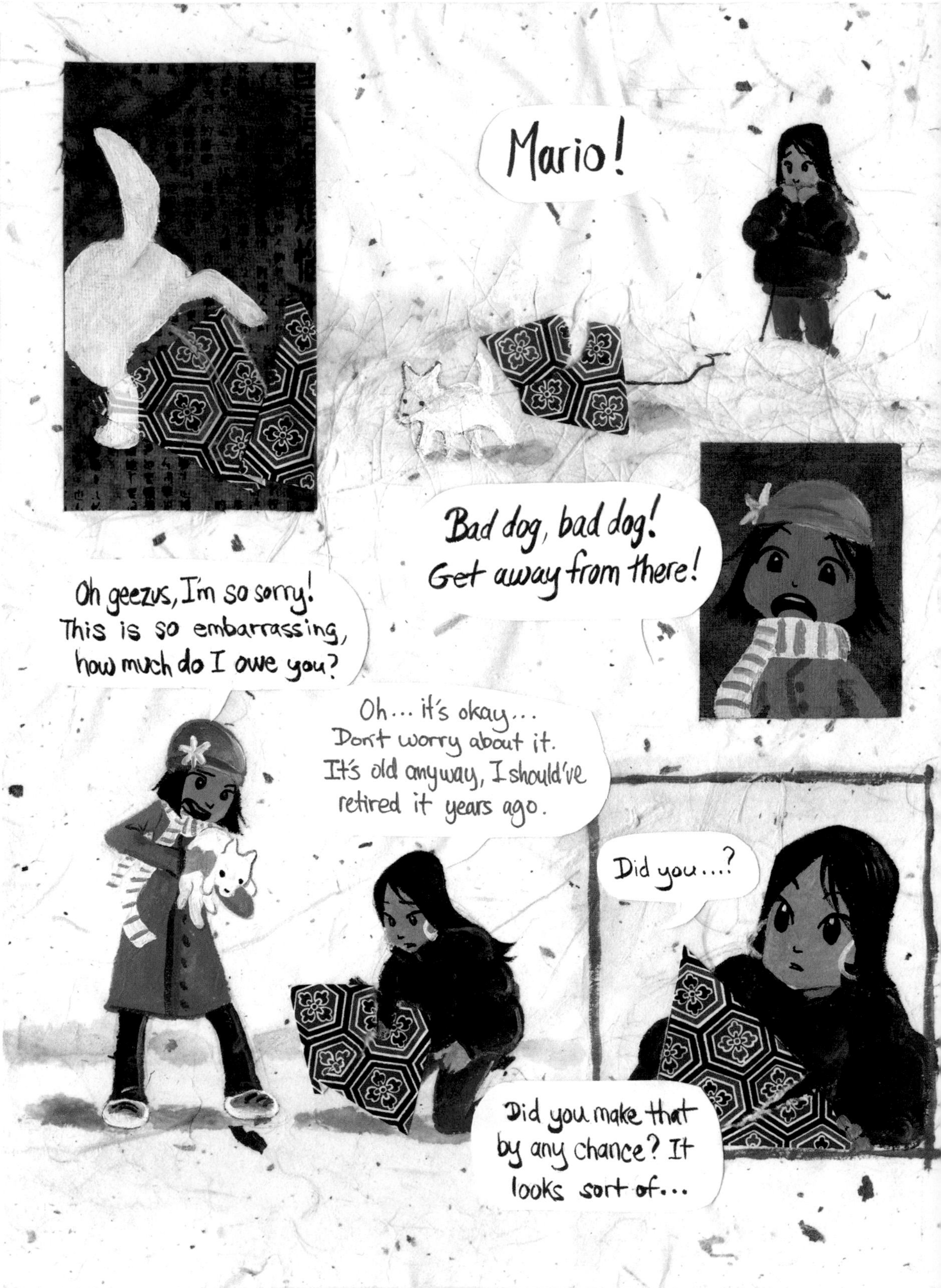
Mario!
Bad dog, bad dog! Get away from there!
Oh geezus, I'm so sorry! This is so embarrassing, how much do I owe you?
Oh... it's okay... Don't worry about it. It's old anyway, I should've retired it years ago.
Did you...?
Did you make that by any chance? It looks sort of...

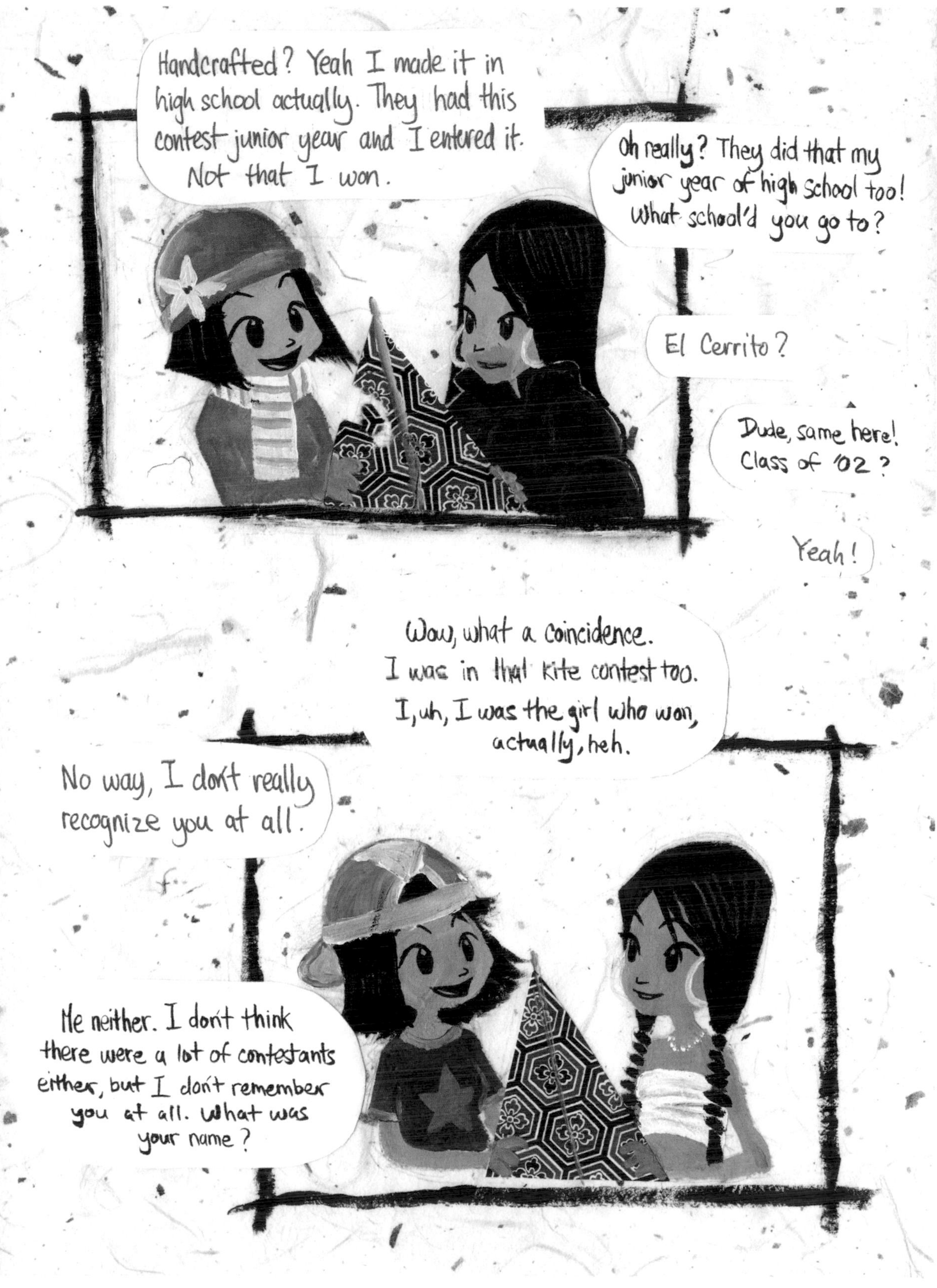
Handcrafted? Yeah I made it in high school actually. They had this contest junior year and I entered it. Not that I won.
Oh really? They did that my junior year of high school too! What school'd you go to?
El Cerrito?
Dude, same here! Class of '02?
Yeah!
Wow, what a coincidence. I was in that kite contest too. I, uh, I was the girl who won, actually, heh.
No way, I don't really recognize you at all.
Me neither. I don't think there were a lot of contestants either, but I don't remember you at all. What was your name?

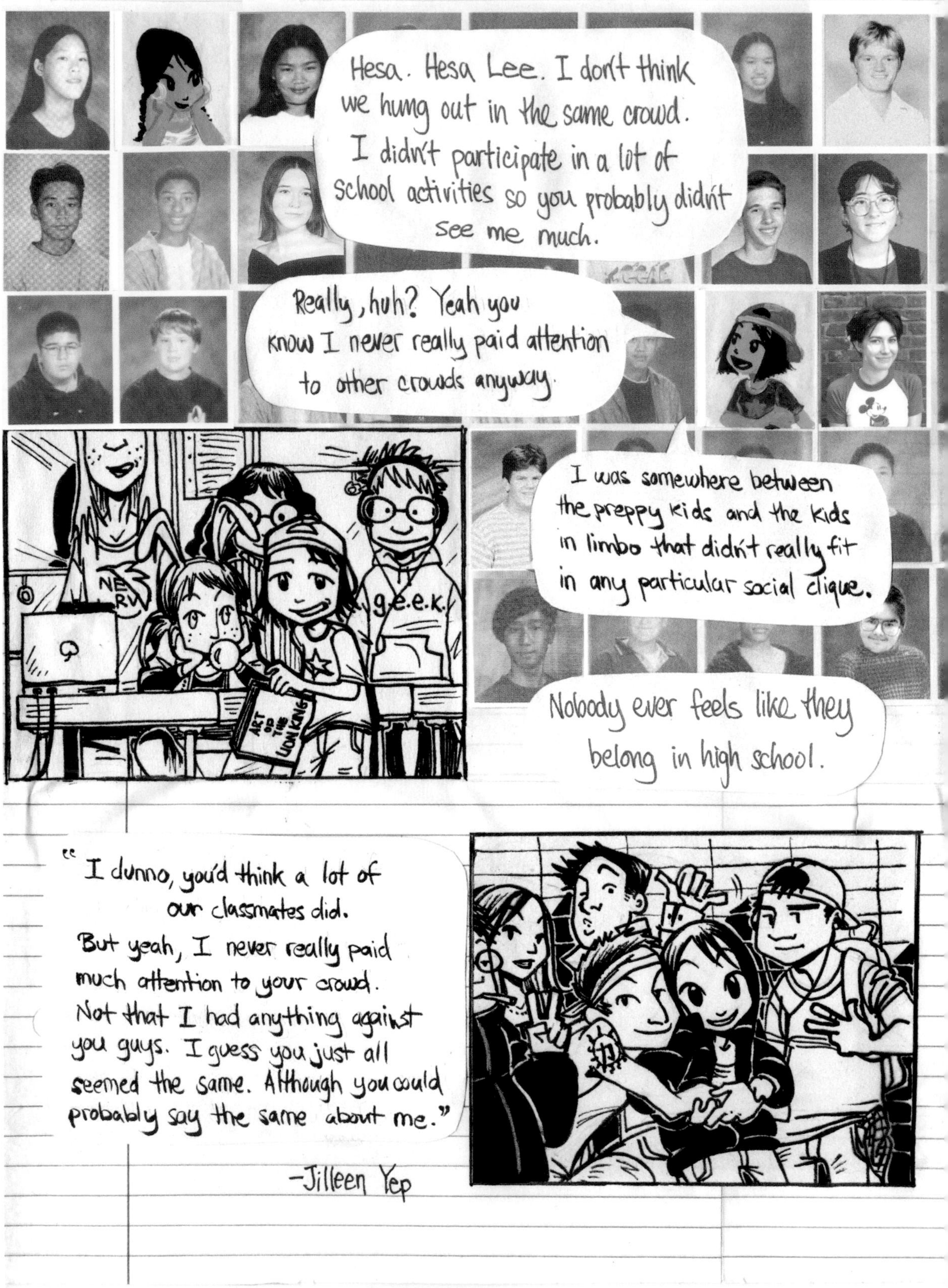
Hesa. Hesa Lee. I don't think we hung out in the same crowd. I didn't participate in a lot of school activities so you probably didn't see me much.
Really, huh? Yeah you know I never really paid attention to other crowds anyway.
I was somewhere between the preppy kids and the kids in limbo that didn't really fit in any particular social clique.
Nobody ever feels like they belong in high school.
NERV
g.e.e.k.
ART OF THE LION KING
"I dunno, you'd think a lot of our classmates did. But yeah, I never really paid much attention to your crowd. Not that I had anything against you guys. I guess you just all seemed the same. Although you could probably say the same about me."
–Jilleen Yep

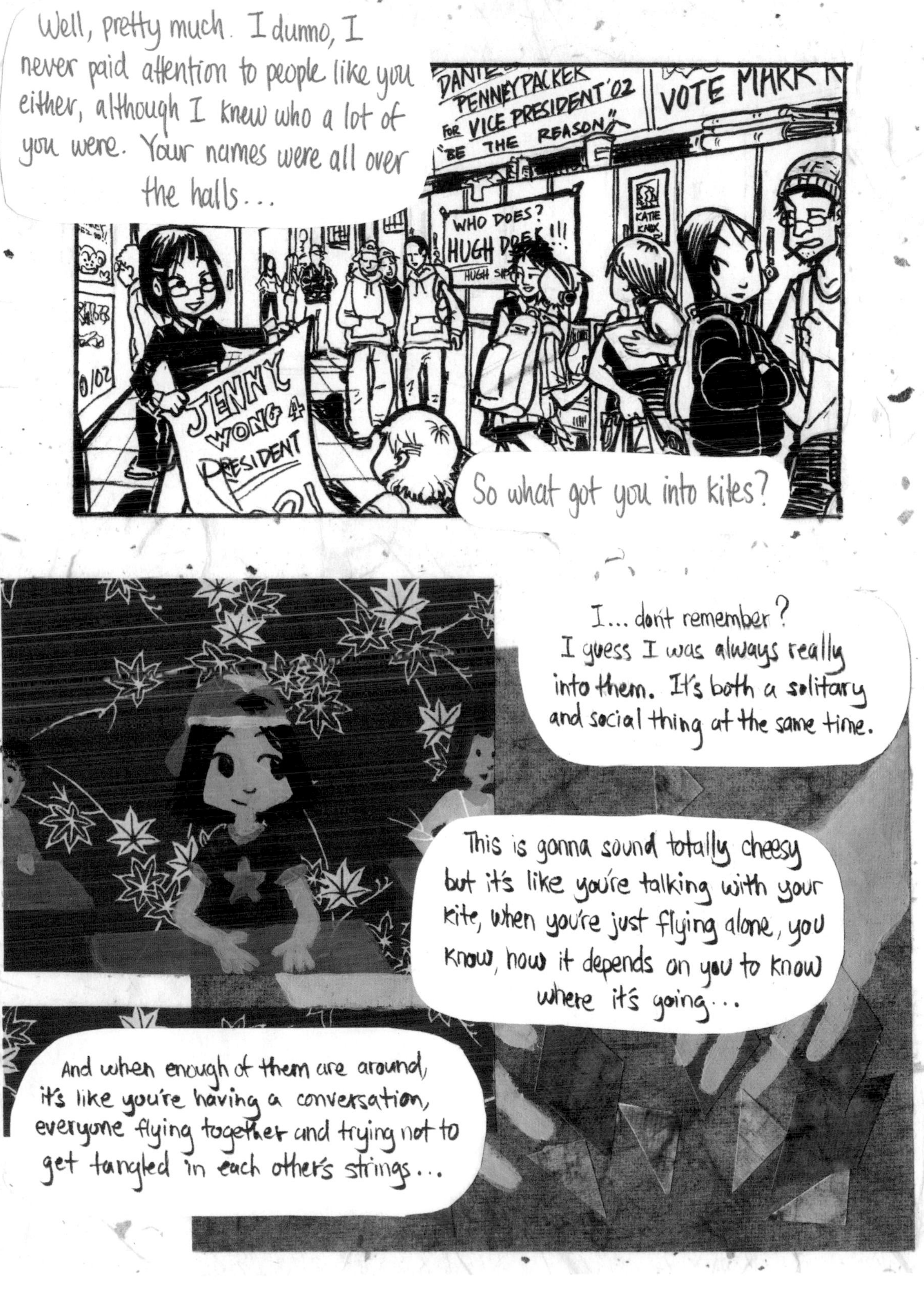

Well, pretty much. I dunno, I never paid attention to people like you either, although I knew who a lot of you were. Your names were all over the halls...
PENNEYPACKER FOR VICE PRESIDENT '02 "BE THE REASON"
VOTE MARK
WHO DOES?
JENNY WONG 4 PRESIDENT
So what got you into kites?
I... don't remember? I guess I was always really into them. It's both a solitary and social thing at the same time.
This is gonna sound totally cheesy but it's like you're talking with your kite, when you're just flying alone, you know, how it depends on you to know where it's going...
And when enough of them are around, it's like you're having a conversation, everyone flying together and trying not to get tangled in each other's strings...

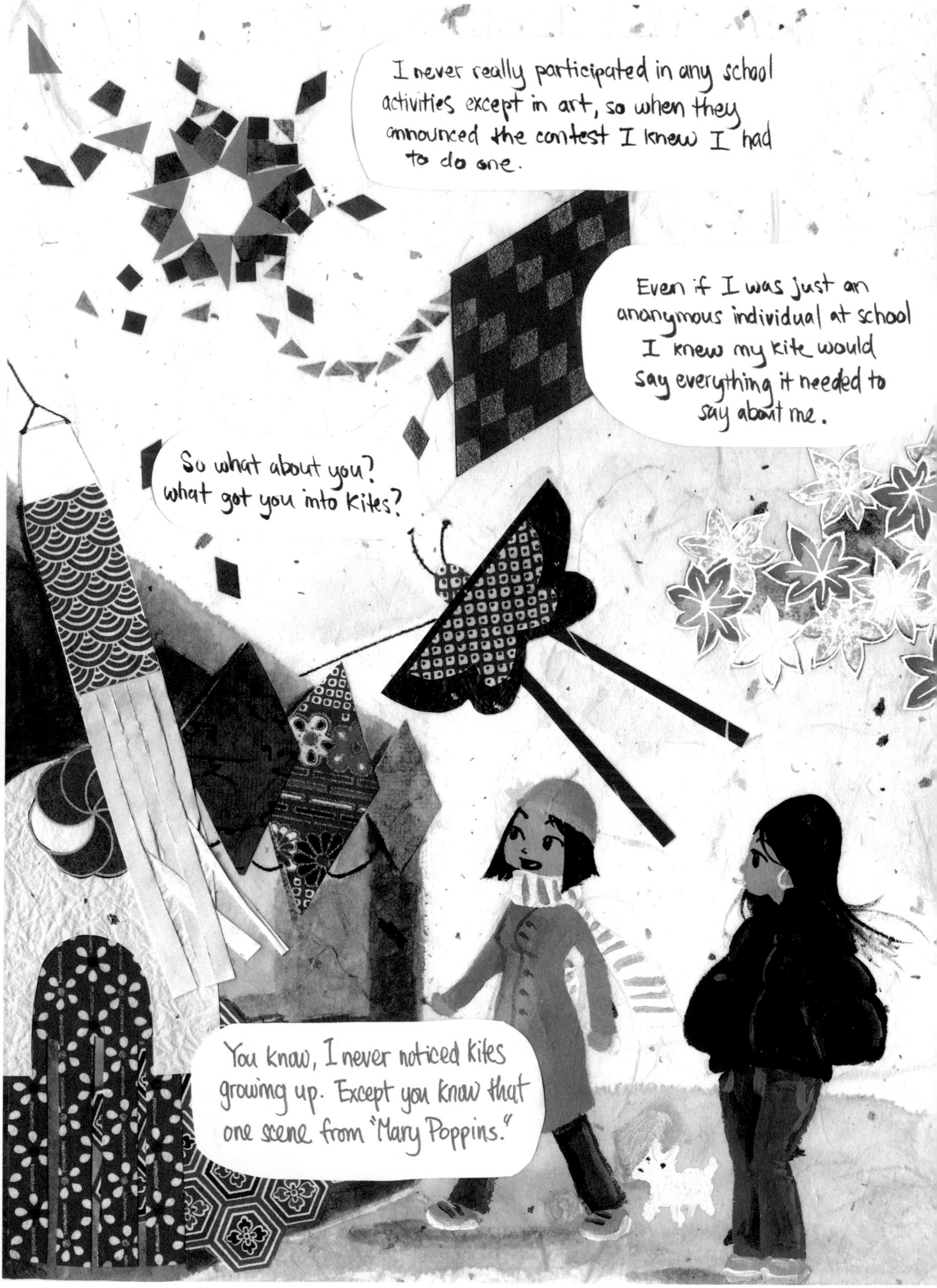

I never really participated in any school activities except in art, so when they announced the contest I knew I had to do one.
Even if I was just an anonymous individual at school I knew my kite would say everything it needed to say about me.
So what about you? what got you into kites?
You know, I never noticed kites growing up. Except you know that one scene from "Mary Poppins."

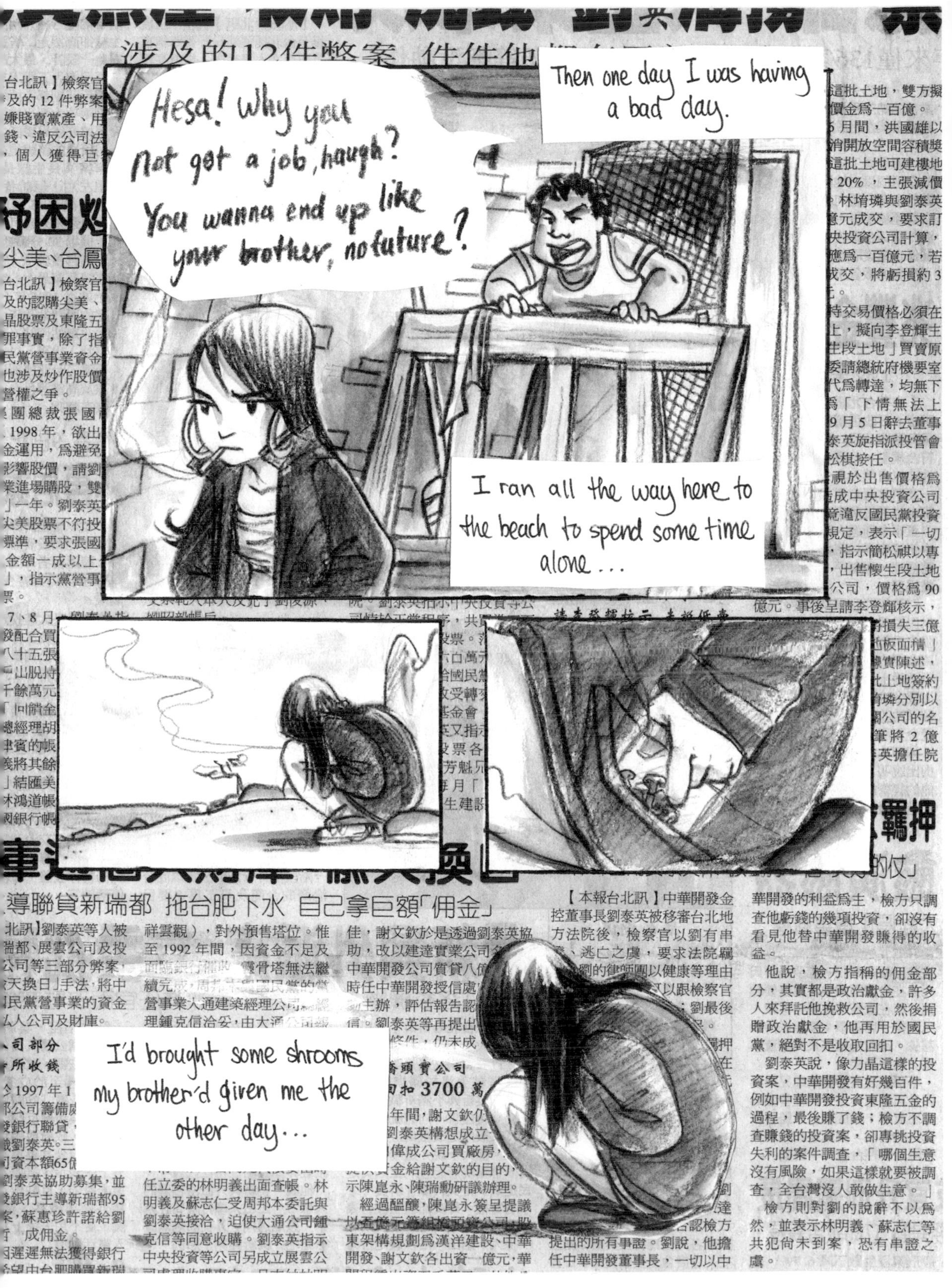
Then one day I was having a bad day.
Hesa! Why you not got a job, haugh? You wanna end up like your brother, no future?
I ran all the way here to the beach to spend some time alone...
I'd brought some shrooms my brother'd given me the other day...

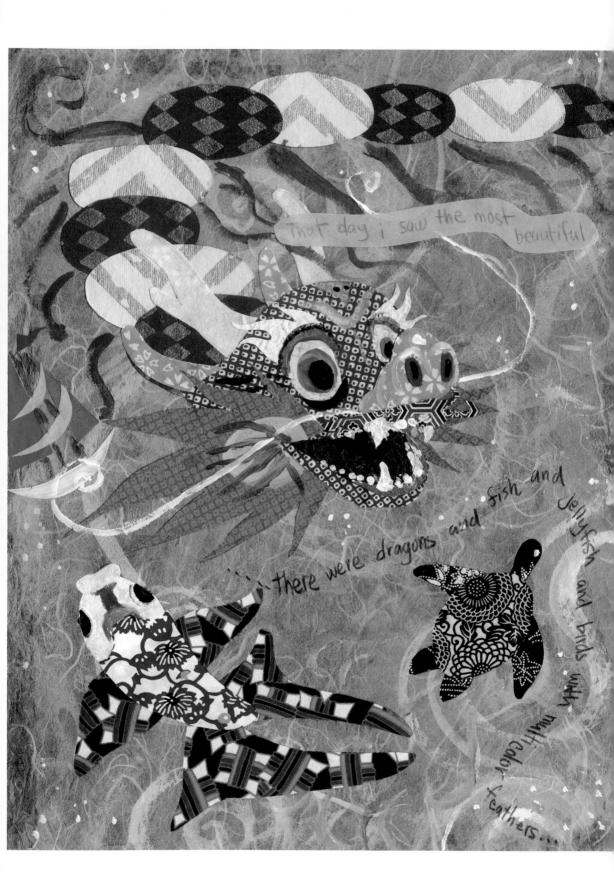

That day i saw the most beautiful

There were dragons and fish and jellyfish and birds with multicolor feathers...

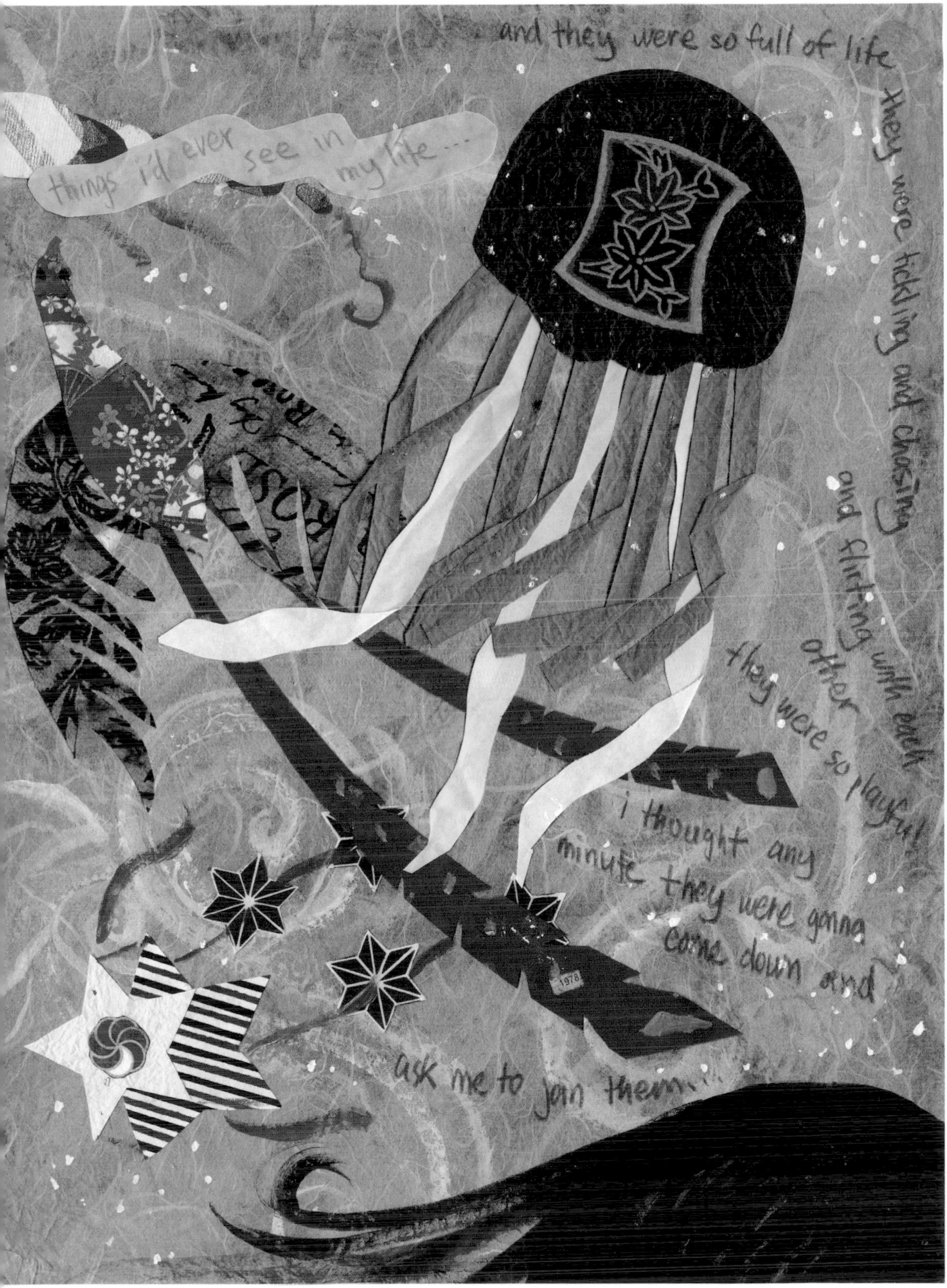
things i'd ever see in my life...
and they were so full of life
they were tickling and chasing
and flirting with each other
they were so playful
i thought any minute they were going come down and
ask me to join them...
1978

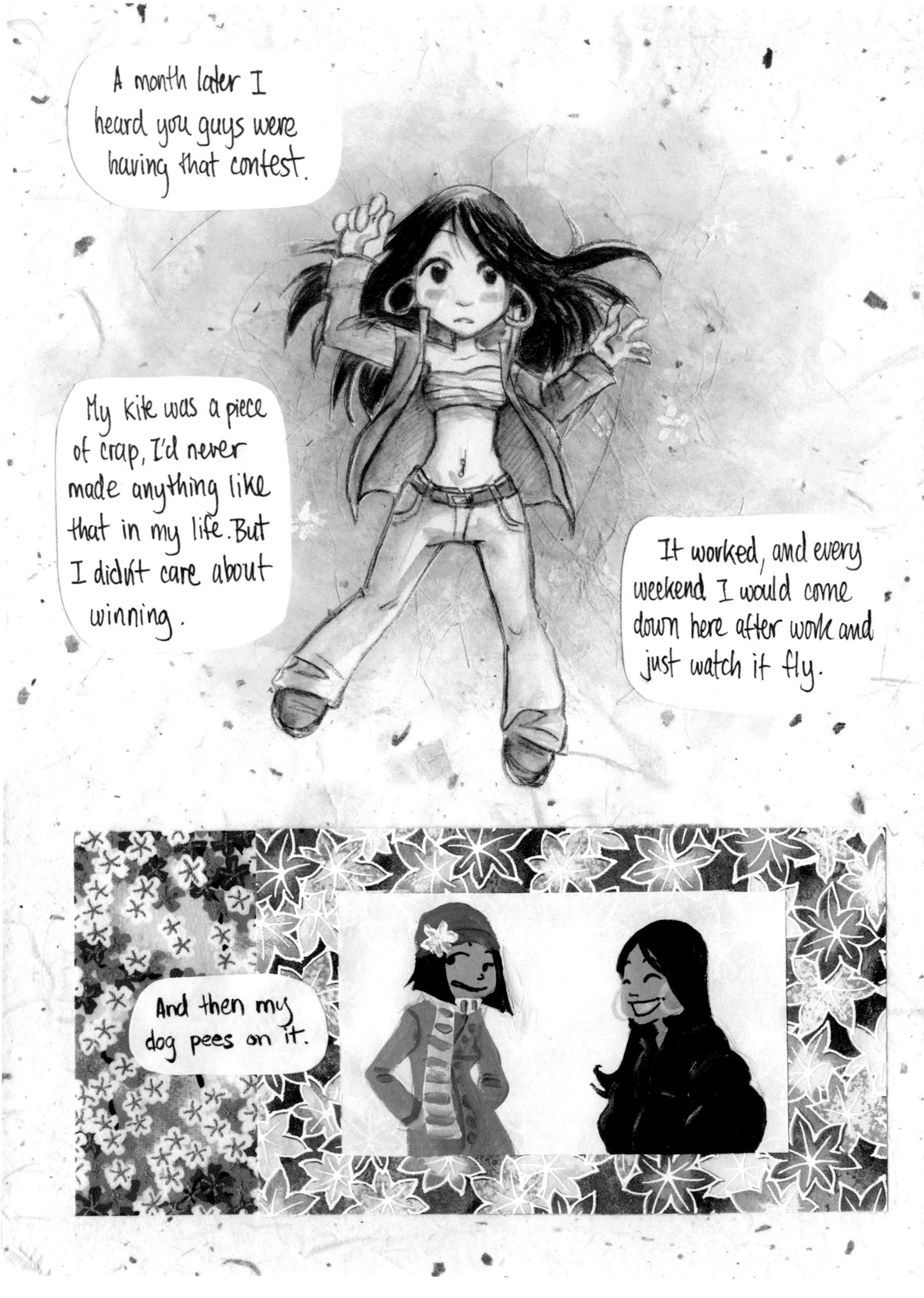
A month later I heard you guys were having that contest.
My kite was a piece of crap, I'd never made anything like that in my life. But I didn't care about winning.
It worked, and every weekend I would come down here after work and just watch it fly.
And then my dog pees on it.

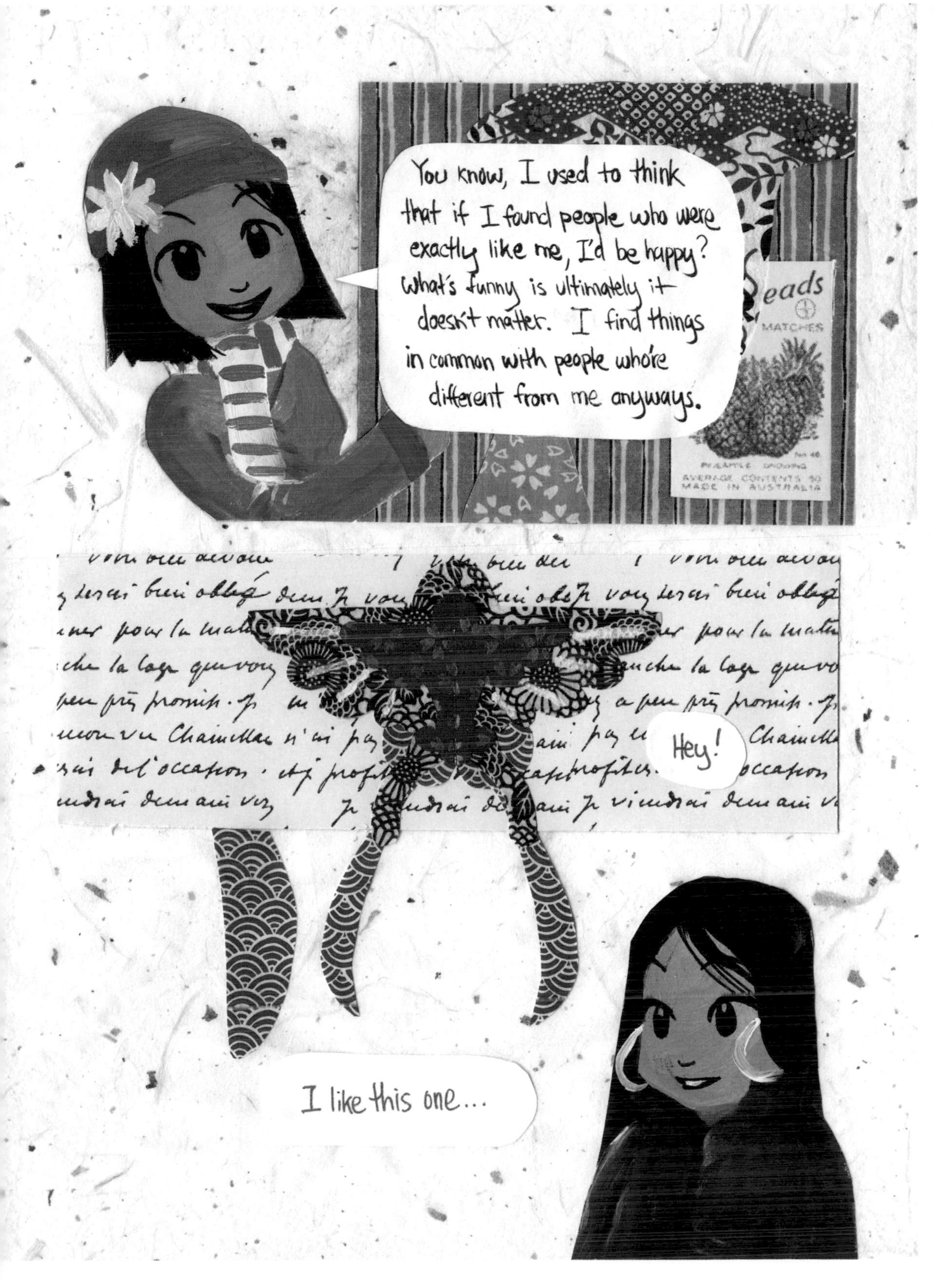
You know, I used to think that if I found people who were exactly like me, I'd be happy? What's funny is ultimately it doesn't matter. I find things in common with people who're different from me anyways.
Hey!
I like this one...

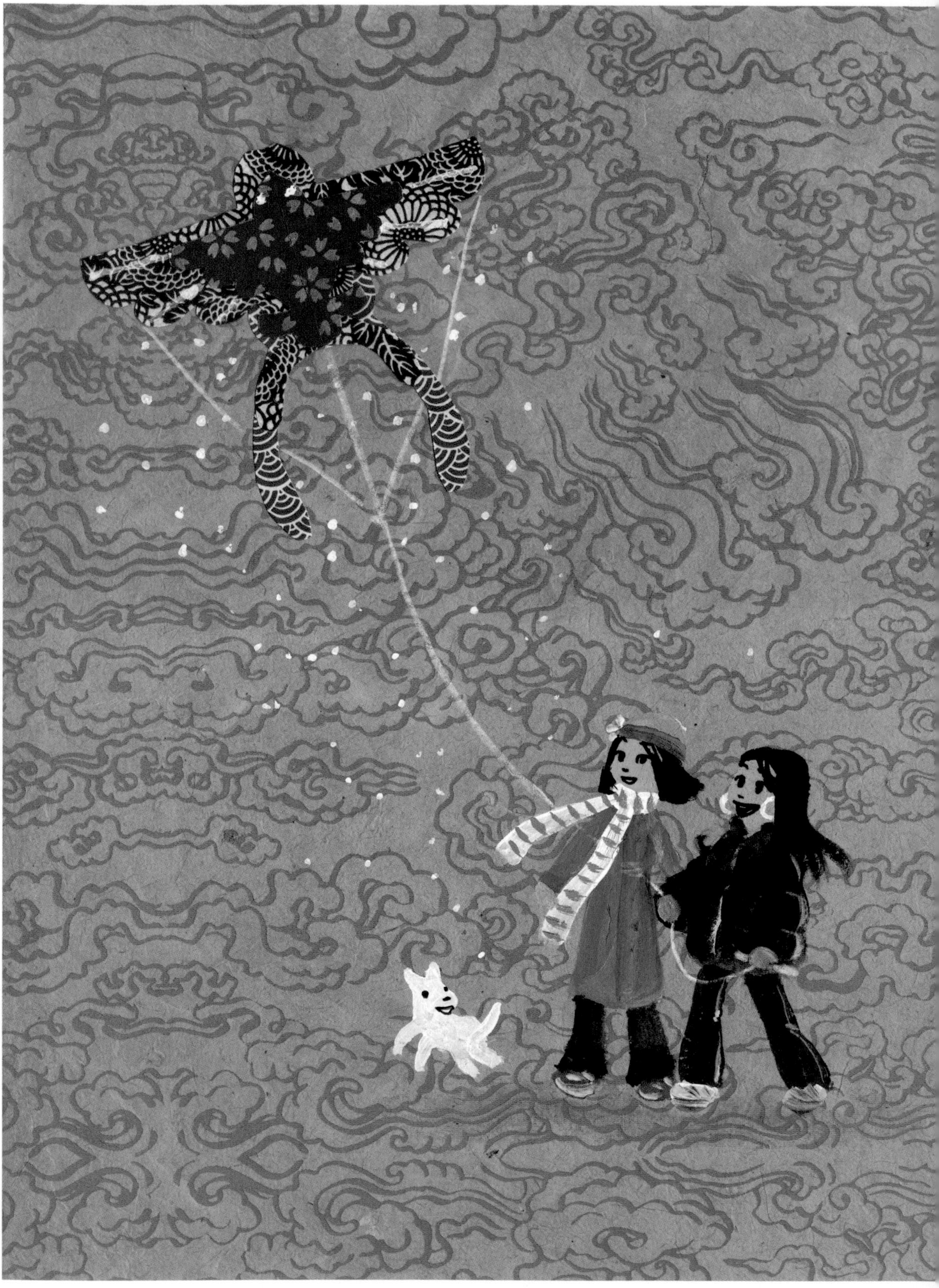

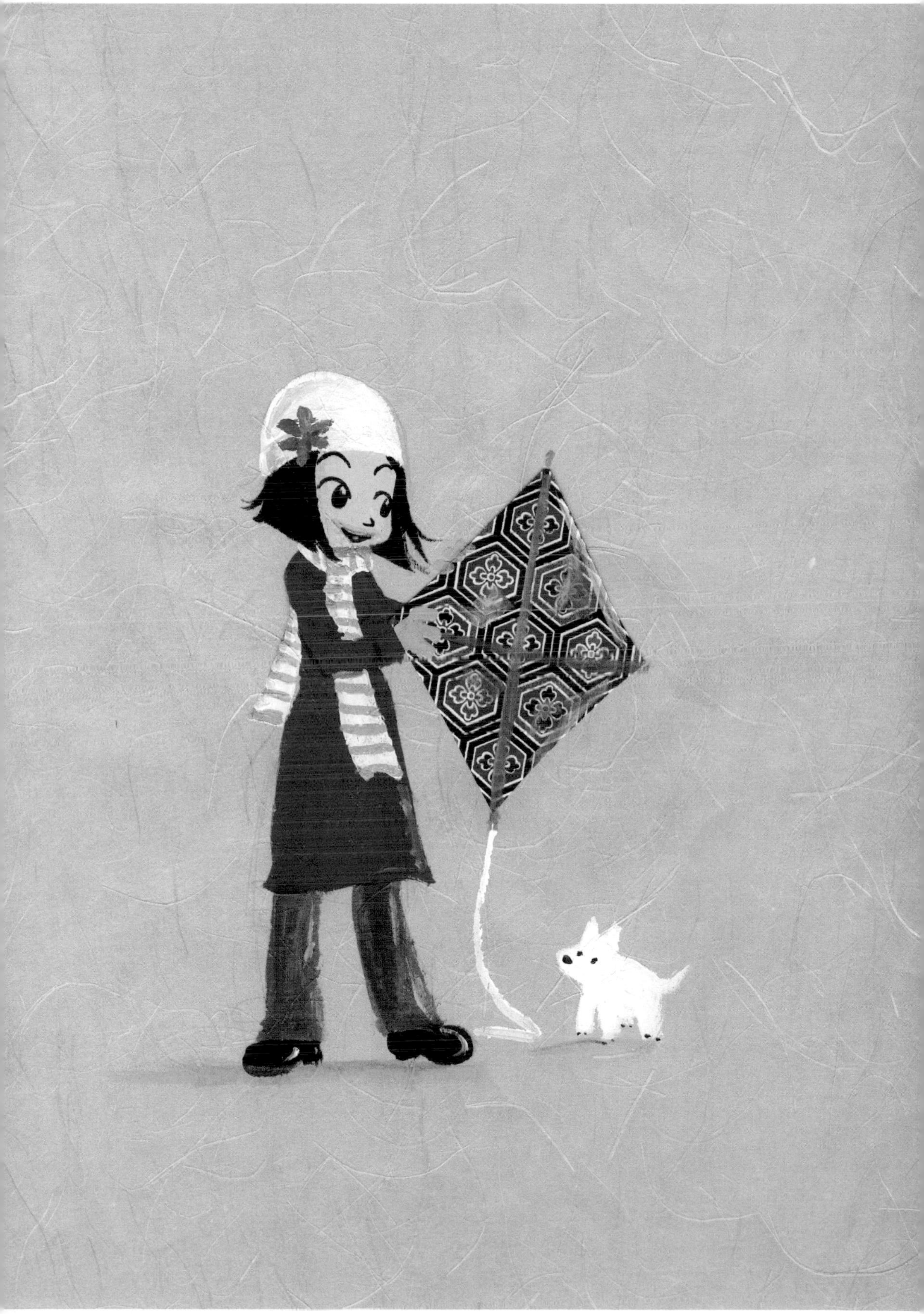

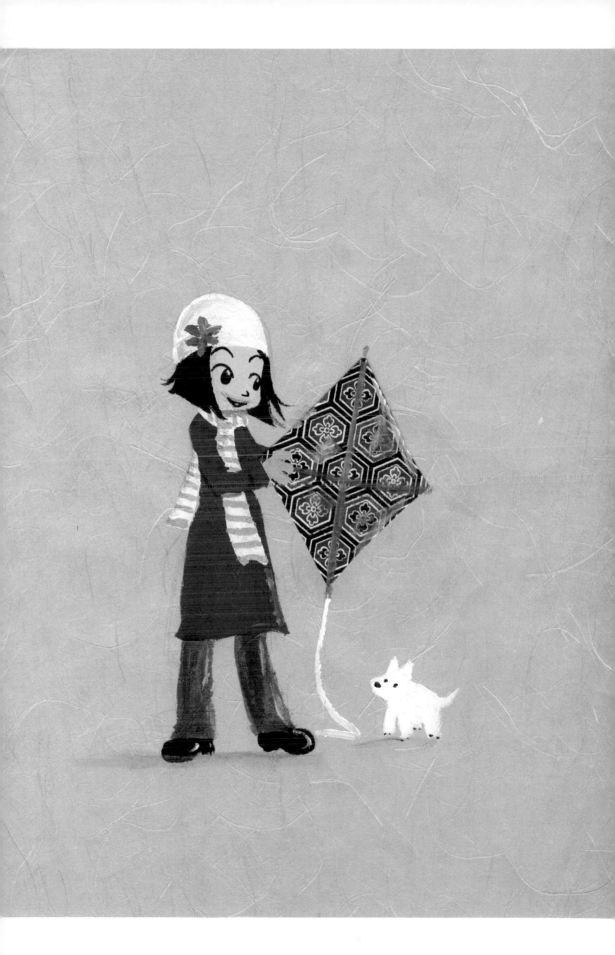

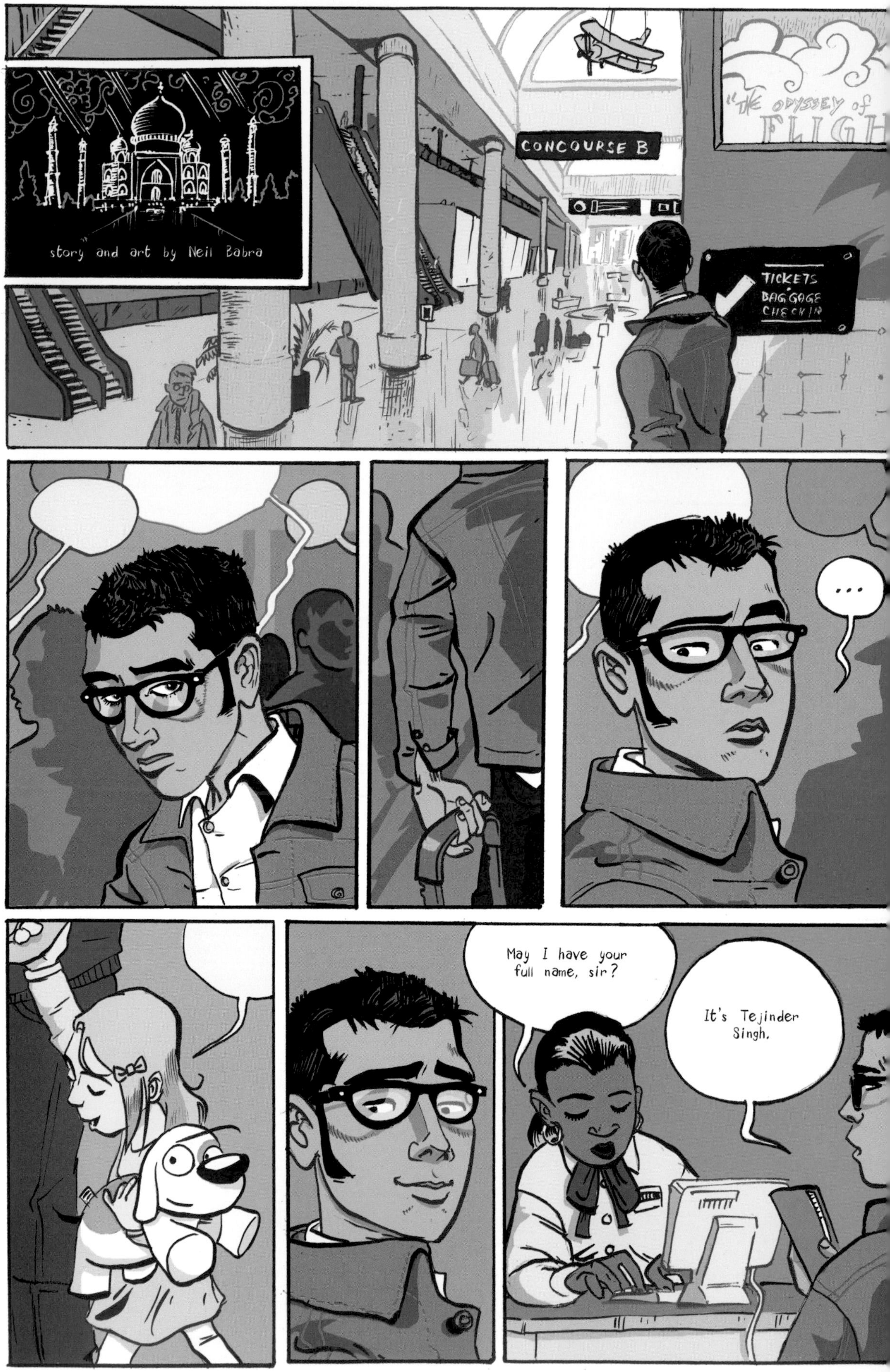
story and art by Neil Babra
CONCOURSE B
TICKETS • BAGGAGE CHECK IN
...
May I have your full name, sir?
It's Tejinder Singh.

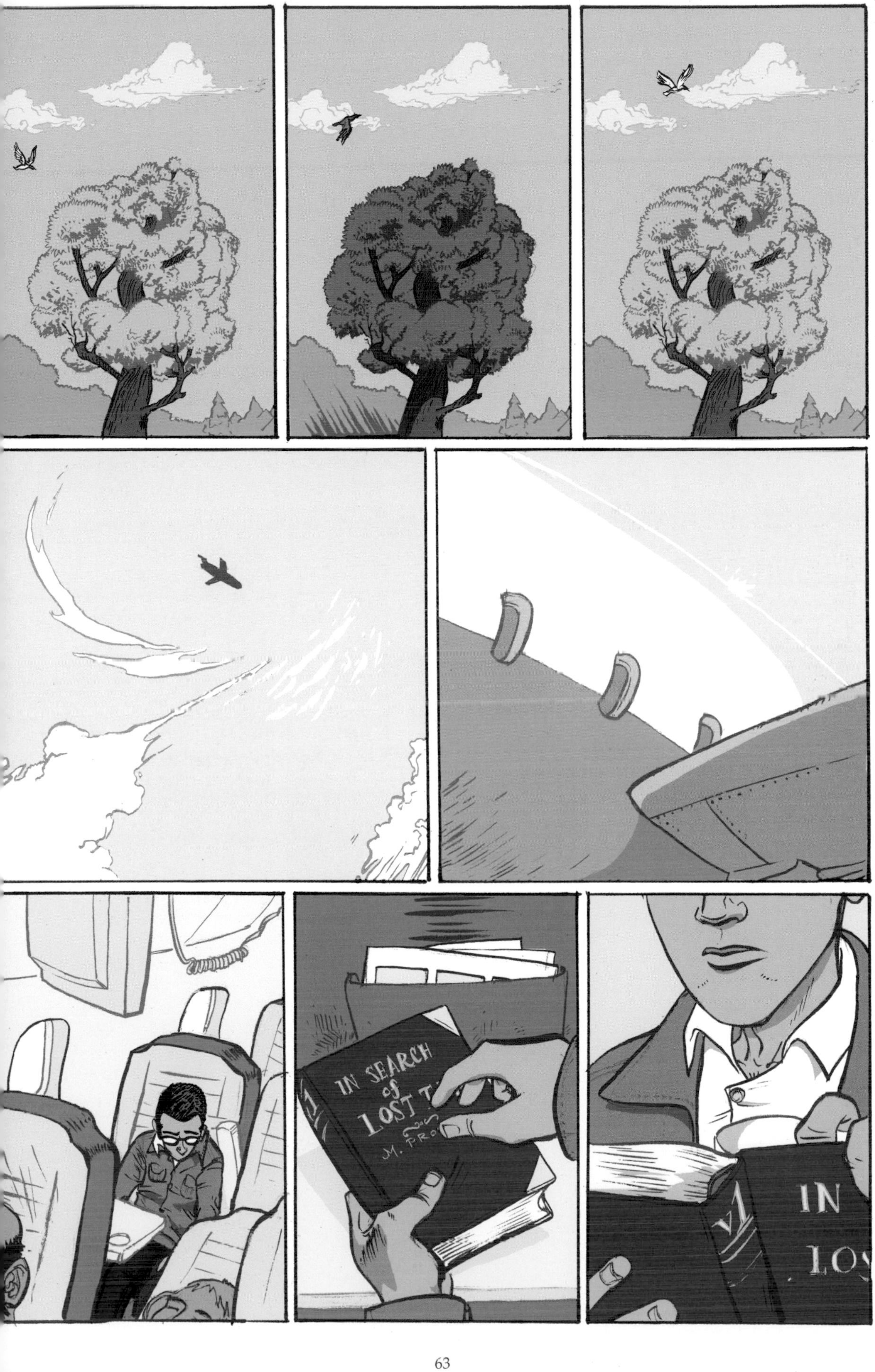
IN SEARCH
of
LOST
IN

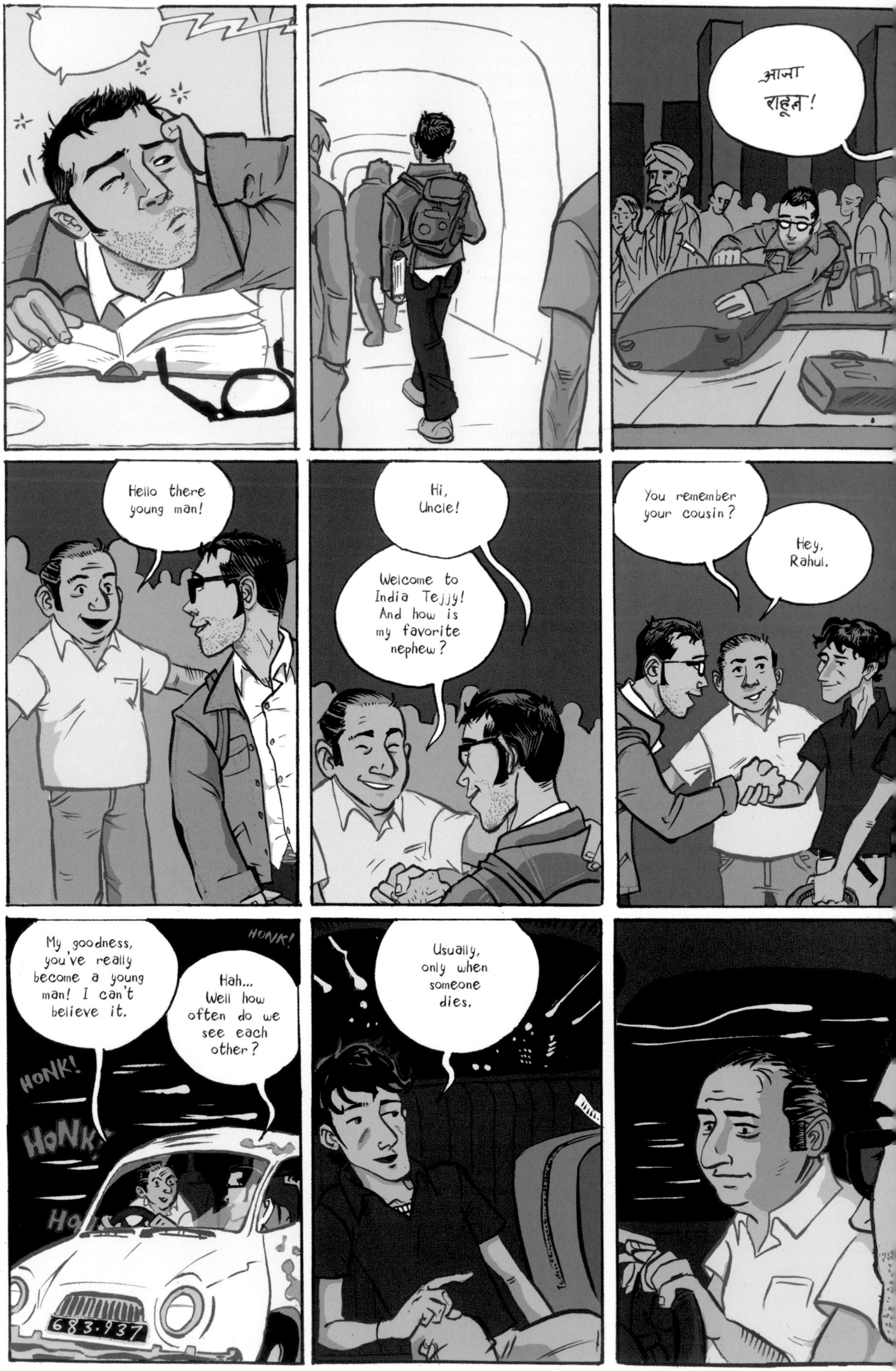
आजा
राहुल!
Hello there young man!
Hi, Uncle!
Welcome to India Tejjy! And how is my favorite nephew?
You remember your cousin?
Hey, Rahul.
My goodness, you've really become a young man! I can't believe it.
HONK!
HONK!
HONK!
Hah... Well how often do we see each other?
683-937
Usually, only when someone dies.

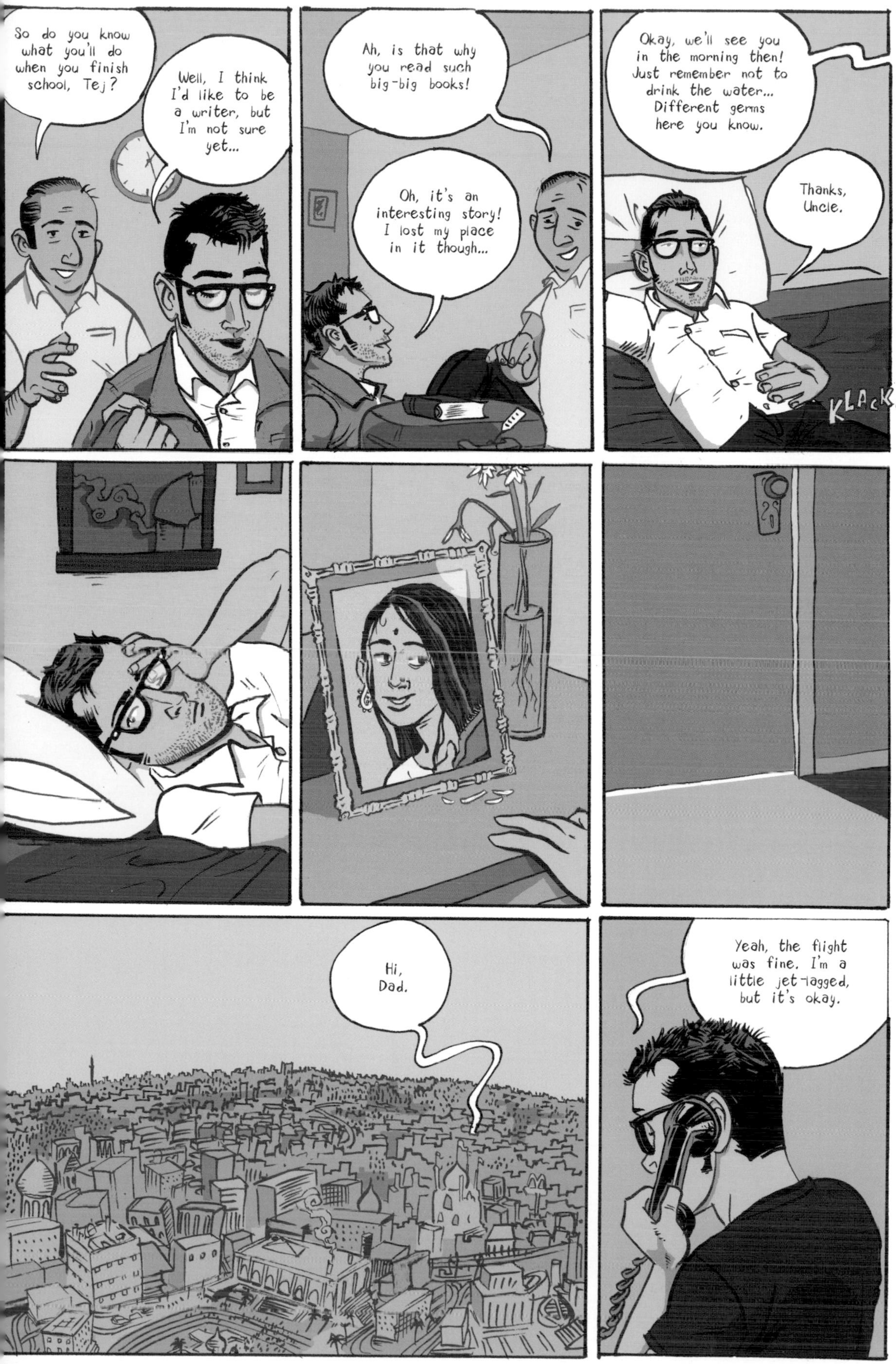
So do you know what you'll do when you finish school, Tej?
Well, I think I'd like to be a writer, but I'm not sure yet...
Ah, is that why you read such big-big books!
Oh, it's an interesting story! I lost my place in it though...
Okay, we'll see you in the morning then! Just remember not to drink the water... Different germs here you know.
Thanks, Uncle.
KLACK.
Hi, Dad.
Yeah, the flight was fine. I'm a little jet-lagged, but it's okay.

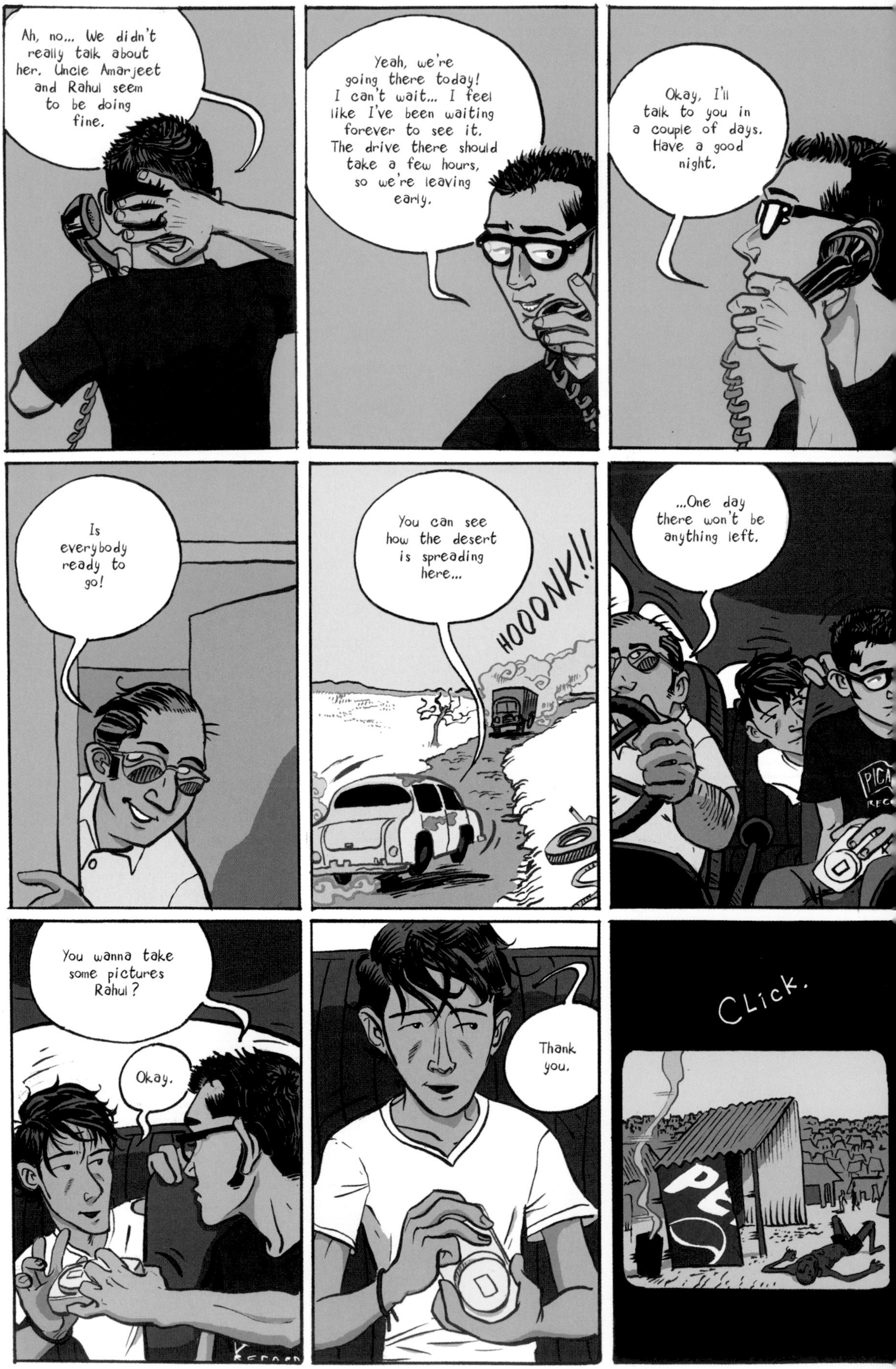
Ah, no... We didn't really talk about her. Uncle Amarjeet and Rahul seem to be doing fine.
Yeah, we're going there today! I can't wait... I feel like I've been waiting forever to see it. The drive there should take a few hours, so we're leaving early.
Okay, I'll talk to you in a couple of days. Have a good night.
Is everybody ready to go!
You can see how the desert is spreading here...
HOOONK!!
...One day there won't be anything left.
You wanna take some pictures Rahul?
Okay.
Thank you.
CLICK.

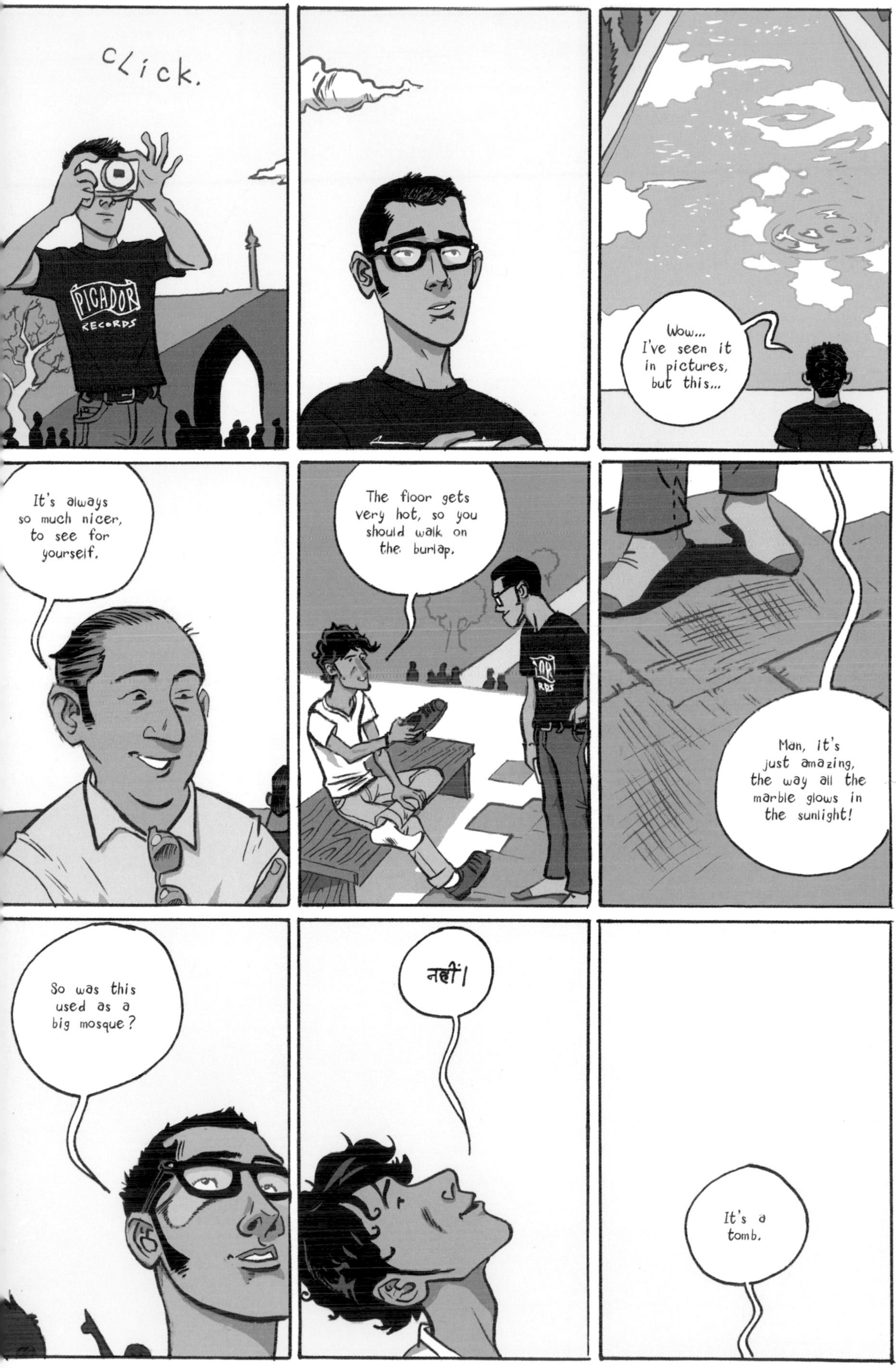
click.
PICADOR RECORDS
Wow... I've seen it in pictures, but this...
It's always so much nicer, to see for yourself.
The floor gets very hot, so you should walk on the burlap.
Man, it's just amazing, the way all the marble glows in the sunlight!
So was this used as a big mosque?
नहीं।
It's a tomb.

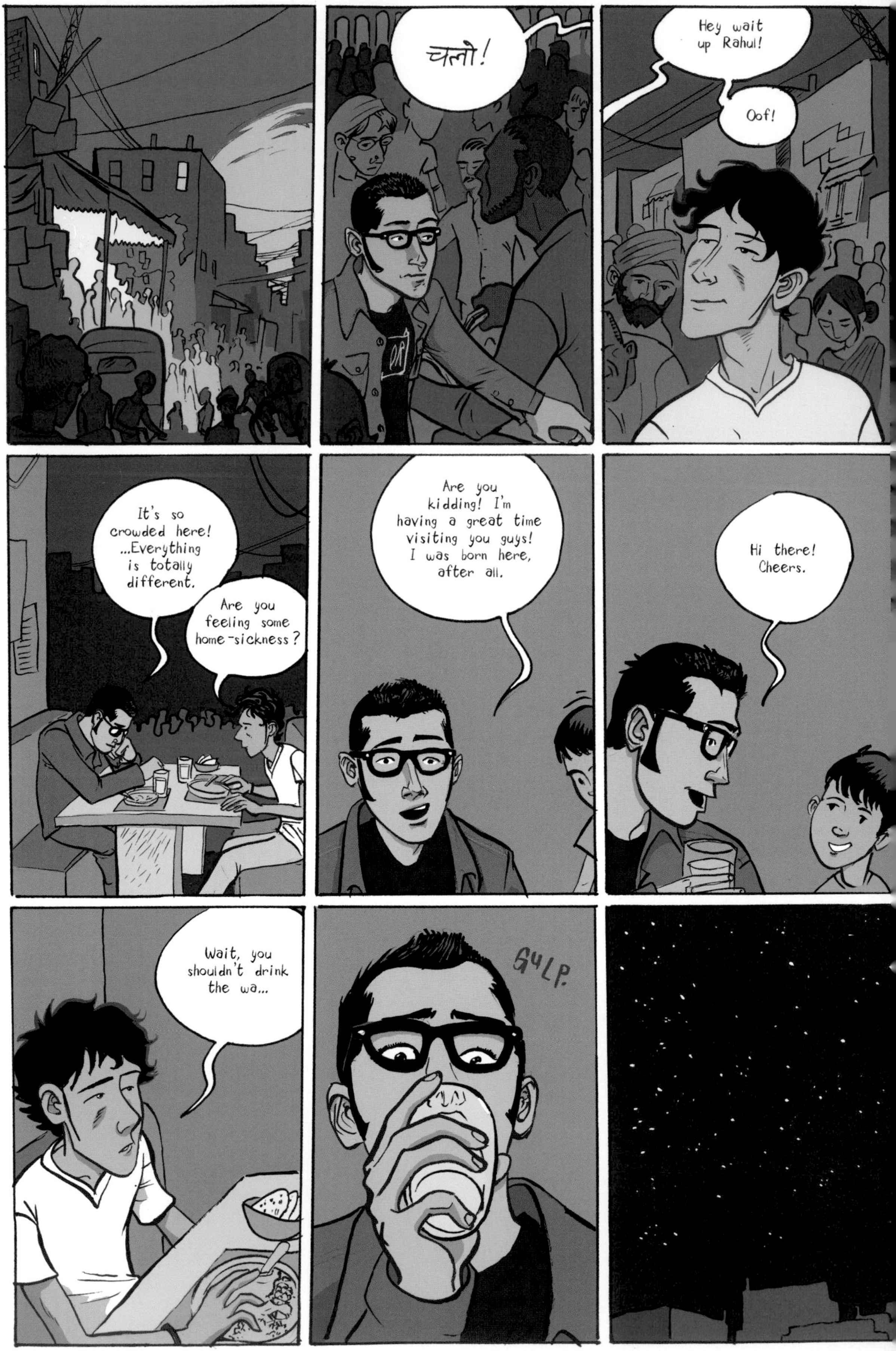
चलो!
Hey wait up Rahul!
Oof!
It's so crowded here! ...Everything is totally different.
Are you feeling some home-sickness?
Are you kidding! I'm having a great time visiting you guys! I was born here, after all.
Hi there! Cheers.
Wait, you shouldn't drink the wa...
GULP.

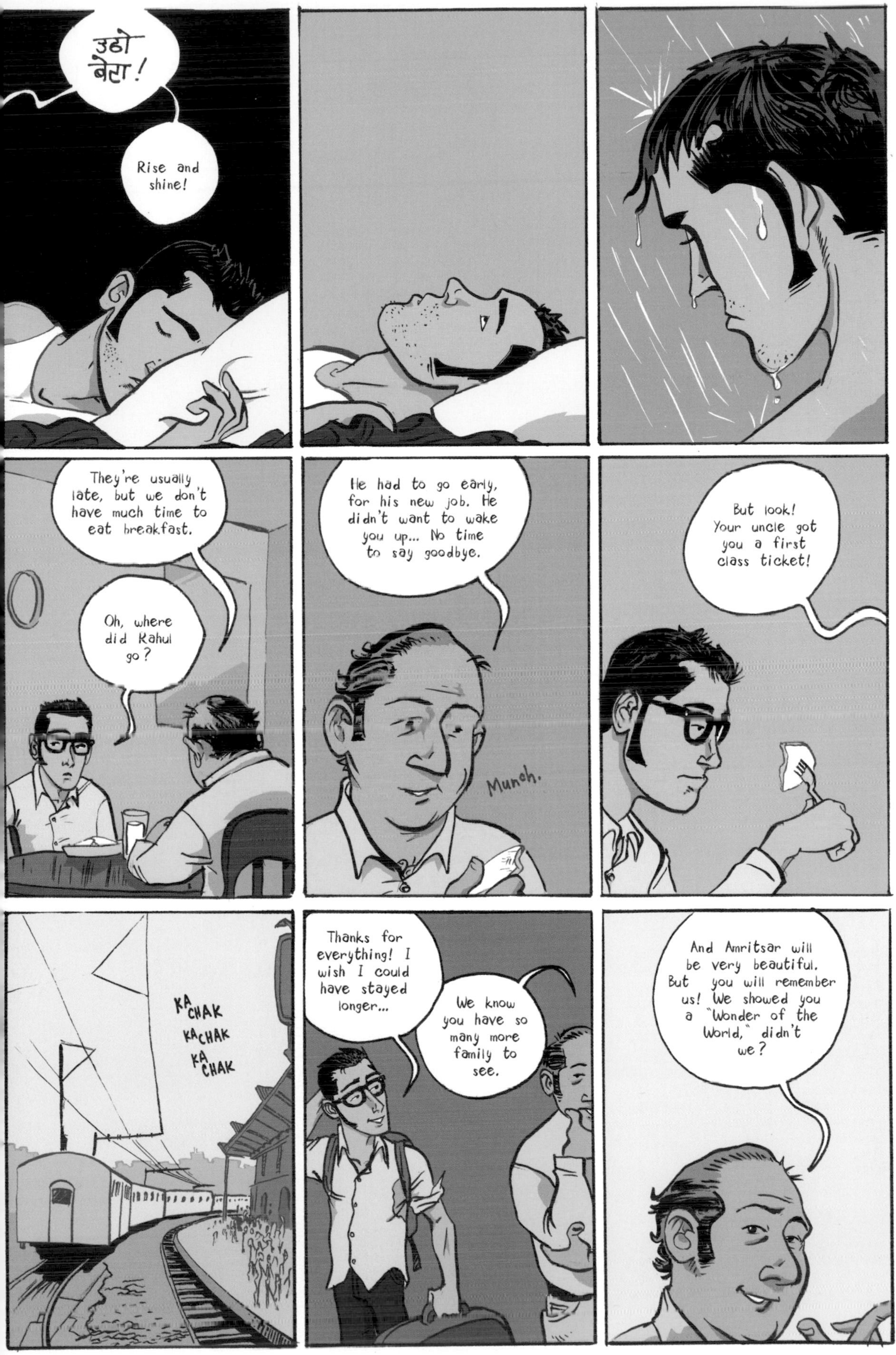

उठो बेटा!
Rise and shine!
They're usually late, but we don't have much time to eat breakfast.
Oh, where did Rahul go?
He had to go early, for his new job. He didn't want to wake you up... No time to say goodbye.
Munch.
But look! Your uncle got you a first class ticket!
KA CHAK
KA CHAK
KA CHAK
Thanks for everything! I wish I could have stayed longer...
We know you have so many more family to see.
And Amritsar will be very beautiful. But you will remember us! We showed you a "Wonder of the World," didn't we?

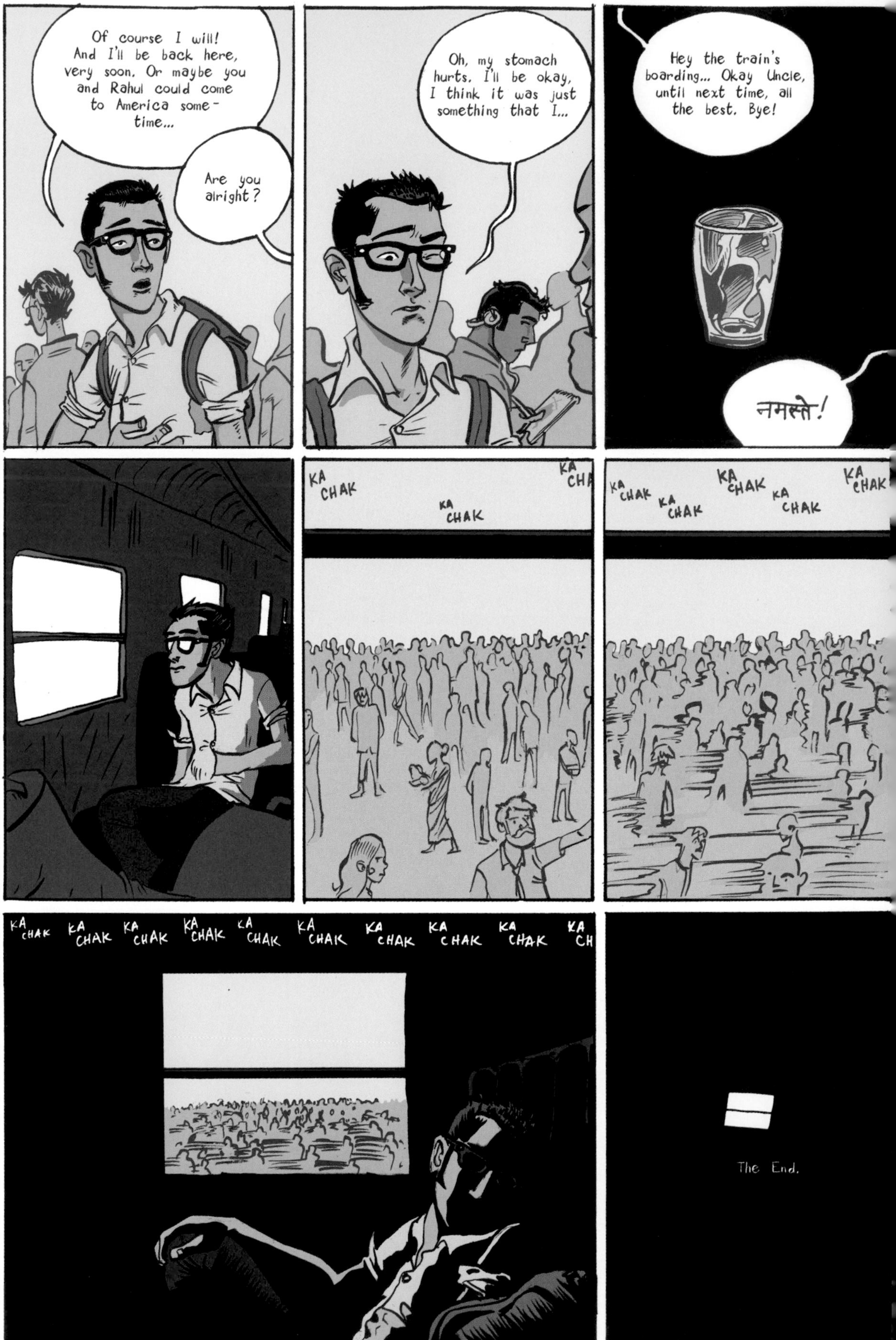
Of course I will! And I'll be back here, very soon. Or maybe you and Rahul could come to America some-time...
Are you alright?
Oh, my stomach hurts. I'll be okay, I think it was just something that I...
Hey the train's boarding... Okay Uncle, until next time, all the best. Bye!
नमस्ते!
KA CHAK
KA CHAK
KA CHA
KA CHAK
KA CHAK
KA CHAK
KA CHAK
KA CHAK
KA CHAK KA CHAK KA CHAK KA CHAK KA CHAK KA CHAK KA CHAK KA CHAK KA CHAK KA CH
The End.

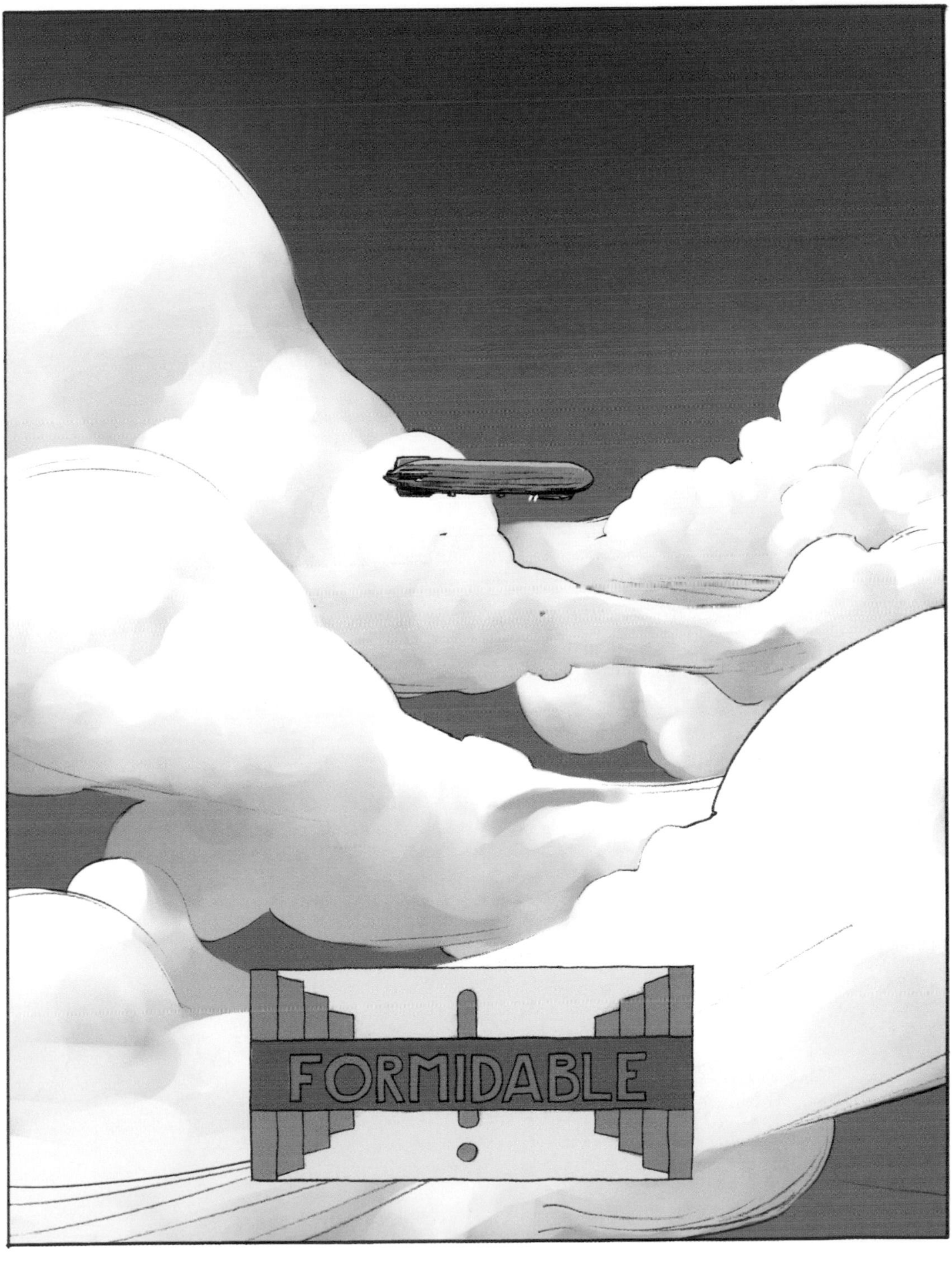
FORMIDABLE

by Bengal

MY FRIENDS, TODAY IS A GREAT DAY INDEED !!!

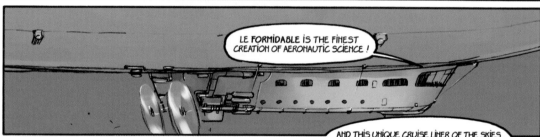

LE FORMIDABLE IS THE FINEST CREATION OF AERONAUTIC SCIENCE !

AND THIS UNIQUE CRUISE LINER OF THE SKIES, WELL WE OWE IT TO ONE MAN, A GREAT MAN, A MAN WHO HAS GIVEN HIS TIME AND MONEY IN ORDER THAT THIS MARVEL COULD BE CREATED.

COUNT FRANÇOIS !

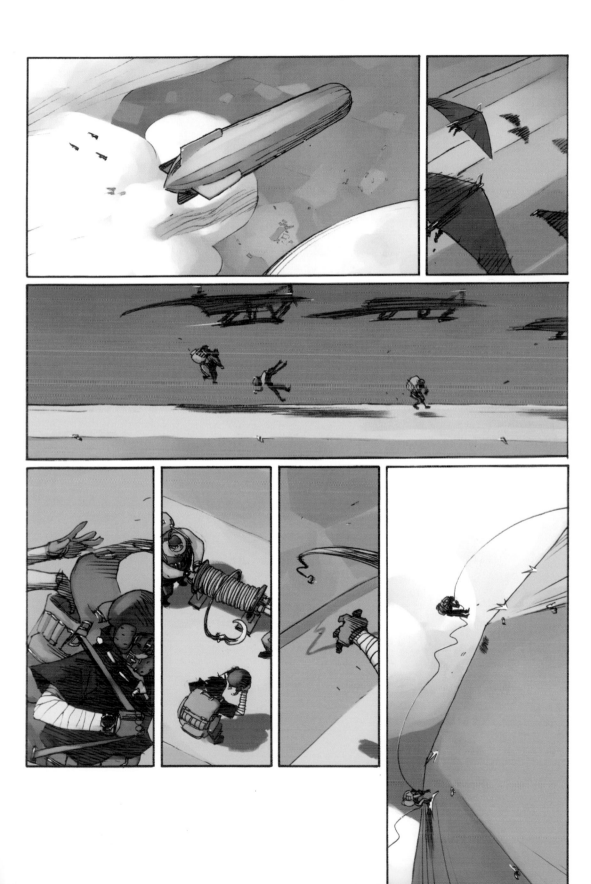

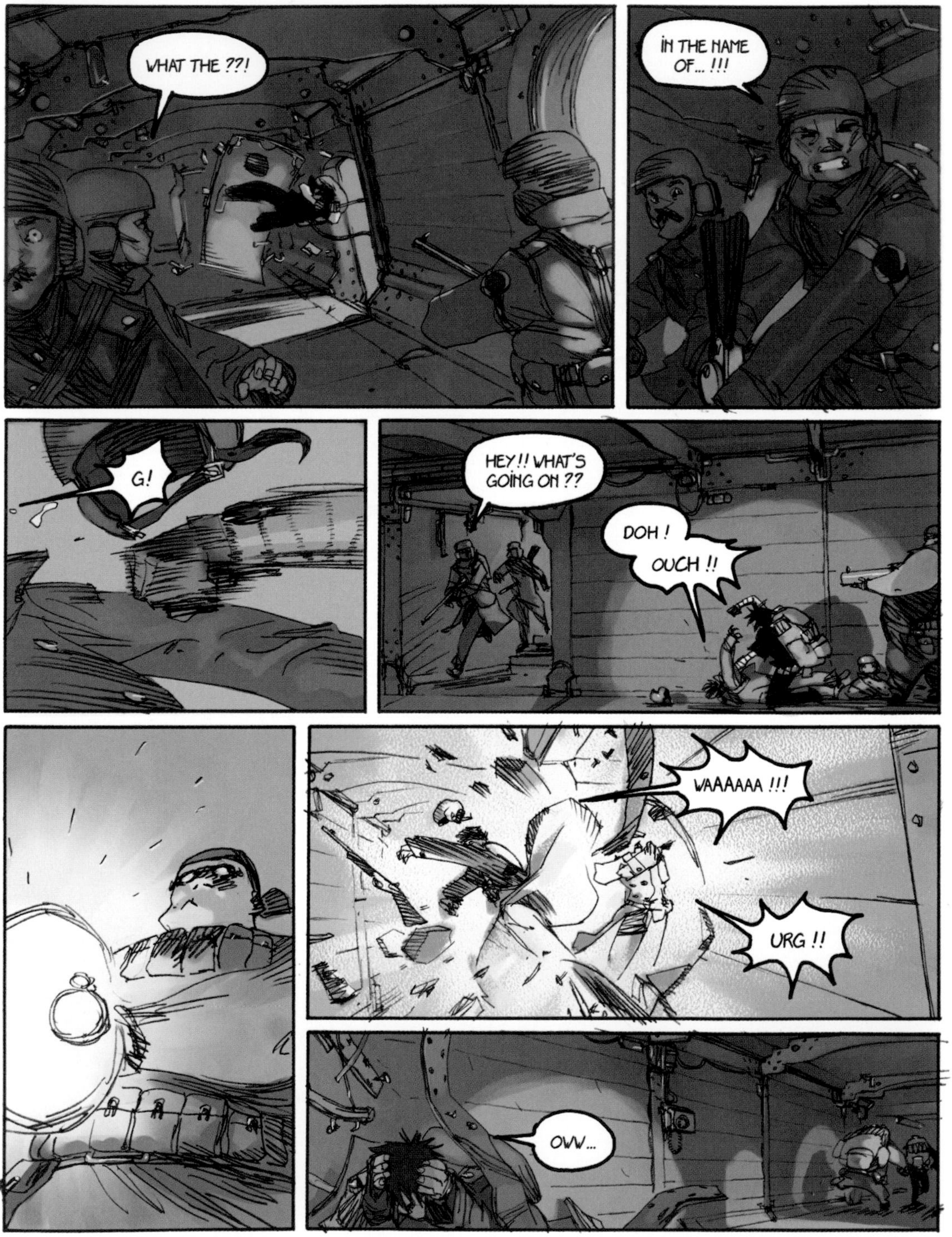
WHAT THE ??!
IN THE NAME OF... !!!
G!
HEY!! WHAT'S GOING ON ??
DOH !
OUCH !!
WAAAAAA !!!
URG !!
OWW...

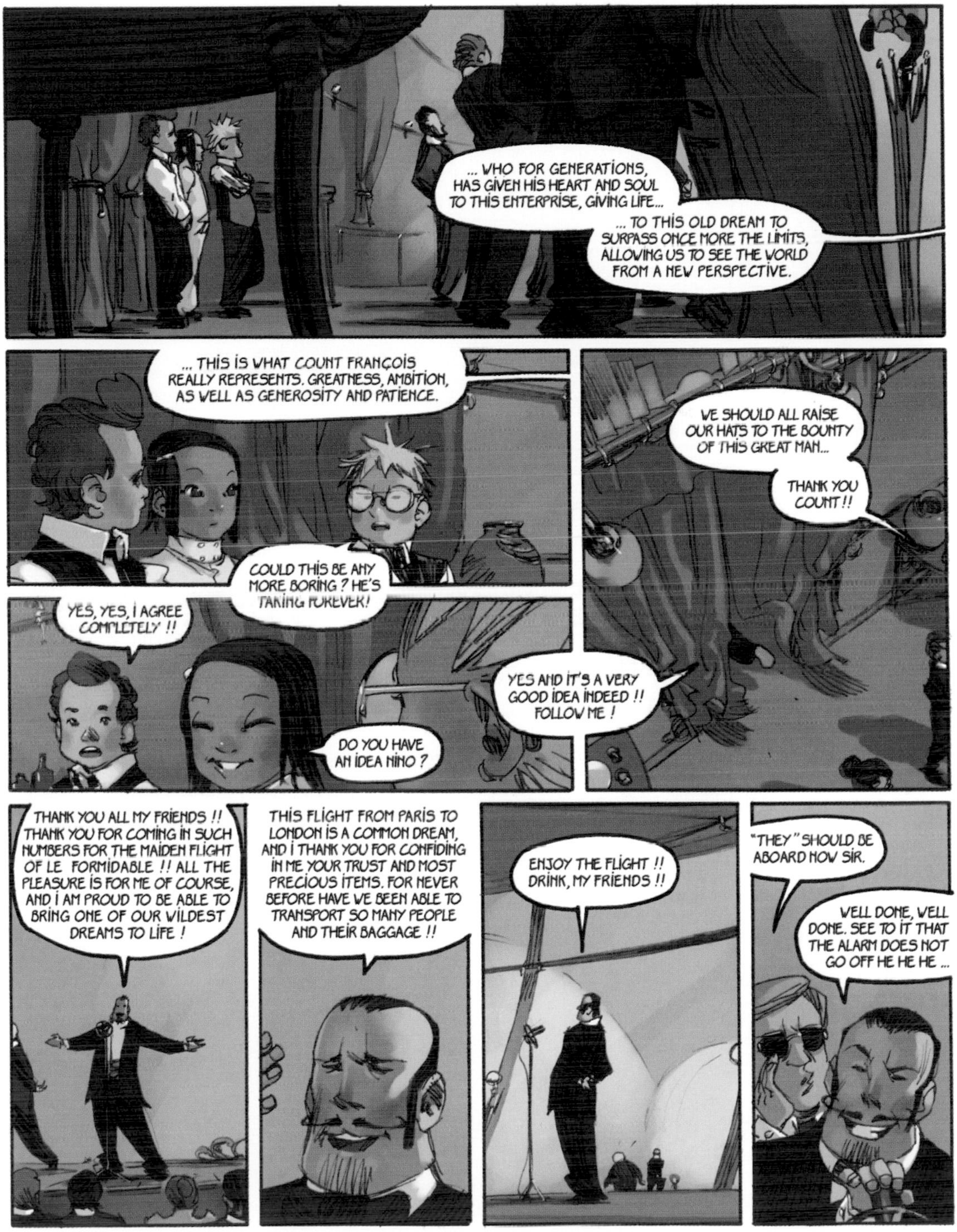
... WHO FOR GENERATIONS, HAS GIVEN HIS HEART AND SOUL TO THIS ENTERPRISE, GIVING LIFE...
... TO THIS OLD DREAM TO SURPASS ONCE MORE THE LIMITS, ALLOWING US TO SEE THE WORLD FROM A NEW PERSPECTIVE.
... THIS IS WHAT COUNT FRANÇOIS REALLY REPRESENTS. GREATNESS, AMBITION, AS WELL AS GENEROSITY AND PATIENCE.
COULD THIS BE ANY MORE BORING ? HE'S TAKING FOREVER!
WE SHOULD ALL RAISE OUR HATS TO THE BOUNTY OF THIS GREAT MAN...
THANK YOU COUNT !!
YES, YES, I AGREE COMPLETELY !!
DO YOU HAVE AN IDEA NINO ?
YES AND IT'S A VERY GOOD IDEA INDEED !! FOLLOW ME !
THANK YOU ALL MY FRIENDS !! THANK YOU FOR COMING IN SUCH NUMBERS FOR THE MAIDEN FLIGHT OF LE FORMIDABLE !! ALL THE PLEASURE IS FOR ME OF COURSE, AND I AM PROUD TO BE ABLE TO BRING ONE OF OUR WILDEST DREAMS TO LIFE !
THIS FLIGHT FROM PARIS TO LONDON IS A COMMON DREAM, AND I THANK YOU FOR CONFIDING IN ME YOUR TRUST AND MOST PRECIOUS ITEMS. FOR NEVER BEFORE HAVE WE BEEN ABLE TO TRANSPORT SO MANY PEOPLE AND THEIR BAGGAGE !!
ENJOY THE FLIGHT !! DRINK, MY FRIENDS !!
"THEY" SHOULD BE ABOARD NOW SIR.
WELL DONE, WELL DONE. SEE TO IT THAT THE ALARM DOES NOT GO OFF HE HE HE ...

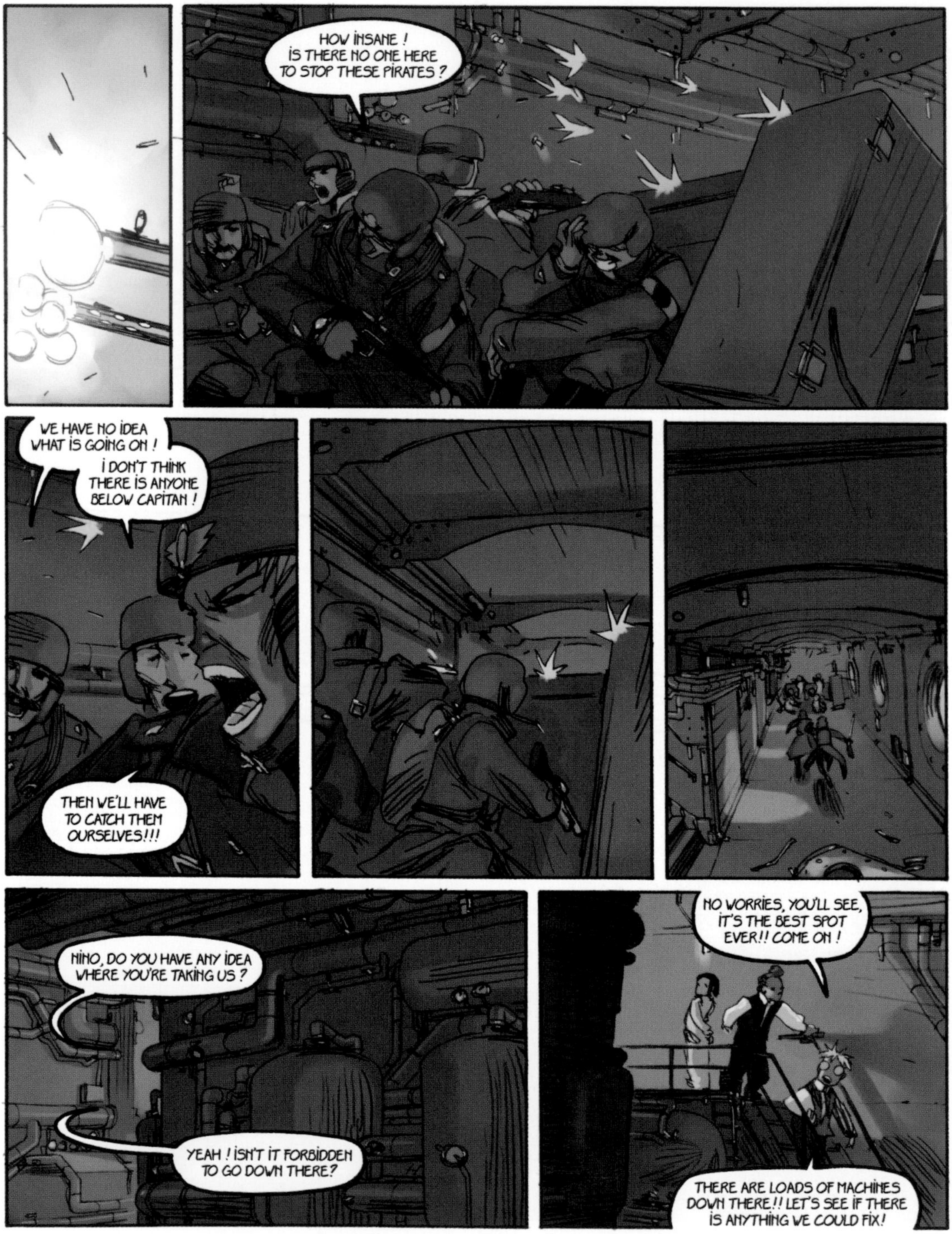

HOW INSANE ! IS THERE NO ONE HERE TO STOP THESE PIRATES ?
WE HAVE NO IDEA WHAT IS GOING ON !
I DON'T THINK THERE IS ANYONE BELOW CAPITAN !
THEN WE'LL HAVE TO CATCH THEM OURSELVES!!!
NINO, DO YOU HAVE ANY IDEA WHERE YOU'RE TAKING US ?
YEAH ! ISN'T IT FORBIDDEN TO GO DOWN THERE?
NO WORRIES, YOU'LL SEE, IT'S THE BEST SPOT EVER!! COME ON !
THERE ARE LOADS OF MACHINES DOWN THERE!! LET'S SEE IF THERE IS ANYTHING WE COULD FIX!

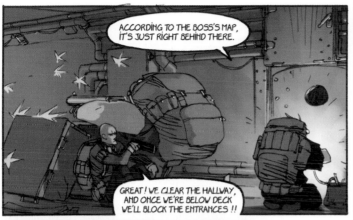

ACCORDING TO THE BOSS'S MAP, IT'S JUST RIGHT BEHIND THERE.

GREAT! WE CLEAR THE HALLWAY, AND ONCE WE'RE BELOW DECK WE'LL BLOCK THE ENTRANCES!!

YES!! THEN WE PREPARE THE PULLYS, THE PARACHUTES FOR THE TREASURES AND OFF WE GO!

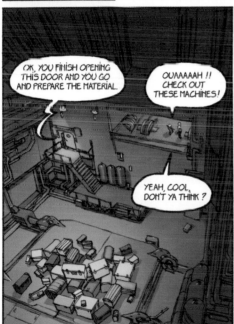

OK, YOU FINISH OPENING THIS DOOR AND YOU GO AND PREPARE THE MATERIAL.

OUAAAAAH!! CHECK OUT THESE MACHINES!

YEAH, COOL, DON'T YA THINK?

IT TAKES ALL THIS TO GET A DIRIGIBLE IN THE AIR?

OH YEAH!! I EVEN KNOW HOW TO MAKE THEM WORK!! I COULD GROW UP TO BE A CAPITAN!

NO WAY, YOU'RE LYING!

NO REALLY!! WATCH I'LL SHOW YOU!!

ACCORDING TO THE TIMING, THEY SHOULD BE NOW DROPPING THE TRUNKS SIR.

I KNOW, DON'T WORRY I'M KEEPING AN EYE OPEN HE HE HE...

THE PLAN IS PERFECT. NO ONE WILL SUSPECT THAT I WAS INVOLVED IN SUCH AN AUDACIOUS THEFT!

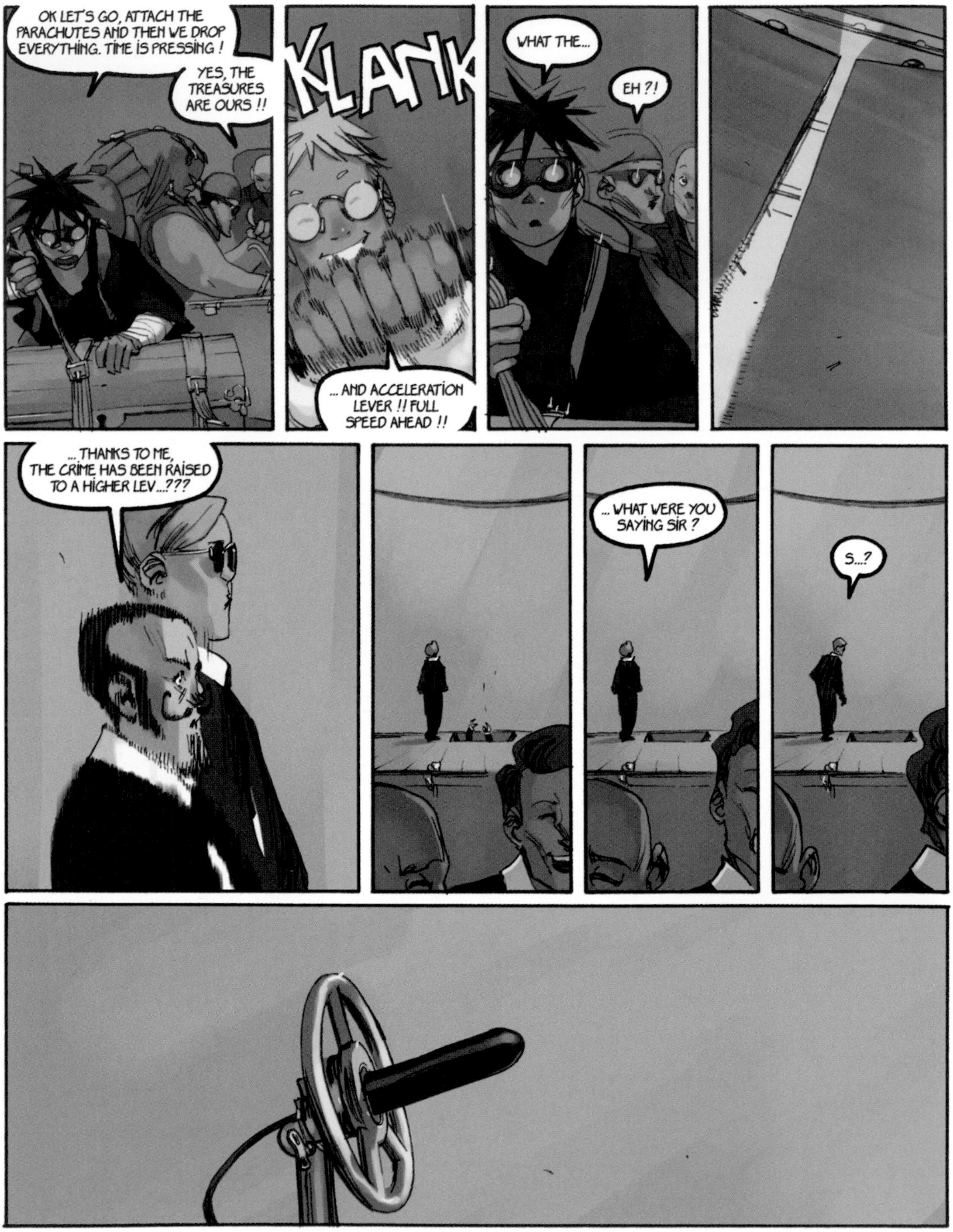
OK LET'S GO, ATTACH THE PARACHUTES AND THEN WE DROP EVERYTHING. TIME IS PRESSING !
YES, THE TREASURES ARE OURS !!
KLANK
... AND ACCELERATION LEVER !! FULL SPEED AHEAD !!
WHAT THE...
EH ?!
... THANKS TO ME, THE CRIME HAS BEEN RAISED TO A HIGHER LEV...???
... WHAT WERE YOU SAYING SIR ?
S...?

"Outside My Window," by Khang Le

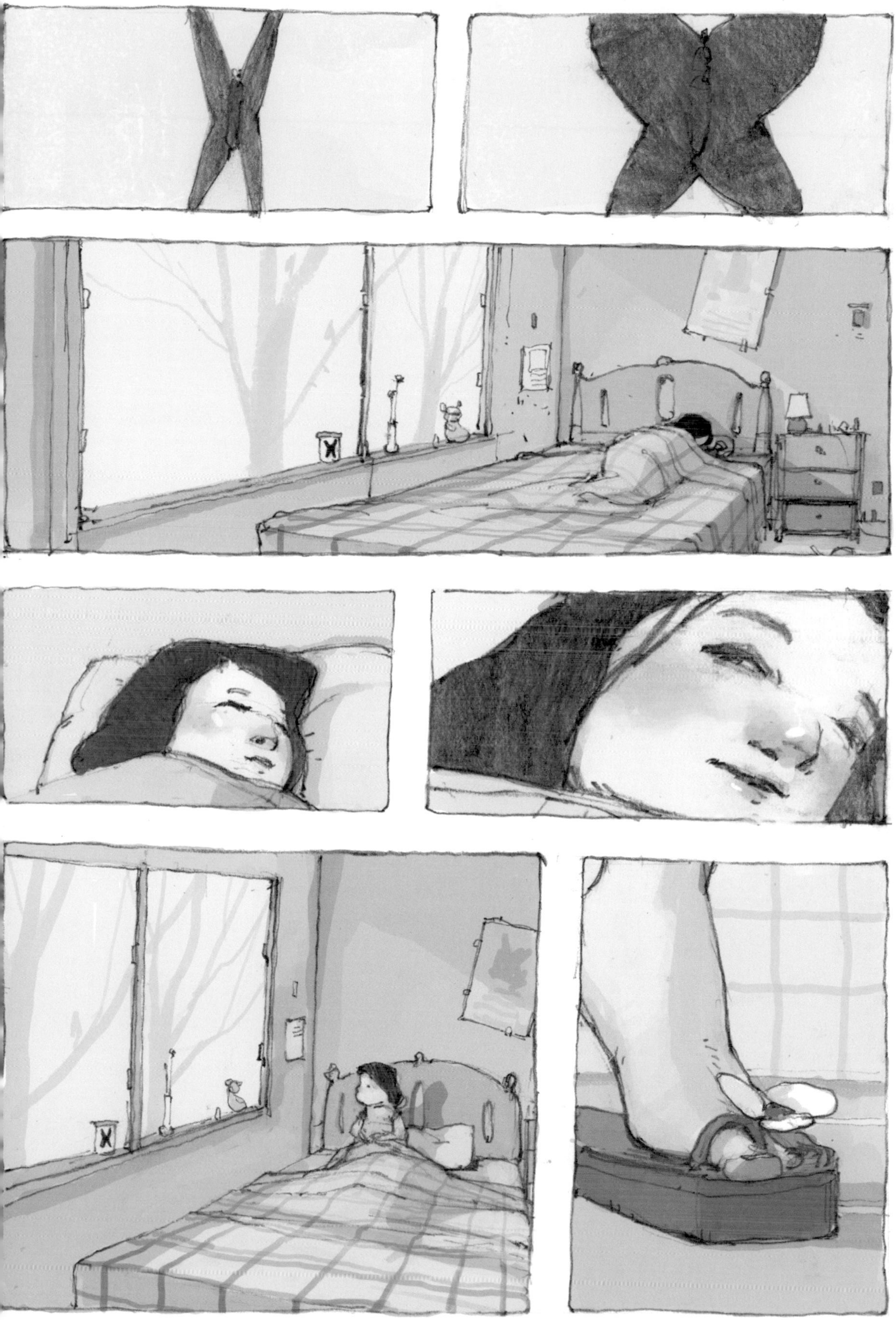

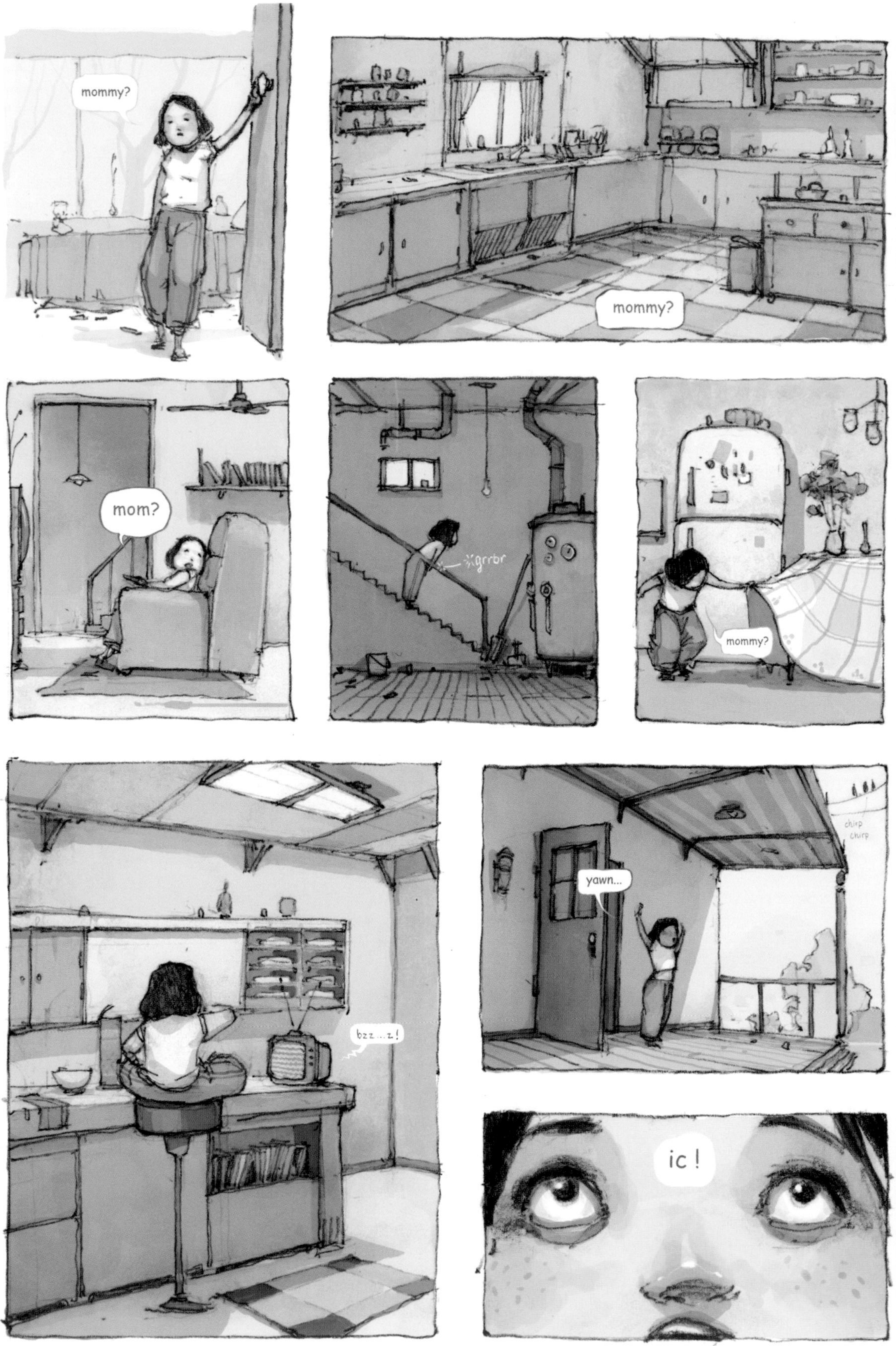
mommy?
mommy?
mom?
grrbr
mommy?
bzz...z!
yawn...
chirp
chirp
ic!

chirp
chirp
Hi!
uh...hello
!

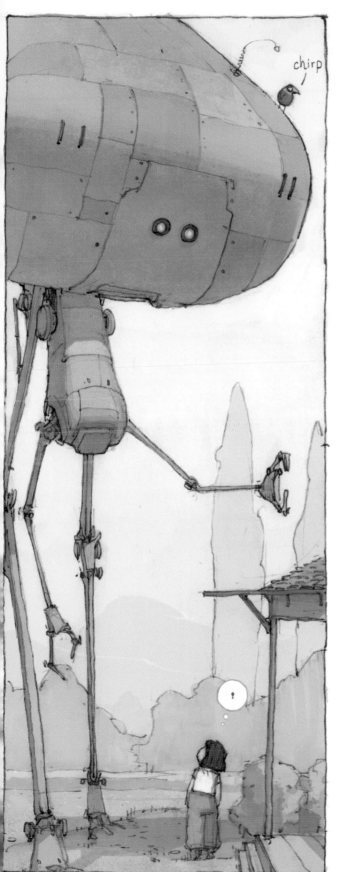

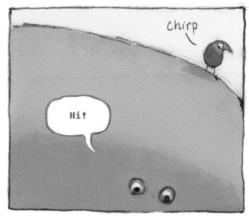

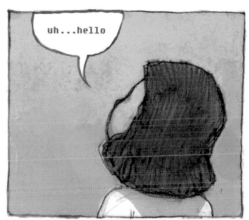

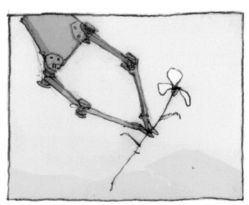

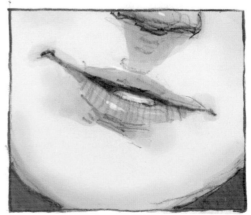

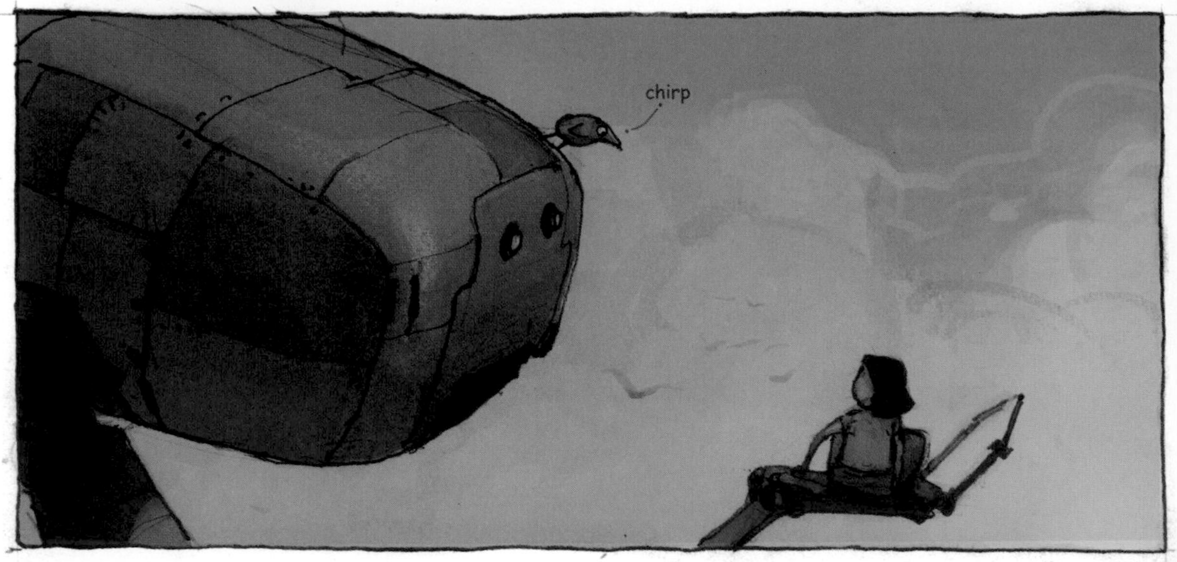
chirp

So what's your name?

Donna. And yours?

Hmm...let's see...you can call me Ulys.

Okay...Ulys. I don't mean to be rude but you're not gonna eat me are you?

Or replace my brain with computer chips and stuff. I saw it on TV once.

Ech...no...of course not. I just want to be your friend. It gets lonely here.

What is this place? I can see my house below but I don't recognize anything else.

Where are my parents? my neighbors? my street?

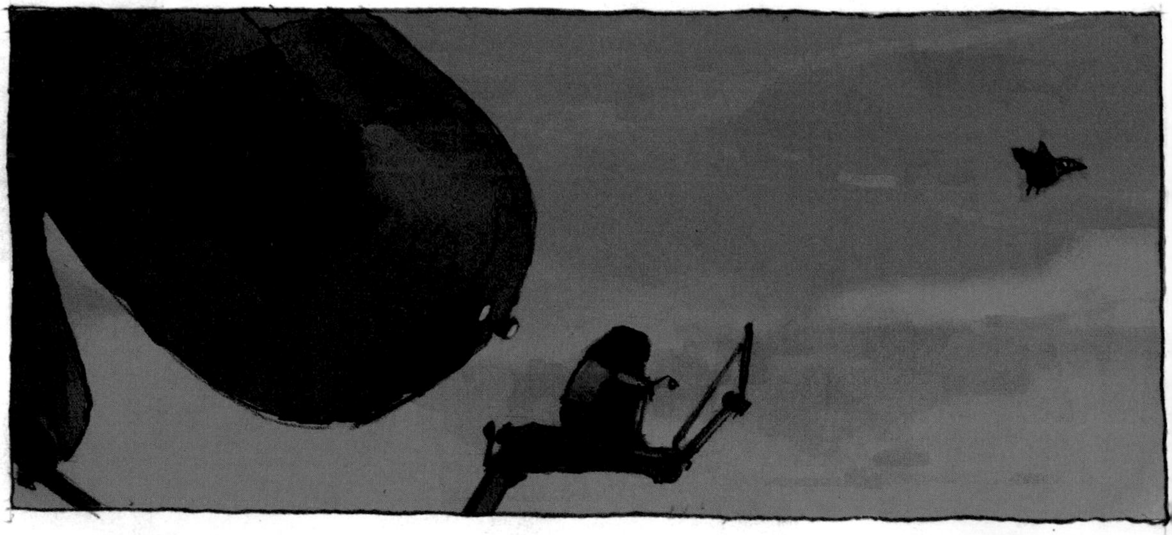

...it's a bit too complicated to explain. I've been watching you, through the glass. And I brought you here.

This is another place.

But my house is right below. That's my home...isn't it?

Donna, this is my world. I built your home from my memory.

I wanted your transition to be a comfortable one.

In this place, I can give you everything...anything you want.

Just as long as you stay.

I want to go home.

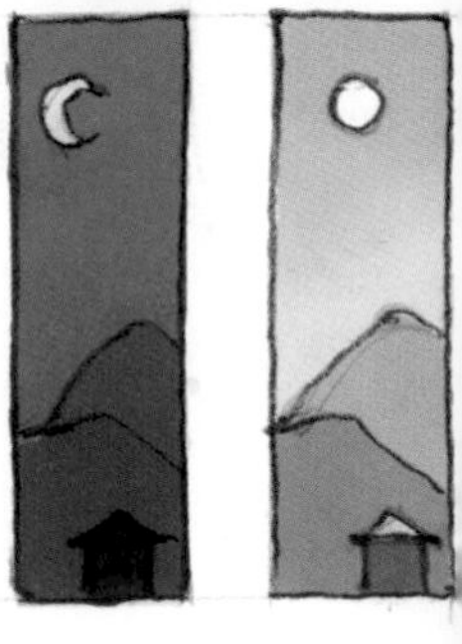

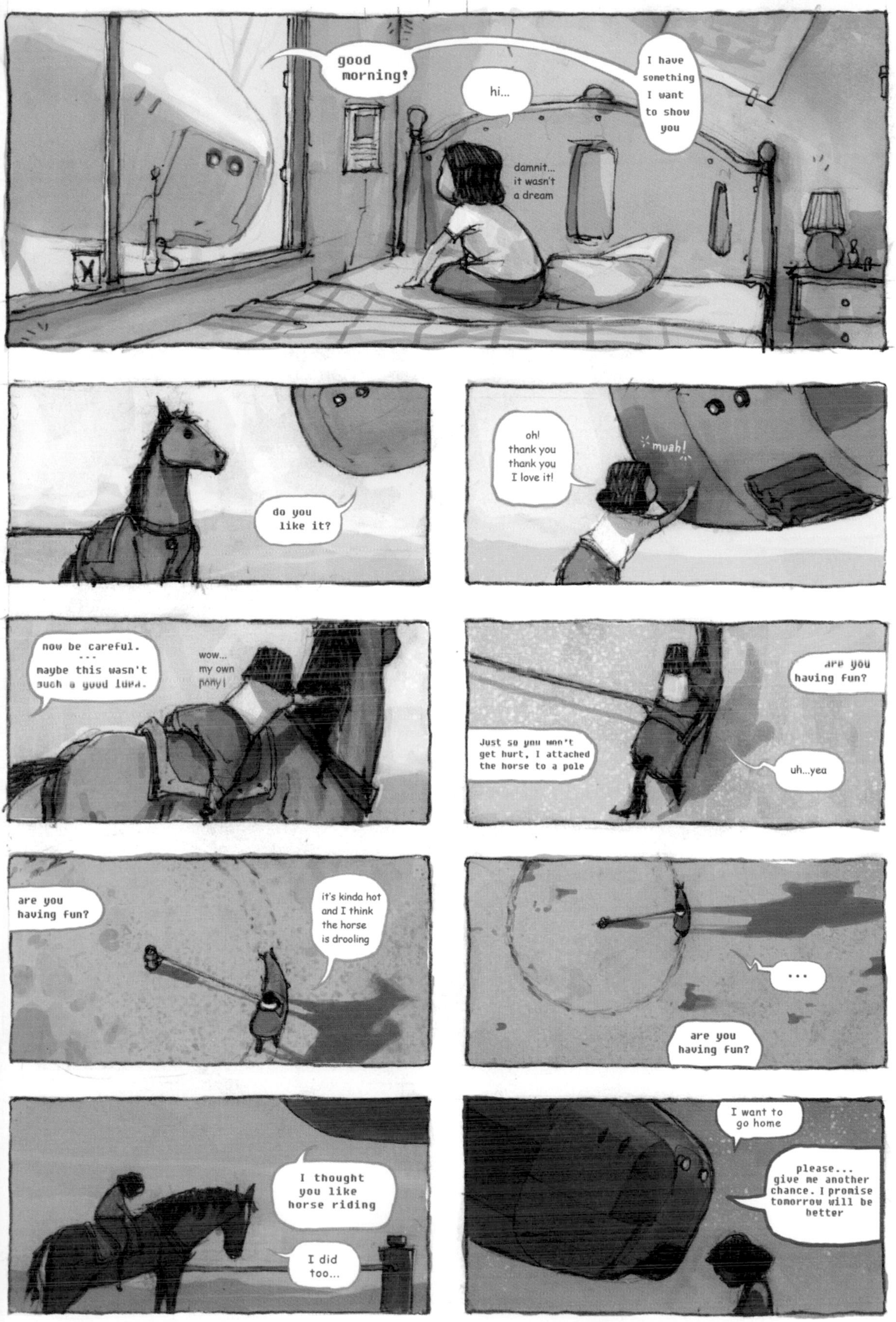
good morning!
hi...
I have something I want to show you
damnit... it wasn't a dream
do you like it?
oh! thank you thank you I love it!
muah!
now be careful. ... maybe this wasn't such a good idea.
wow... my own pony!
are you having fun?
Just so you won't get hurt, I attached the horse to a pole
uh...yea
are you having fun?
it's kinda hot and I think the horse is drooling
...
are you having fun?
I thought you like horse riding
I did too...
I want to go home
please... give me another chance. I promise tomorrow will be better

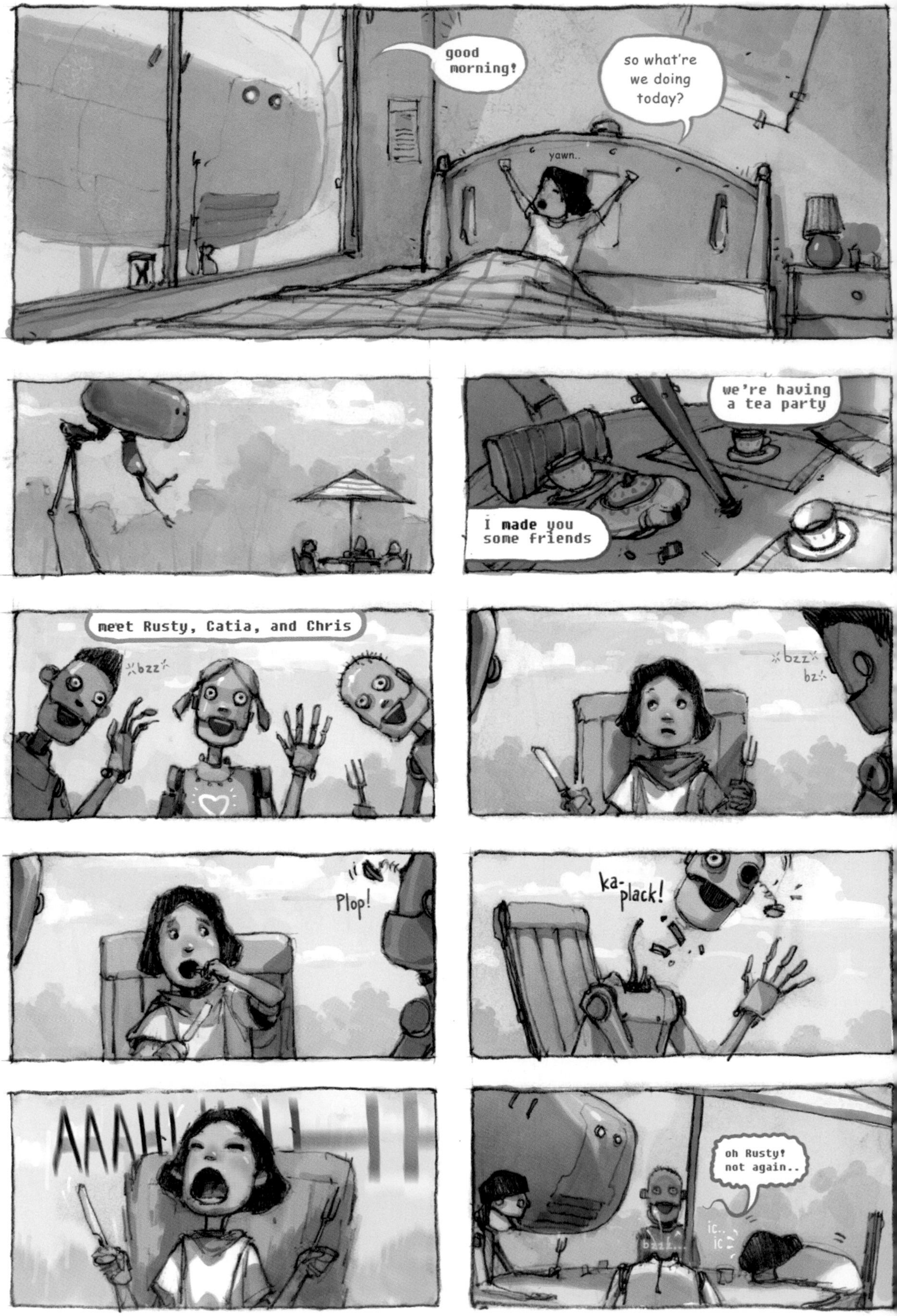
good morning!
so what're we doing today?
yawn..
we're having a tea party
I made you some friends
meet Rusty, Catia, and Chris
bzz
bzz bz
Plop!
ka-plack!
AAAH
oh Rusty! not again..
ic.. ic

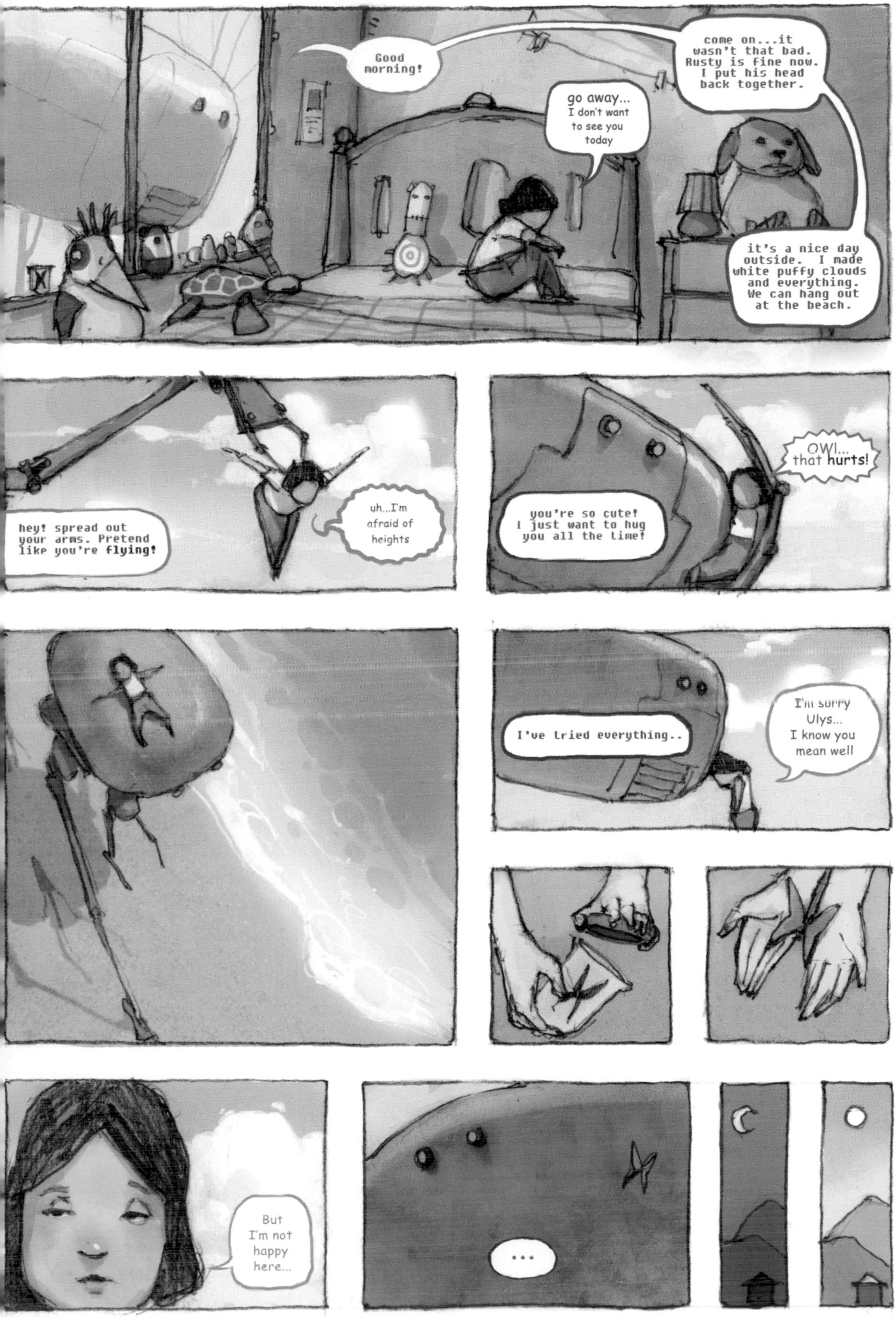
Good morning!
go away... I don't want to see you today
come on...it wasn't that bad. Rusty is fine now. I put his head back together.
it's a nice day outside. I made white puffy clouds and everything. We can hang out at the beach.
hey! spread out your arms. Pretend like you're flying!
uh...I'm afraid of heights
you're so cute! I just want to hug you all the time!
OW!... that hurts!
I've tried everything..
I'm sorry Ulys... I know you mean well
But I'm not happy here...
...

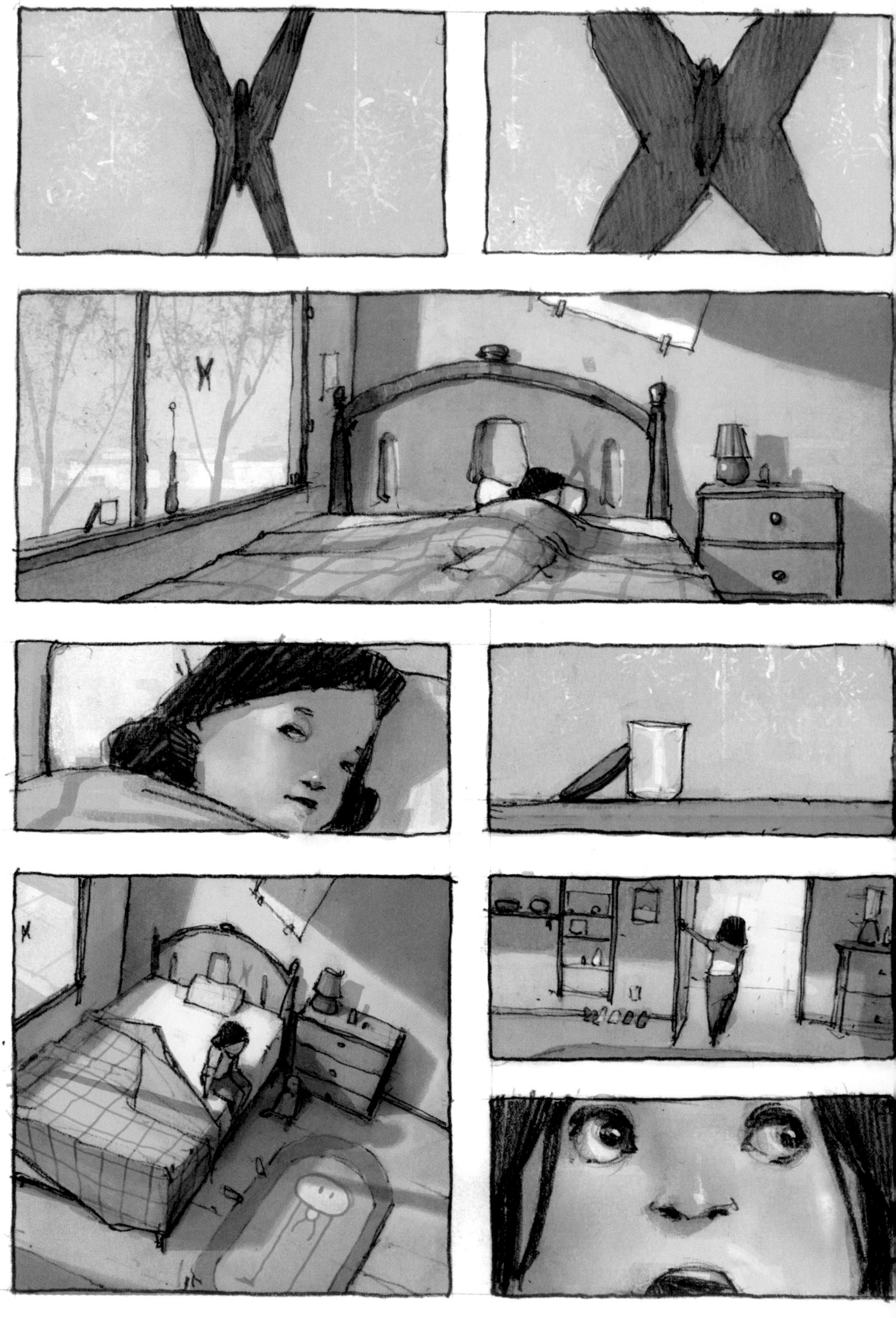

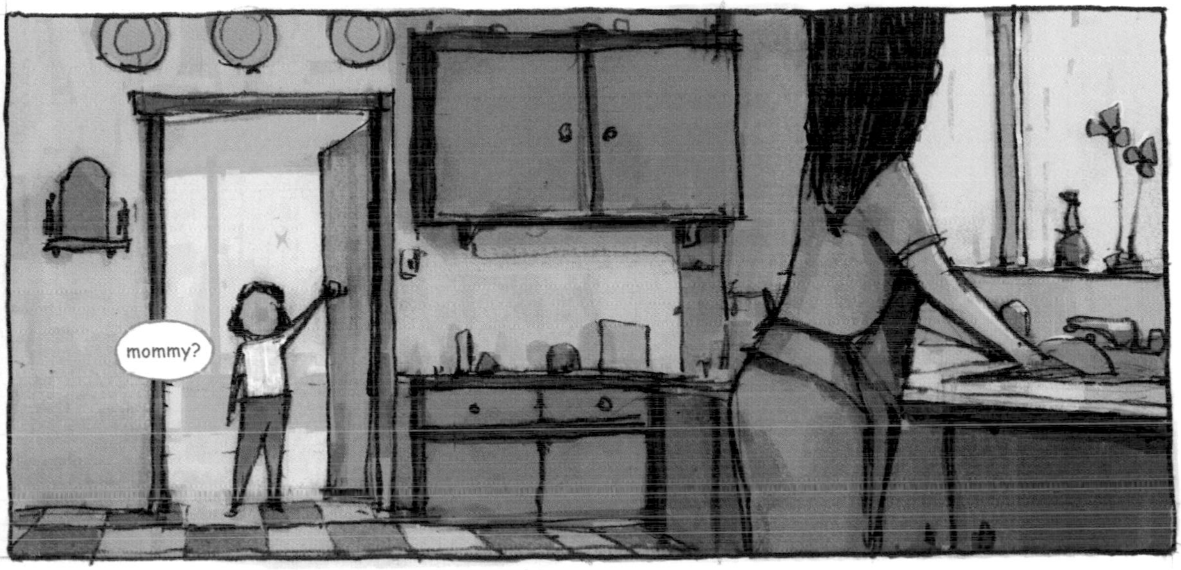
mommy?

THE END

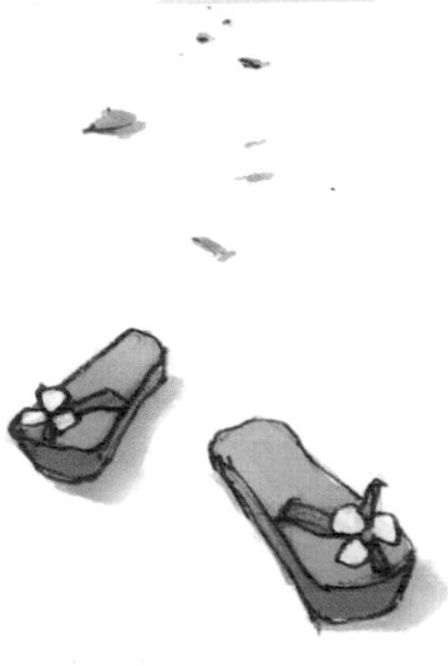

Story and pictures by Chris Appelhans

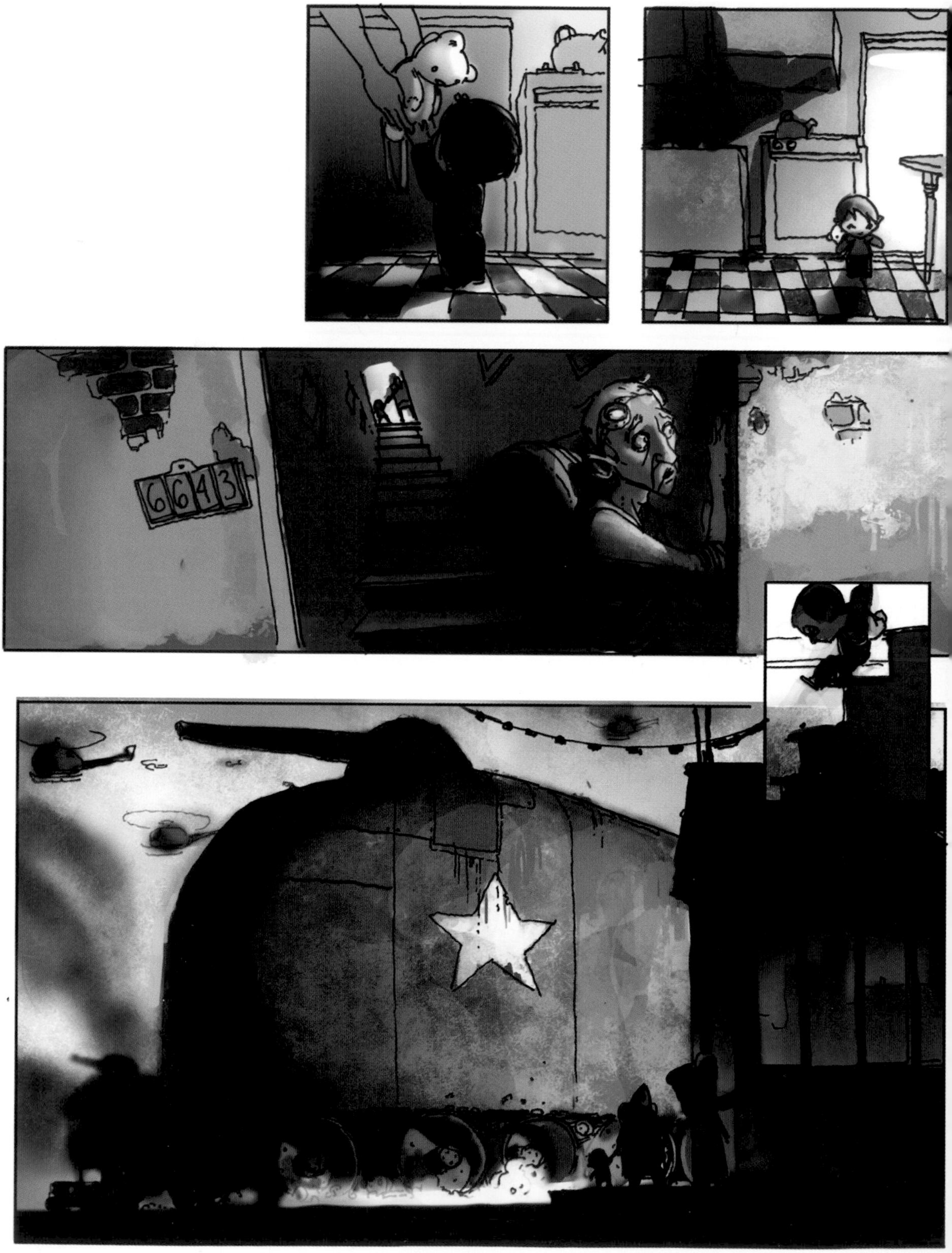
6643

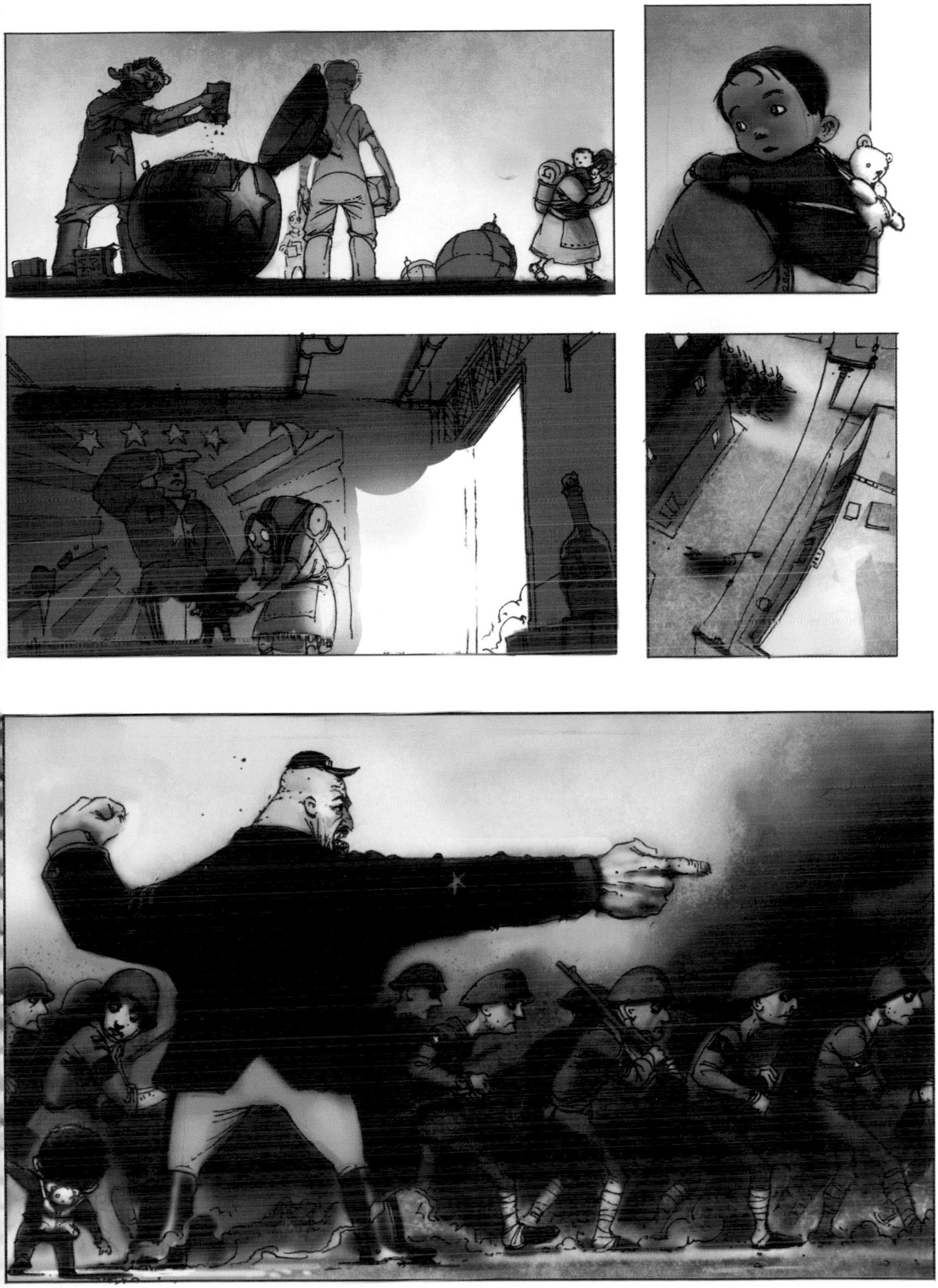

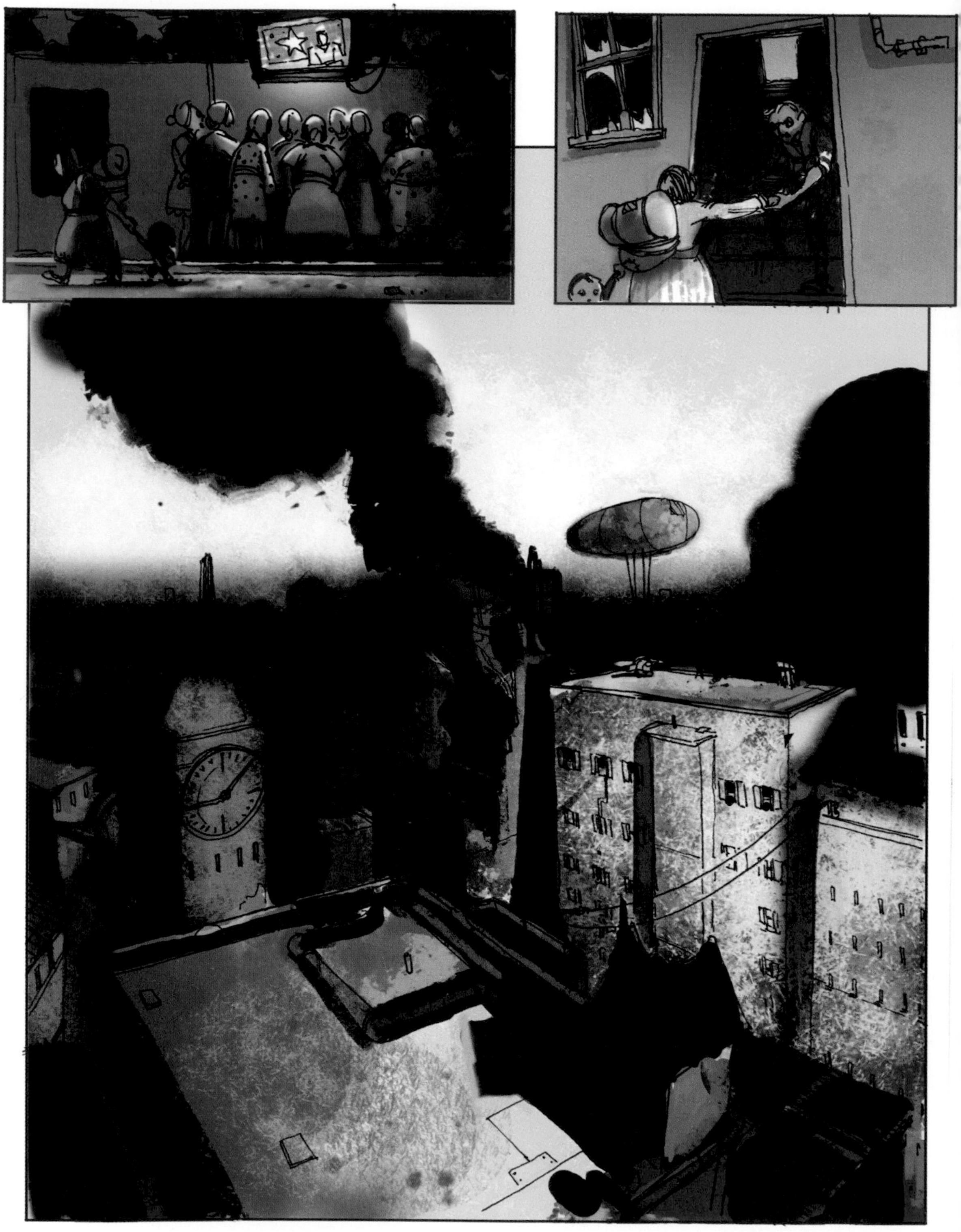

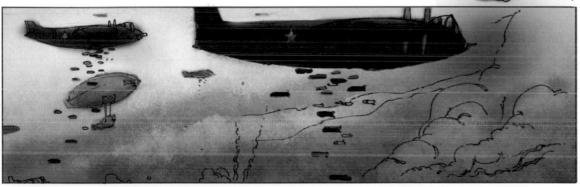

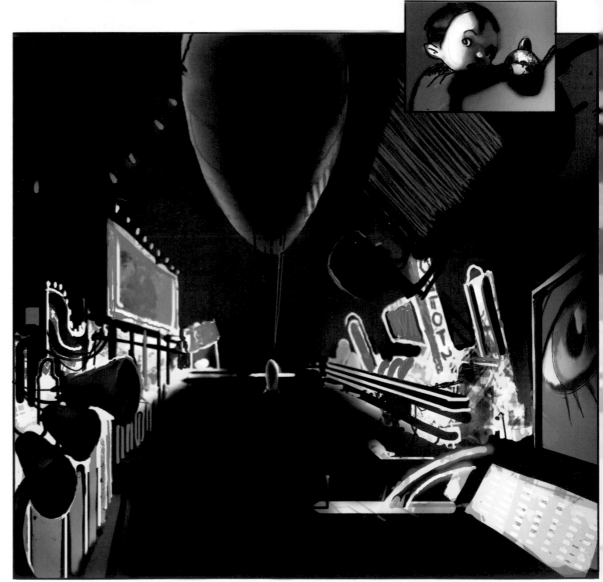

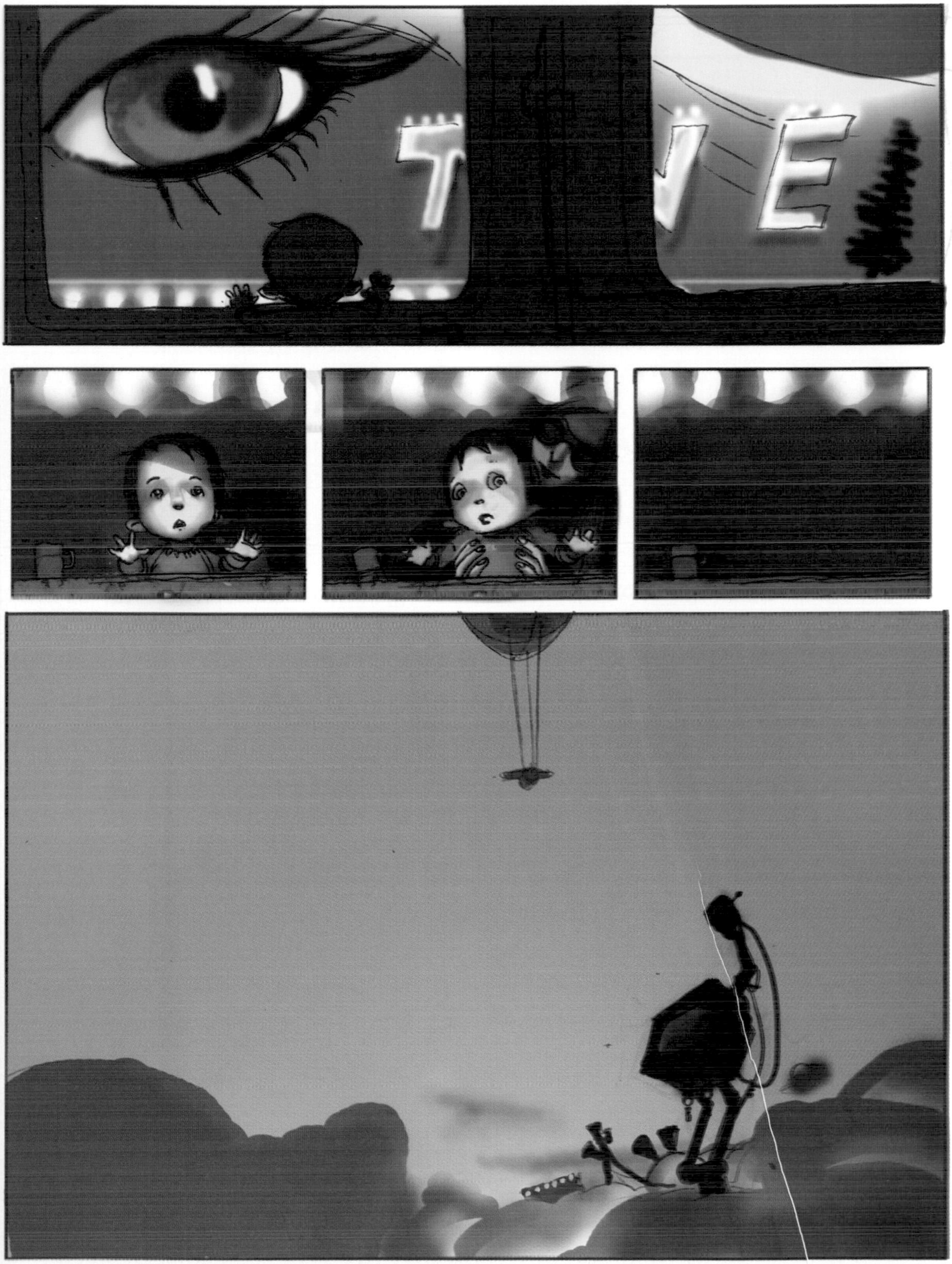

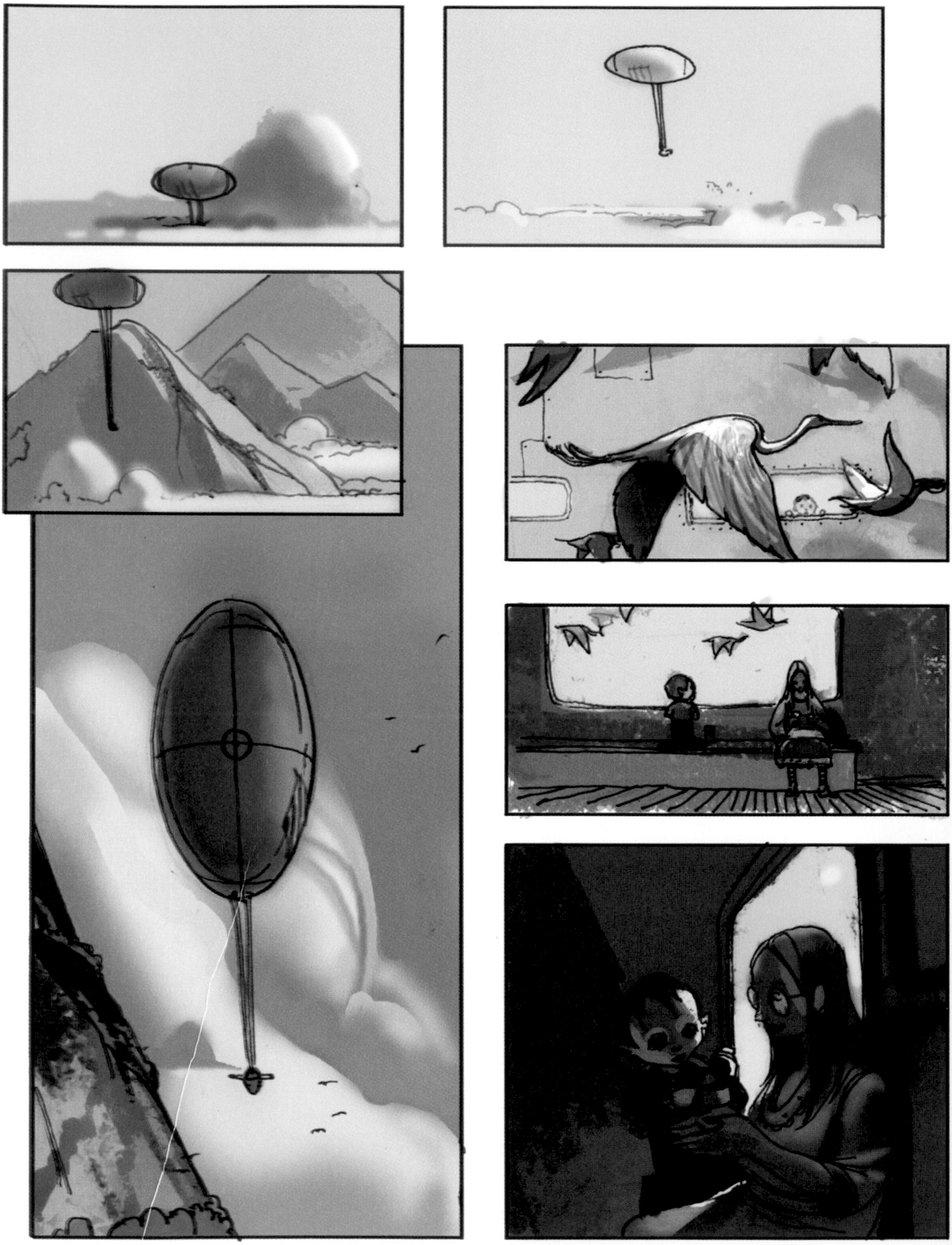

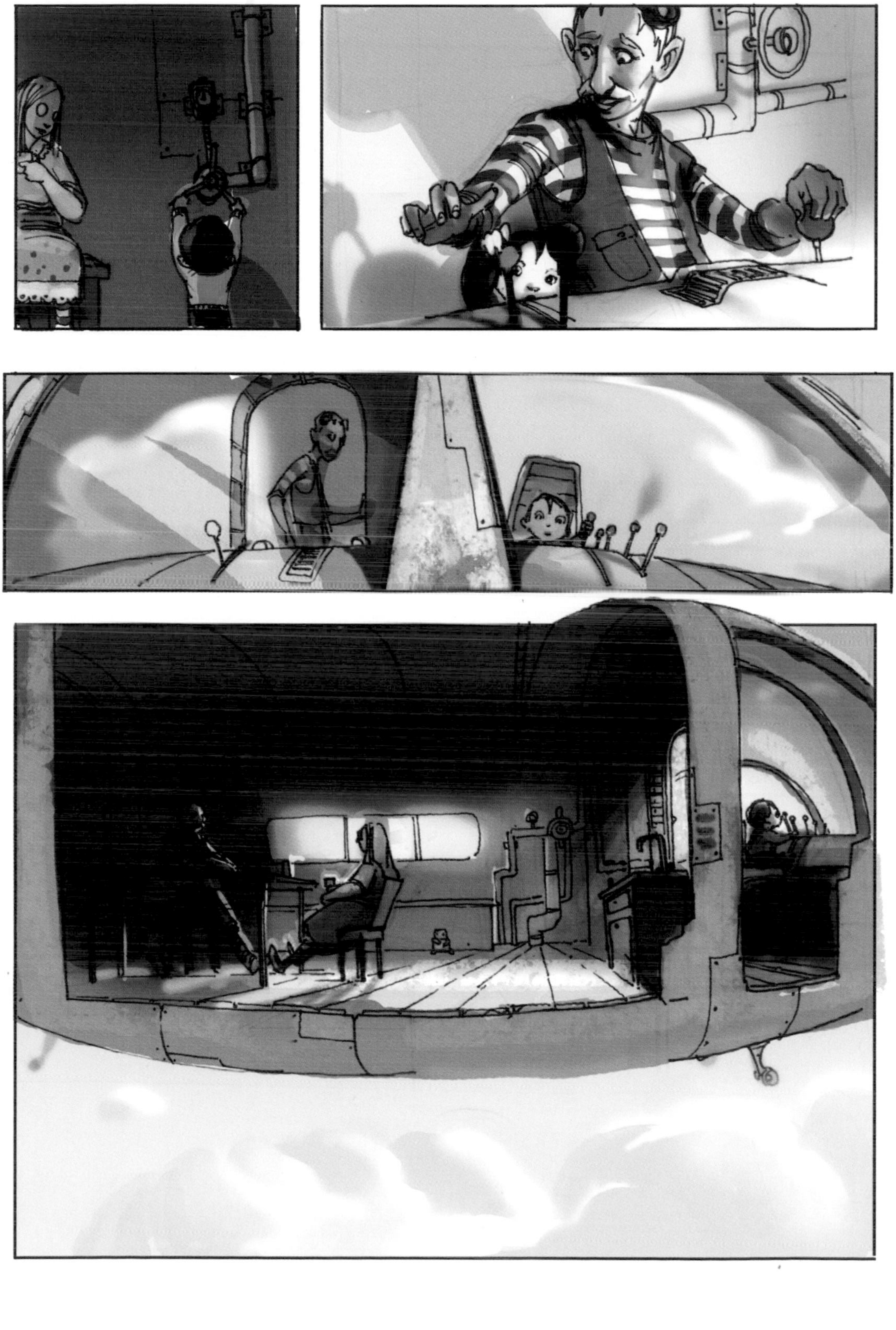

for MOM and DAD

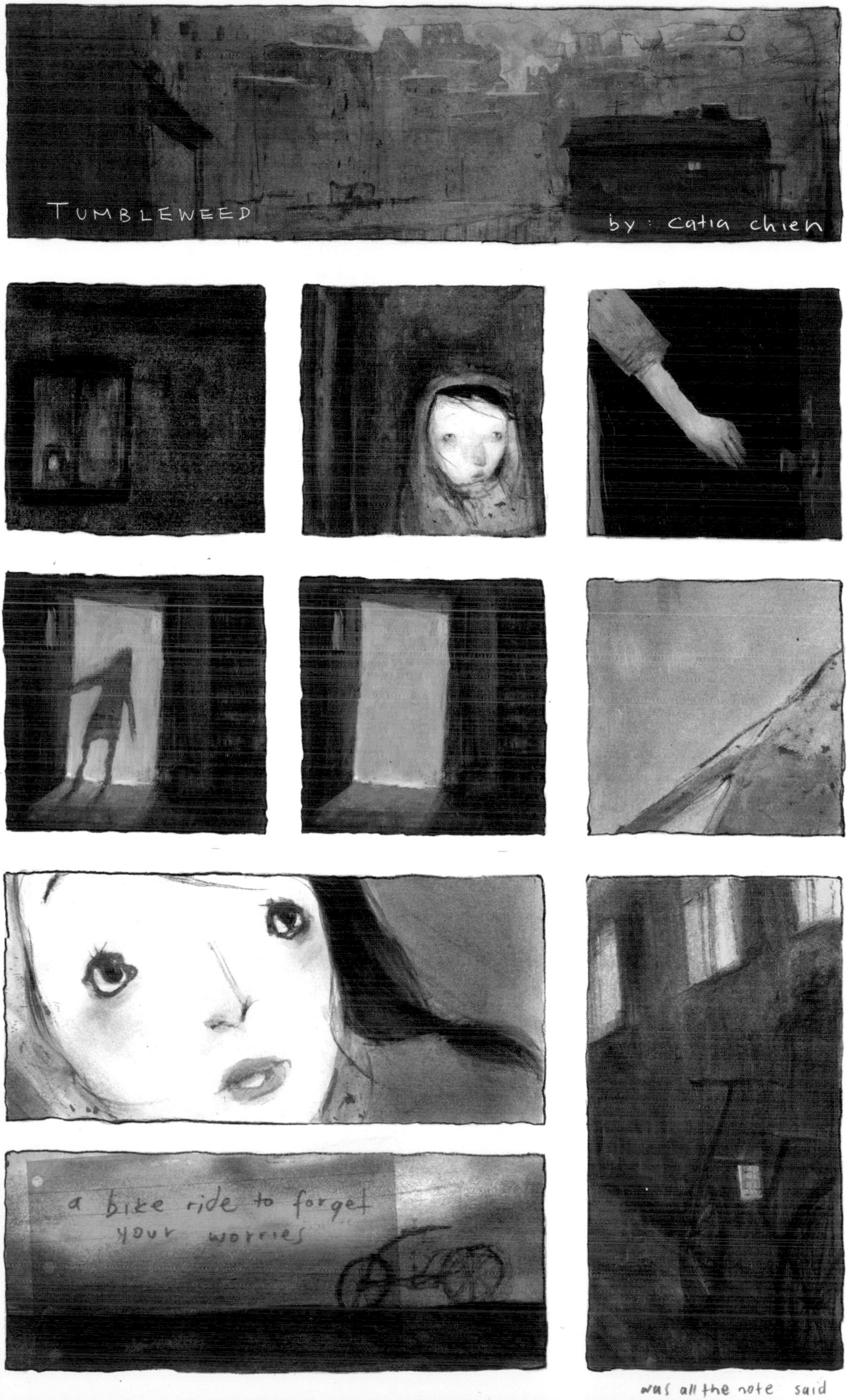
TUMBLEWEED
by: catia chien
a bike ride to forget your worries
was all the note said

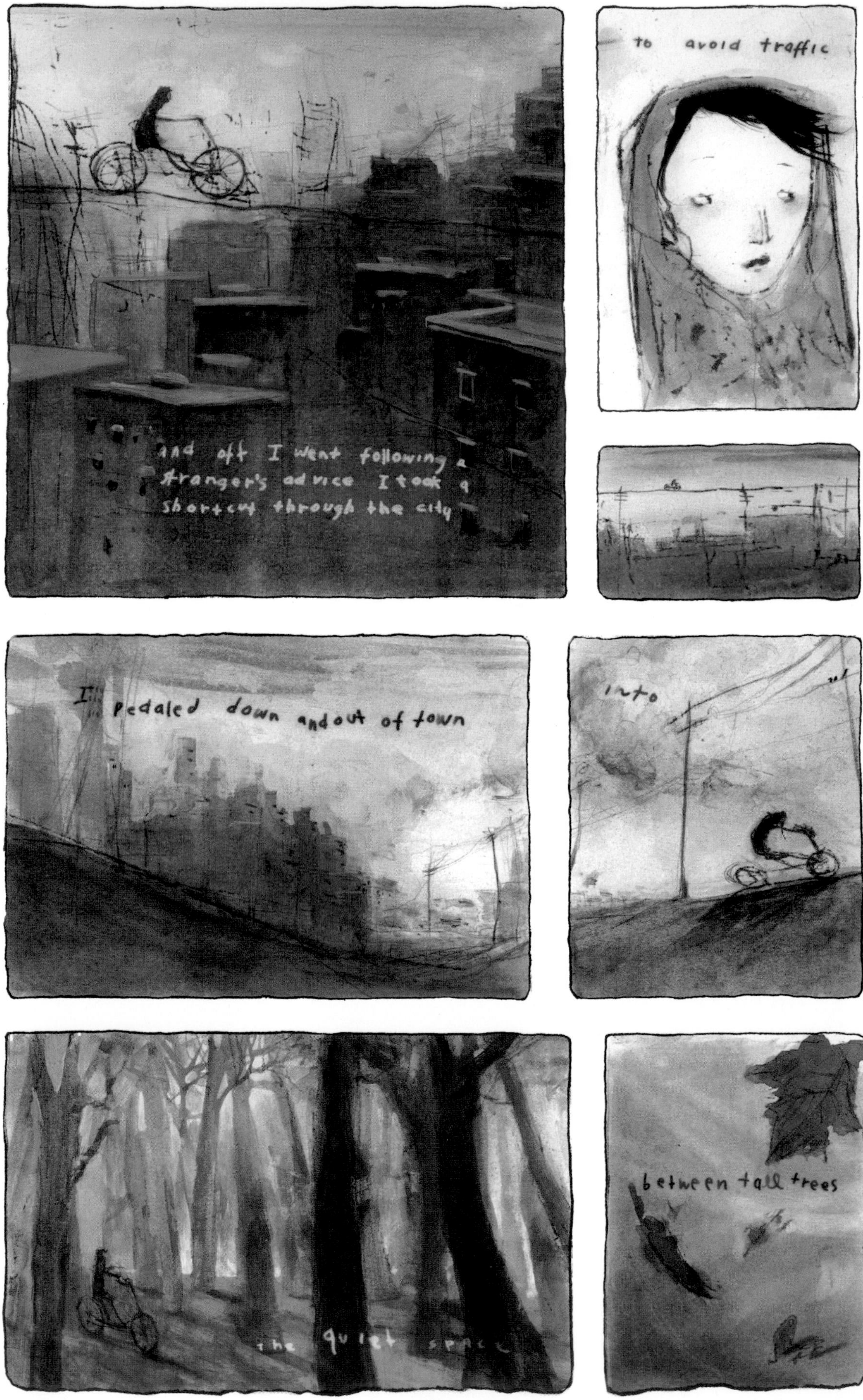
and off I went following a
stranger's advice I took a
shortcut through the city
to avoid traffic
I pedaled down and out of town
into
the quiet space
between tall trees

Shhhh

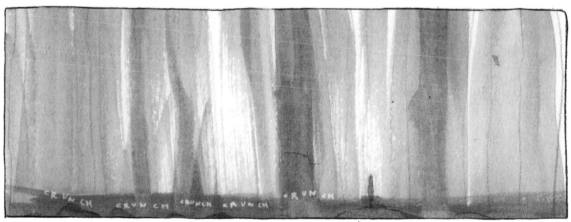

CRUNCH CRUNCH CRUNCH CRUNCH CRUNCH

I filled my pockets full of leaves

to set the music for the rest of the ride

CRUNCH
CRUNCH
CRUN
CRUNCH
CRUNCH
CRUNCH
SPLASH

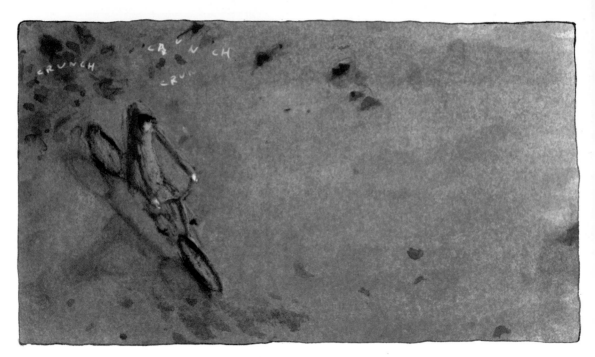

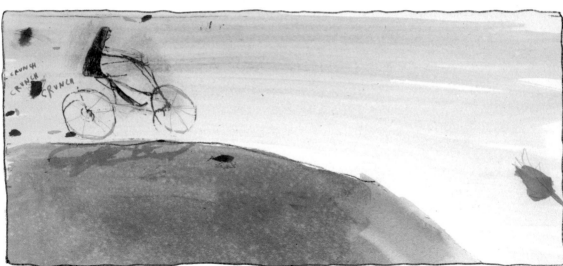

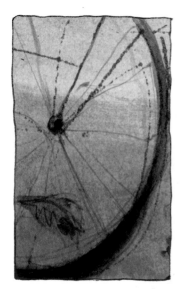

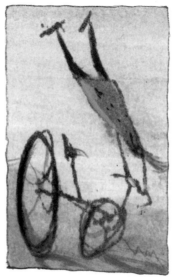

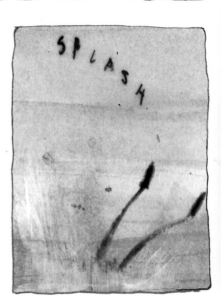

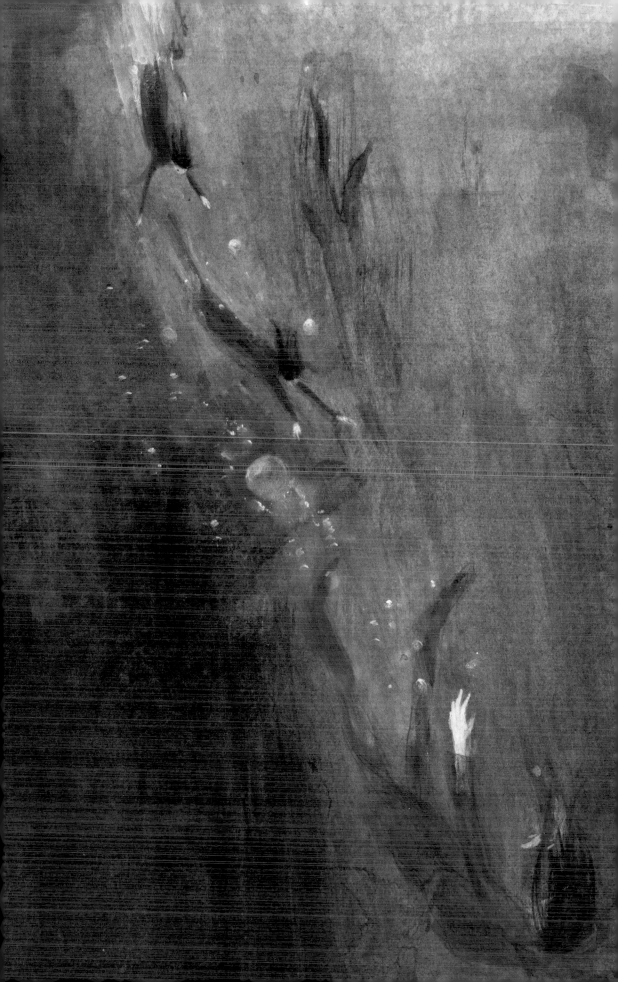

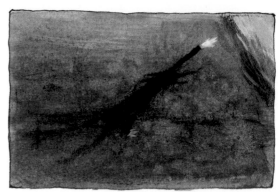

HELLO?

NO ONE

'CEPT . . .

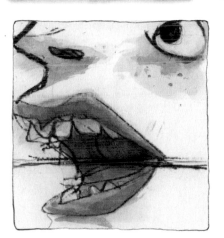

a cat

held.

with a string

SNAP

I followed the string

till our hands met in a light handshake

A sudden Raincloud passed

and our attention was turned towards finding shelter from the downpour

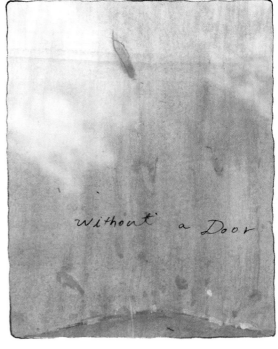

without a Door

We found a lit room

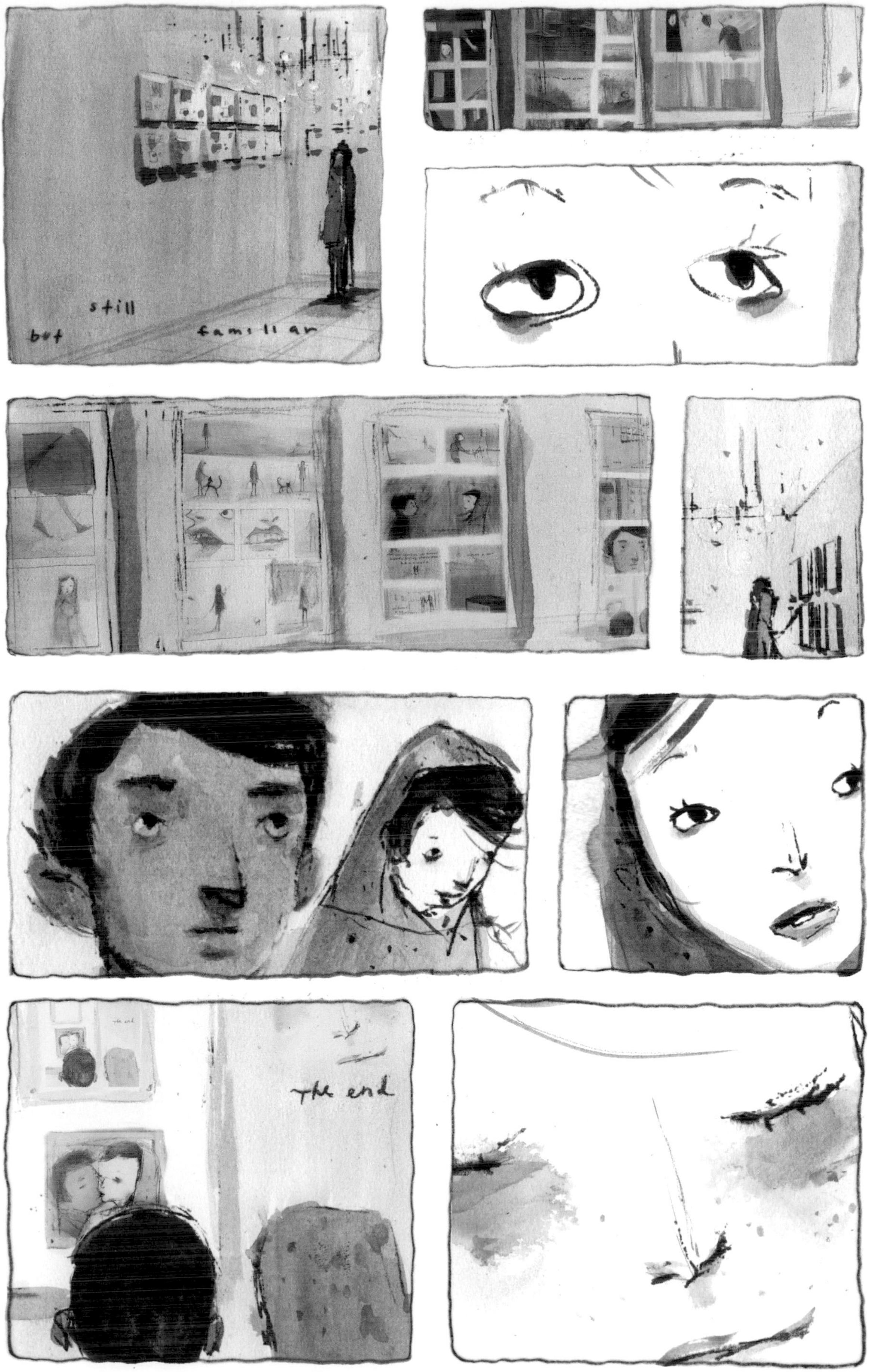
but still familiar
the end

Fall

by: Catia chien

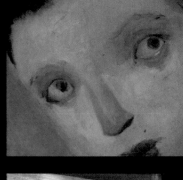

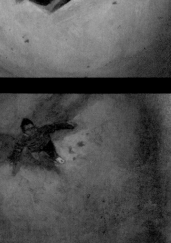

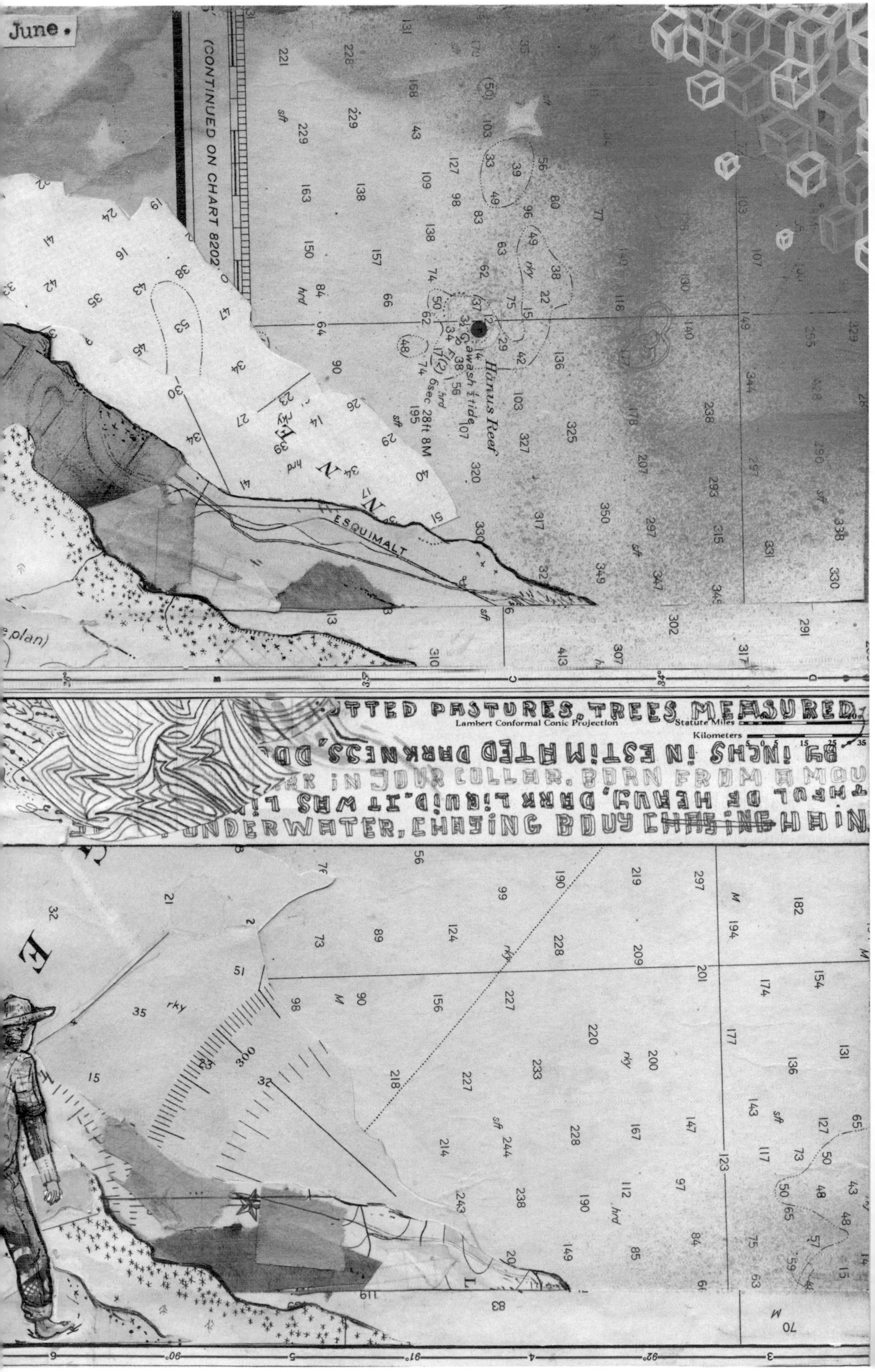
June.
(CONTINUED ON CHART 8202)
Hanus Reef
ESQUIMALT
TTED PASTURES, TREES MEASURED
Lambert Conformal Conic Projection
Statute Miles
Kilometers
BY INCHS IN ESTIMATED DARKNESS, DD
RK IN YOUR COLLAR, BORN FROM A MOU
THFUL OF HEAVY, DARK LIQUID. IT WAS LI
UNDERWATER, CHASING BOUY CHASING A IN

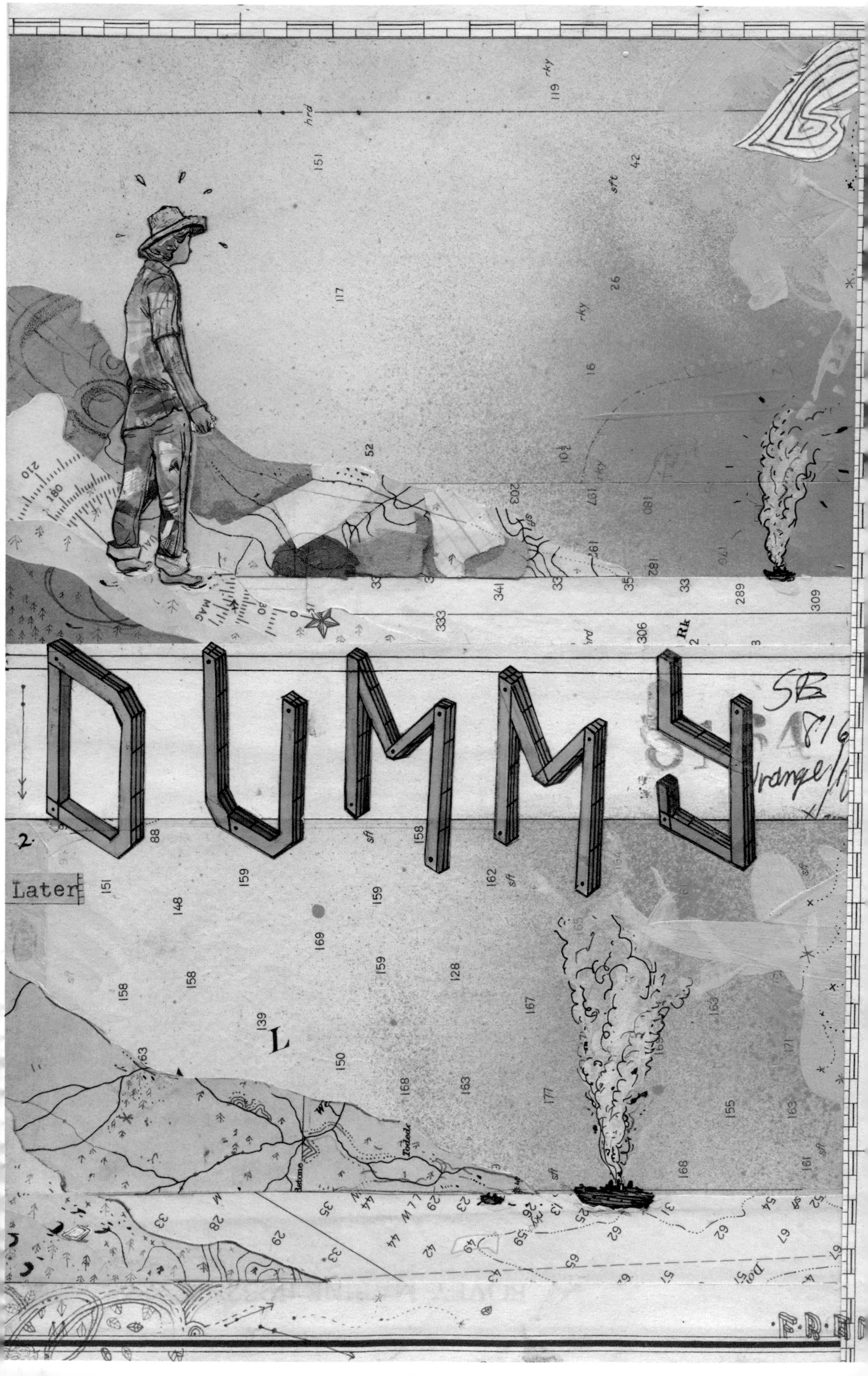
DUMMY
Later

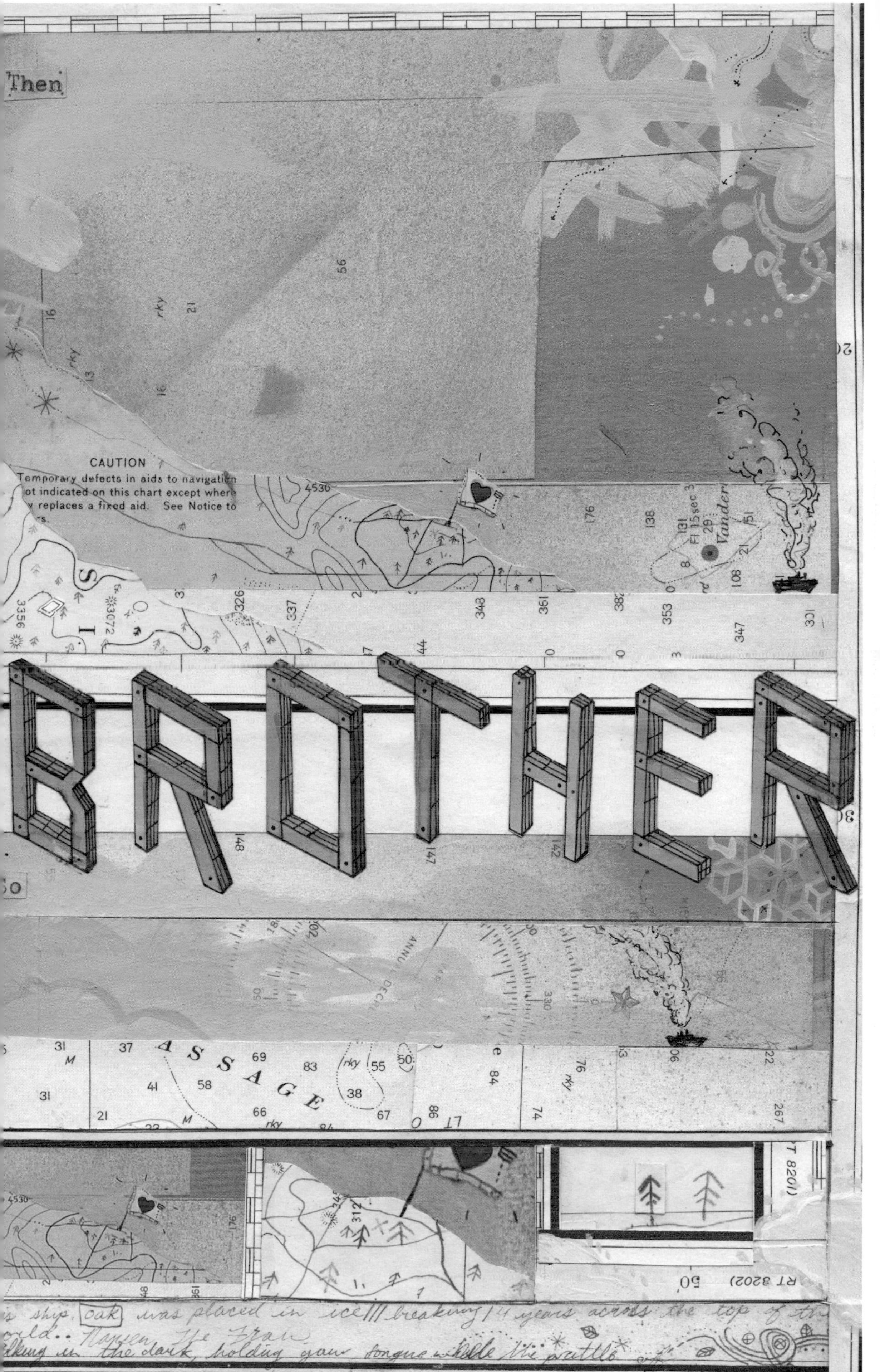
Then
CAUTION
Temporary defects in aids to navigation
not indicated on this chart except where
replaces a fixed aid. See Notice to
BROTHER
ASSAGE
s ship Oak was placed in ice /// breaking 14 years across the top of the
world.. Nansen The Fram
lking in the dark, holding your tongue while the prattle

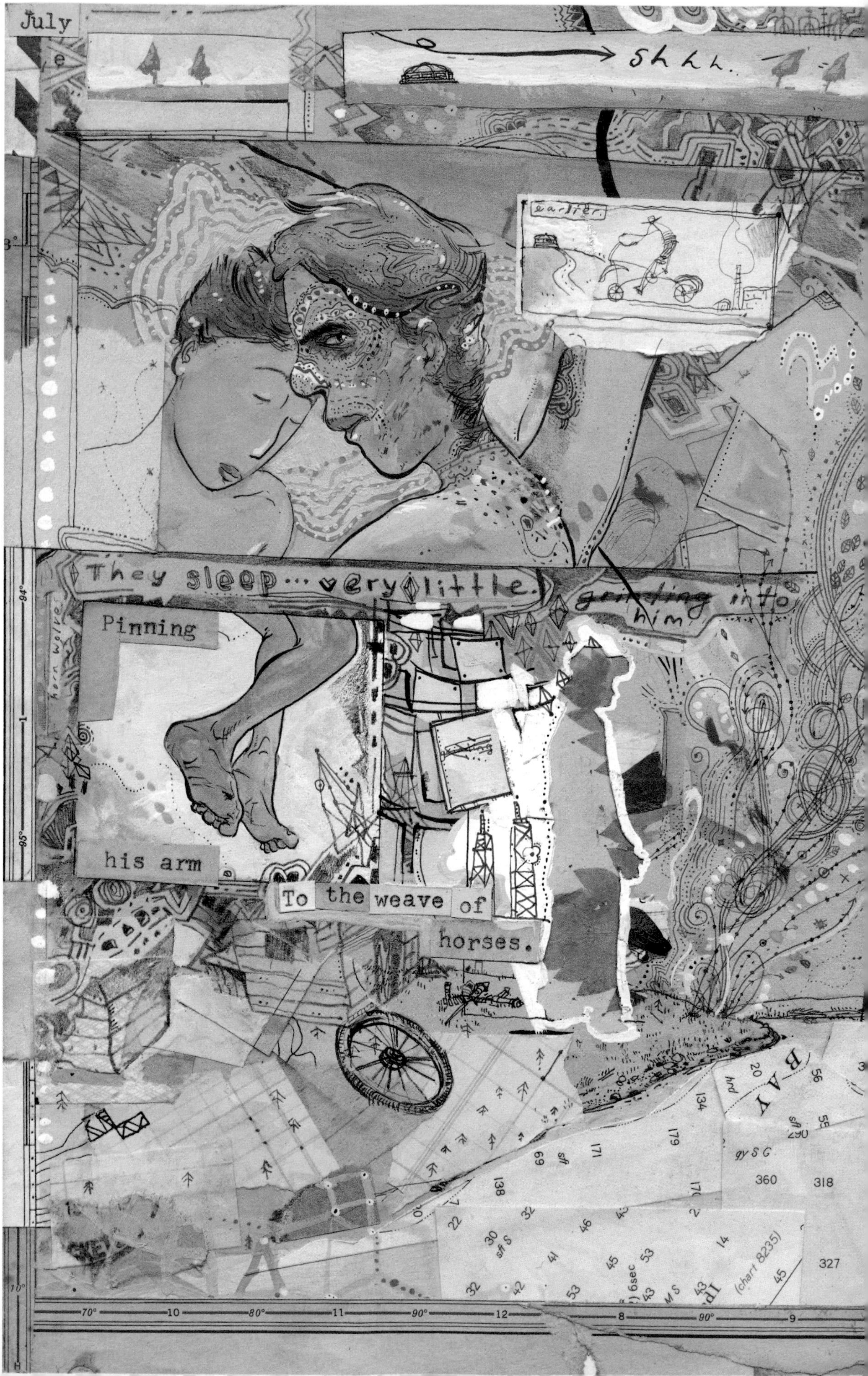

July
Shhh.
earlier.
They sleep... very little.
grinding into him
Pinning
his arm
To the weave of
horses.
BAY
(chart 8235)

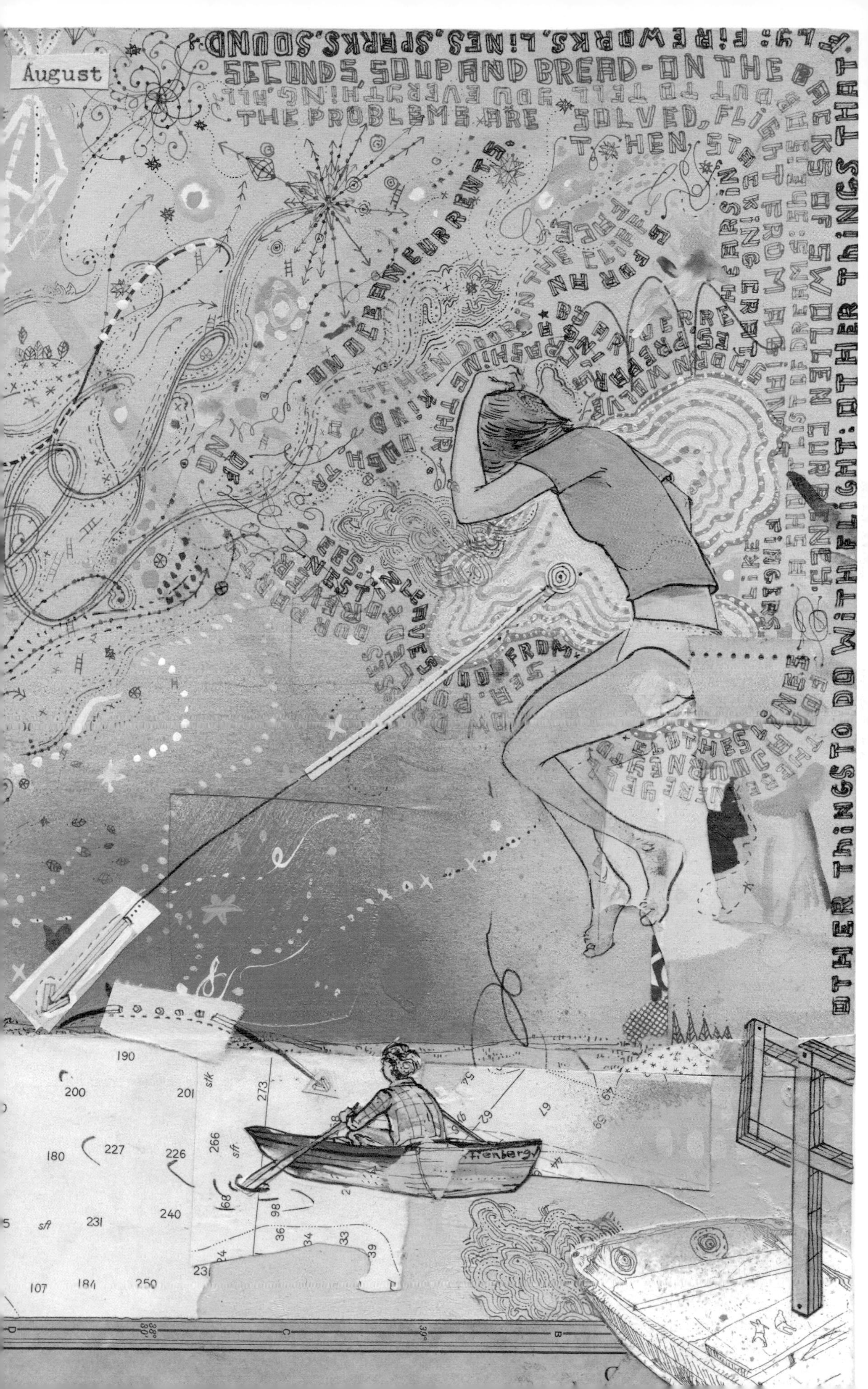

August
SECONDS, SOUP AND BREAD—ON THE
THE PROBLEMS ARE SOLVED,

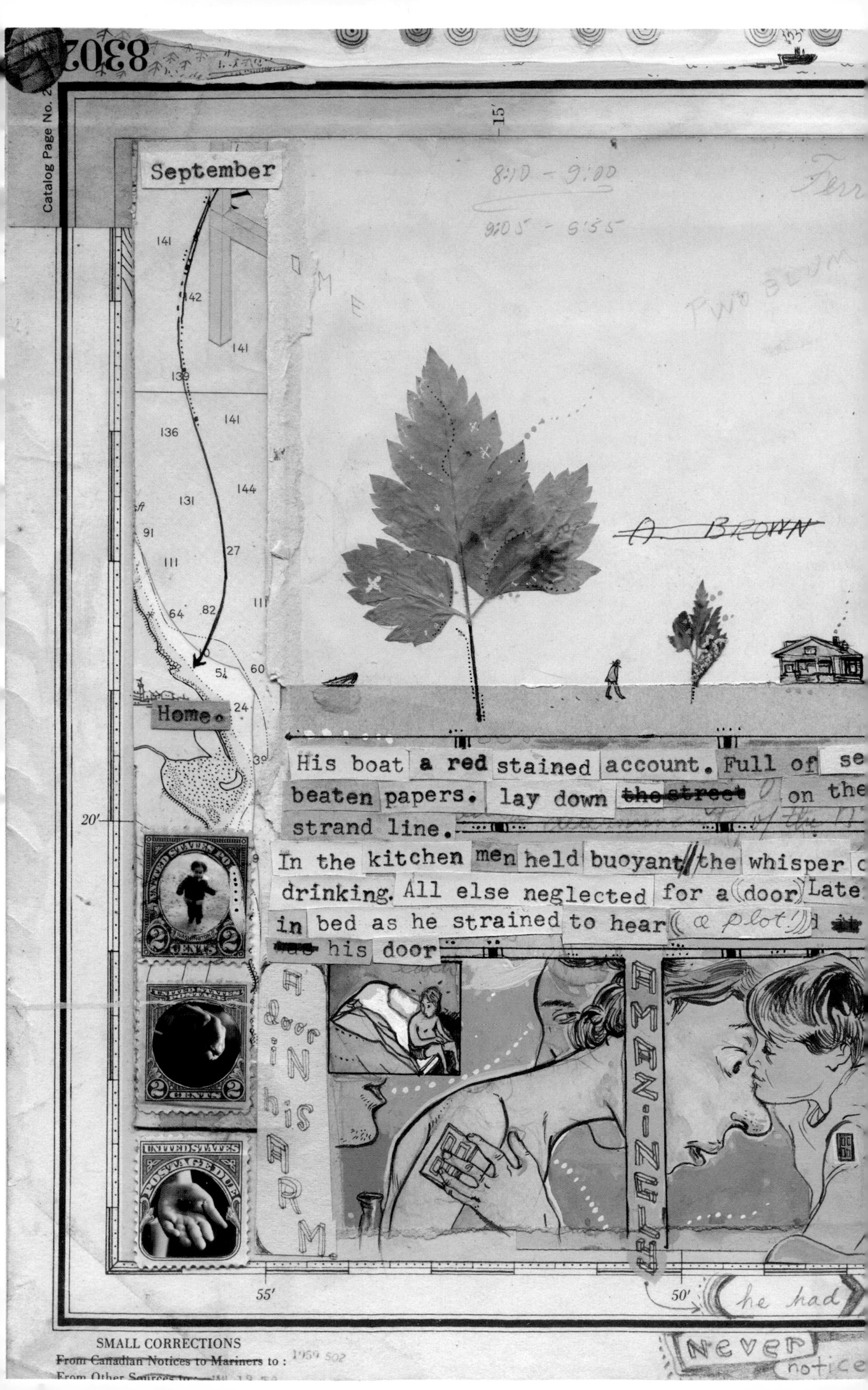
8302
Catalog Page No. 2
15'
September
8:10 - 9:00
9:05 - 5:55
Home.
A. BROWN
His boat a red stained account. Full of se
beaten papers. lay down the street on the
strand line.
In the kitchen men held buoyant the whisper c
drinking. All else neglected for a door Late
in bed as he strained to hear (a plot!)
his door
A door in his ARM
UNITED STATES POSTAGE DUE
20'
55'
50'
he had
never
notice
SMALL CORRECTIONS
From Canadian Notices to Mariners to :

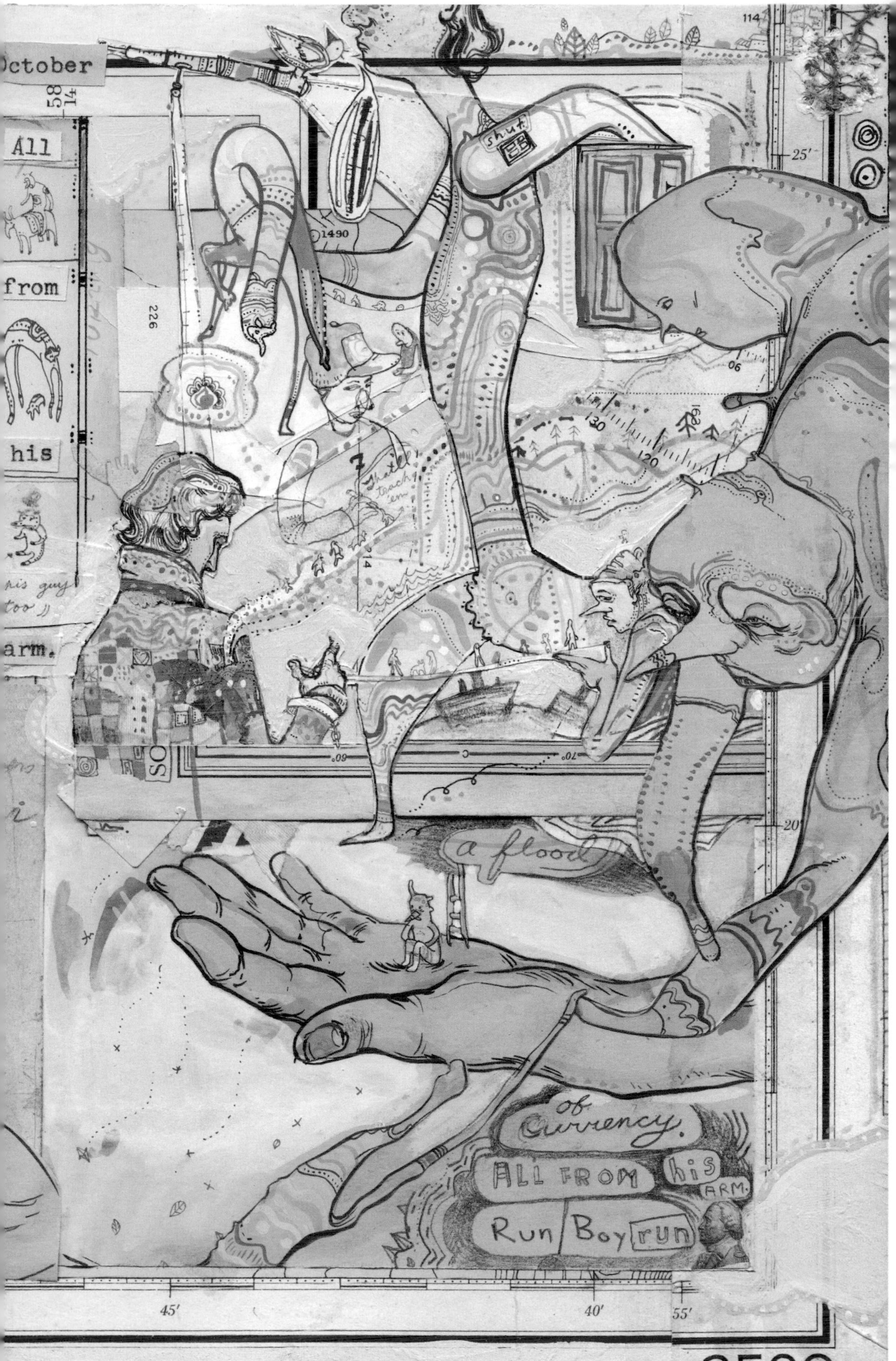
October
All
from
his
his guy
too
arm.
shut
a flood
of Currency.
ALL FROM his ARM.
Run Boy run

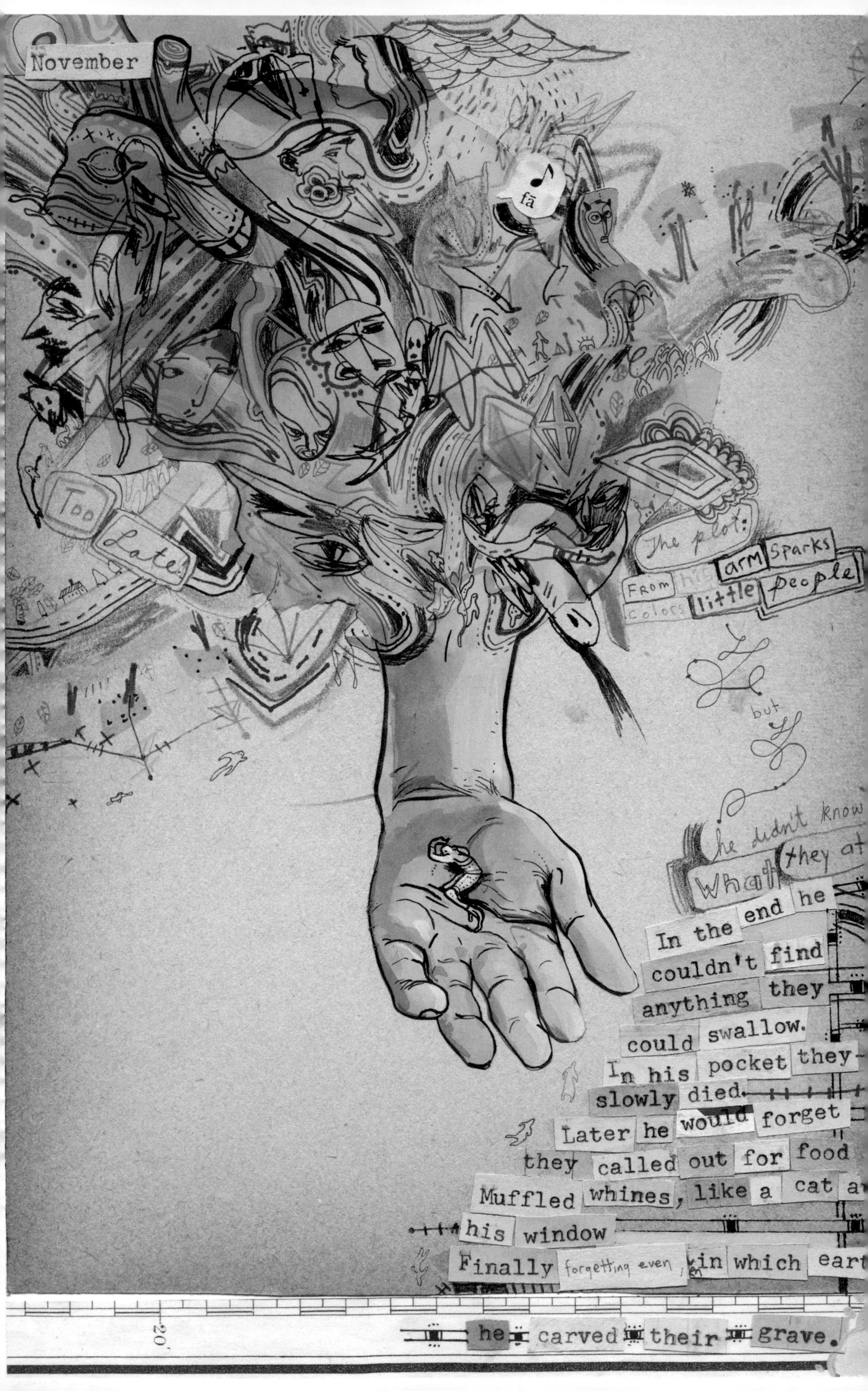
November
fā
Too Late
The plot:
From his arm sparks
colors little people
but
he didn't know
What they at
In the end he
couldn't find
anything they
could swallow.
In his pocket they
slowly died.
Later he would forget
they called out for food
Muffled whines, like a cat a
his window
Finally forgetting even in which eart
20
he carved their grave.

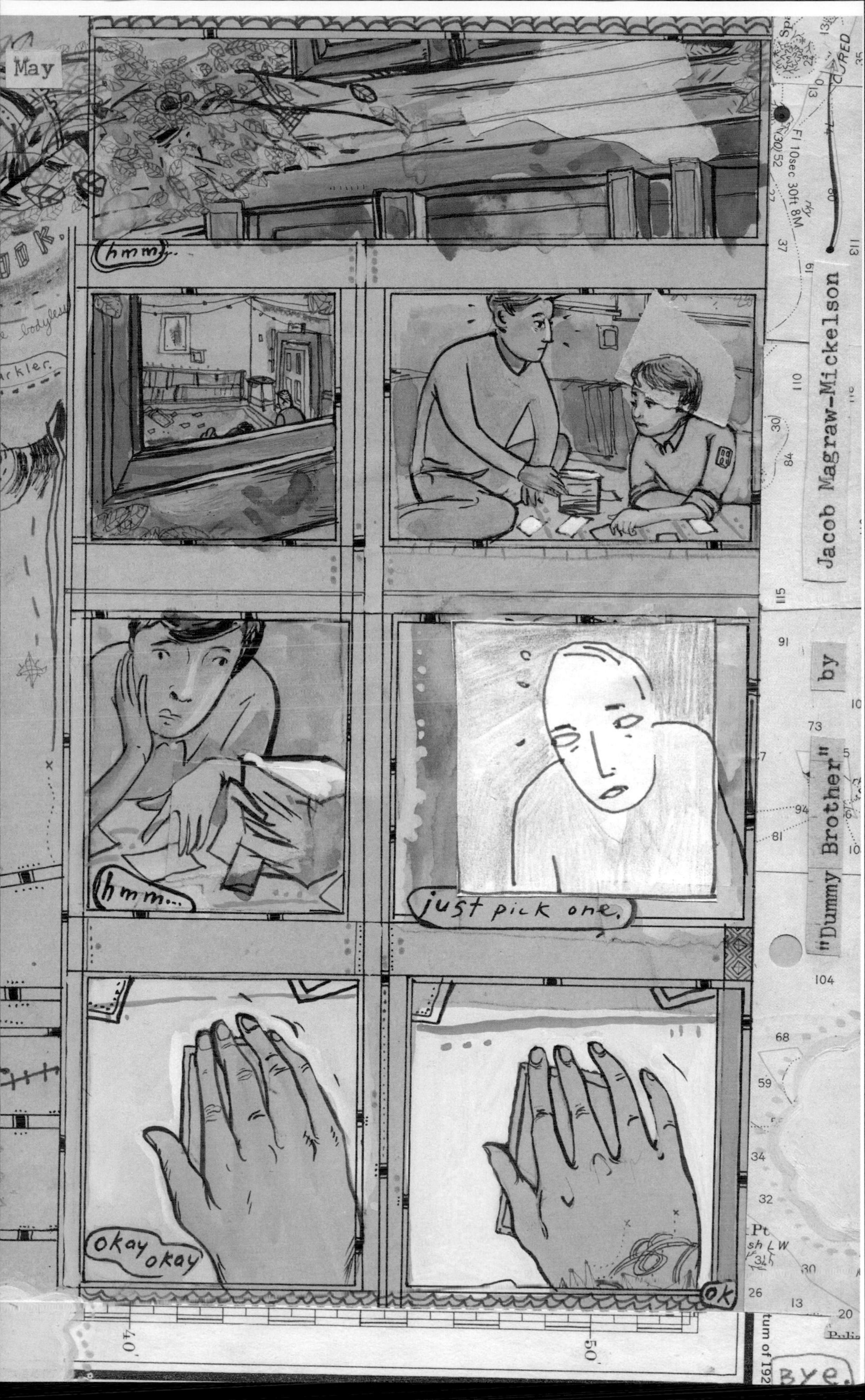
May
hmm...
"Dummy Brother" by
Jacob Magraw-Mickelson
hmm...
just pick one.
okay okay
ok
Bye.

"All-Time Low," Story by Dylan Meconis Pictures by Bill Mudron

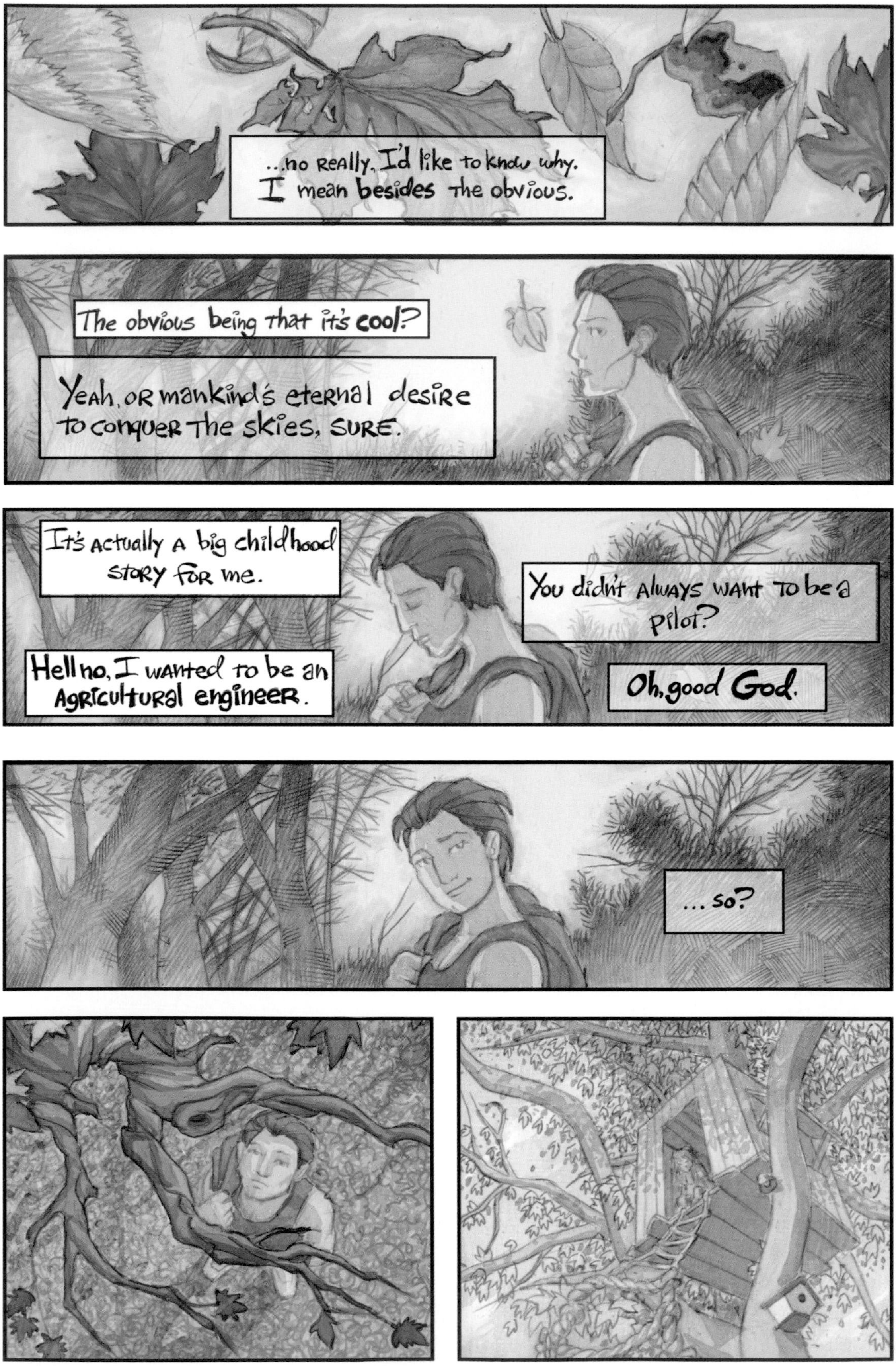

...no really, I'd like to know why. I mean besides the obvious.
The obvious being that it's cool?
Yeah, or mankind's eternal desire to conquer the skies, sure.
It's actually a big childhood story for me.
You didn't always want to be a pilot?
Hell no, I wanted to be an agricultural engineer.
Oh, good God.
...so?

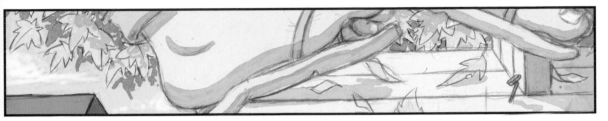

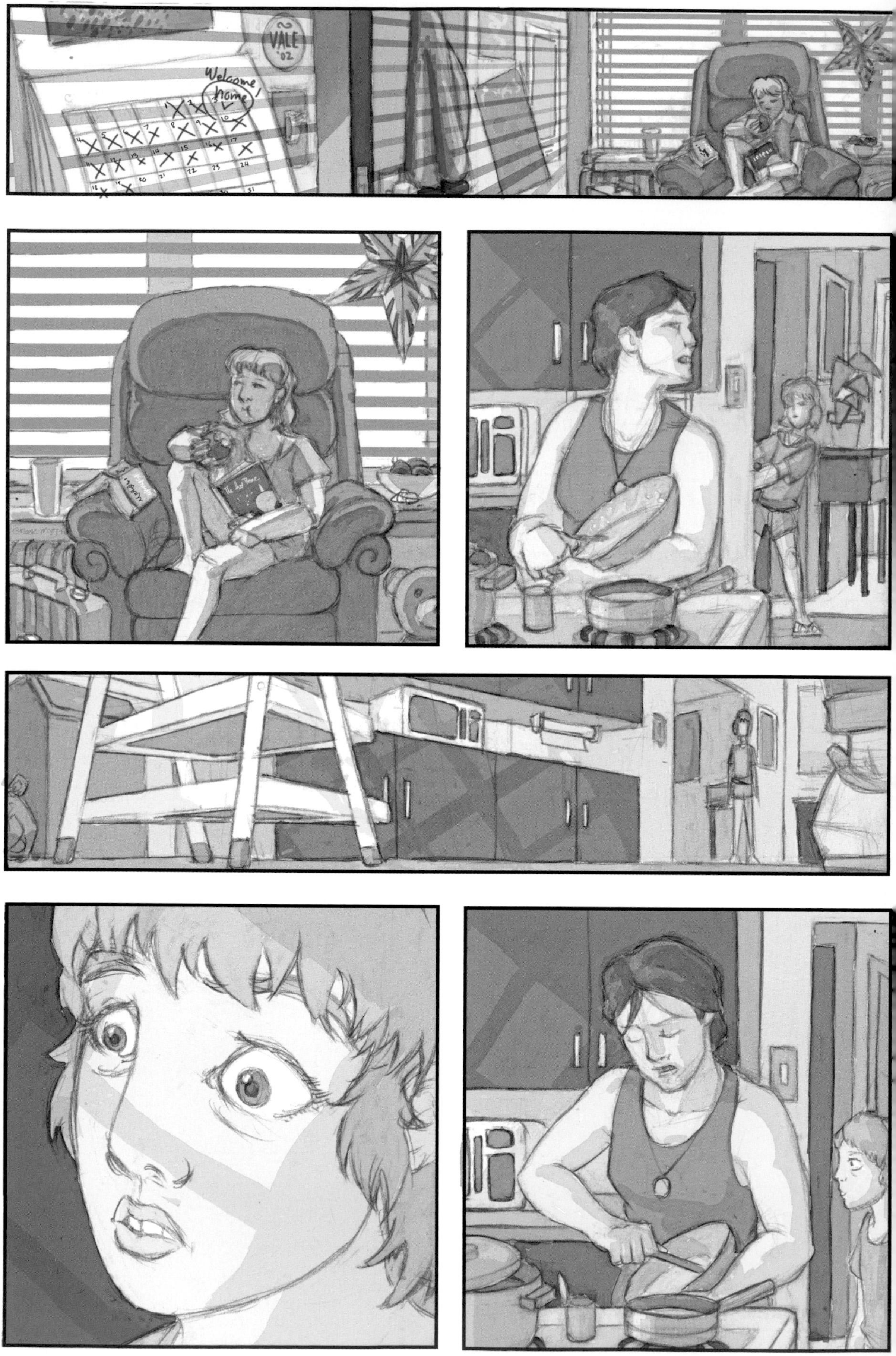
VALE '02
Welcome home!

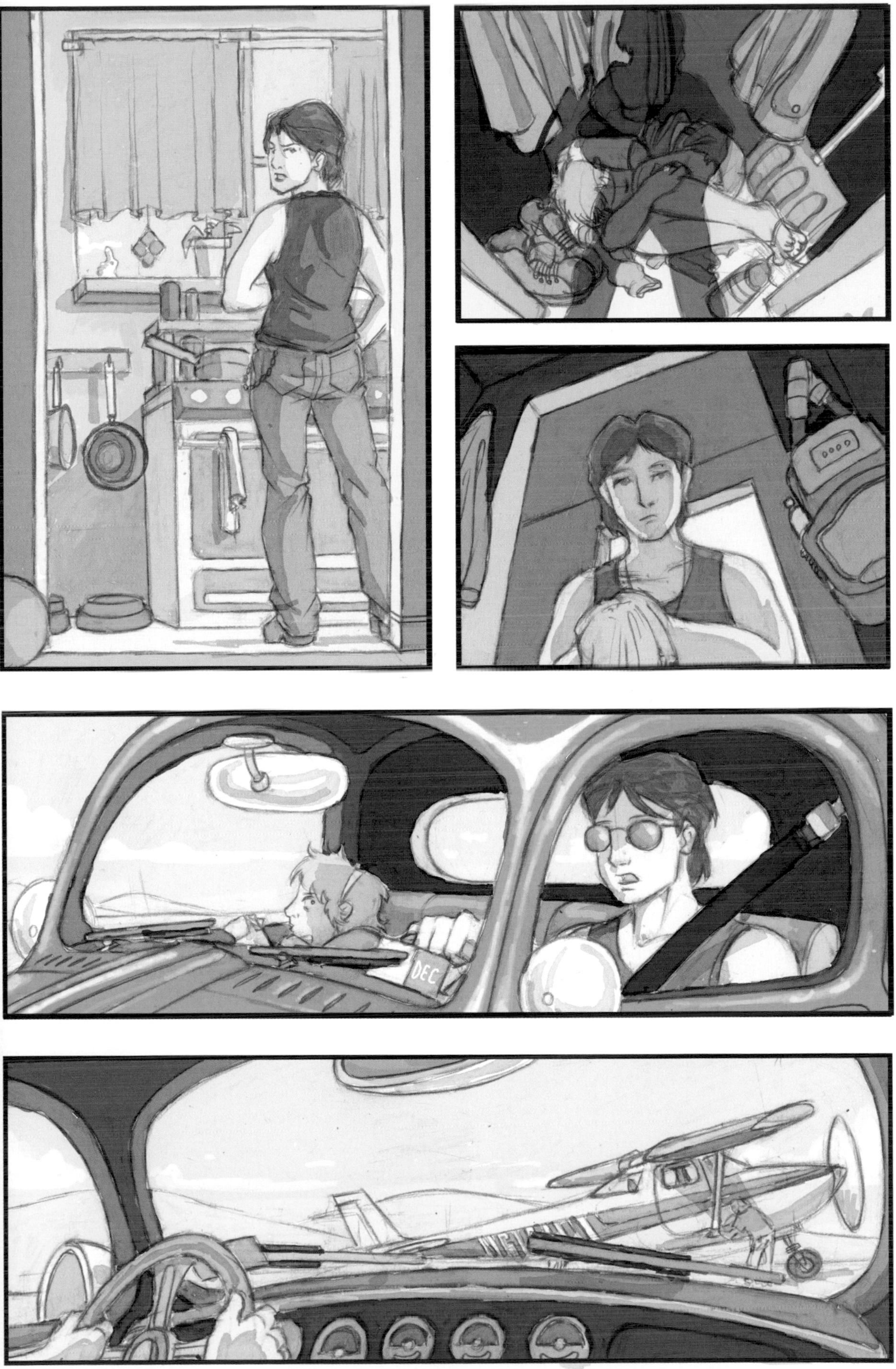
DEC

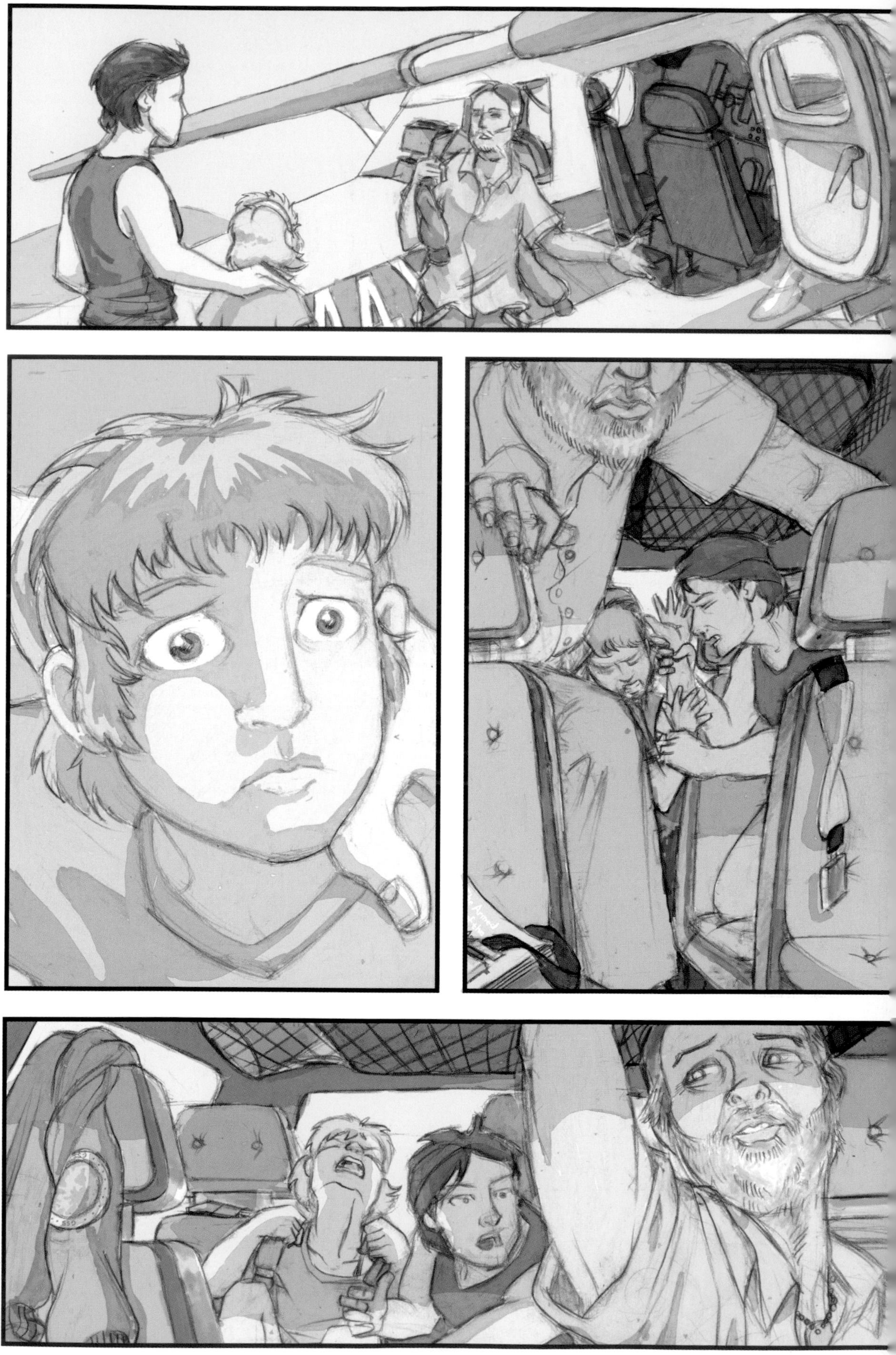

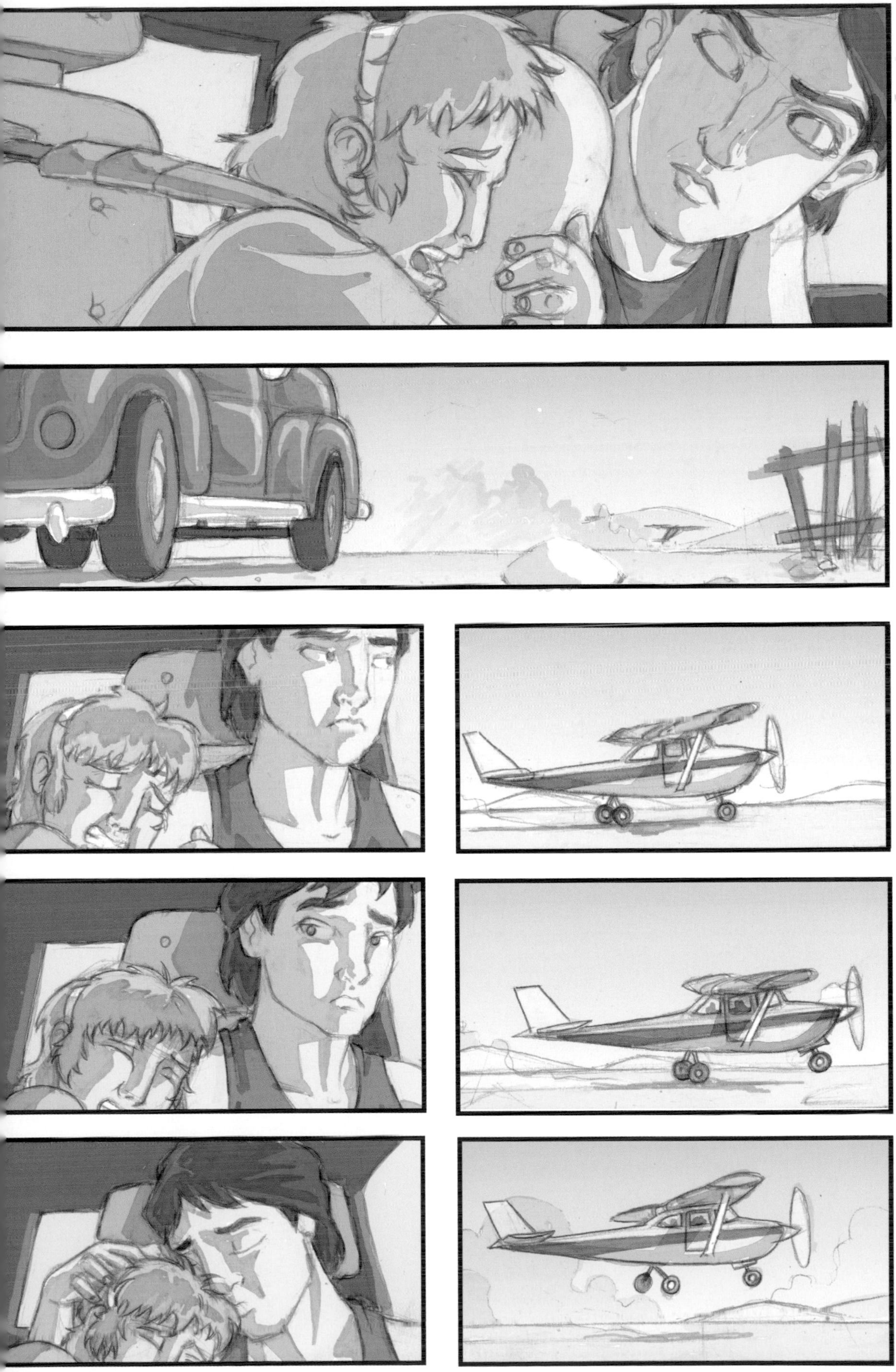

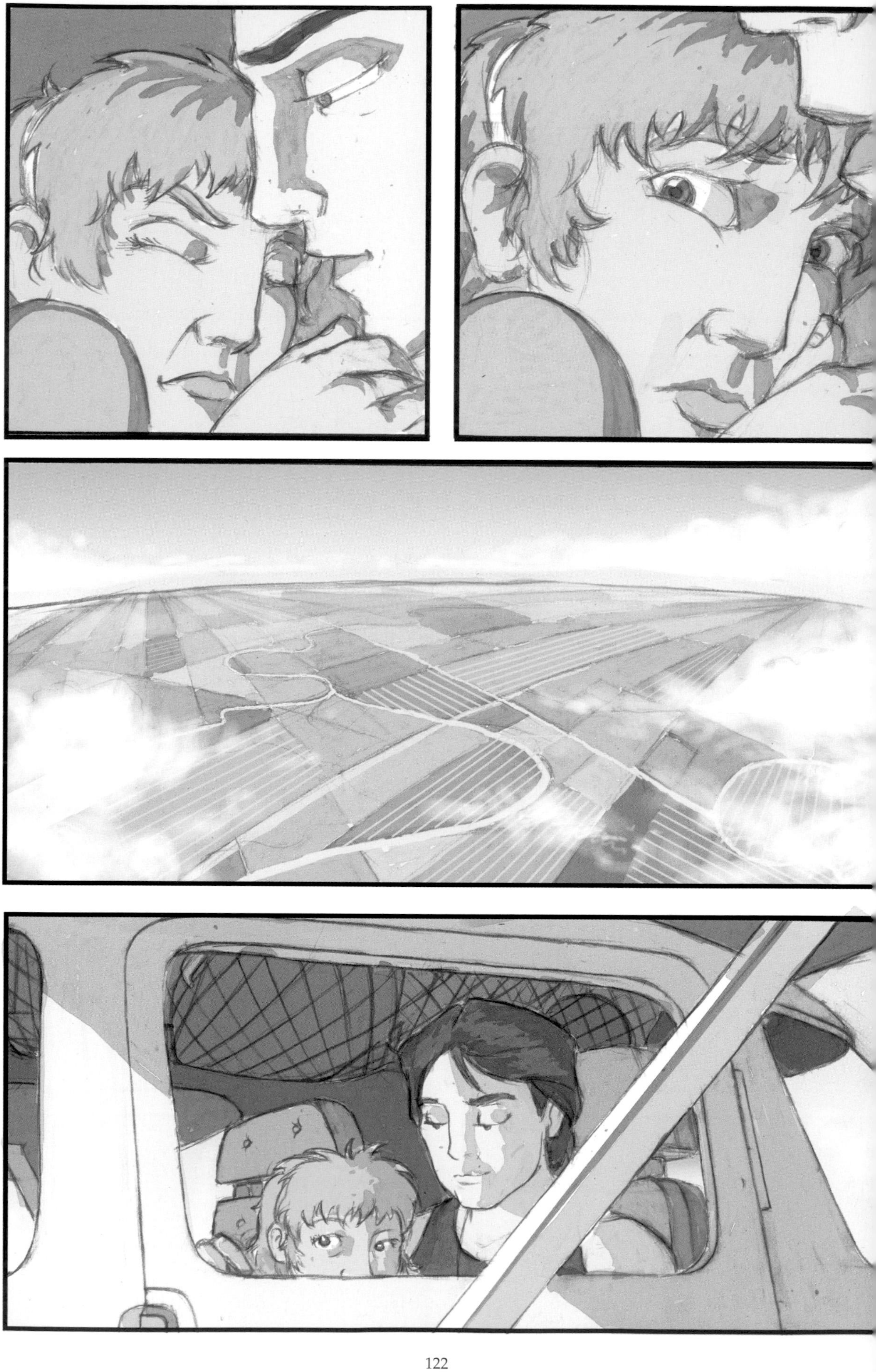

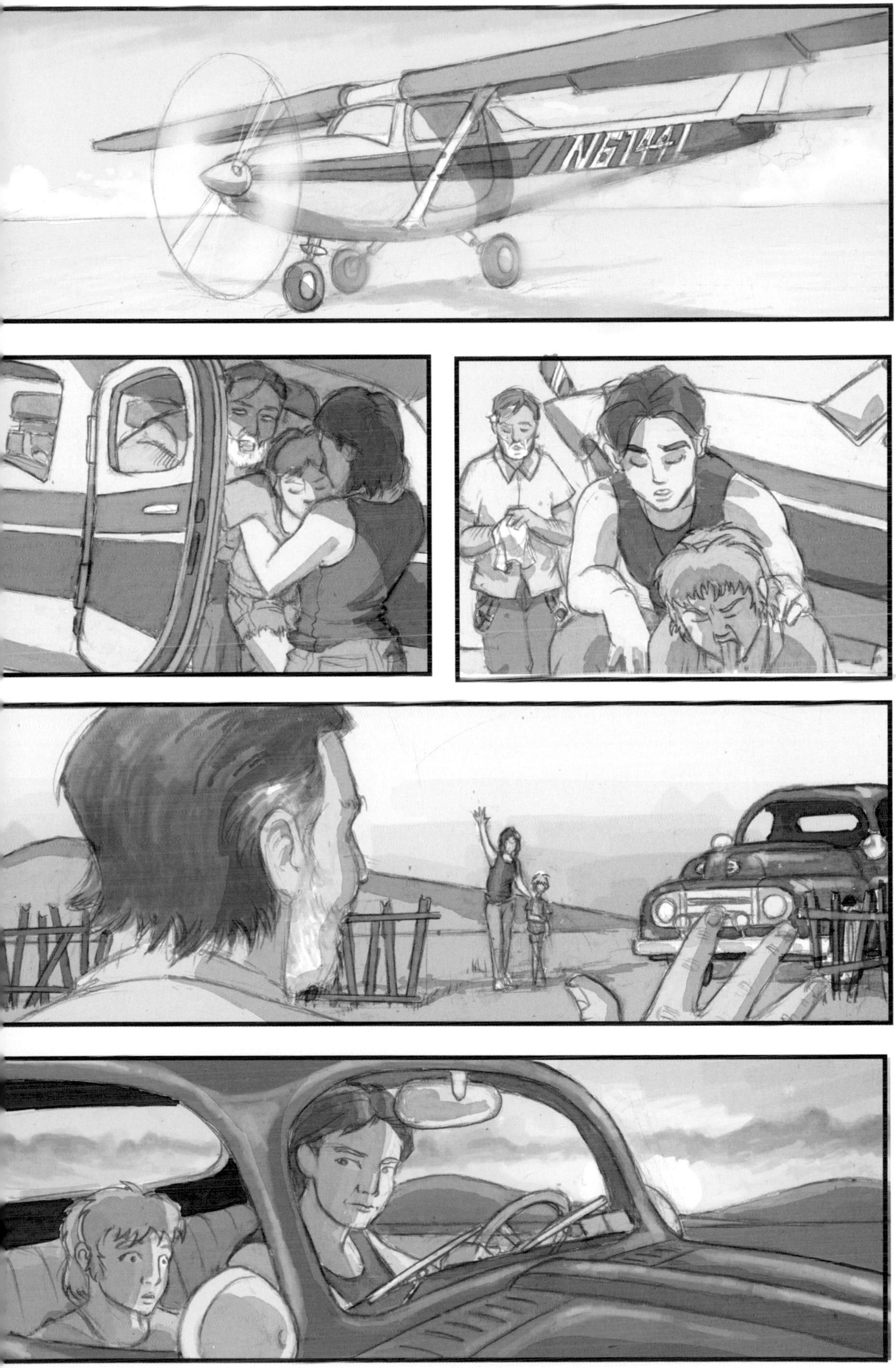
N67441

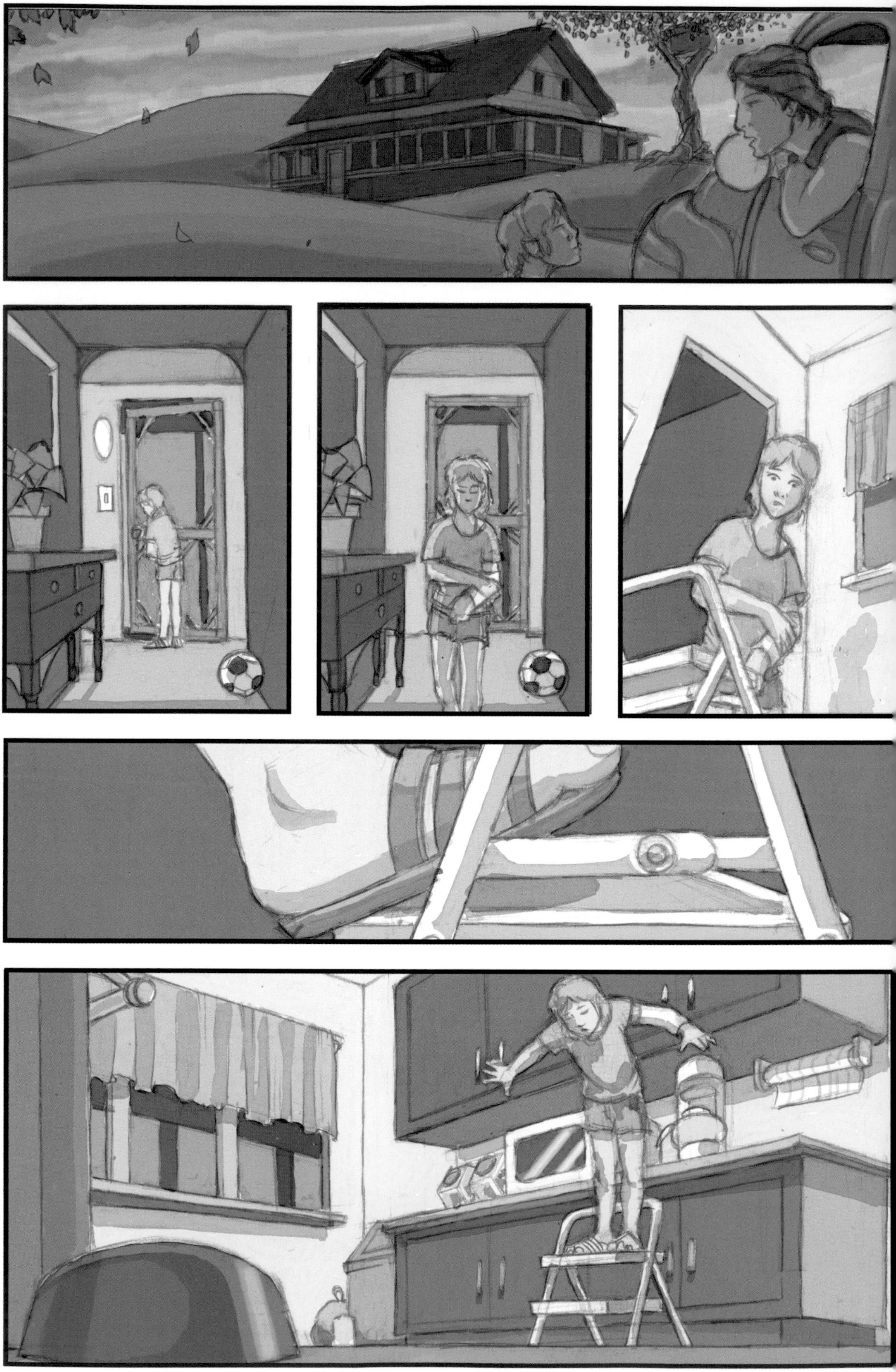

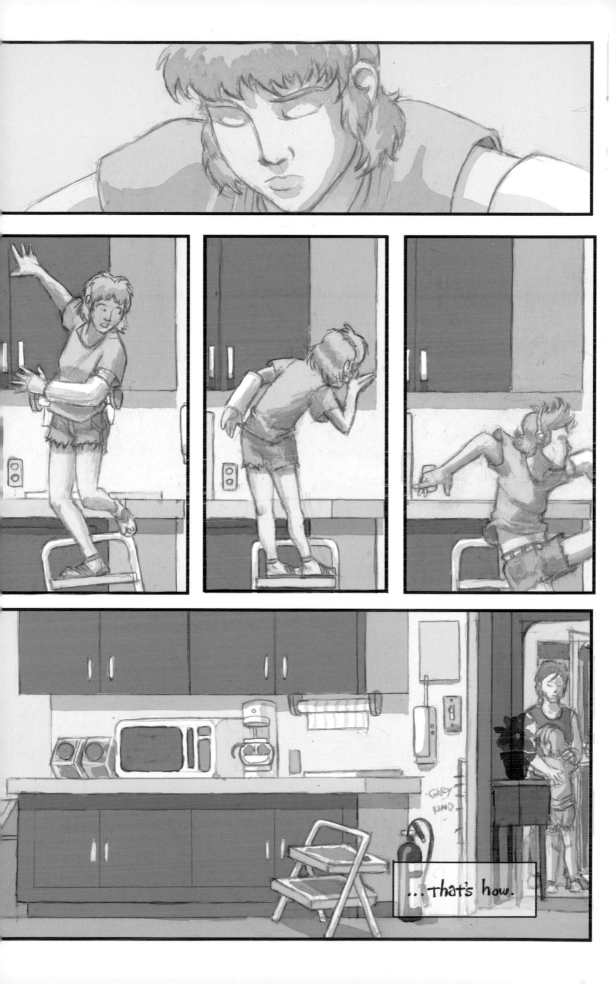

...that's how.

The Maiden and the River Spirit

by Derek Kirk Kim

Once upon a time, a maiden was drinking coffee on the bank of a river after a hard day's work.

Exhausted, she accidentally dropped her thermos into the river. As she knelt by the water's edge lamenting her loss, the River Spirit appeared and asked her the cause of her distress.

Out of pity, the River Spirit dove into the river to retrieve the thermos upon learning what had happened. He resurfaced with a thermos made of pure gold and asked the maiden if it was the one she had lost.

Excited, she was about to claim ownership of the golden thermos when she remembered Aesop's fable "Mercury and the Woodman."

A WOODMAN was felling a tree on the bank of a river, when his axe, glancing off the trunk, flew out of his hands and fell into the water. As he stood by the water's edge lamenting his loss, Mercury appeared and asked him the reason for his grief; and on learning what had happened, out of pity for his distress he dived into the river and, bringing up a gold axe, asked him if that was the one he had lost. The Woodman replied that it was not, and Mercury then dived a second time, and, bringing up a silver axe, asked if that was his. "No, that is not mine either," said the Woodman. Once more Mercury dived into the river, and brought up the missing axe. The Woodman was overjoyed at recovering his property, and thanked his benefactor warmly; and the latter was so pleased with his honesty that he made him a present of the other two axes. When the Woodman told the story to his companions, one of these was filled with envy of his good fortune and determined to try his luck for himself. So he went and began to fell a tree at the edge of the river, and presently contrived to let his axe drop into the water. Mercury appeared as before, and, on learning that his axe had fallen in, he dived and brought up a golden axe, as he had done on the previous occasion. Without waiting to be asked

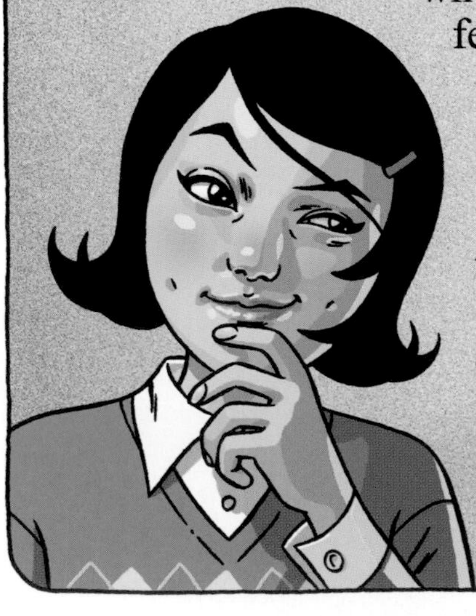

whether it was his or not the fellow cried, "That's mine, that's mine," and stretched out his hand eagerly for the prize: but Mercury was so disgusted at his dishonesty that he not only declined to give him the golden axe, but also refused to recover for him the one he had let fall into the stream.

Moral: Honesty is the best policy.

So, following the Woodman's example, she told the truth instead. The River Spirit dove in a second time and this time brought up a thermos made of pure silver.

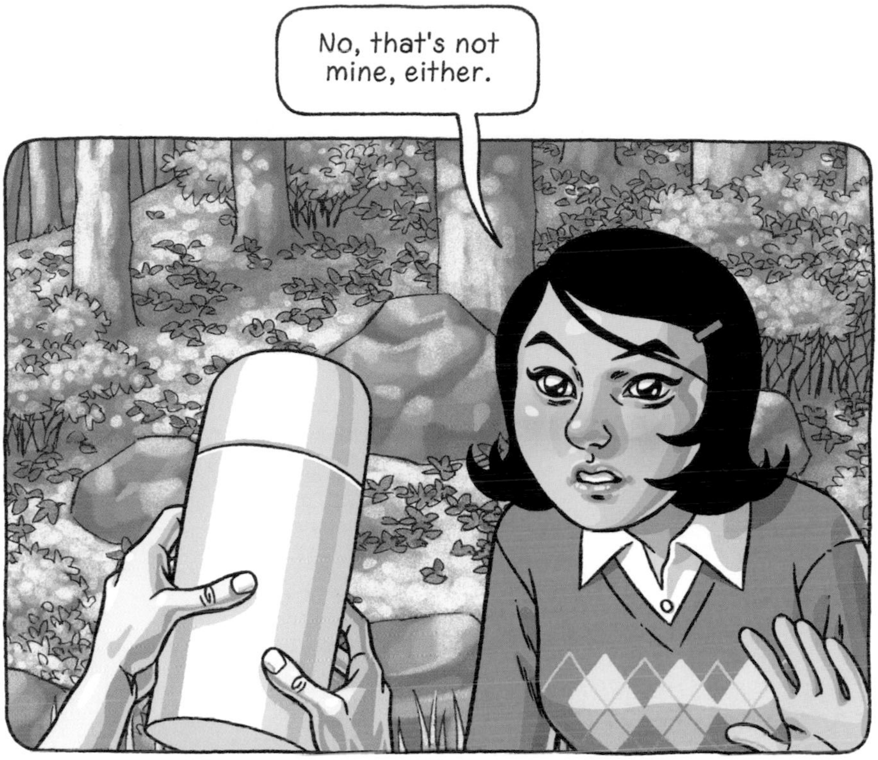
No, that's not mine, either.

One more time the River Spirit dove into the river and this time he brought up the Maiden's thermos.

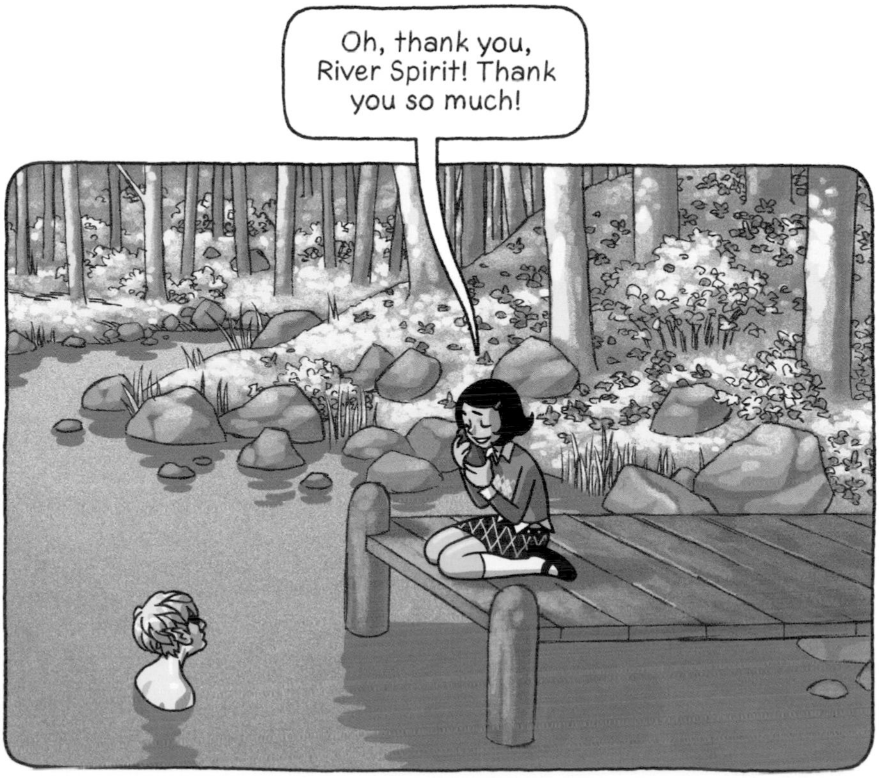
Oh, thank you, River Spirit! Thank you so much!

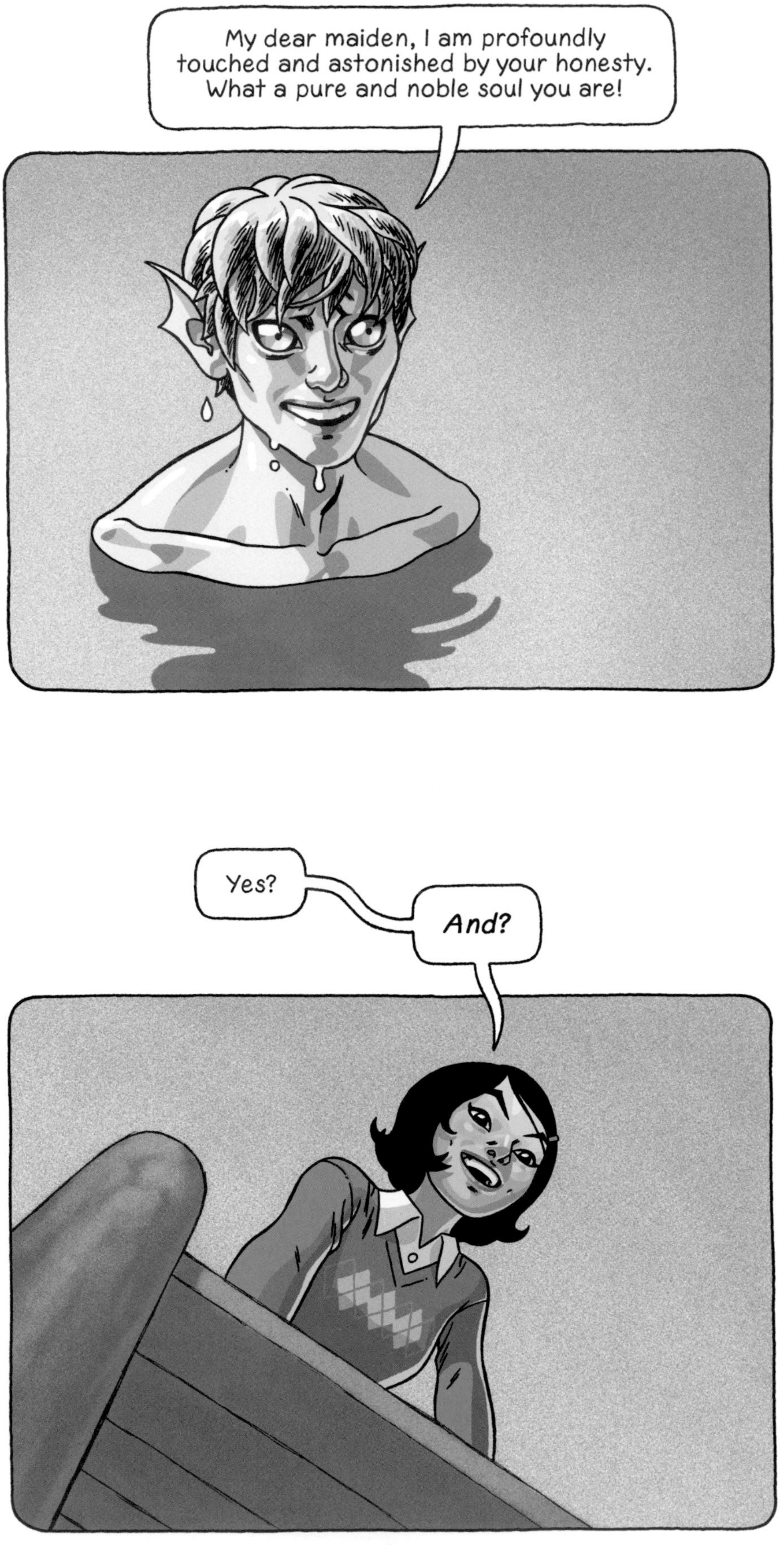
My dear maiden, I am profoundly touched and astonished by your honesty. What a pure and noble soul you are!
Yes?
And?

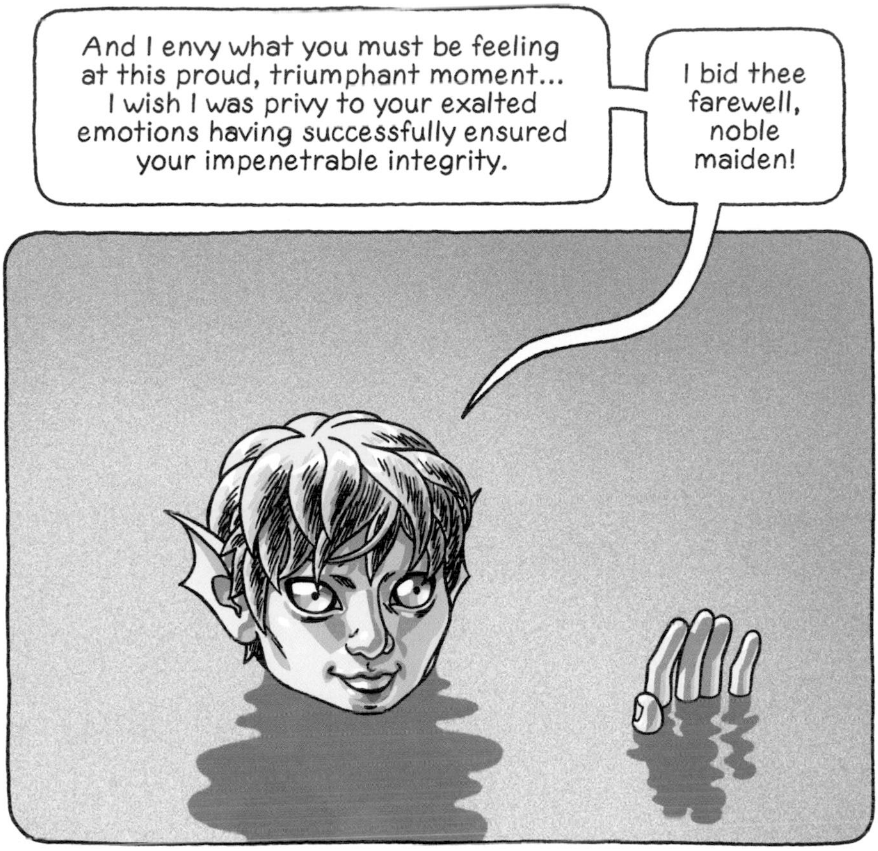
And I envy what you must be feeling at this proud, triumphant moment... I wish I was privy to your exalted emotions having successfully ensured your impenetrable integrity.
I bid thee farewell, noble maiden!

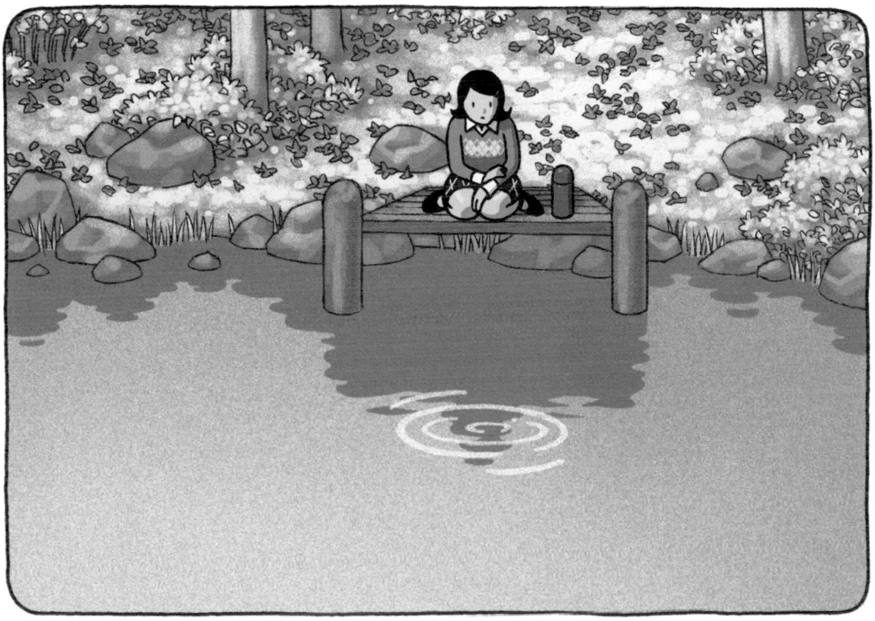

Moral: Aesop is great on paper.

"Beneath the Leaves: Jump," by Rad Sechrist

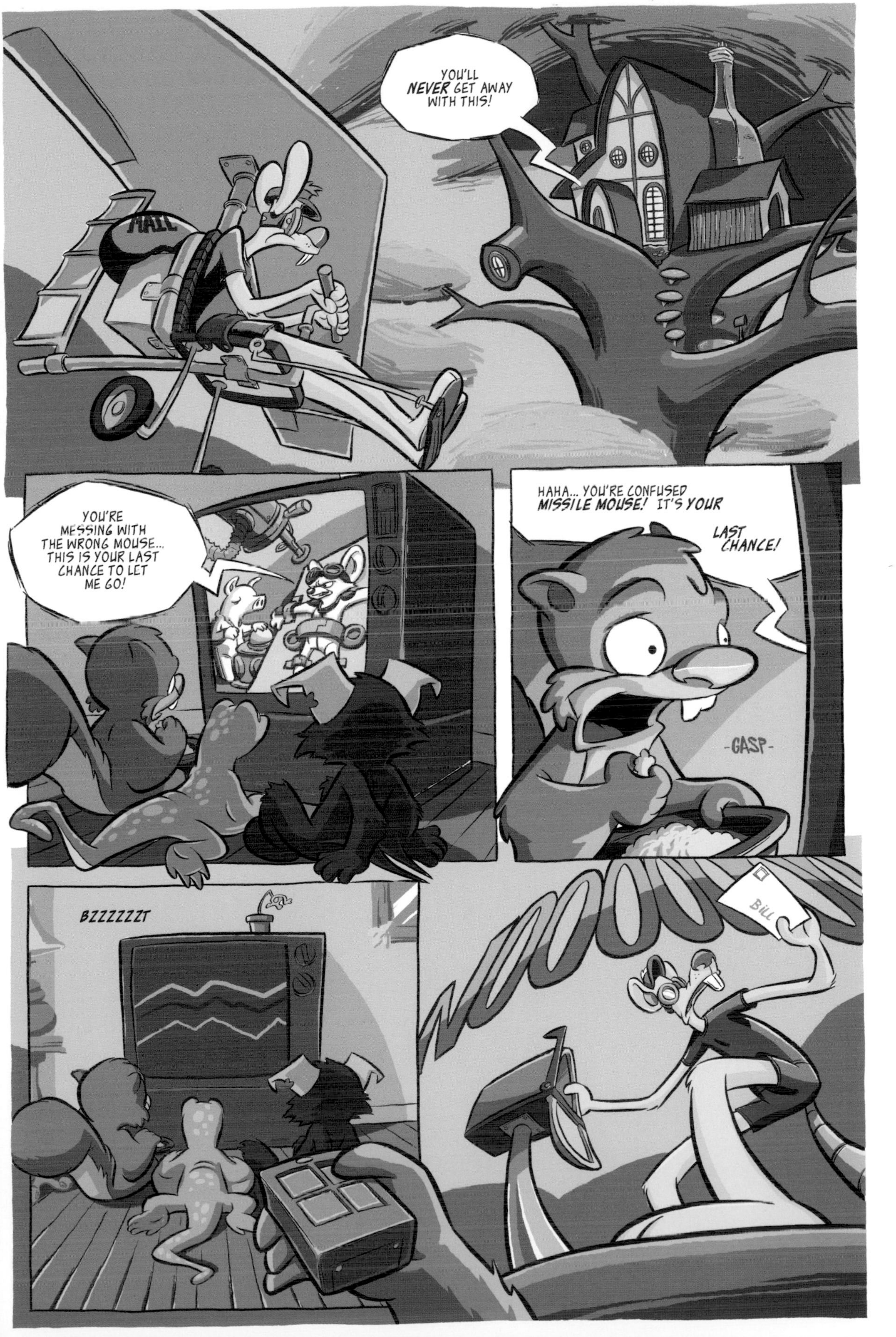
YOU'LL NEVER GET AWAY WITH THIS!
YOU'RE MESSING WITH THE WRONG MOUSE... THIS IS YOUR LAST CHANCE TO LET ME GO!
HAHA... YOU'RE CONFUSED MISSILE MOUSE! IT'S YOUR LAST CHANCE!
-GASP-
BZZZZZZT
BILL

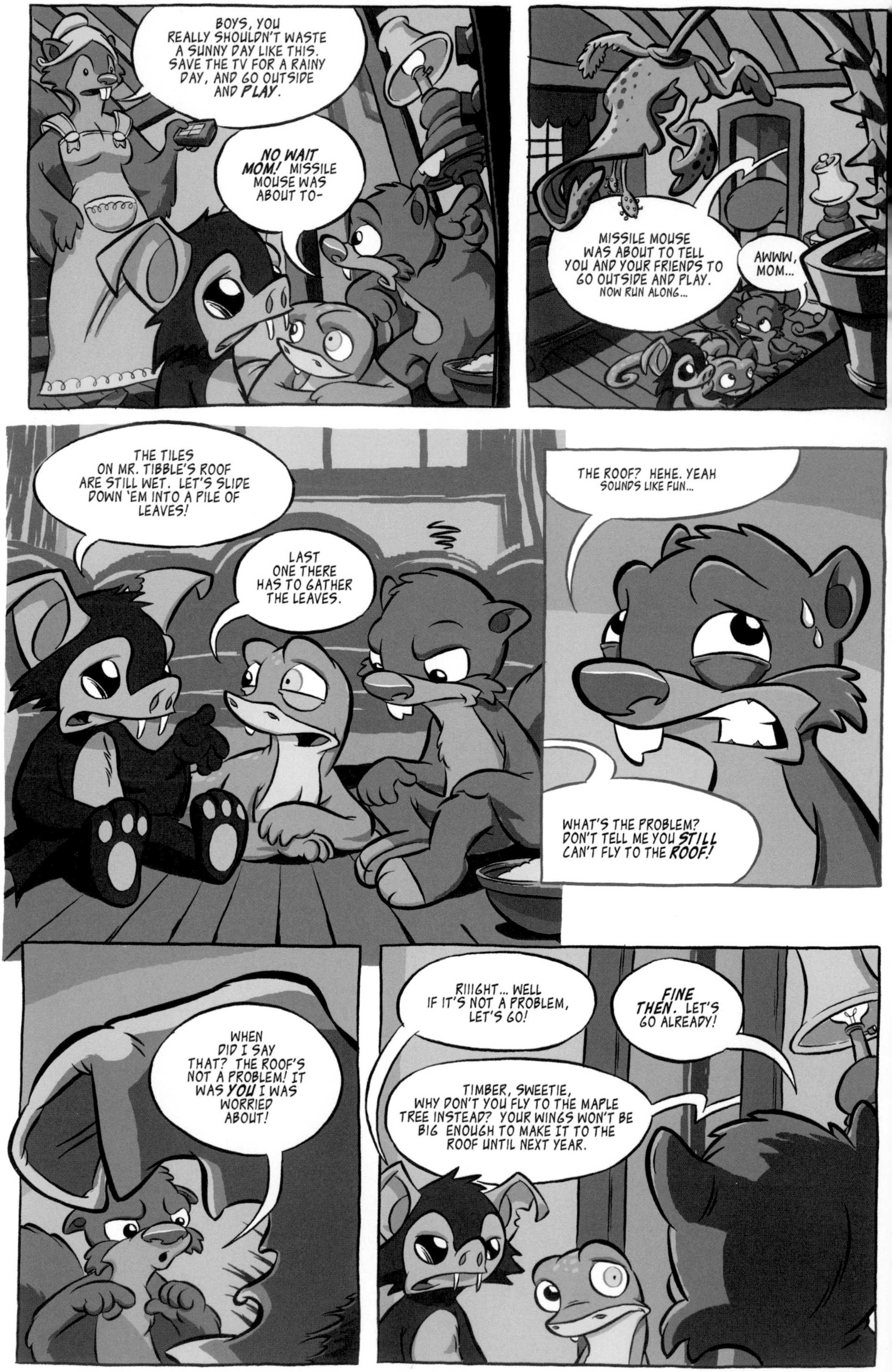
BOYS, YOU REALLY SHOULDN'T WASTE A SUNNY DAY LIKE THIS. SAVE THE TV FOR A RAINY DAY, AND GO OUTSIDE AND PLAY.
NO WAIT MOM! MISSILE MOUSE WAS ABOUT TO-
MISSILE MOUSE WAS ABOUT TO TELL YOU AND YOUR FRIENDS TO GO OUTSIDE AND PLAY. NOW RUN ALONG...
AWWW, MOM...
THE TILES ON MR. TIBBLE'S ROOF ARE STILL WET. LET'S SLIDE DOWN 'EM INTO A PILE OF LEAVES!
LAST ONE THERE HAS TO GATHER THE LEAVES.
THE ROOF? HEHE. YEAH SOUNDS LIKE FUN...
WHAT'S THE PROBLEM? DON'T TELL ME YOU STILL CAN'T FLY TO THE ROOF!
WHEN DID I SAY THAT? THE ROOF'S NOT A PROBLEM! IT WAS YOU I WAS WORRIED ABOUT!
RIIIGHT... WELL IF IT'S NOT A PROBLEM, LET'S GO!
FINE THEN. LET'S GO ALREADY!
TIMBER, SWEETIE, WHY DON'T YOU FLY TO THE MAPLE TREE INSTEAD? YOUR WINGS WON'T BE BIG ENOUGH TO MAKE IT TO THE ROOF UNTIL NEXT YEAR.

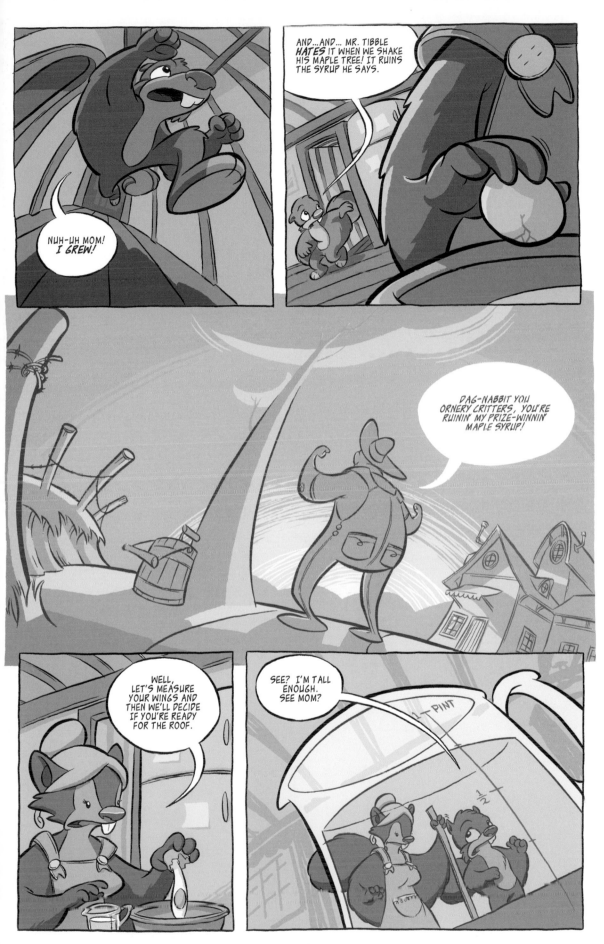

NUH-UH MOM! I *GREW!*

AND...AND... MR. TIBBLE *HATES* IT WHEN WE SHAKE HIS MAPLE TREE! IT RUINS THE SYRUP HE SAYS.

DAG-NABBIT YOU ORNERY CRITTERS, YOU'RE RUININ' MY PRIZE-WINNIN' MAPLE SYRUP!

WELL, LET'S MEASURE YOUR WINGS AND THEN WE'LL DECIDE IF YOU'RE READY FOR THE ROOF.

SEE? I'M TALL ENOUGH. SEE MOM?

1 PINT

½

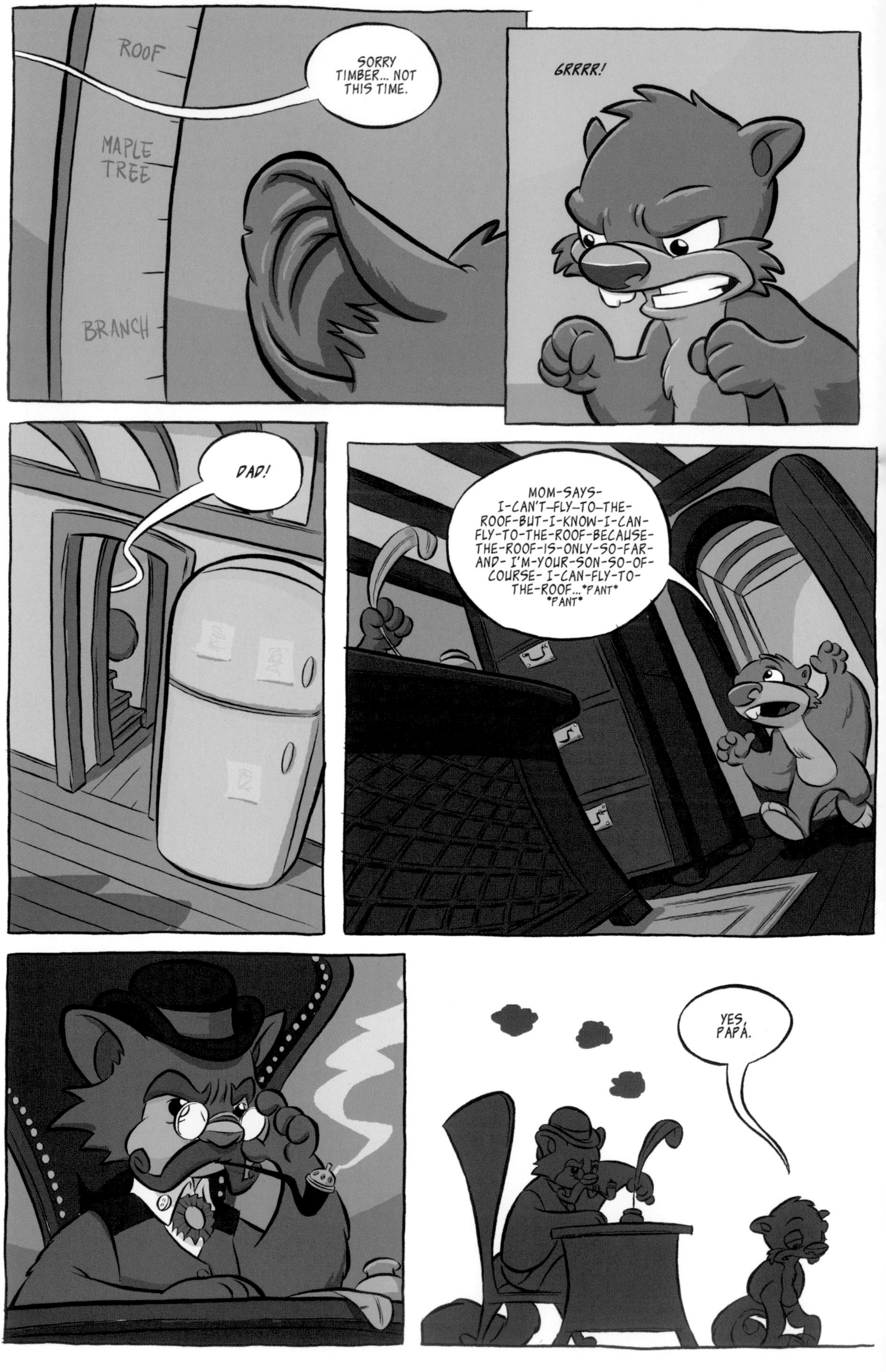
ROOF
MAPLE TREE
BRANCH
SORRY TIMBER... NOT THIS TIME.
GRRRR!
DAD!
MOM-SAYS-I-CAN'T-FLY-TO-THE-ROOF-BUT-I-KNOW-I-CAN-FLY-TO-THE-ROOF-BECAUSE-THE-ROOF-IS-ONLY-SO-FAR-AND- I'M-YOUR-SON-SO-OF-COURSE- I-CAN-FLY-TO-THE-ROOF...*PANT* *PANT*
YES, PAPA.

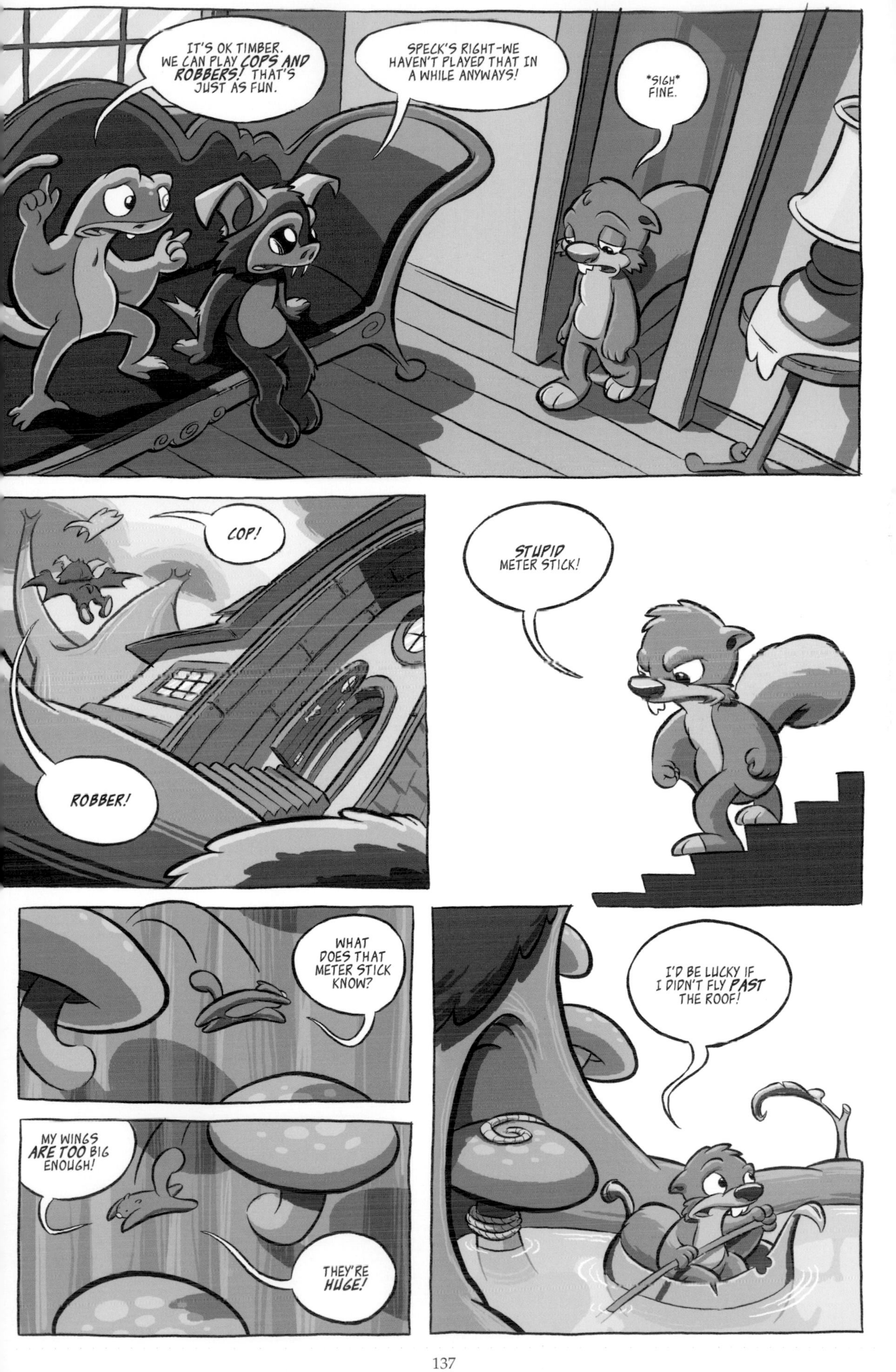
IT'S OK TIMBER. WE CAN PLAY COPS AND ROBBERS! THAT'S JUST AS FUN.
SPECK'S RIGHT—WE HAVEN'T PLAYED THAT IN A WHILE ANYWAYS!
SIGH FINE.
COP!
ROBBER!
STUPID METER STICK!
WHAT DOES THAT METER STICK KNOW?
MY WINGS ARE TOO BIG ENOUGH!
THEY'RE HUGE!
I'D BE LUCKY IF I DIDN'T FLY PAST THE ROOF!

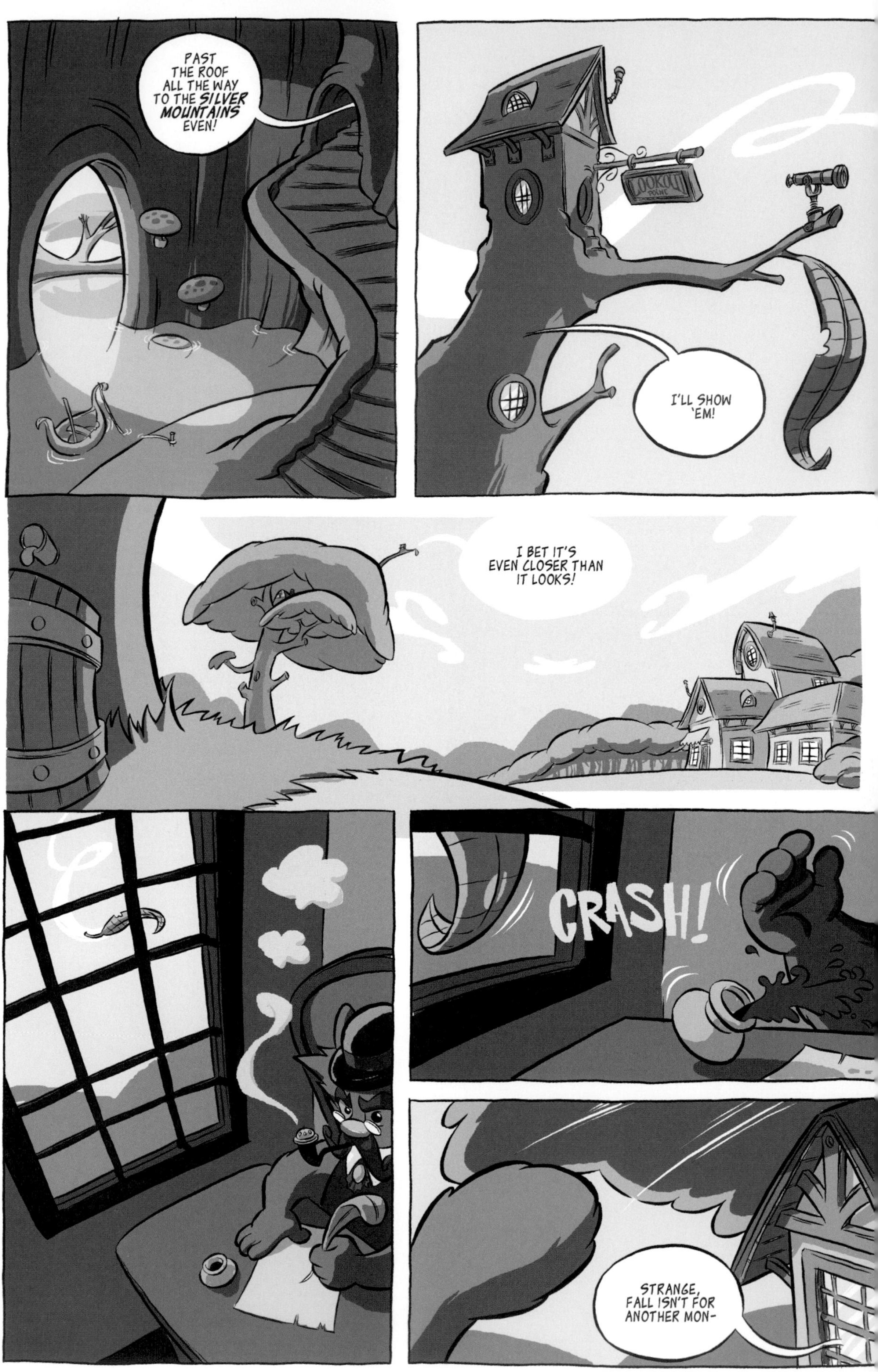
PAST THE ROOF ALL THE WAY TO THE SILVER MOUNTAINS EVEN!
LOOKOUT
I'LL SHOW 'EM!
I BET IT'S EVEN CLOSER THAN IT LOOKS!
CRASH!
STRANGE, FALL ISN'T FOR ANOTHER MON-

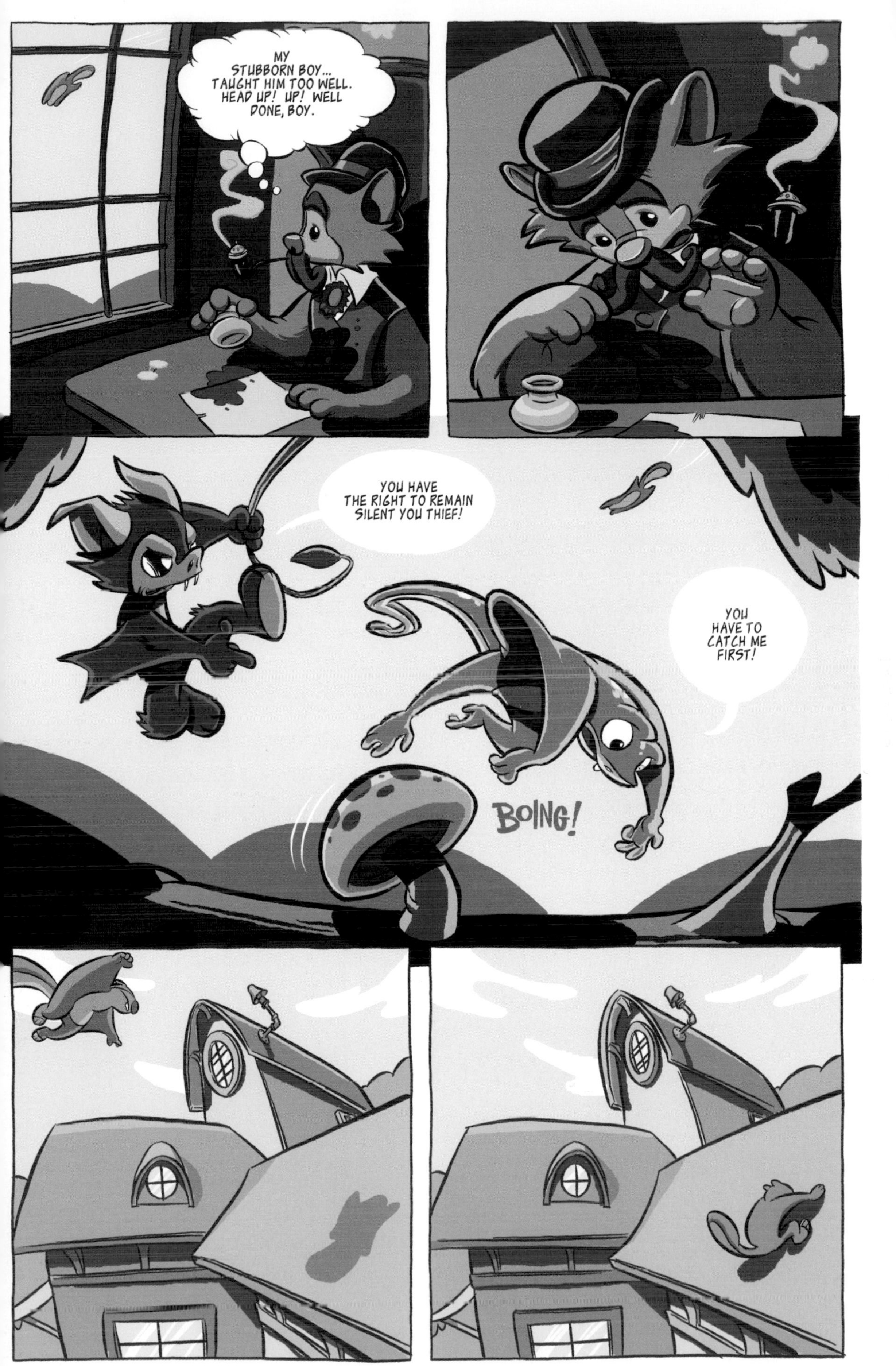
MY STUBBORN BOY... TAUGHT HIM TOO WELL. HEAD UP! UP! WELL DONE, BOY.
YOU HAVE THE RIGHT TO REMAIN SILENT YOU THIEF!
YOU HAVE TO CATCH ME FIRST!
BOING!

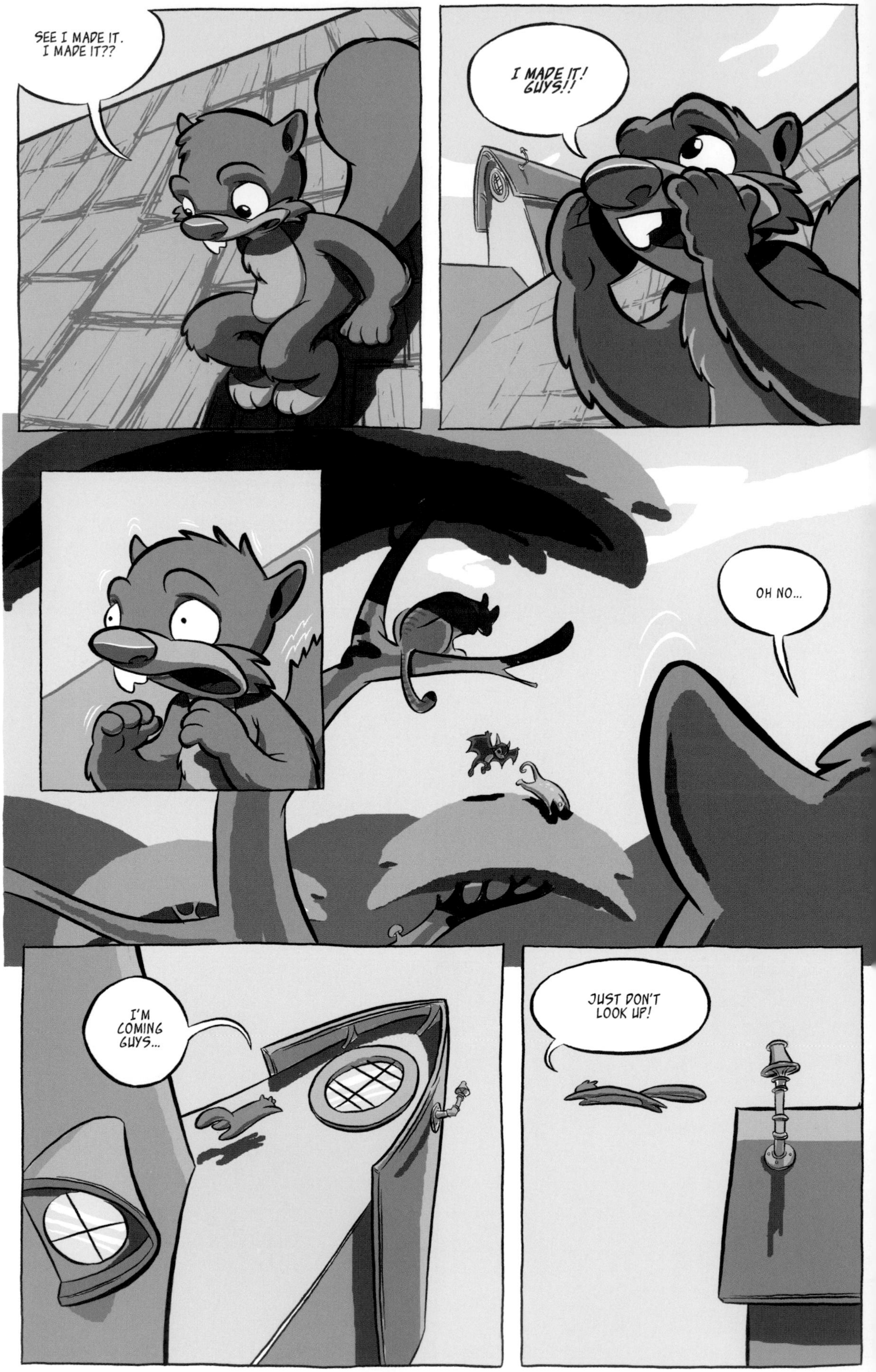
SEE I MADE IT. I MADE IT??
I MADE IT! GUYS!!
OH NO...
I'M COMING GUYS...
JUST DON'T LOOK UP!

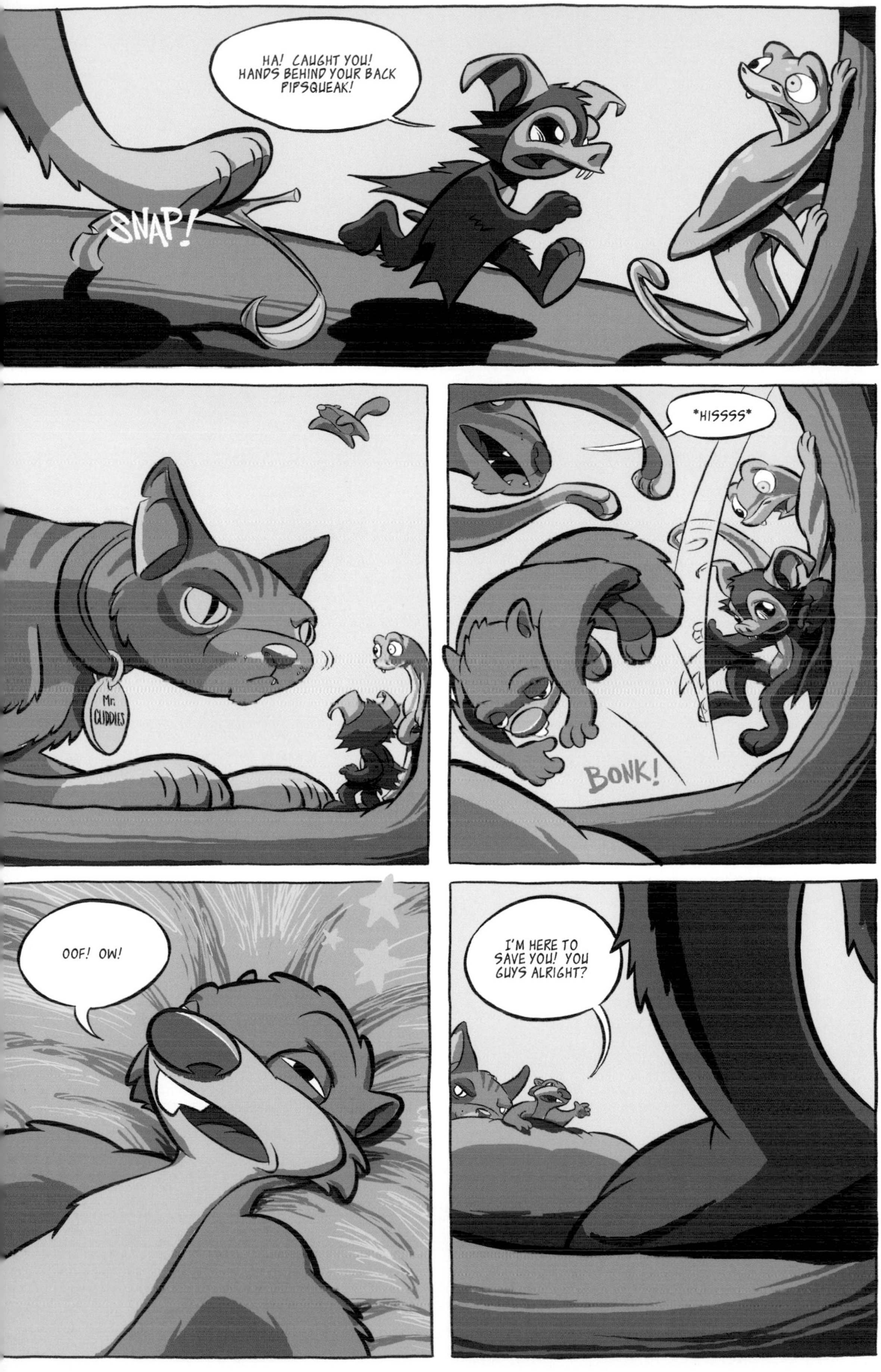
HA! CAUGHT YOU! HANDS BEHIND YOUR BACK PIPSQUEAK!
SNAP!
Mr. CUDDLES
HISSSS
BONK!
OOF! OW!
I'M HERE TO SAVE YOU! YOU GUYS ALRIGHT?

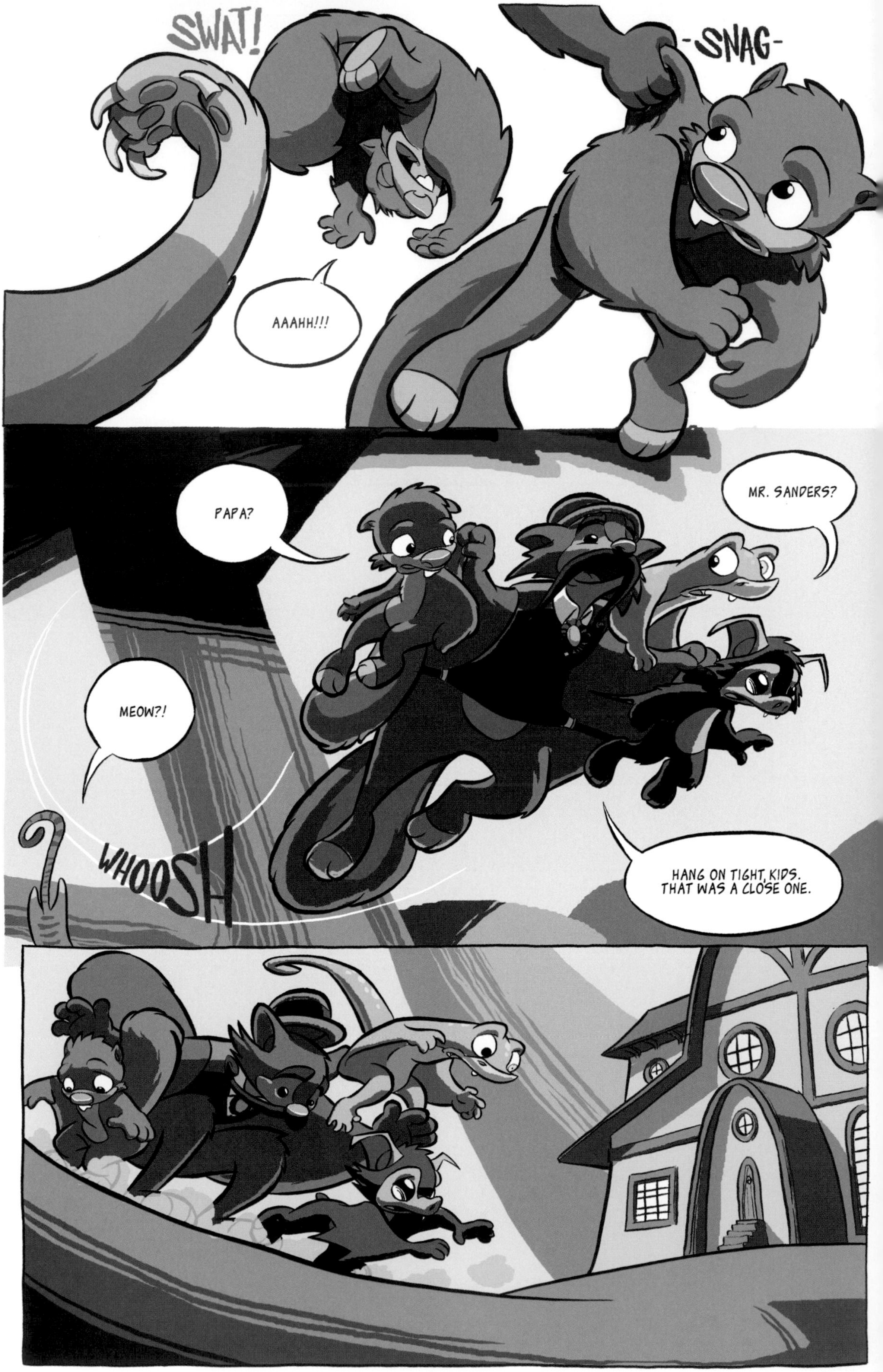
SWAT!
-SNAG-
AAAHH!!!
PAPA?
MR. SANDERS?
MEOW?!
WHOOSH
HANG ON TIGHT, KIDS.
THAT WAS A CLOSE ONE.

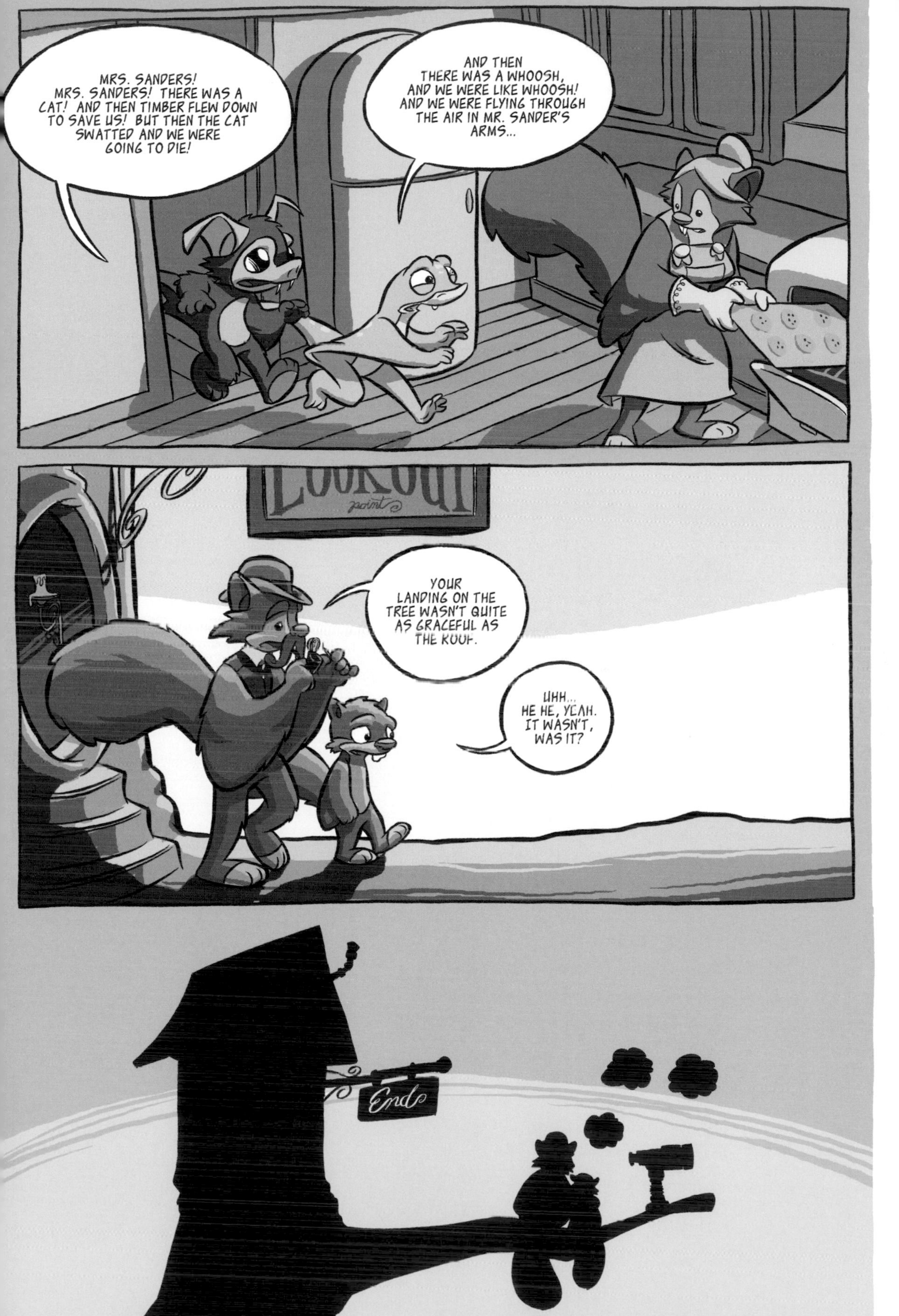
MRS. SANDERS! MRS. SANDERS! THERE WAS A CAT! AND THEN TIMBER FLEW DOWN TO SAVE US! BUT THEN THE CAT SWATTED AND WE WERE GOING TO DIE!
AND THEN THERE WAS A WHOOSH, AND WE WERE LIKE WHOOSH! AND WE WERE FLYING THROUGH THE AIR IN MR. SANDER'S ARMS...
LOOKOUT point
YOUR LANDING ON THE TREE WASN'T QUITE AS GRACEFUL AS THE ROOF.
UHH... HE HE, YEAH. IT WASN'T, WAS IT?
End

"Tug McTaggart, Circus Detective," by Phil Craven

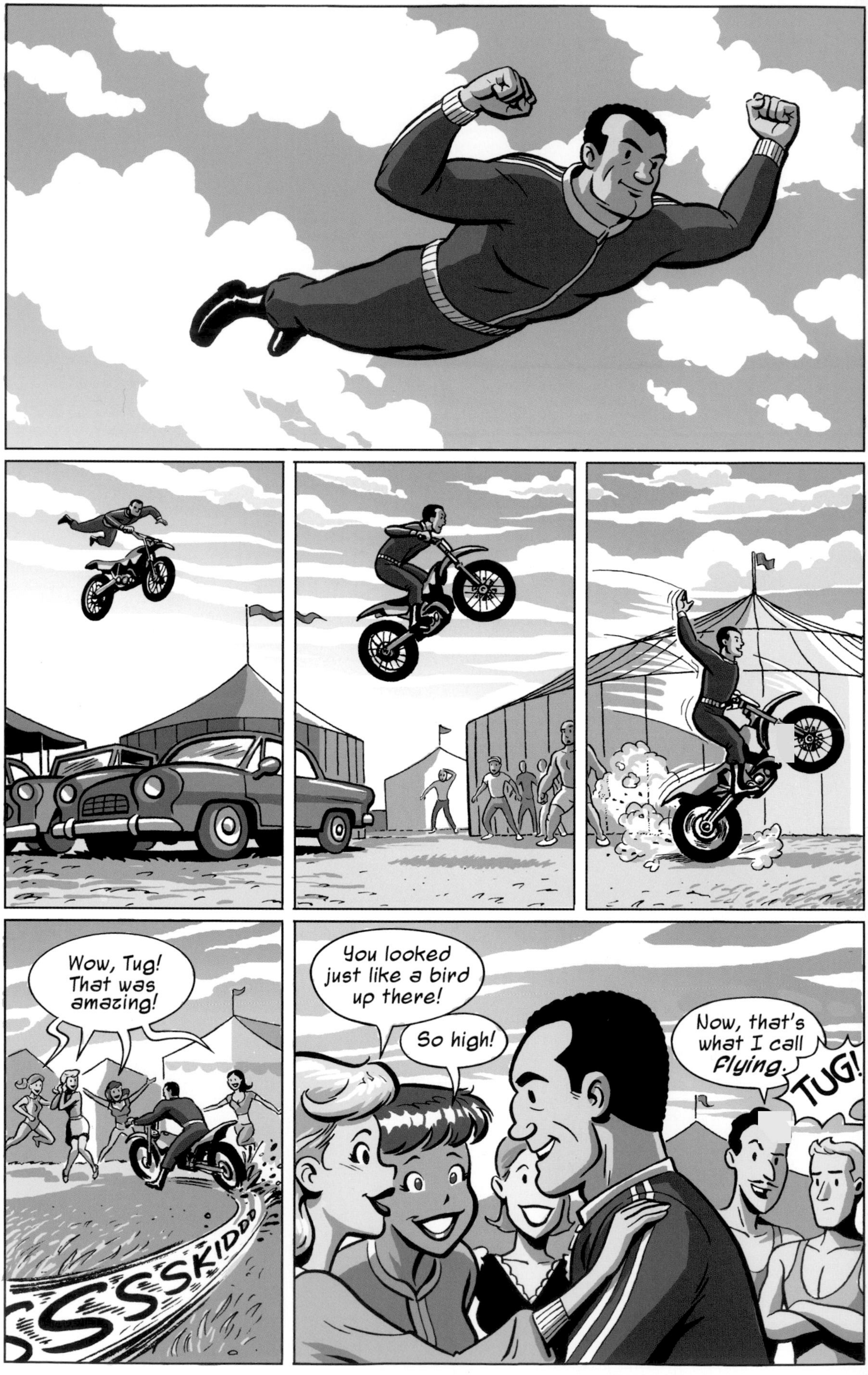
Wow, Tug! That was amazing!
SSSSKIDDD
You looked just like a bird up there!
So high!
Now, that's what I call *flying.*
TUG!

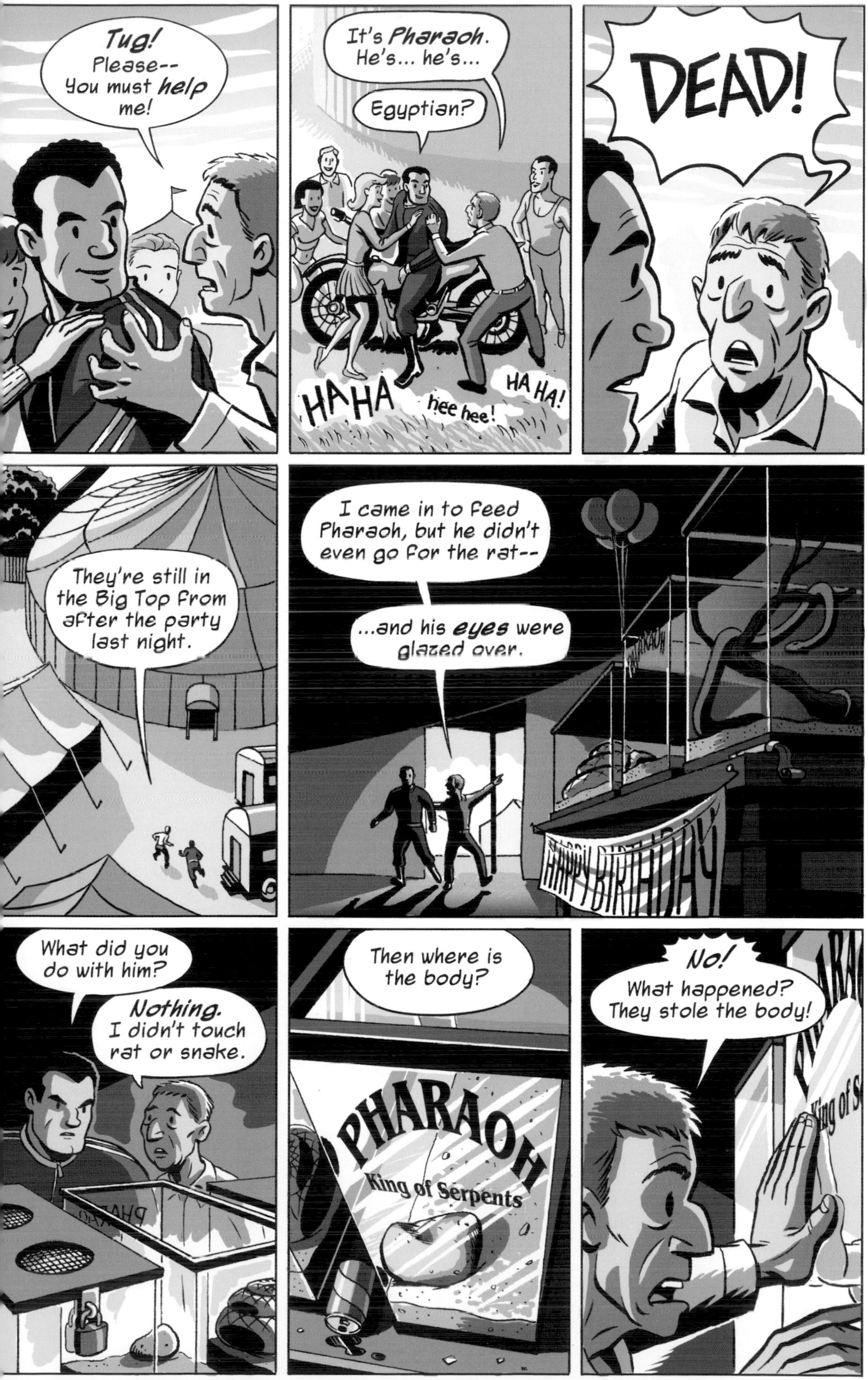
Tug! Please-- You must help me!
It's Pharaoh. He's... he's...
Egyptian?
HAHA
hee hee!
HA HA!
DEAD!
They're still in the Big Top from after the party last night.
I came in to feed Pharaoh, but he didn't even go for the rat--
...and his eyes were glazed over.
HAPPY BIRTHDAY
What did you do with him?
Nothing. I didn't touch rat or snake.
Then where is the body?
PHARAOH
King of Serpents
No! What happened? They stole the body!

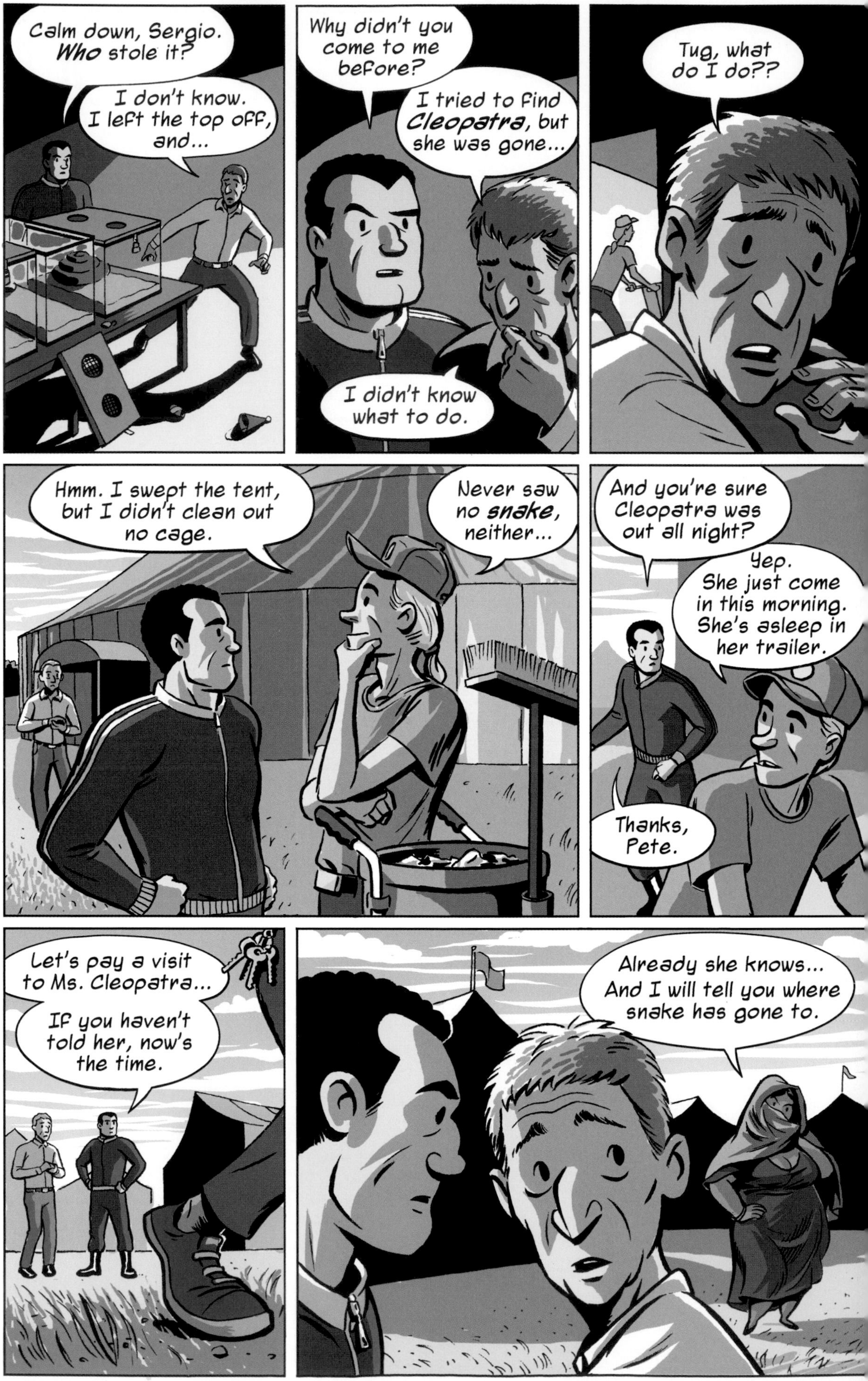

Calm down, Sergio. Who stole it?
I don't know. I left the top off, and...
Why didn't you come to me before?
I tried to find Cleopatra, but she was gone...
I didn't know what to do.
Tug, what do I do??
Hmm. I swept the tent, but I didn't clean out no cage.
Never saw no snake, neither...
And you're sure Cleopatra was out all night?
Yep. She just come in this morning. She's asleep in her trailer.
Thanks, Pete.
Let's pay a visit to Ms. Cleopatra...
If you haven't told her, now's the time.
Already she knows... And I will tell you where snake has gone to.

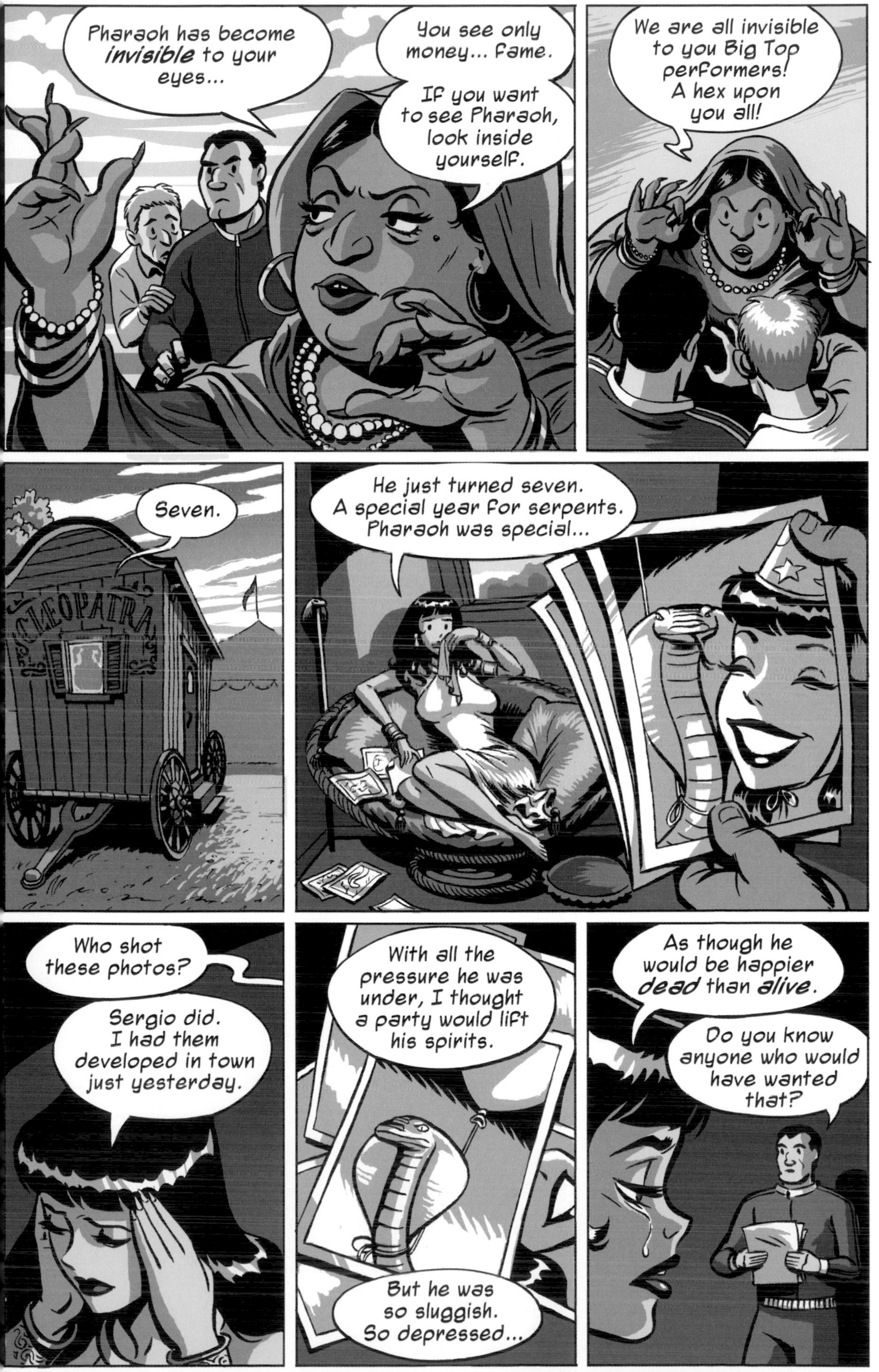
Pharaoh has become *invisible* to your eyes...
You see only money... fame.
If you want to see Pharaoh, look inside yourself.
We are all invisible to you Big Top performers! A hex upon you all!
Seven.
CLEOPATRA
He just turned seven. A special year for serpents. Pharaoh was special...
Who shot these photos?
Sergio did. I had them developed in town just yesterday.
With all the pressure he was under, I thought a party would lift his spirits.
But he was so sluggish. So depressed...
As though he would be happier *dead* than *alive*.
Do you know anyone who would have wanted that?

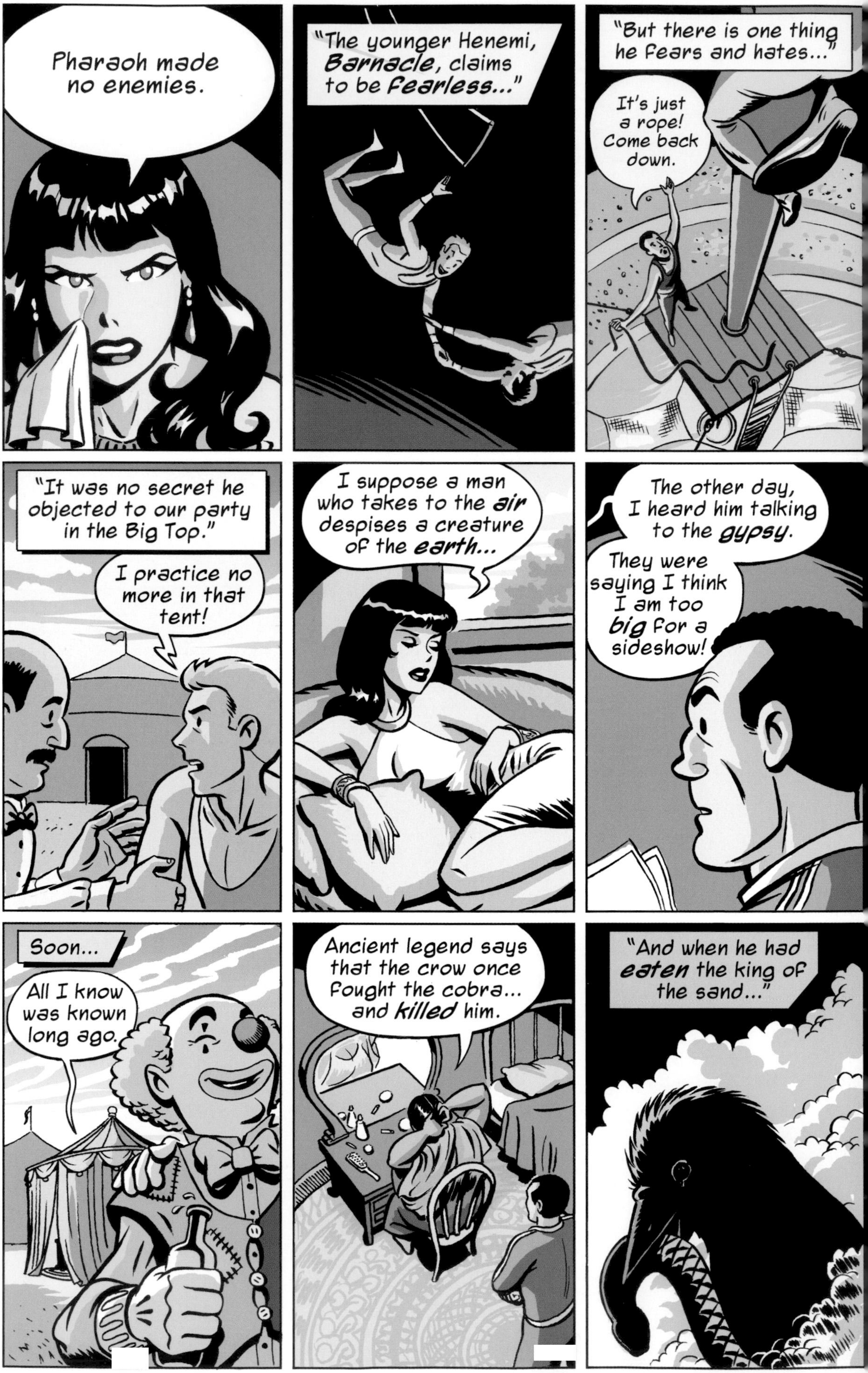
Pharaoh made no enemies.
"The younger Henemi, Barnacle, claims to be fearless..."
"But there is one thing he fears and hates..."
It's just a rope! Come back down.
"It was no secret he objected to our party in the Big Top."
I practice no more in that tent!
I suppose a man who takes to the air despises a creature of the earth...
The other day, I heard him talking to the gypsy.
They were saying I think I am too big for a sideshow!
Soon...
All I know was known long ago.
Ancient legend says that the crow once fought the cobra... and killed him.
"And when he had eaten the king of the sand..."

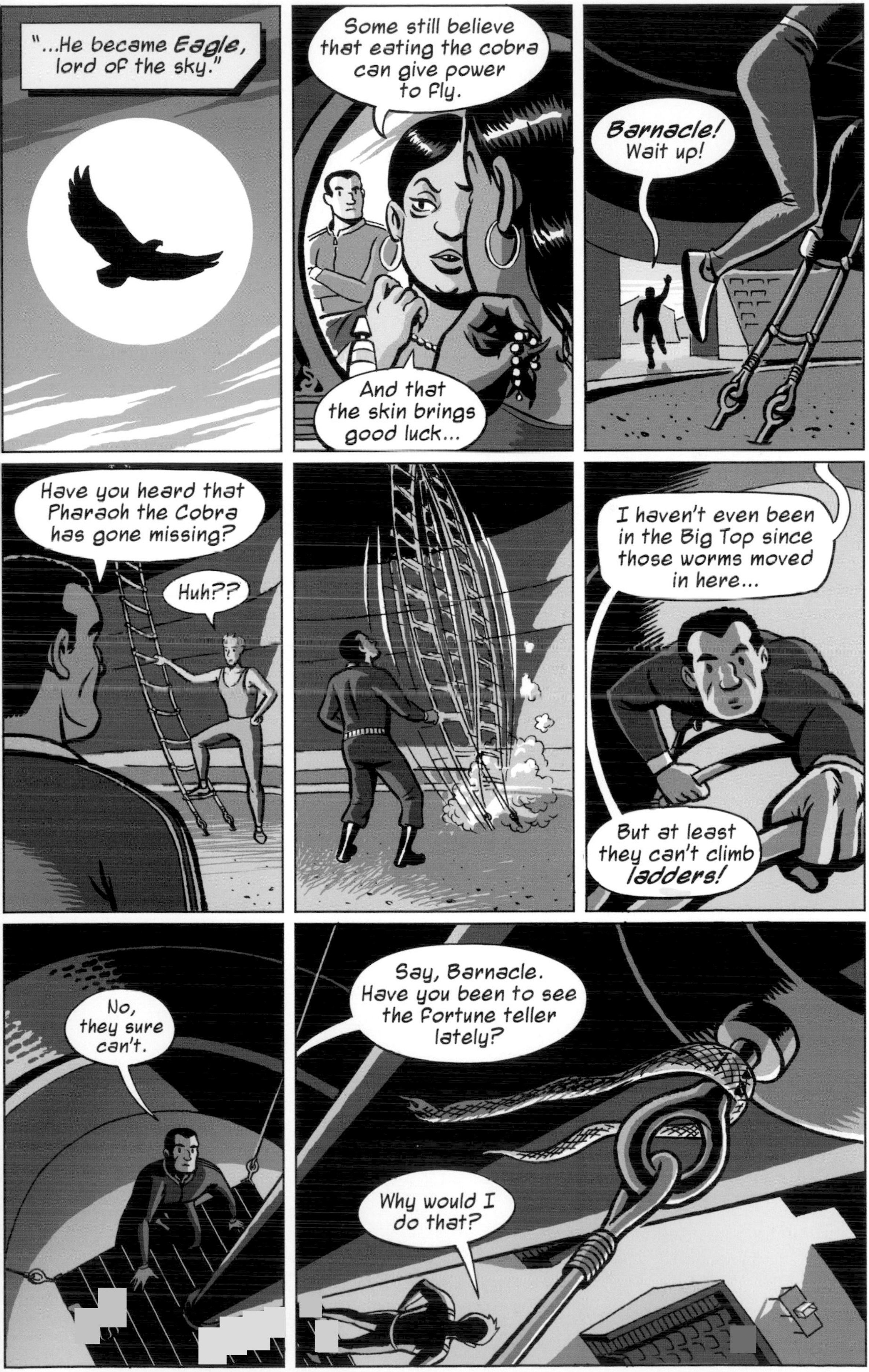

"...He became *Eagle*, lord of the sky."
Some still believe that eating the cobra can give power to fly.
And that the skin brings good luck...
Barnacle! Wait up!
Have you heard that Pharaoh the Cobra has gone missing?
Huh??
I haven't even been in the Big Top since those worms moved in here...
But at least they can't climb *ladders!*
No, they sure can't.
Say, Barnacle. Have you been to see the fortune teller lately?
Why would I do that?

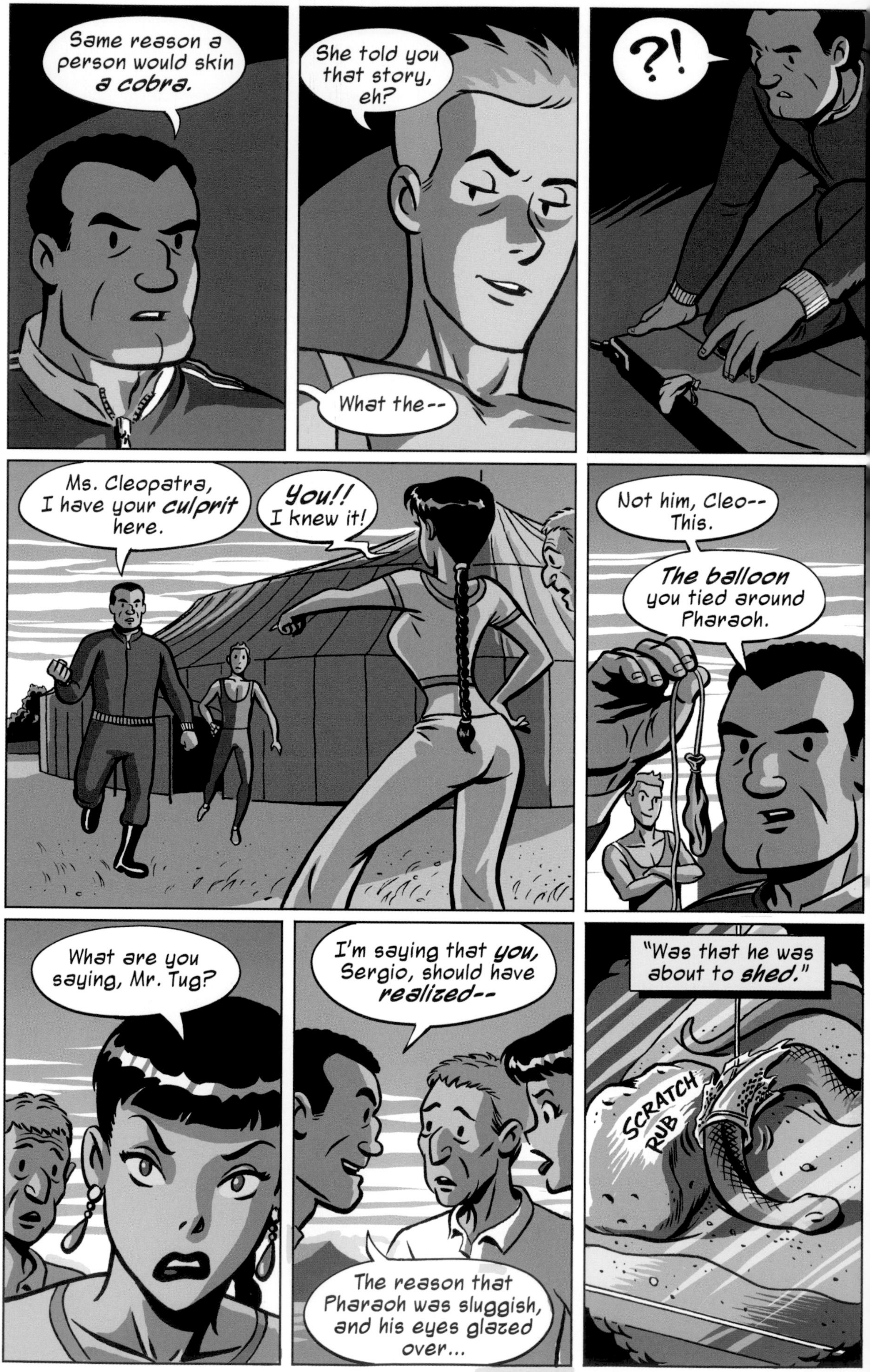

Same reason a person would skin a cobra.
She told you that story, eh?
What the--
?!
Ms. Cleopatra, I have your culprit here.
You!! I knew it!
Not him, Cleo-- This.
The balloon you tied around Pharaoh.
What are you saying, Mr. Tug?
I'm saying that you, Sergio, should have realized--
The reason that Pharaoh was sluggish, and his eyes glazed over...
"Was that he was about to shed."
SCRATCH
RUB

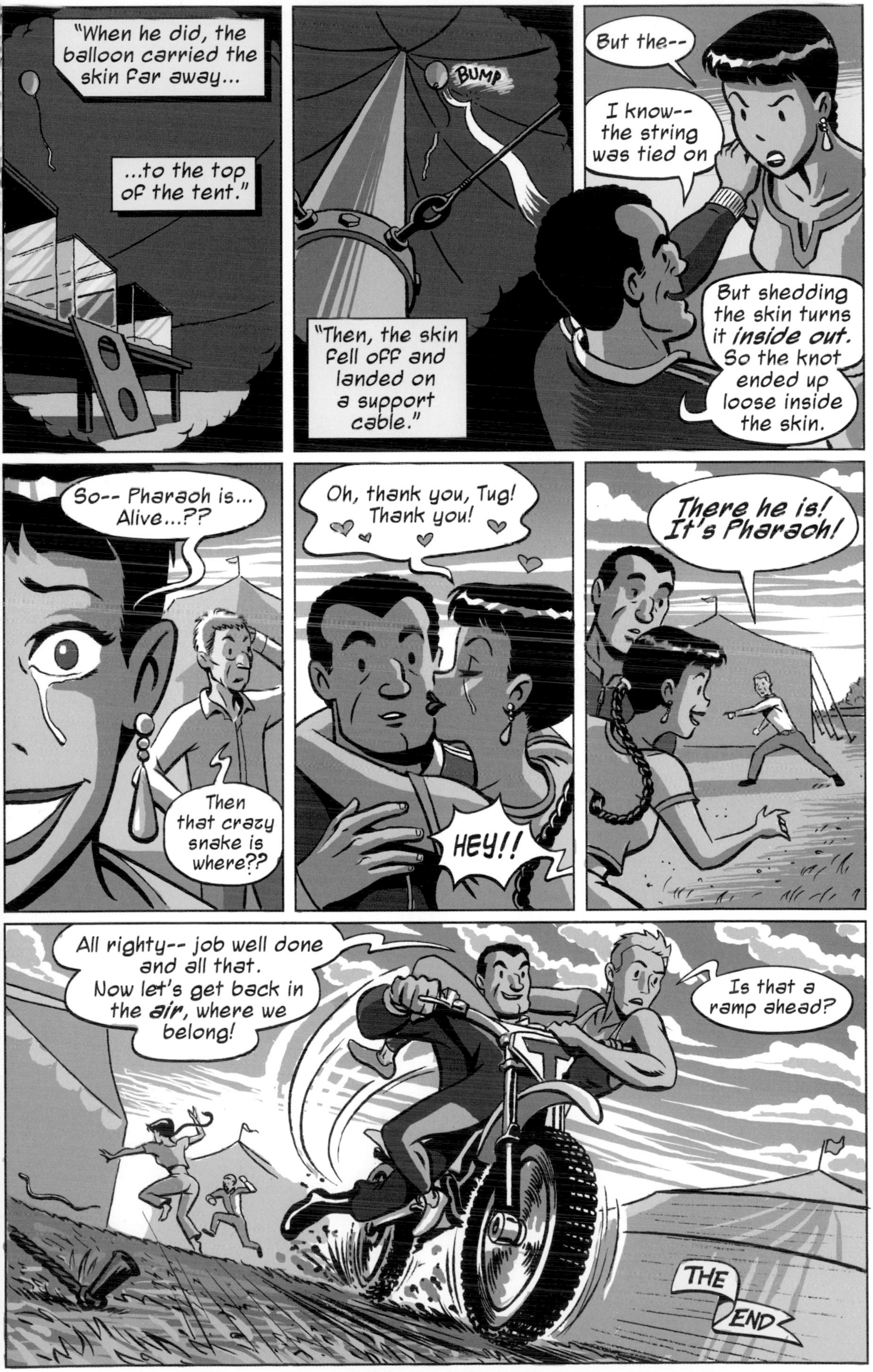
"When he did, the balloon carried the skin far away...
...to the top of the tent."
BUMP
"Then, the skin fell off and landed on a support cable."
But the--
I know-- the string was tied on
But shedding the skin turns it *inside out.* So the knot ended up loose inside the skin.
So-- Pharaoh is... Alive...??
Then that crazy snake is where??
Oh, thank you, Tug! Thank you!
HEY!!
There he is! It's Pharaoh!
All righty-- job well done and all that. Now let's get back in the *air*, where we belong!
Is that a ramp ahead?
THE END

“Deep Blue,” by Phil Craven

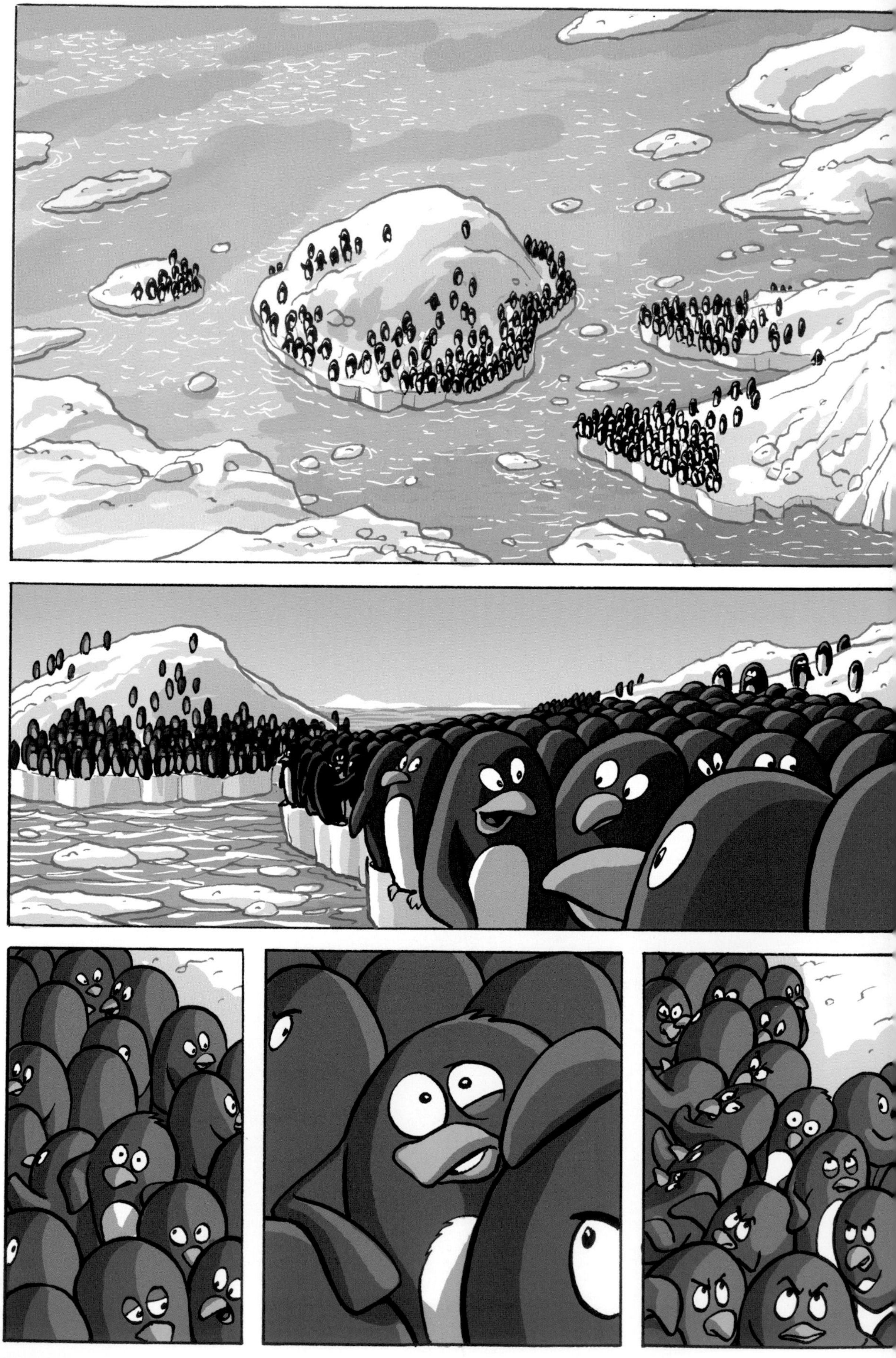

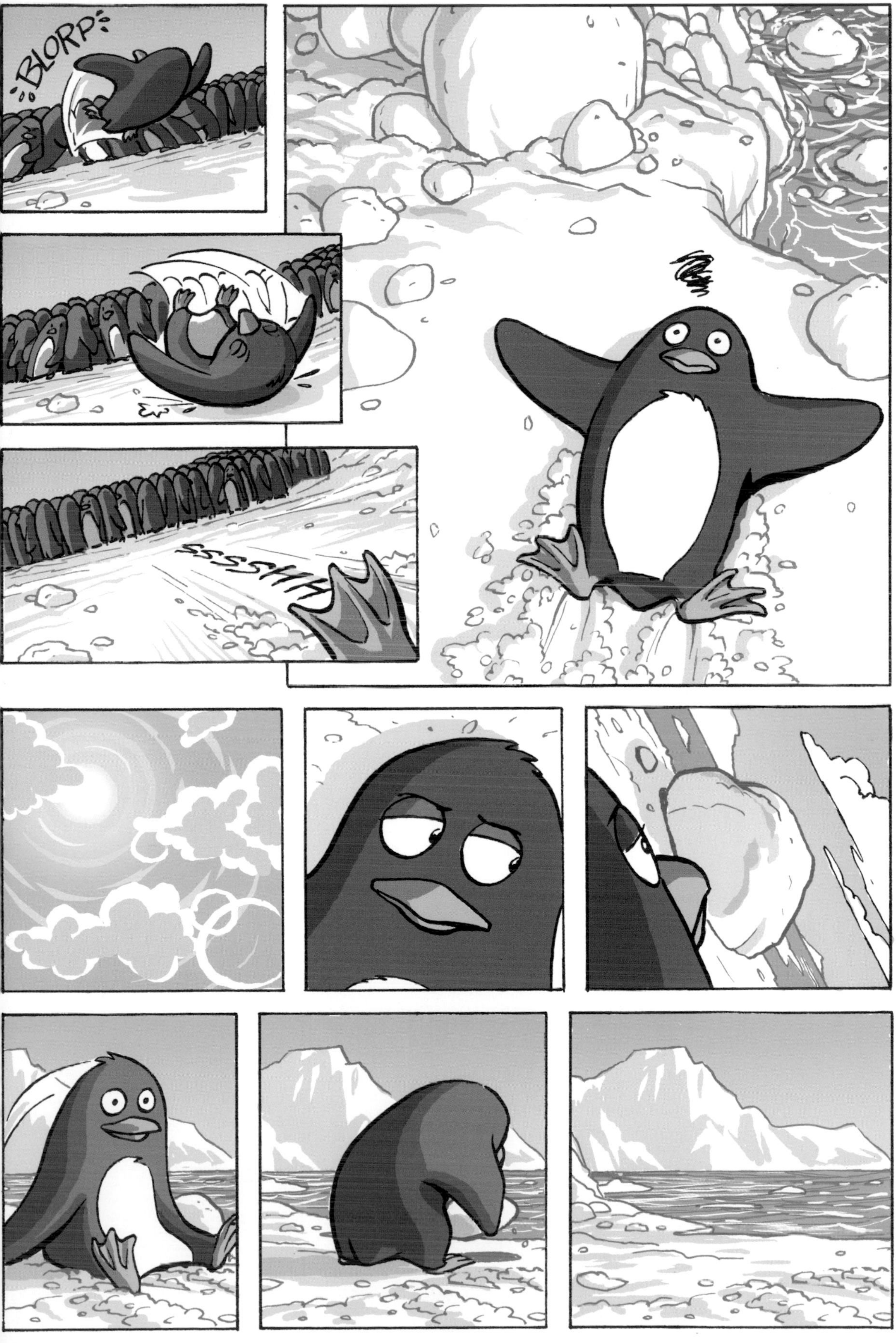
BLORP
SSSSHH

PLOINK!... PLOINK!... PLOINK!... PLOINK!

PLOINK!

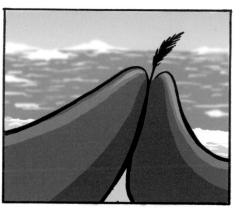

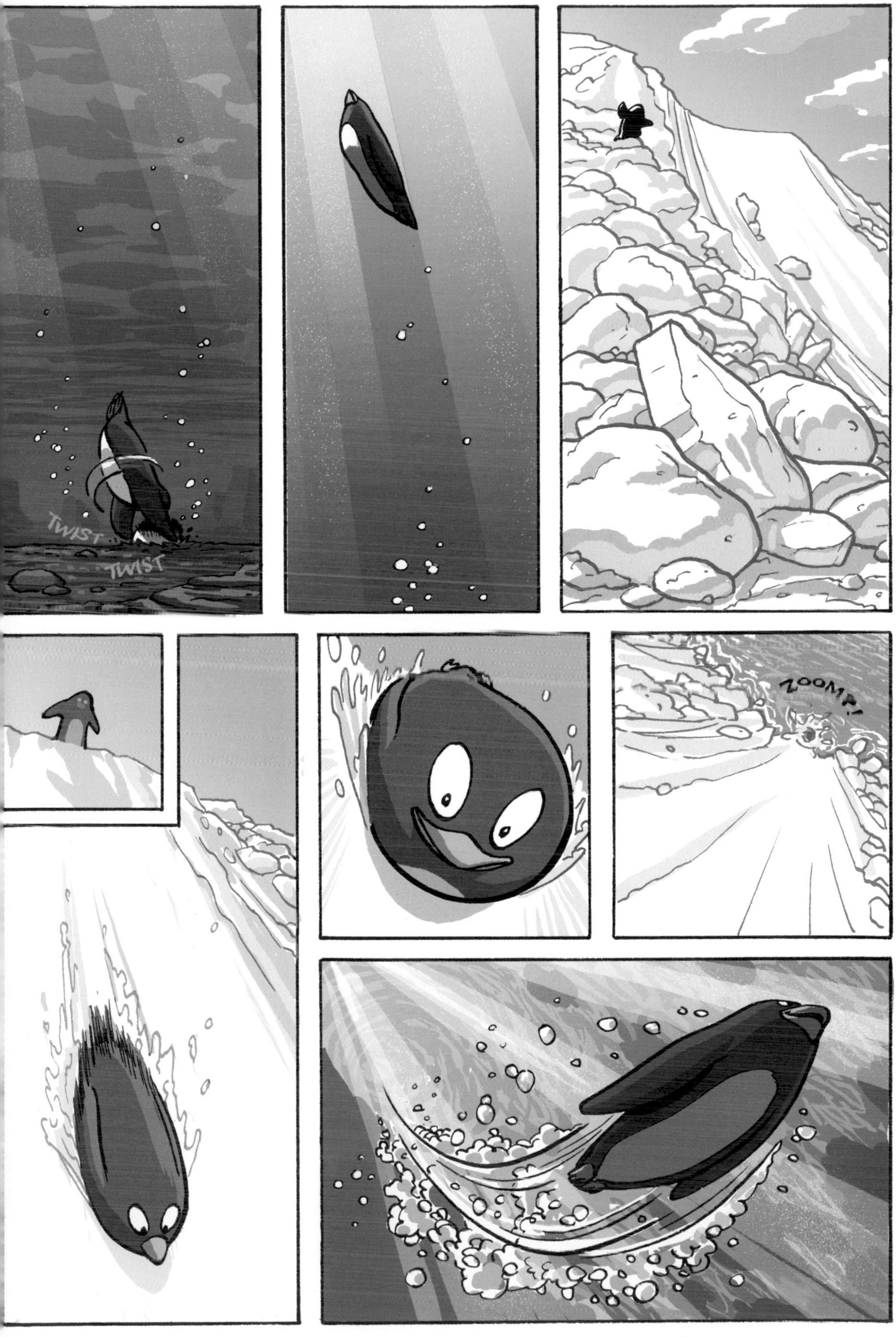
TWIST
TWIST
ZOOMP!

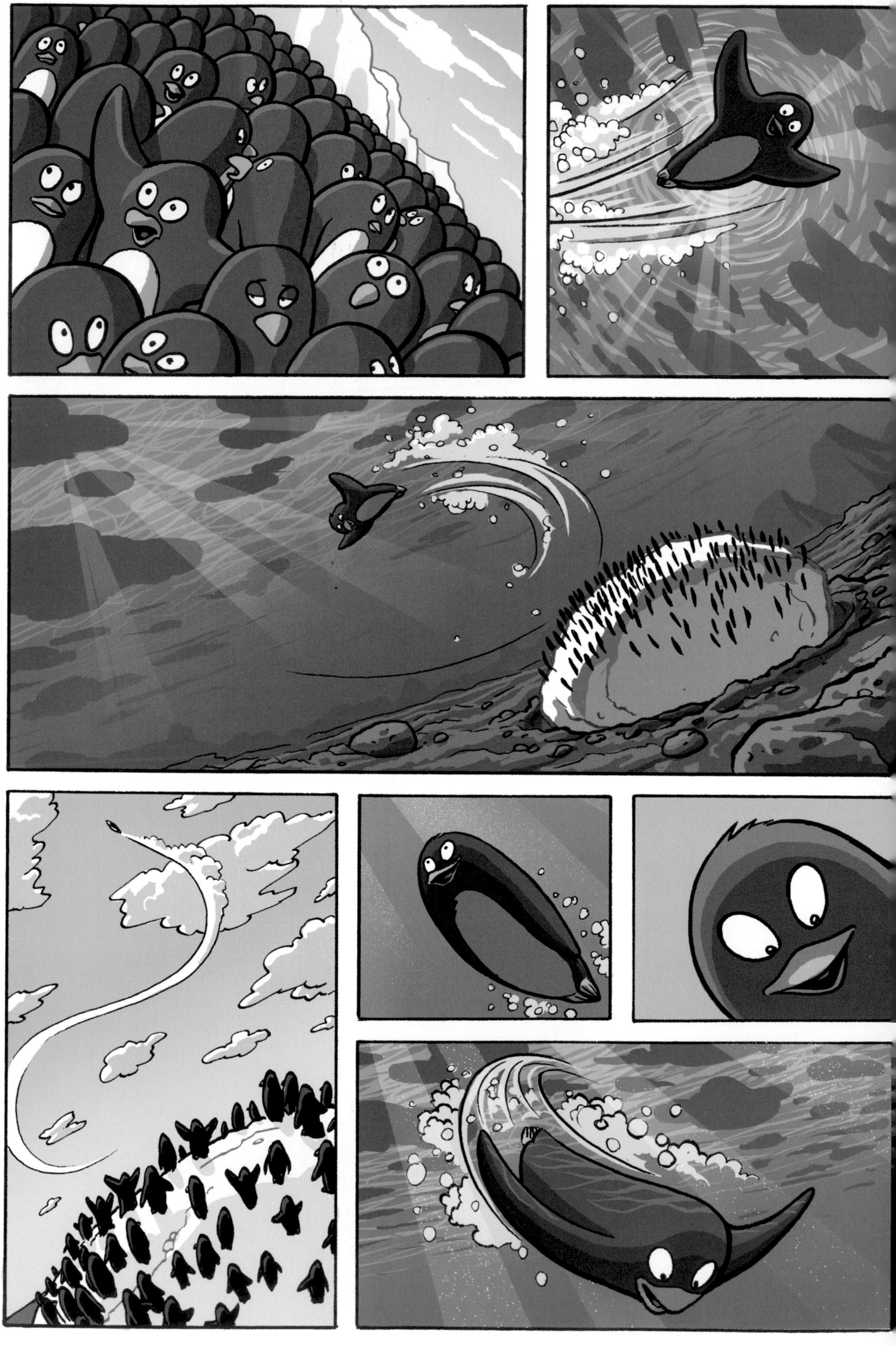

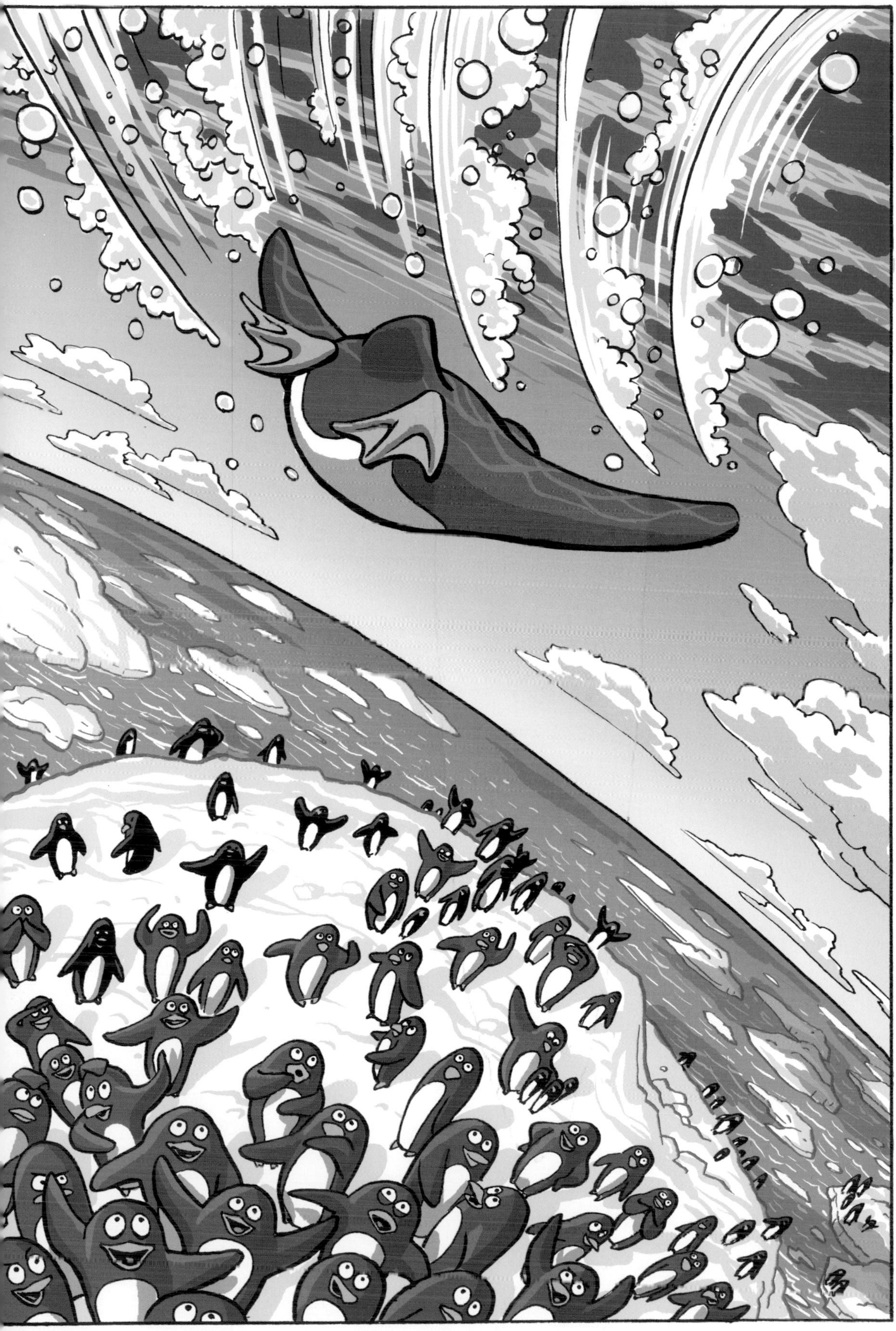

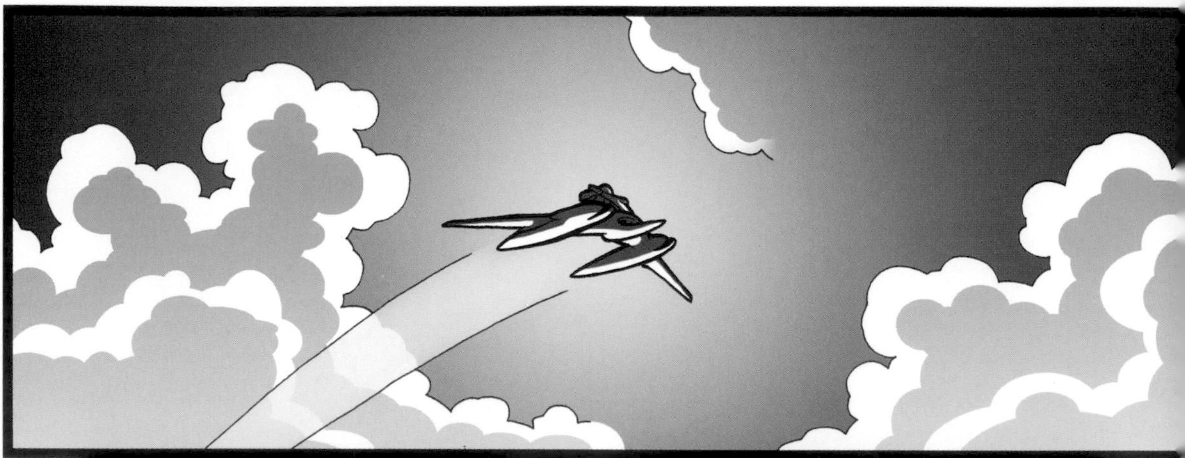

WING

JOEL CARROLL

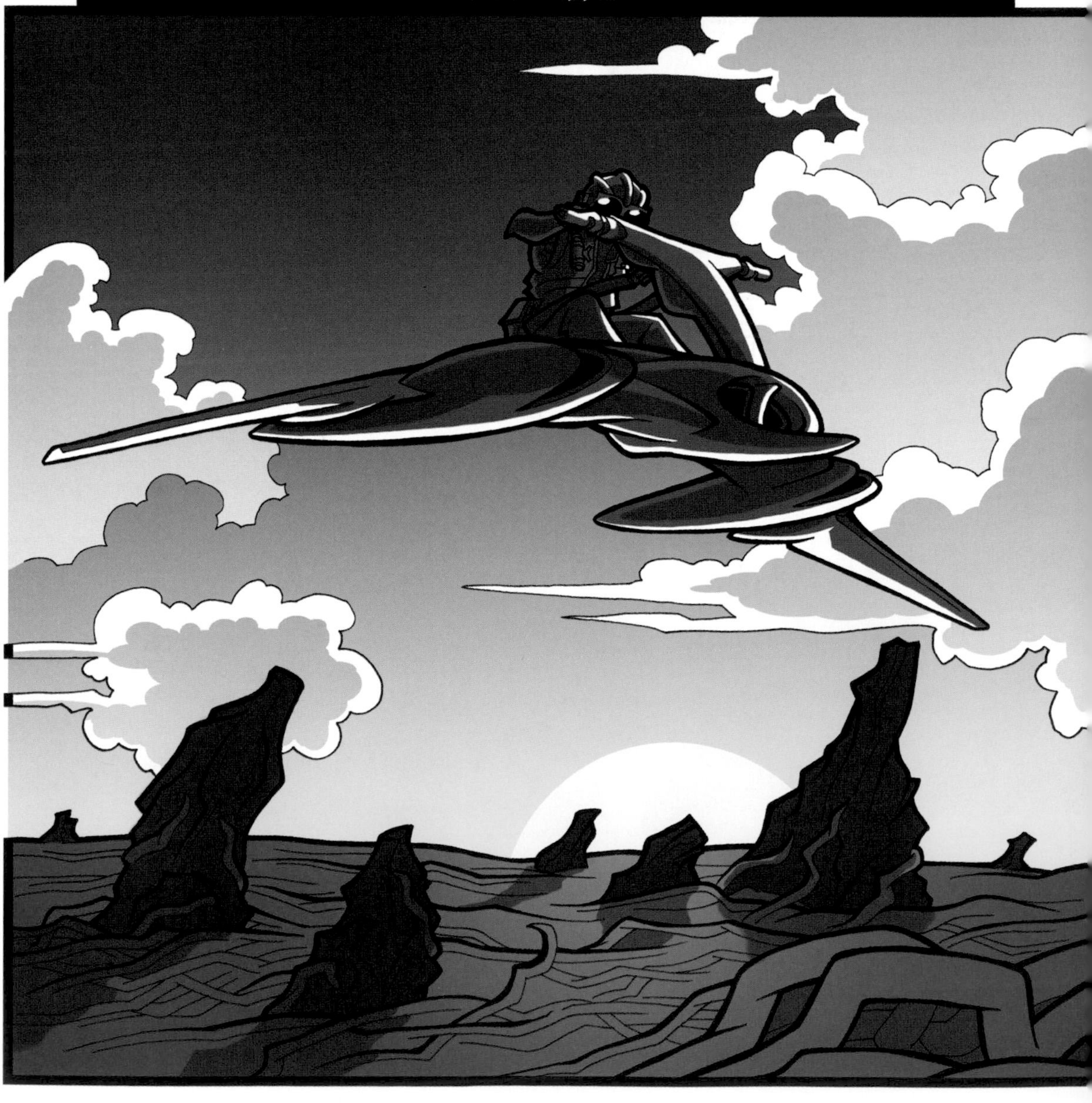

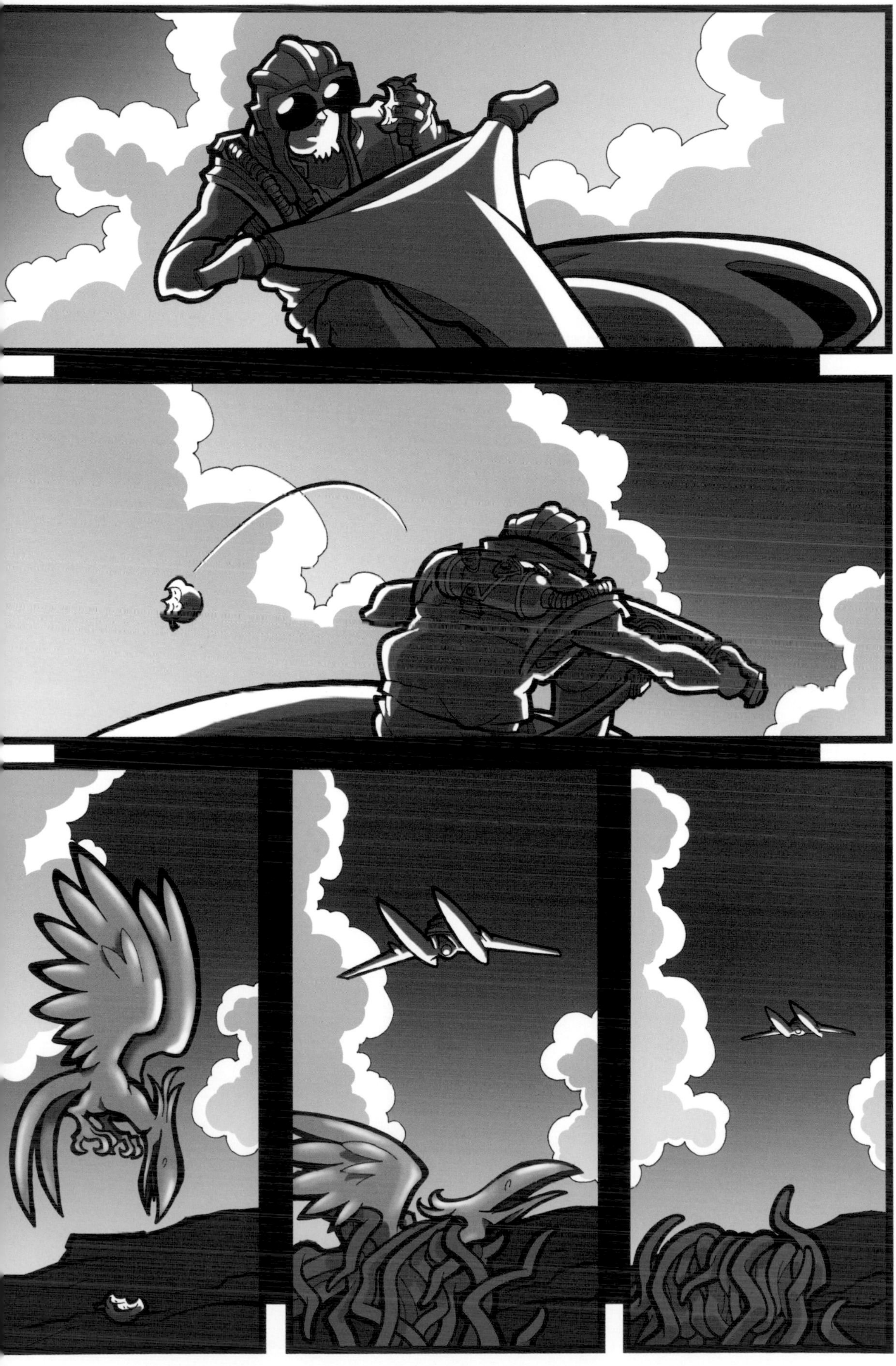

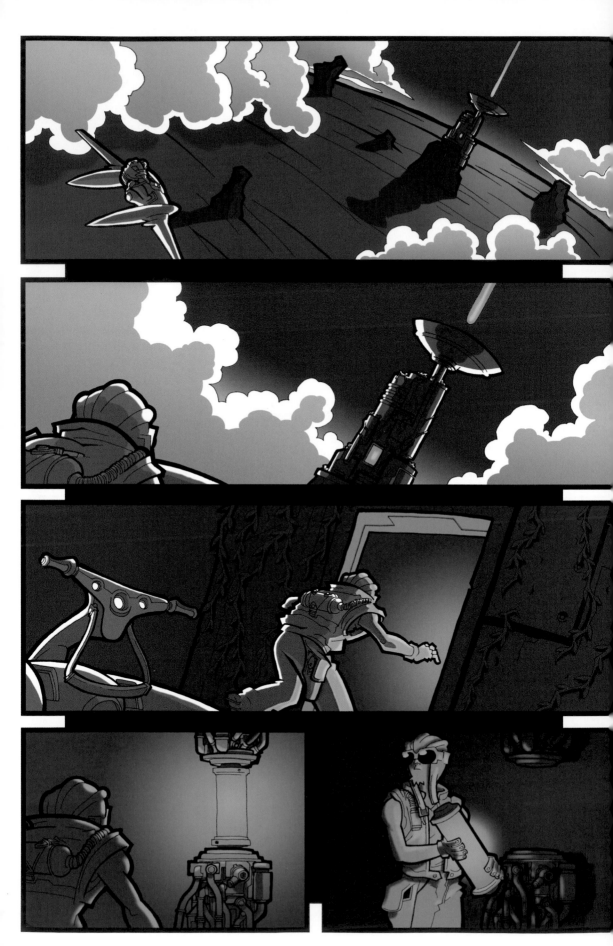

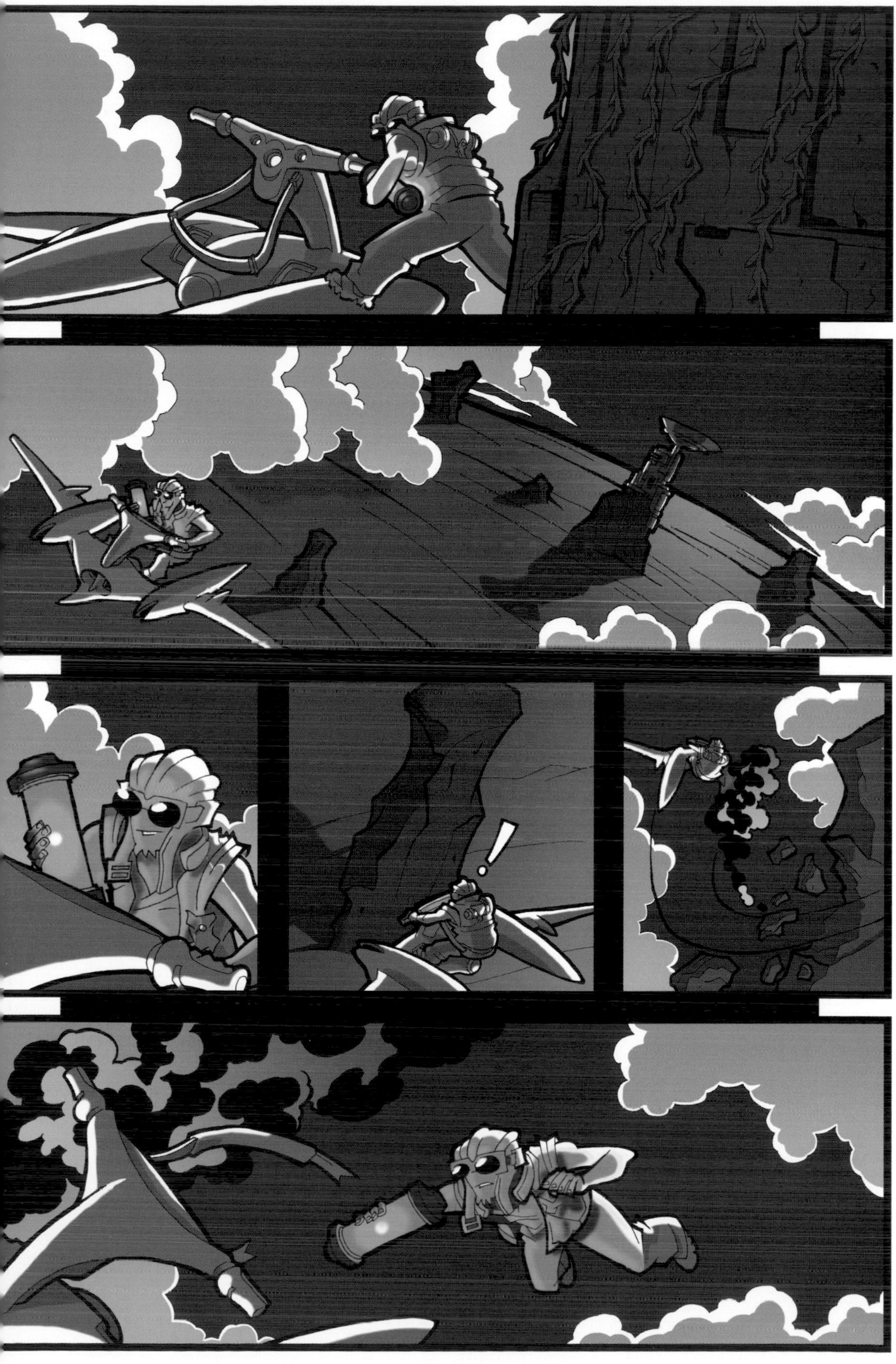
!

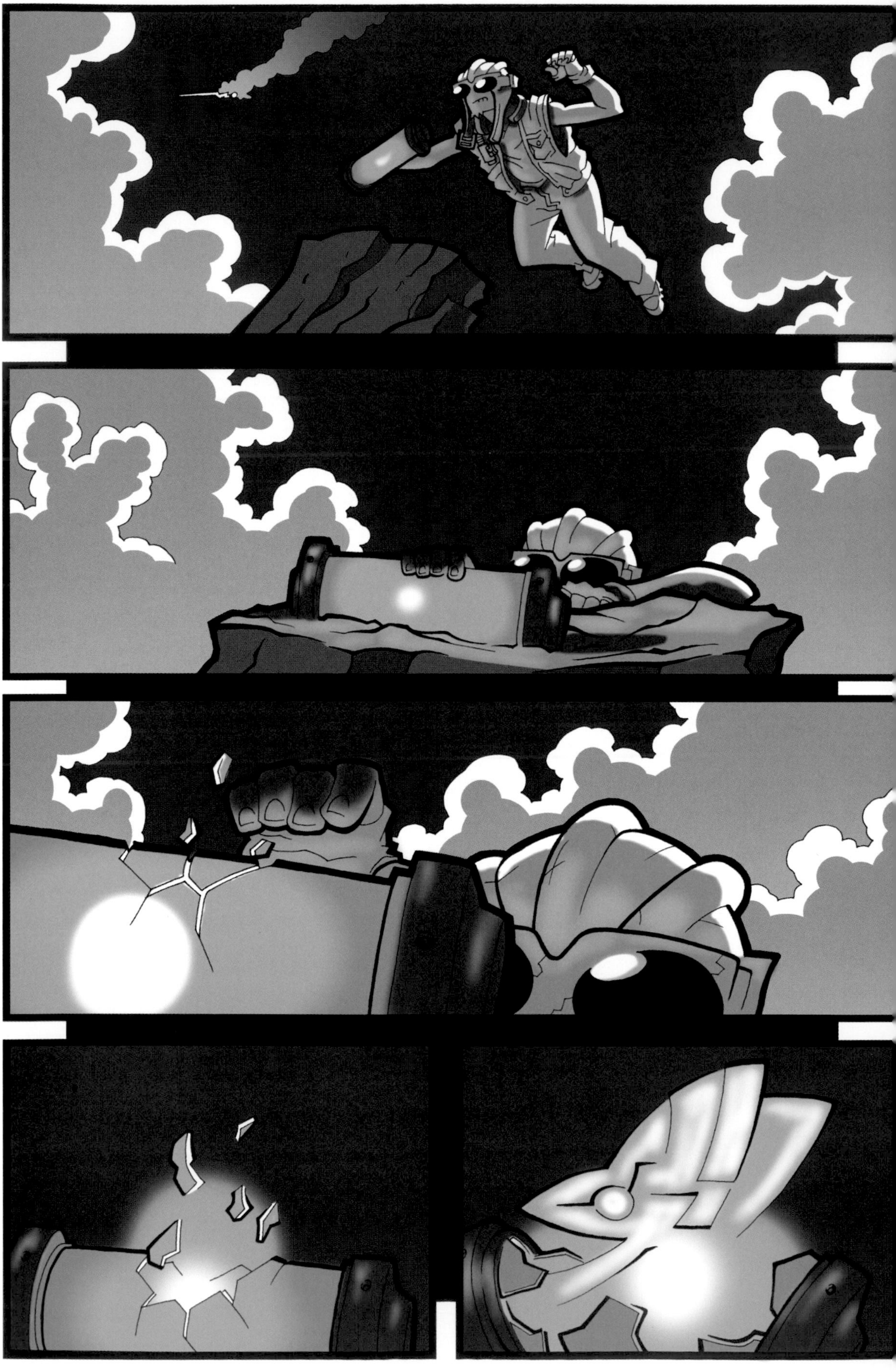

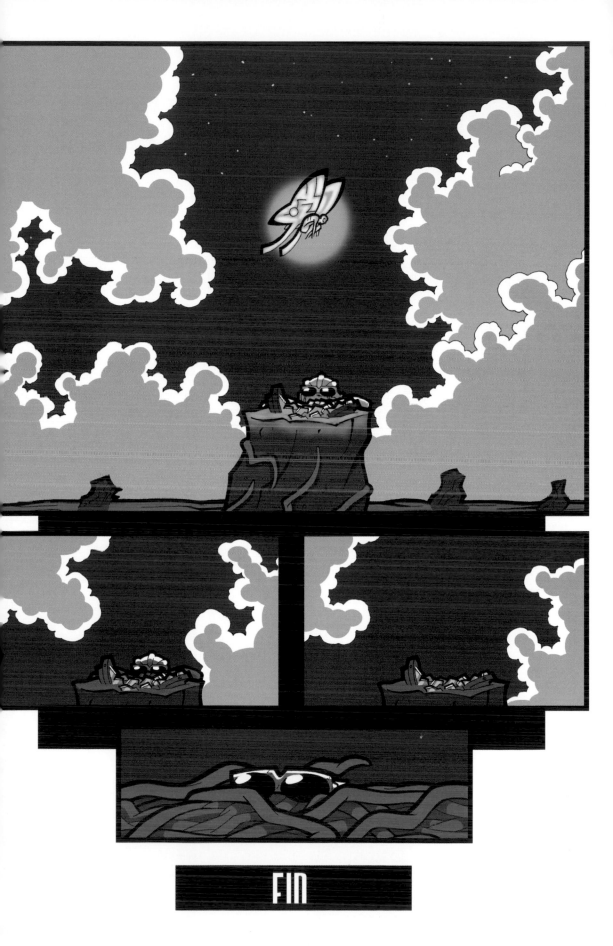

FIN

MIGRATIONS

by Kean Soo

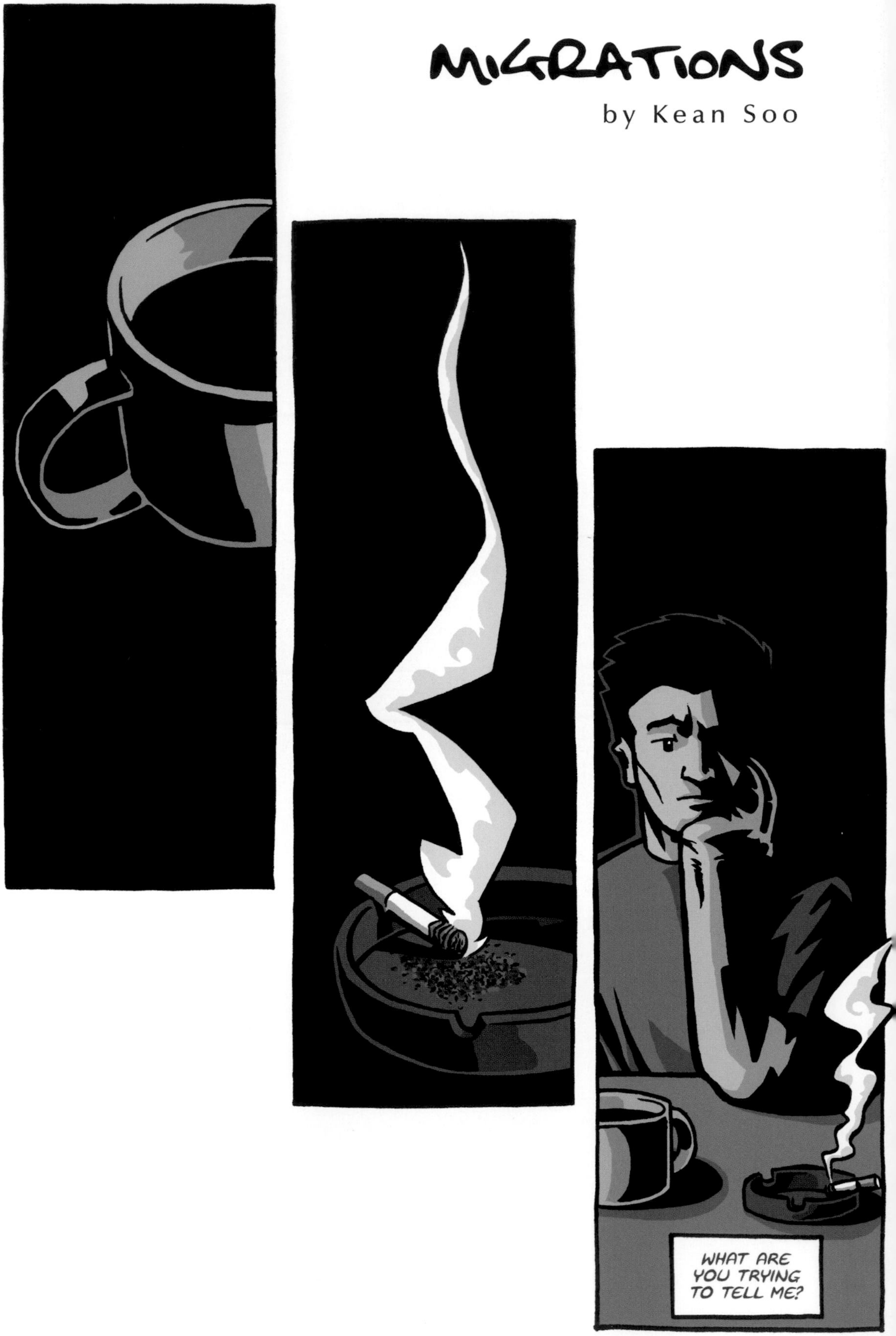
WHAT ARE YOU TRYING TO TELL ME?

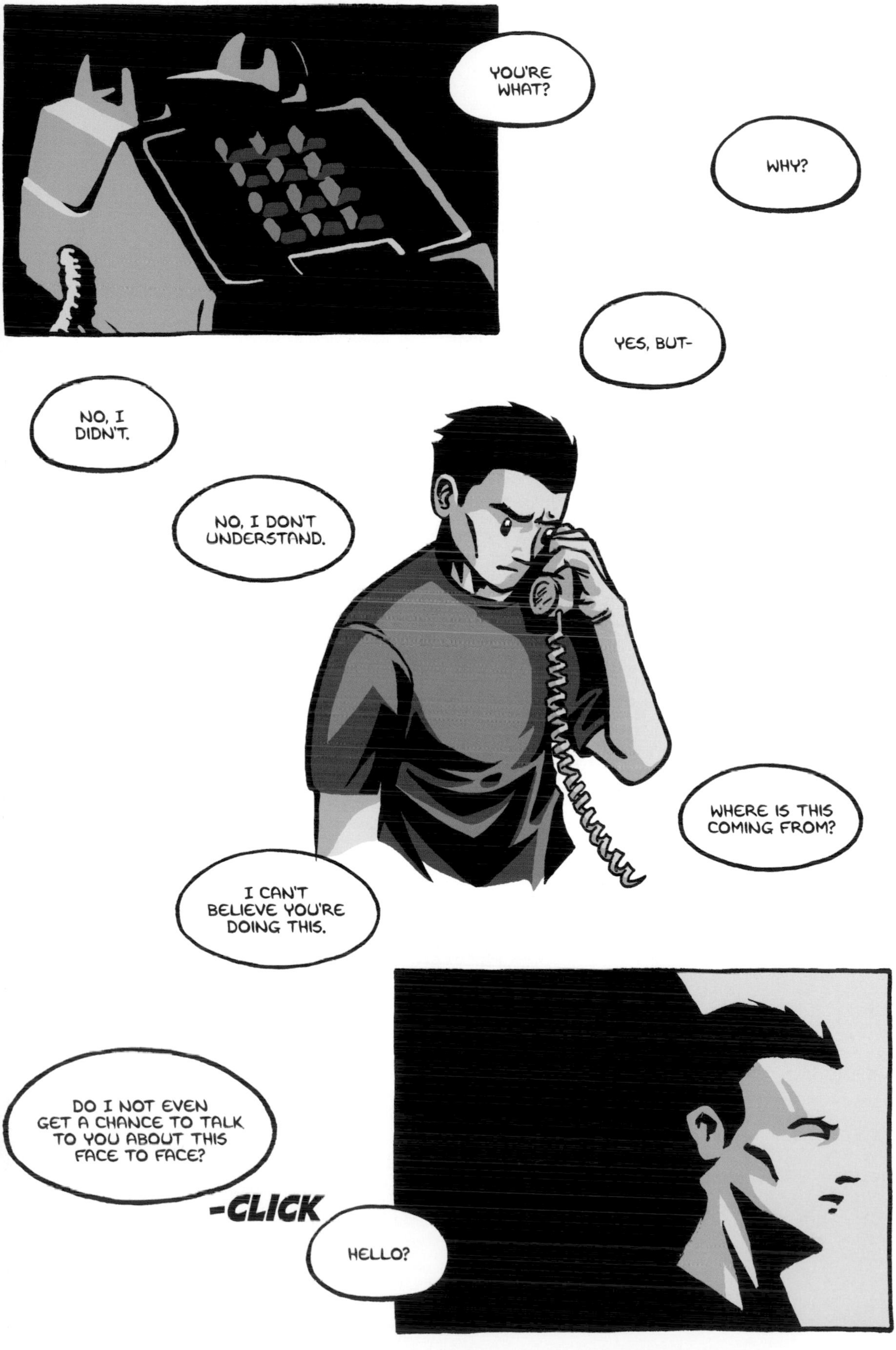
YOU'RE WHAT?
WHY?
YES, BUT-
NO, I DIDN'T.
NO, I DON'T UNDERSTAND.
WHERE IS THIS COMING FROM?
I CAN'T BELIEVE YOU'RE DOING THIS.
DO I NOT EVEN GET A CHANCE TO TALK TO YOU ABOUT THIS FACE TO FACE?
-CLICK
HELLO?

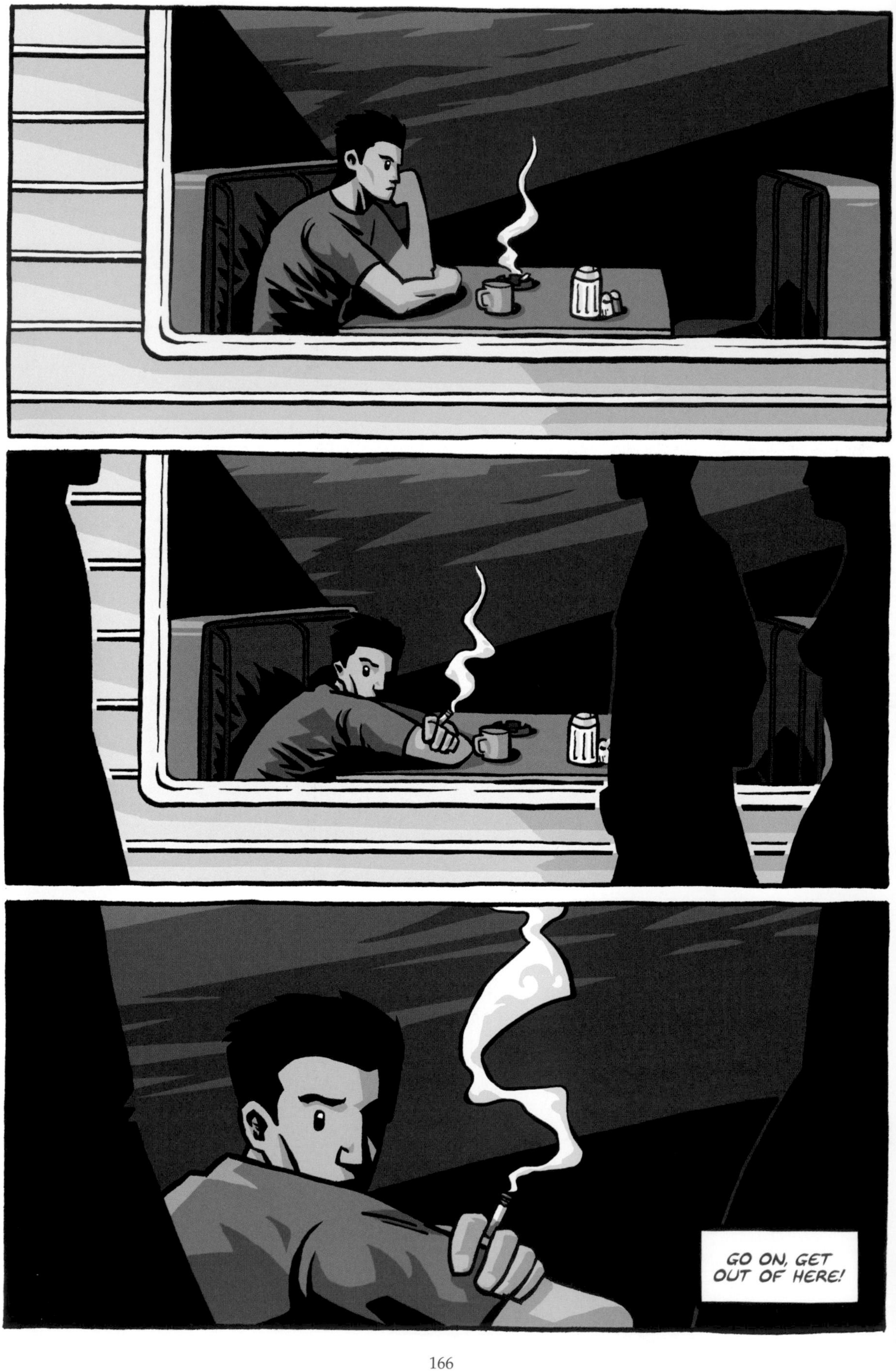
GO ON, GET OUT OF HERE!

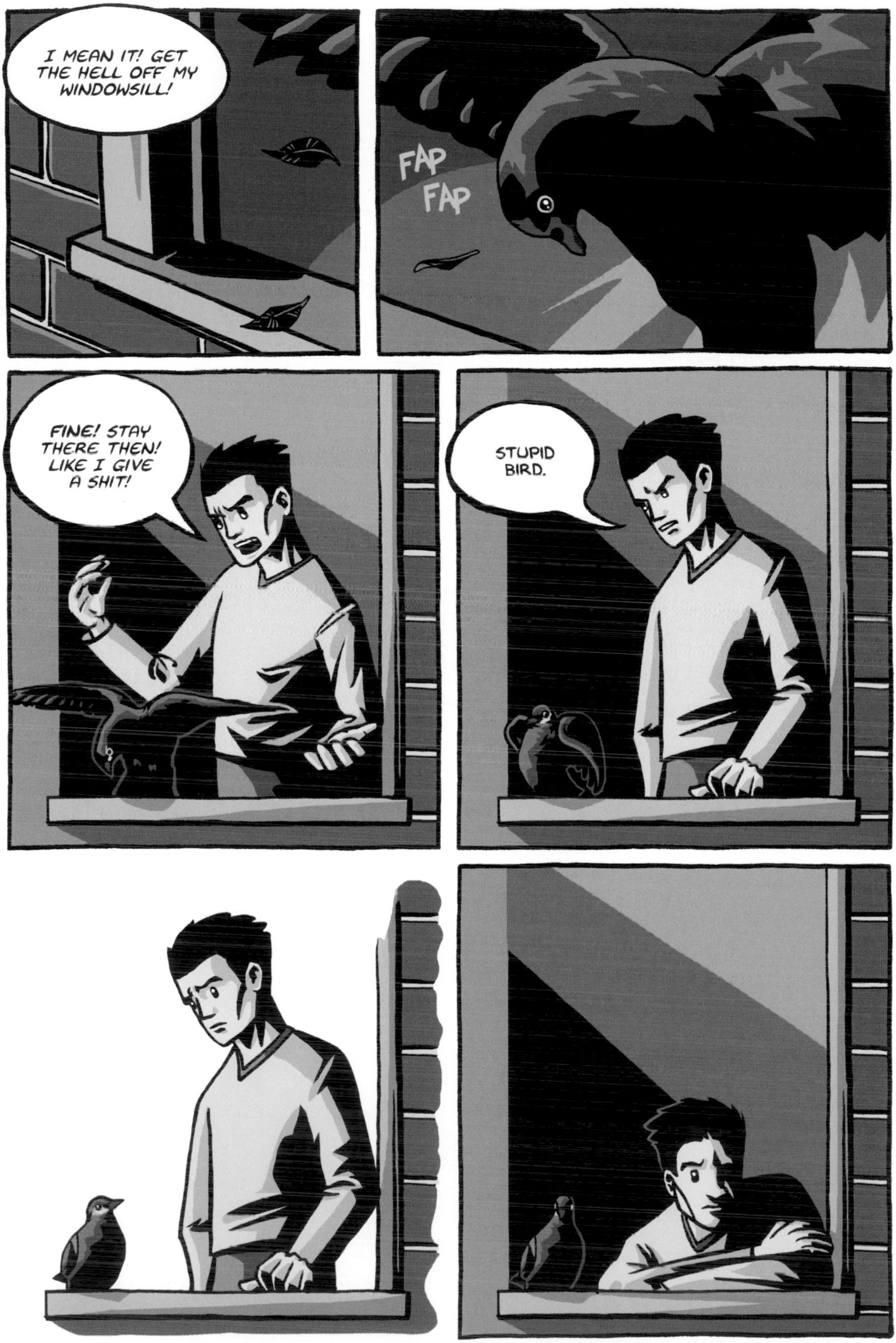
I MEAN IT! GET THE HELL OFF MY WINDOWSILL!
FAP FAP
FINE! STAY THERE THEN! LIKE I GIVE A SHIT!
STUPID BIRD.

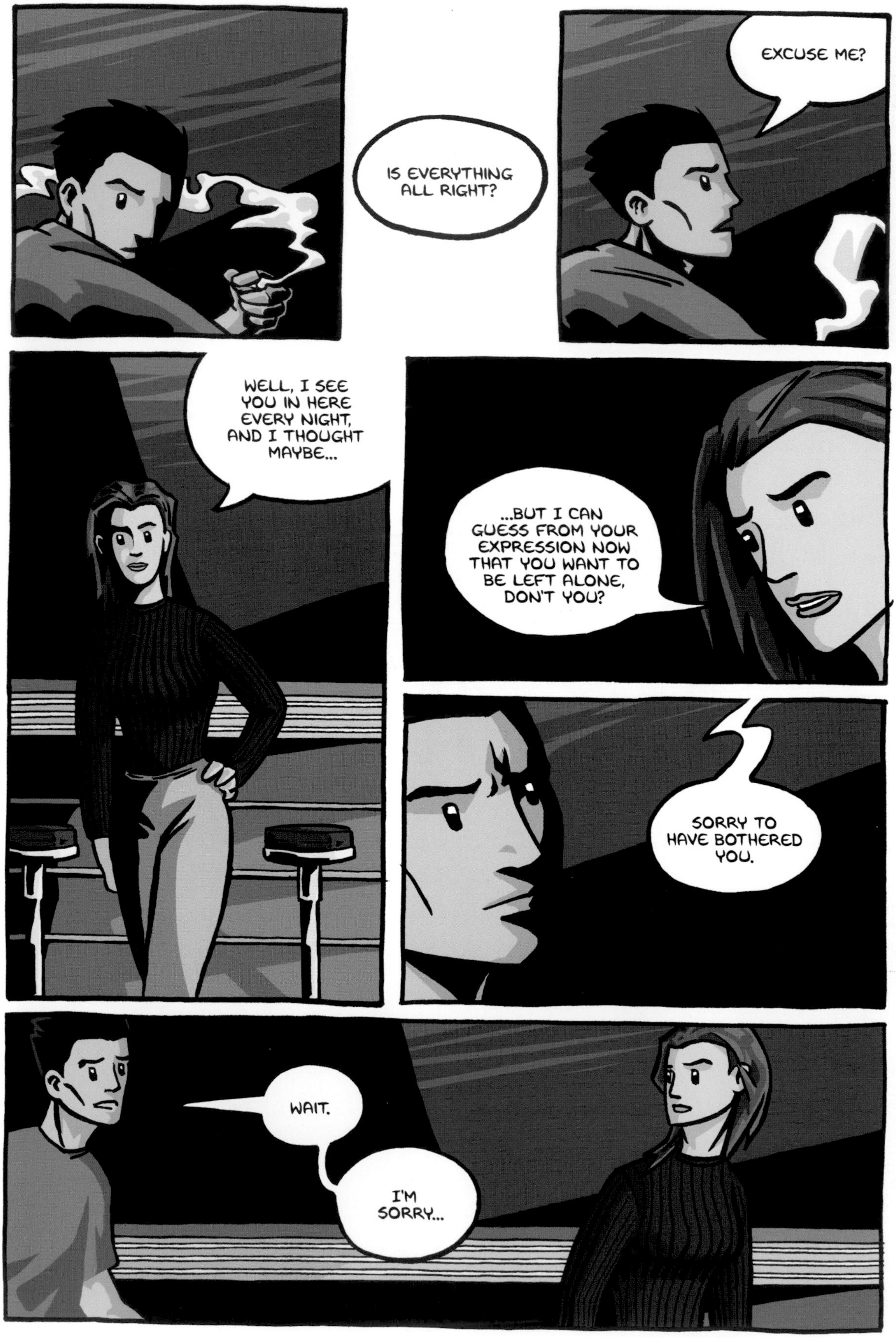
IS EVERYTHING ALL RIGHT?
EXCUSE ME?
WELL, I SEE YOU IN HERE EVERY NIGHT, AND I THOUGHT MAYBE...
...BUT I CAN GUESS FROM YOUR EXPRESSION NOW THAT YOU WANT TO BE LEFT ALONE, DON'T YOU?
SORRY TO HAVE BOTHERED YOU.
WAIT.
I'M SORRY...

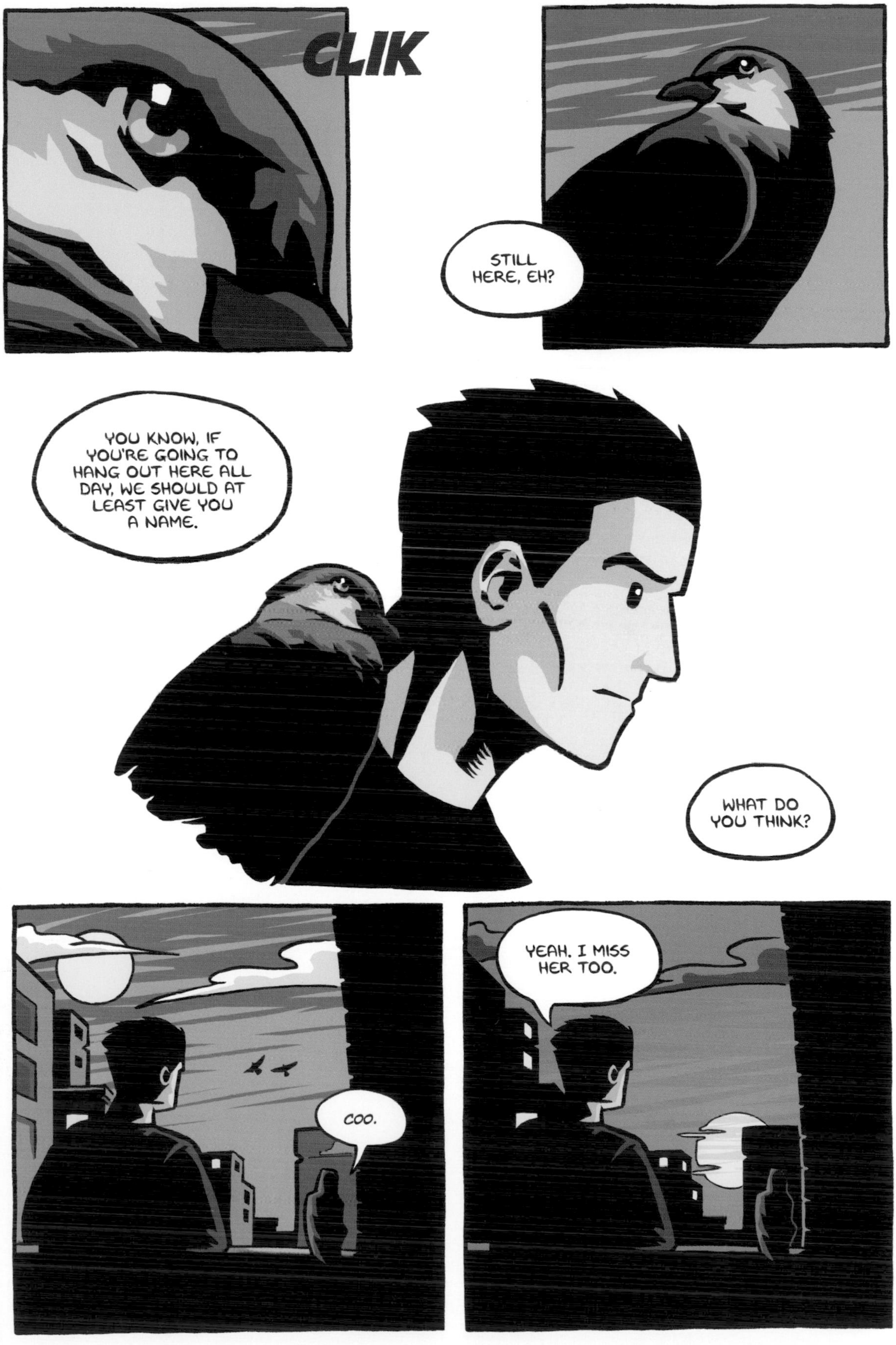
CLIK
STILL HERE, EH?
YOU KNOW, IF YOU'RE GOING TO HANG OUT HERE ALL DAY, WE SHOULD AT LEAST GIVE YOU A NAME.
WHAT DO YOU THINK?
COO.
YEAH. I MISS HER TOO.

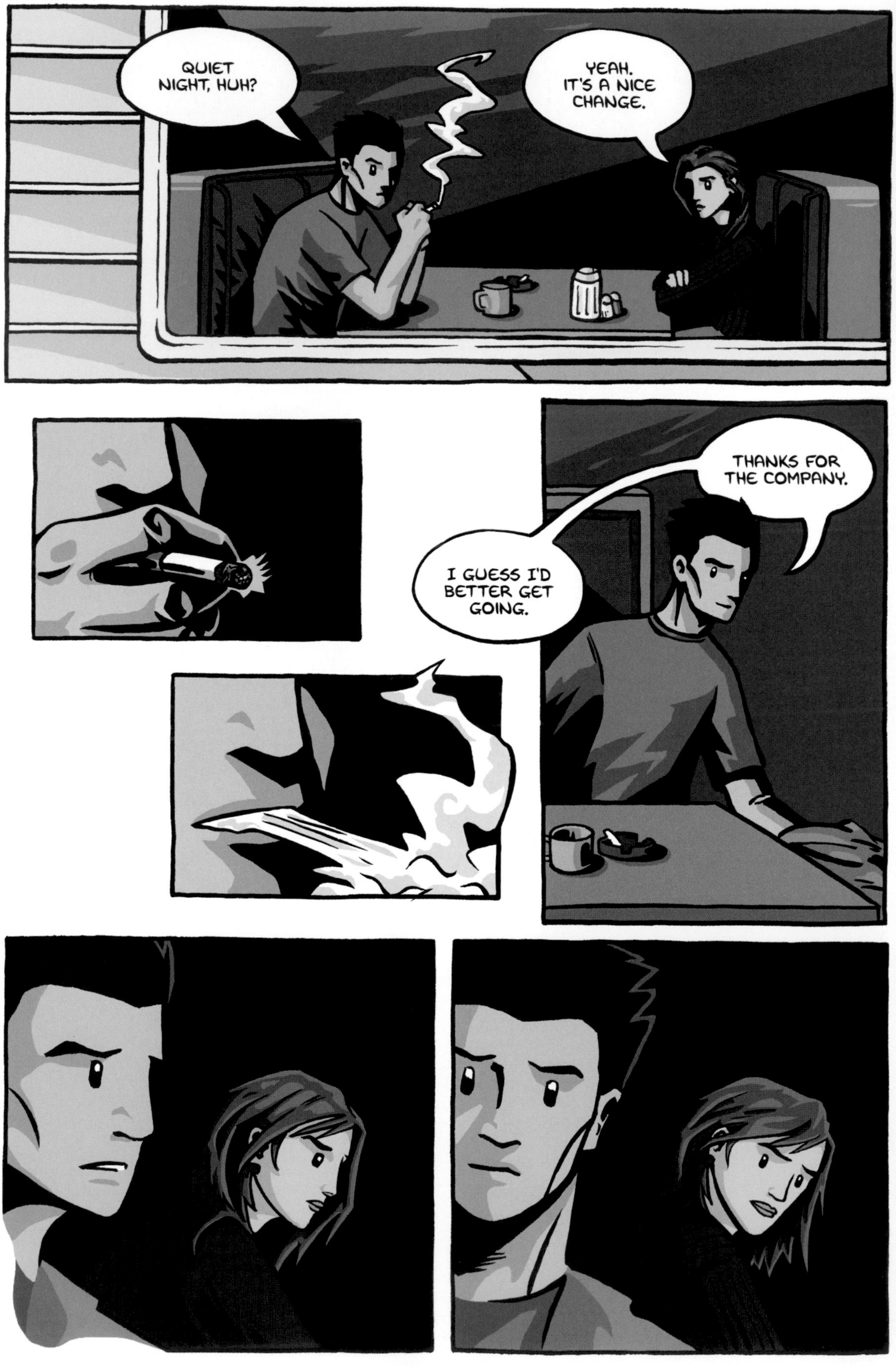
QUIET NIGHT, HUH?
YEAH. IT'S A NICE CHANGE.
THANKS FOR THE COMPANY.
I GUESS I'D BETTER GET GOING.

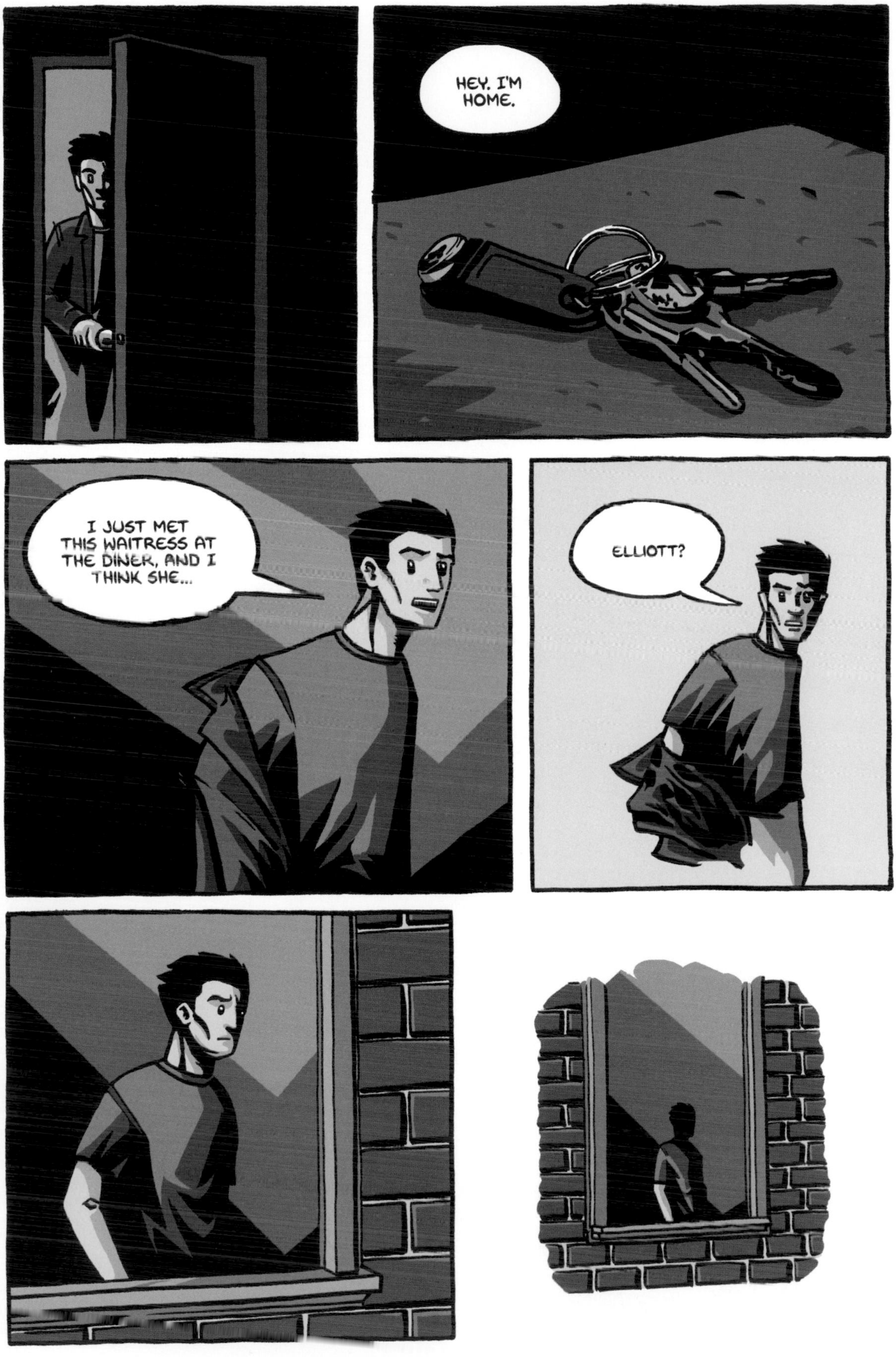
HEY. I'M HOME.
I JUST MET THIS WAITRESS AT THE DINER, AND I THINK SHE...
ELLIOTT?

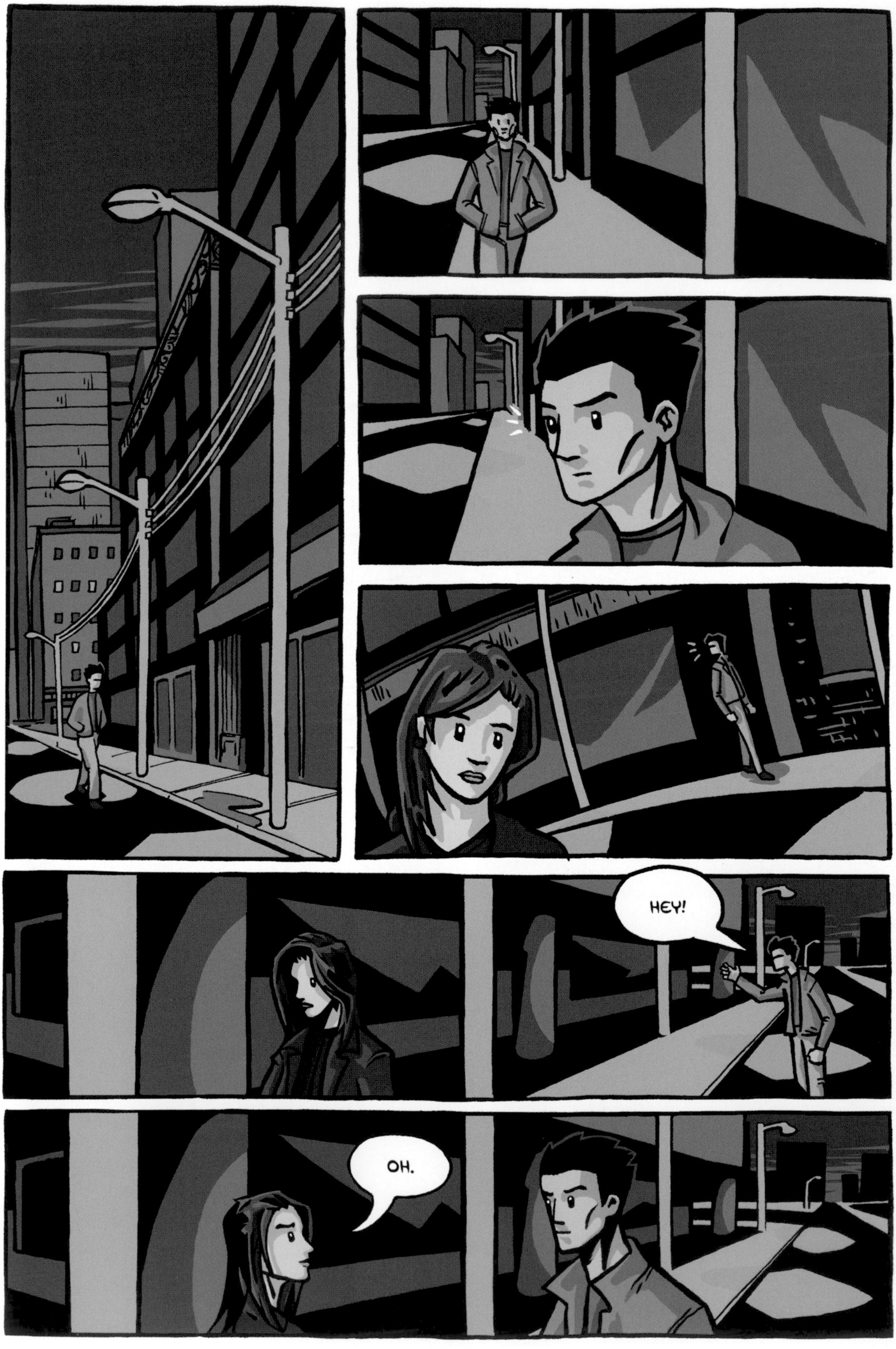
HEY!
OH.

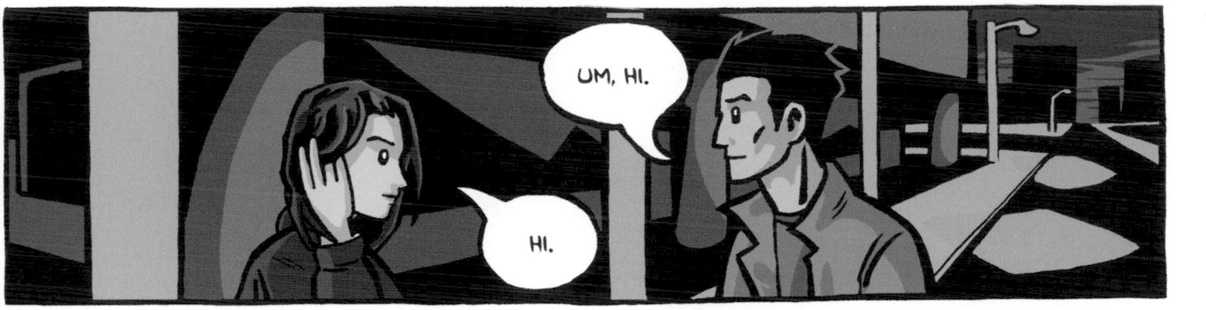
UM, HI.
HI.

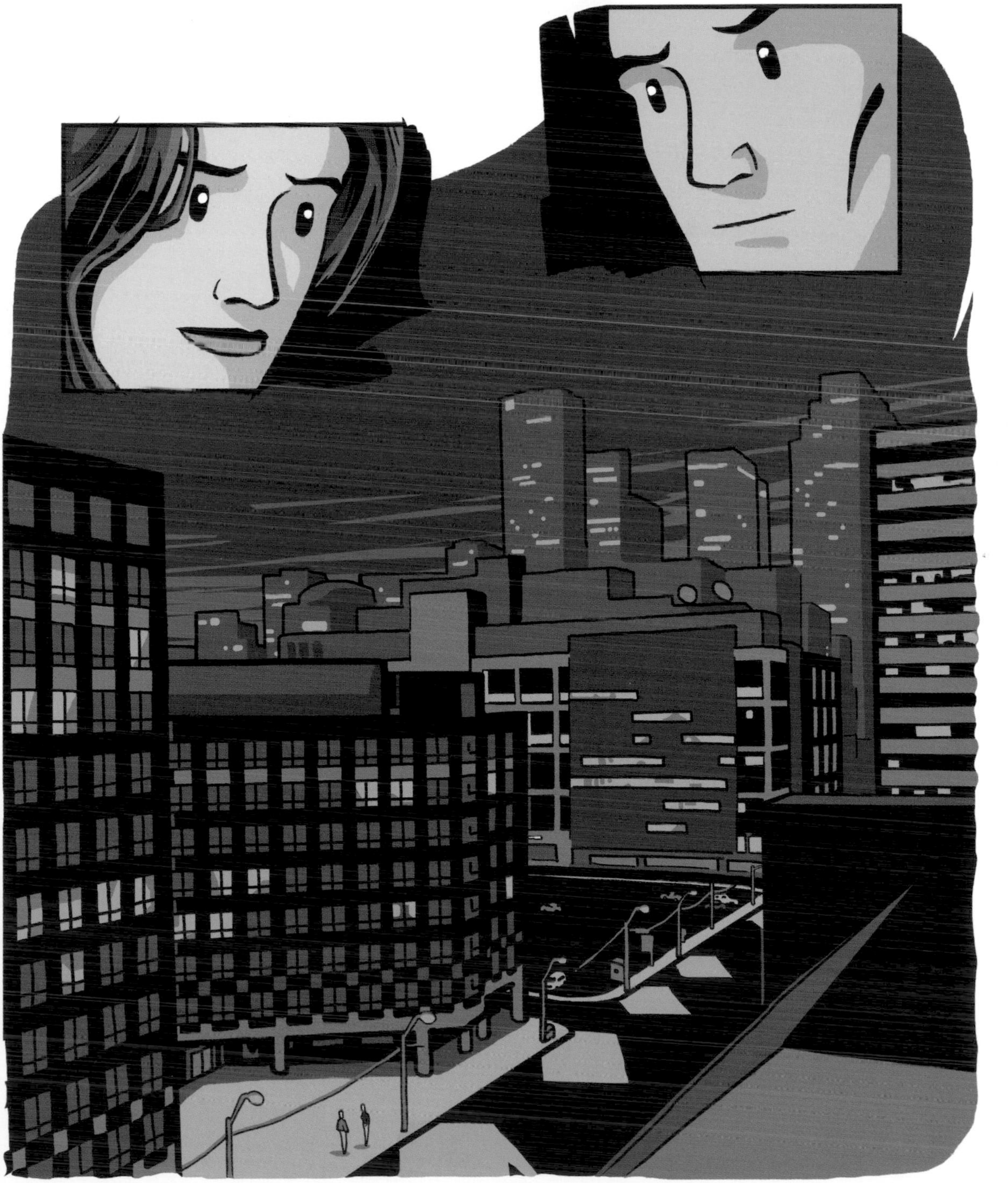

"Faith," by Erika Moen Colors by Hope Larson

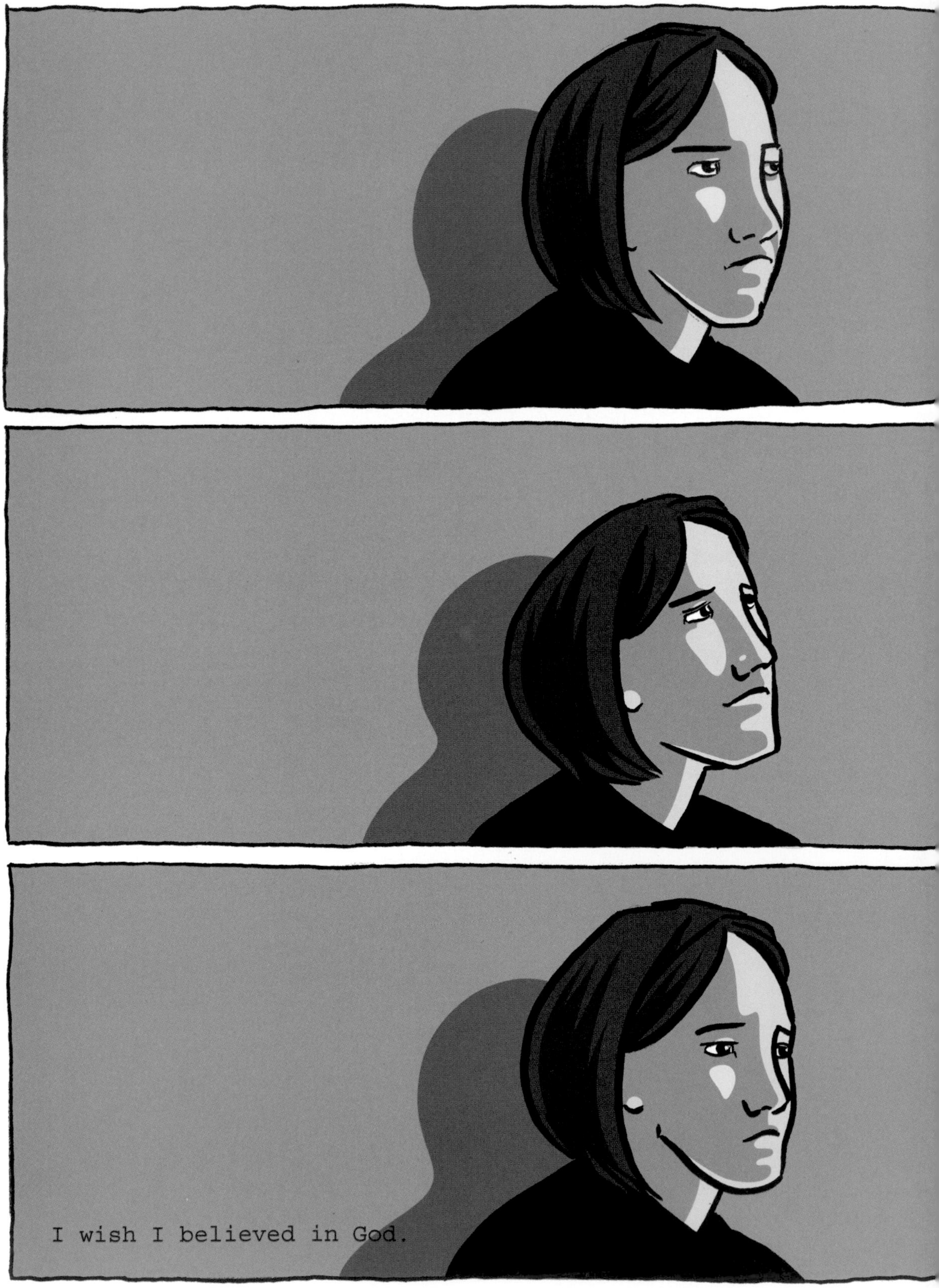
I wish I believed in God.

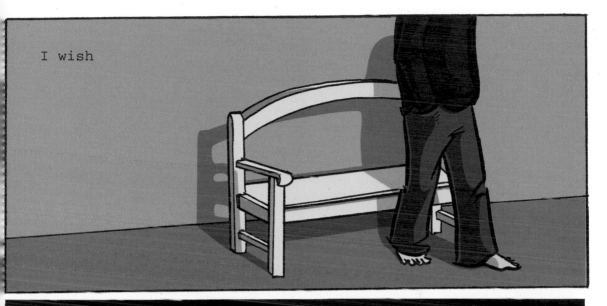

I wish

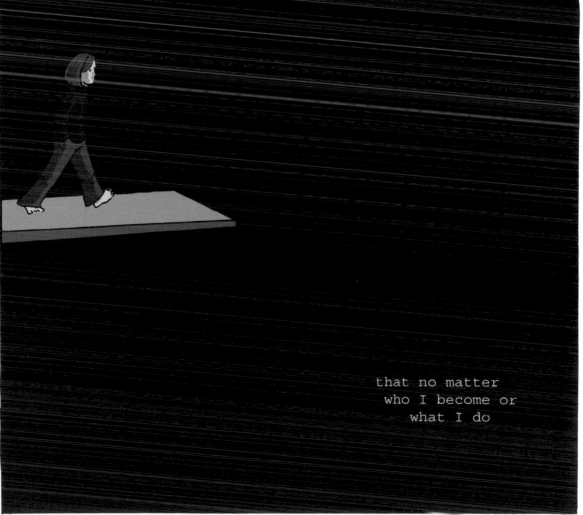

that no matter
who I become or
what I do

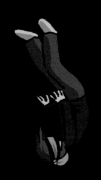

that something

   big and powerful

were watching out

      for me.

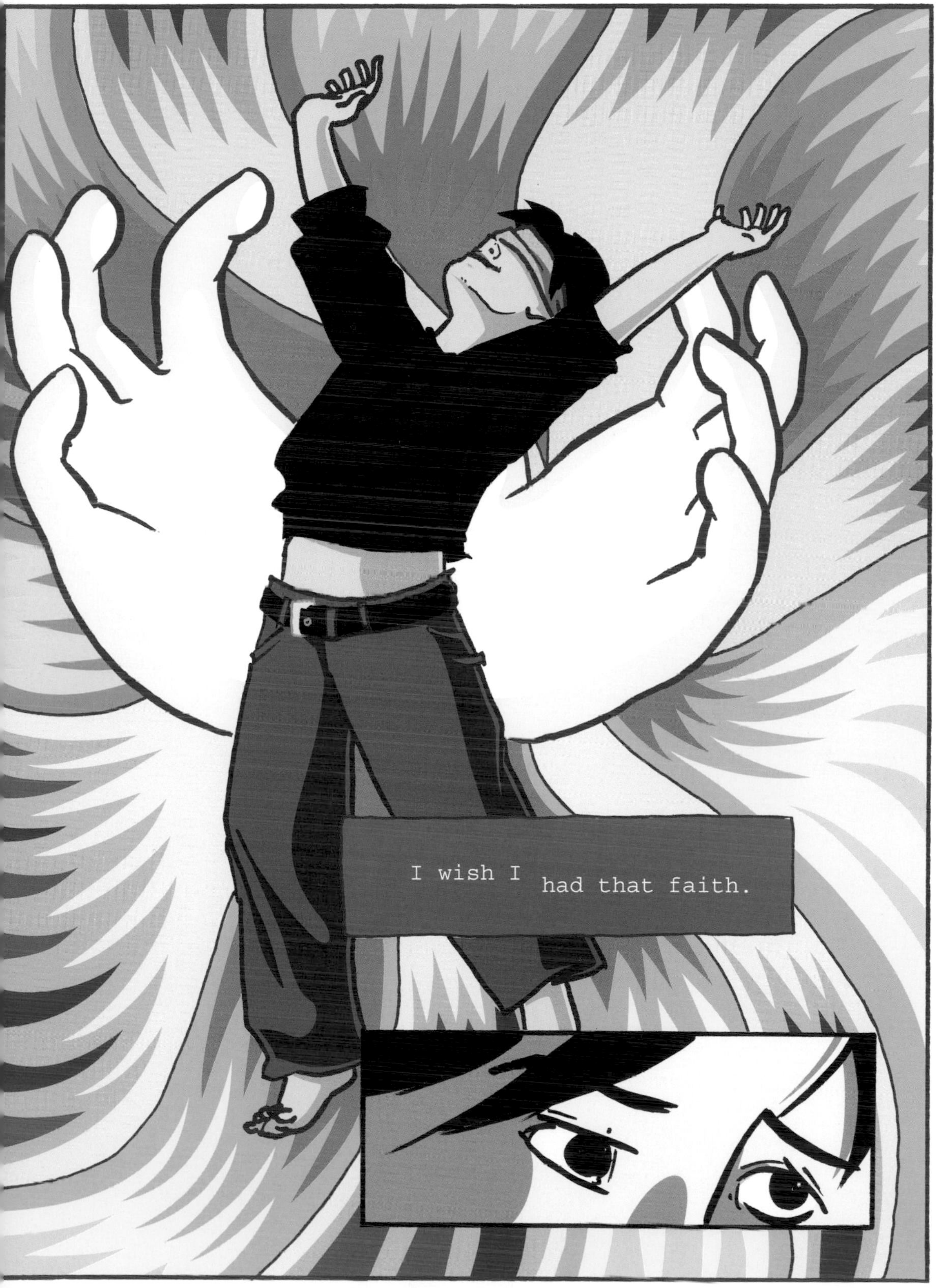
I wish I had that faith.

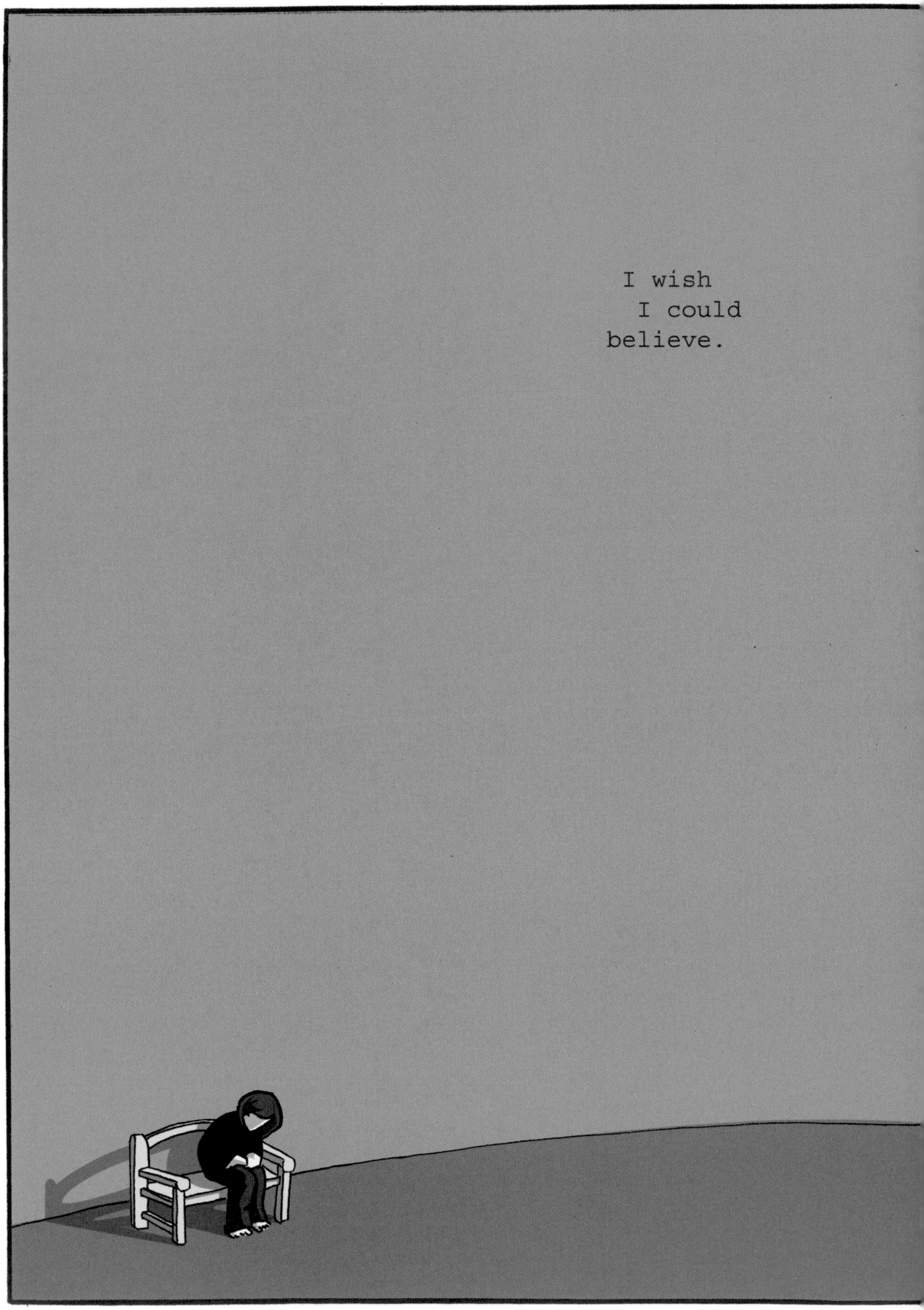
I wish
I could
believe.

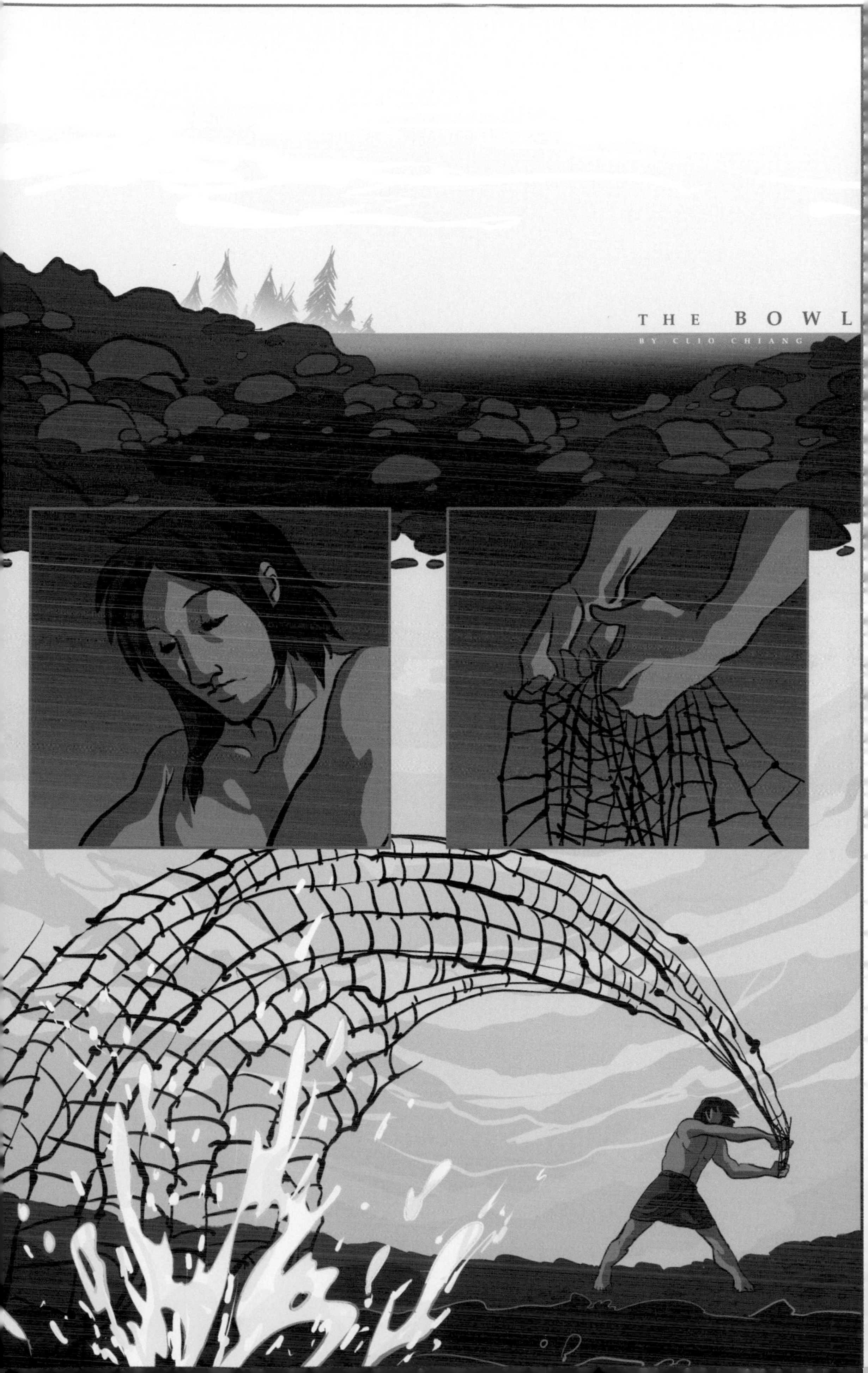
THE BOWL
BY CLIO CHIANG

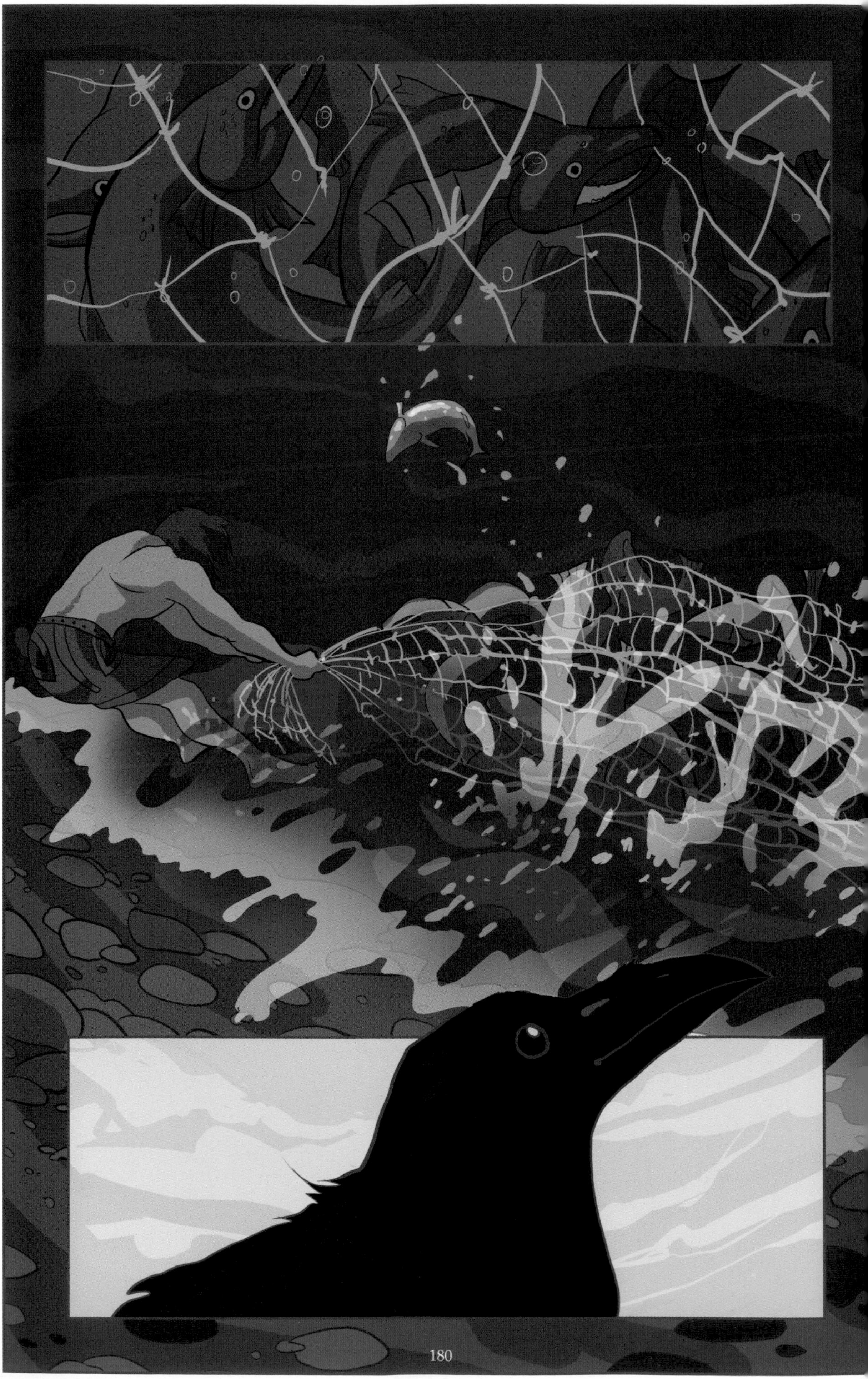

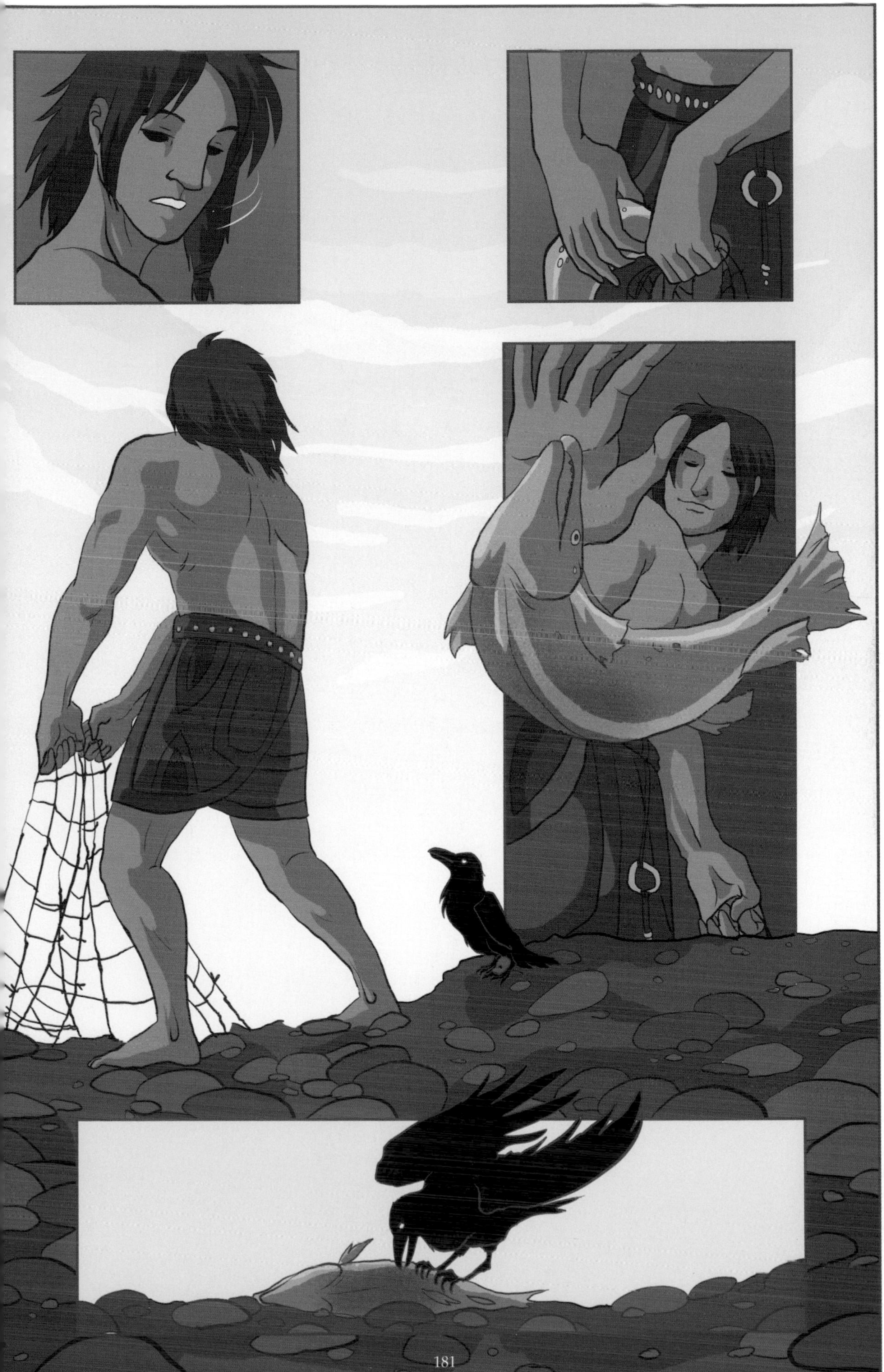

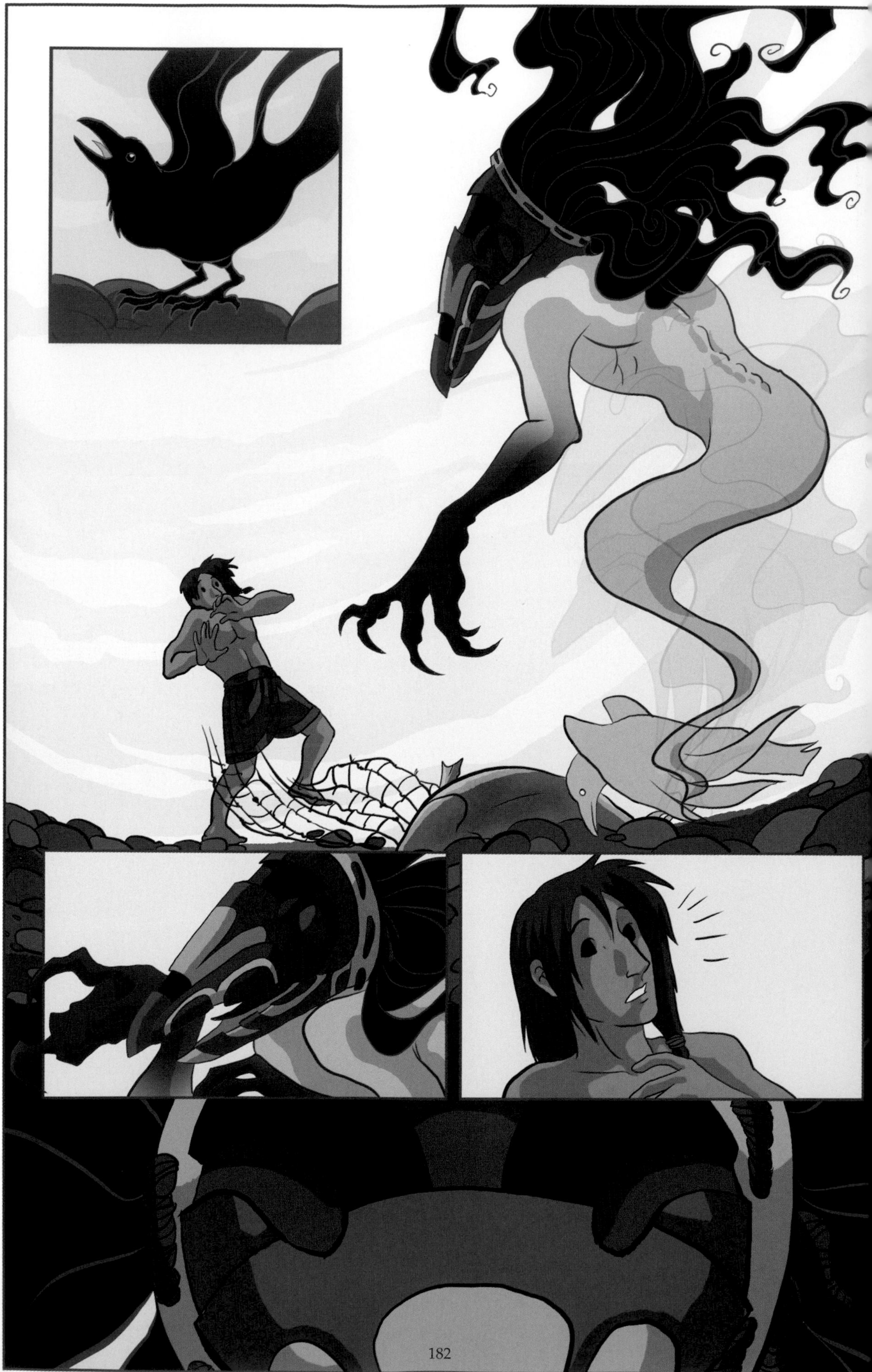

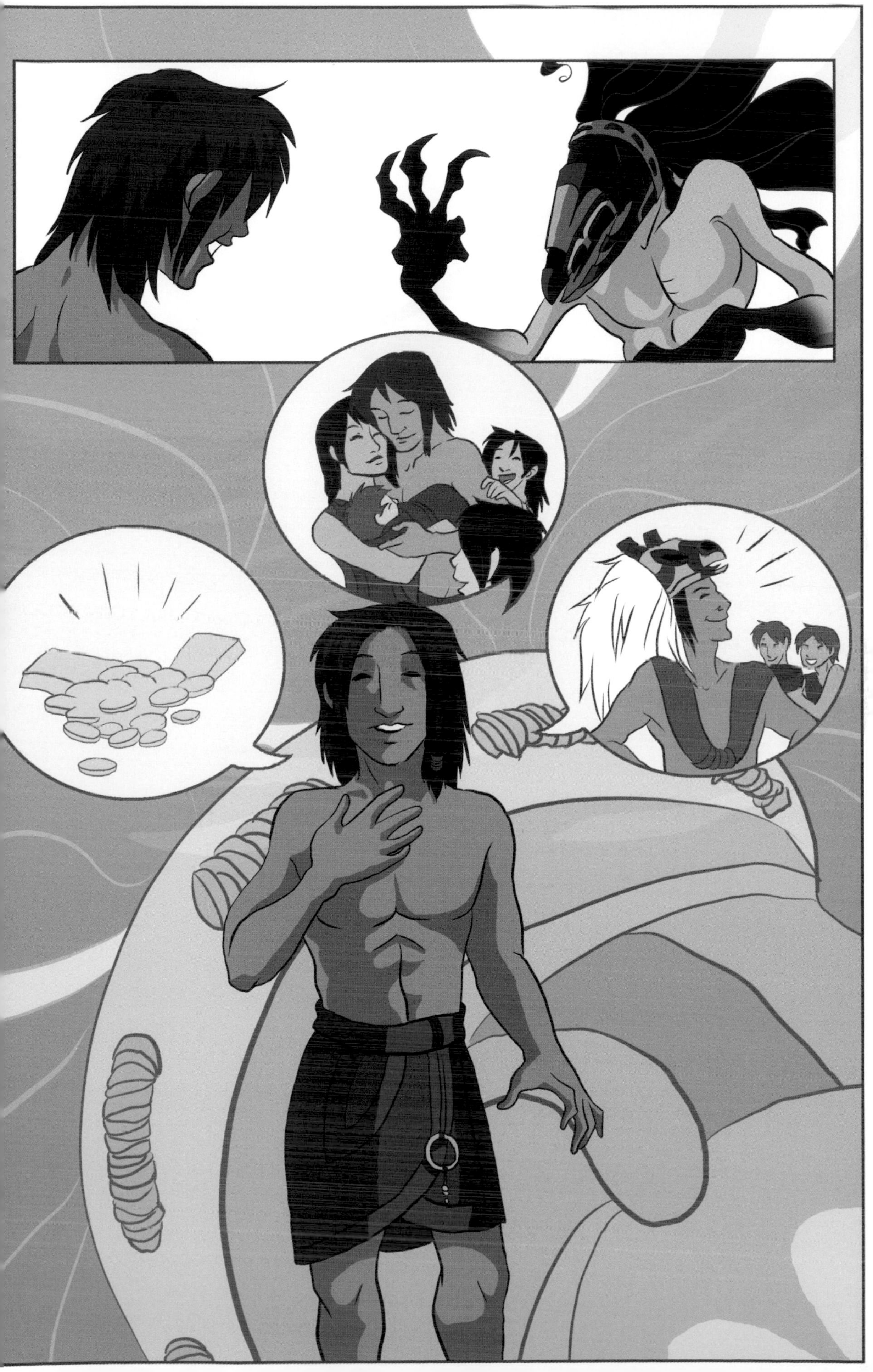

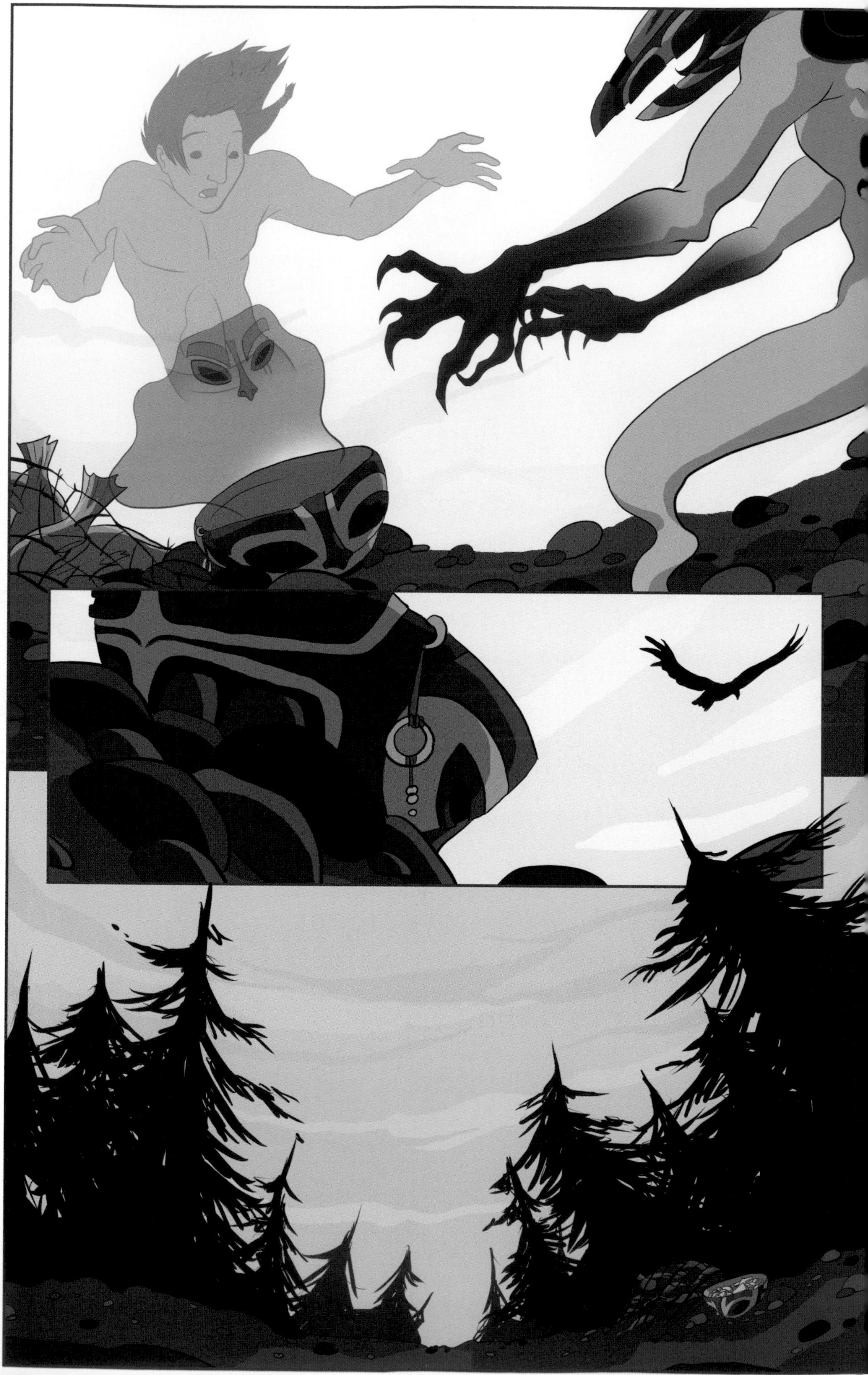

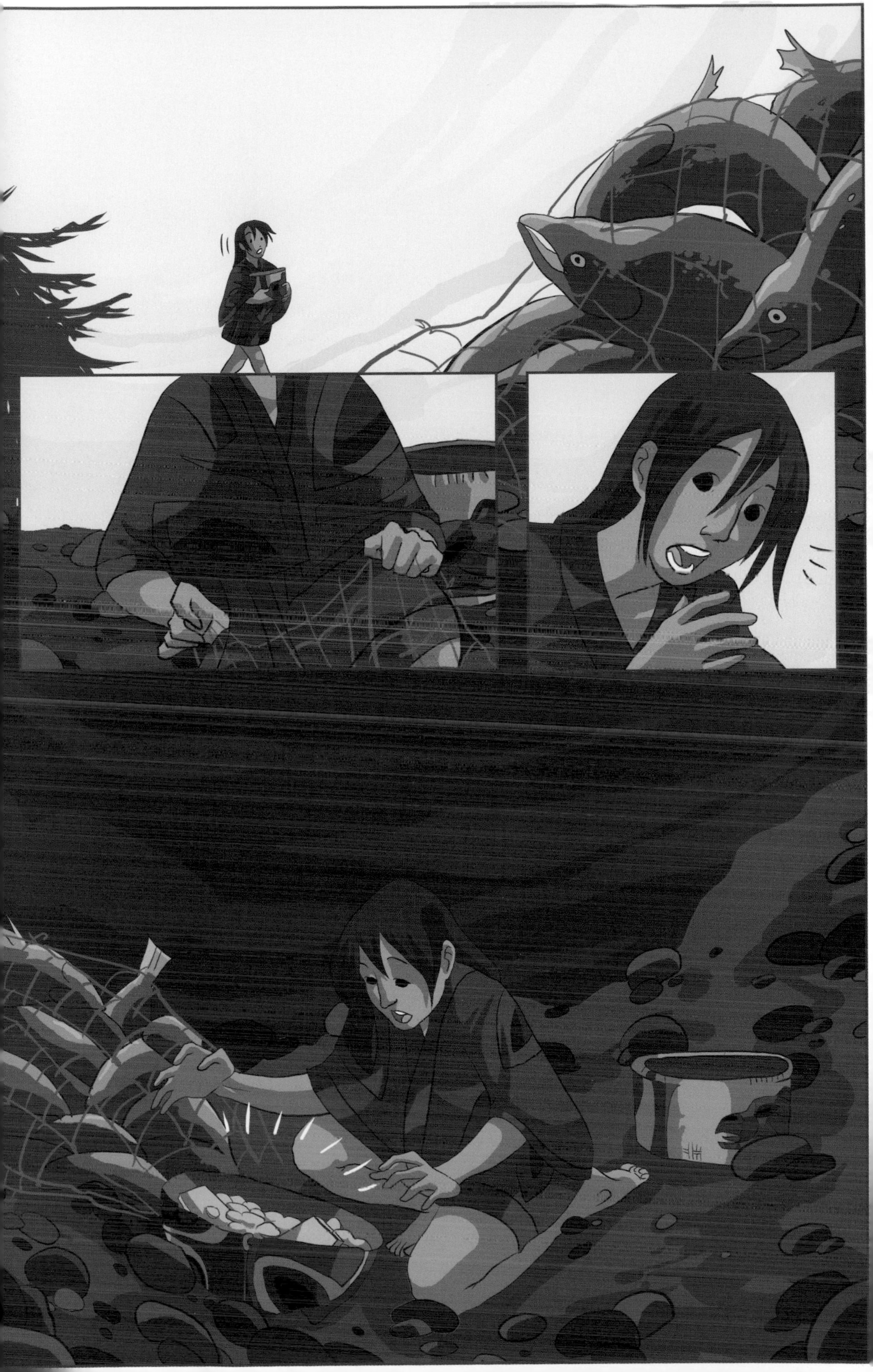

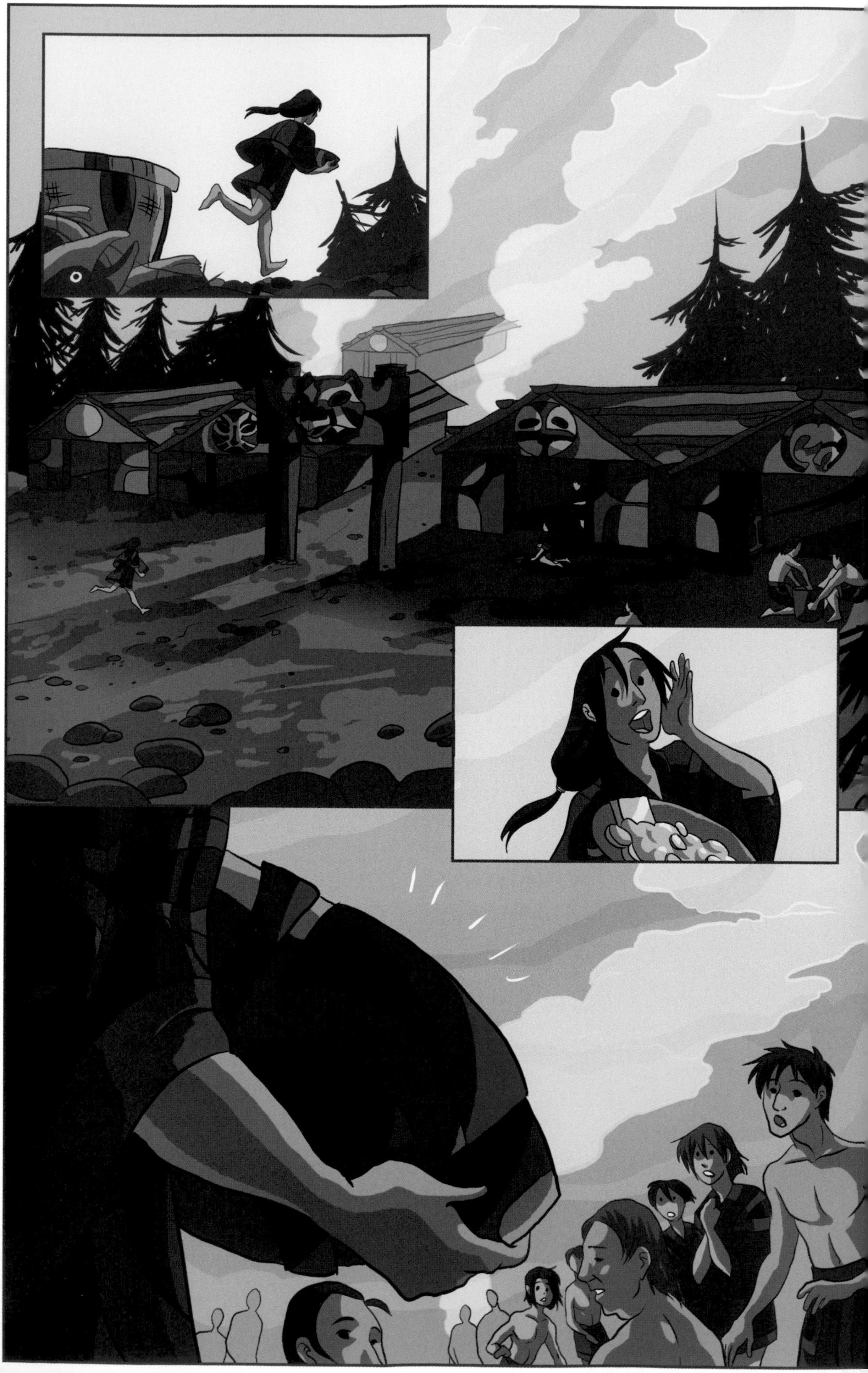

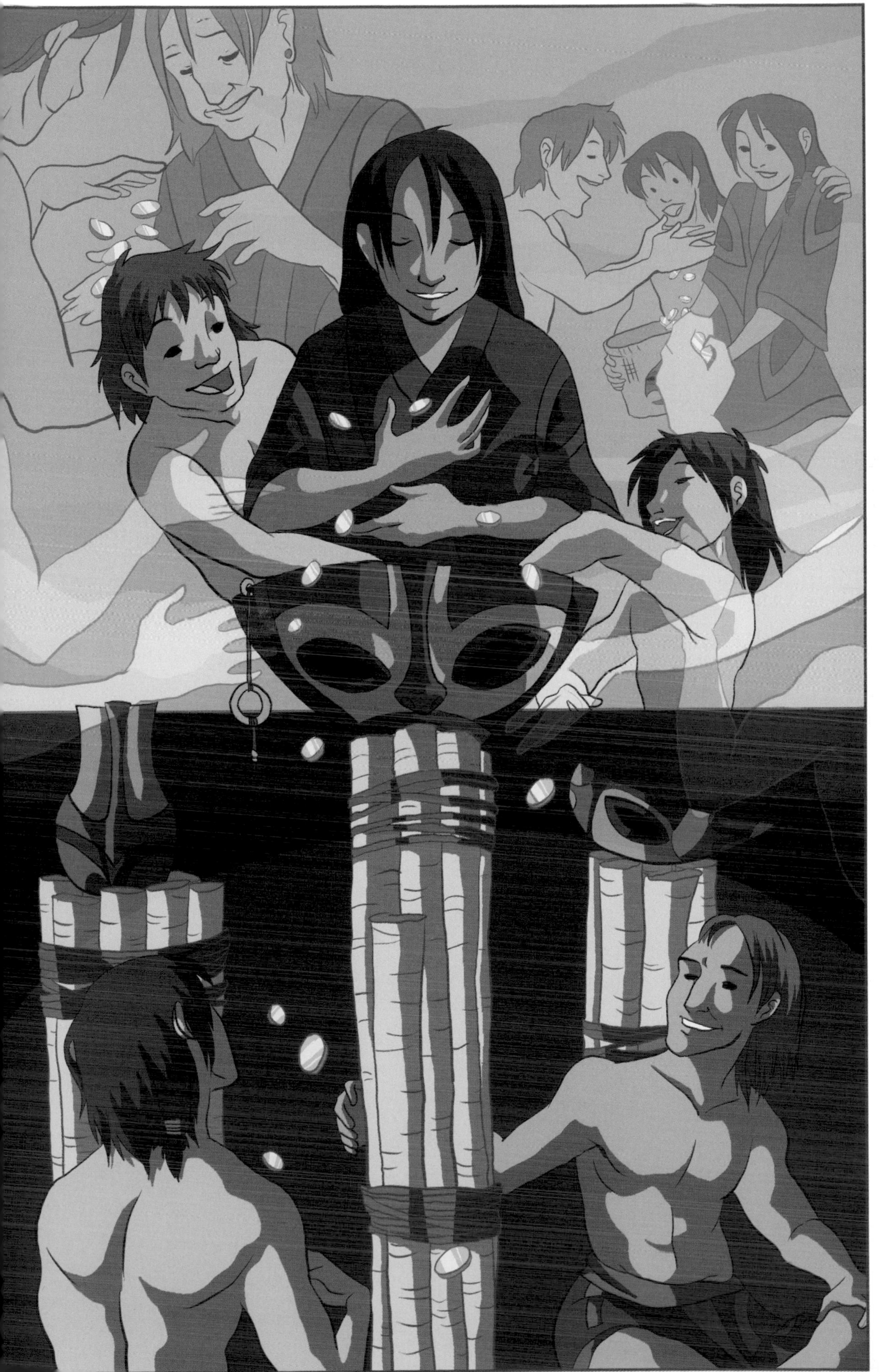

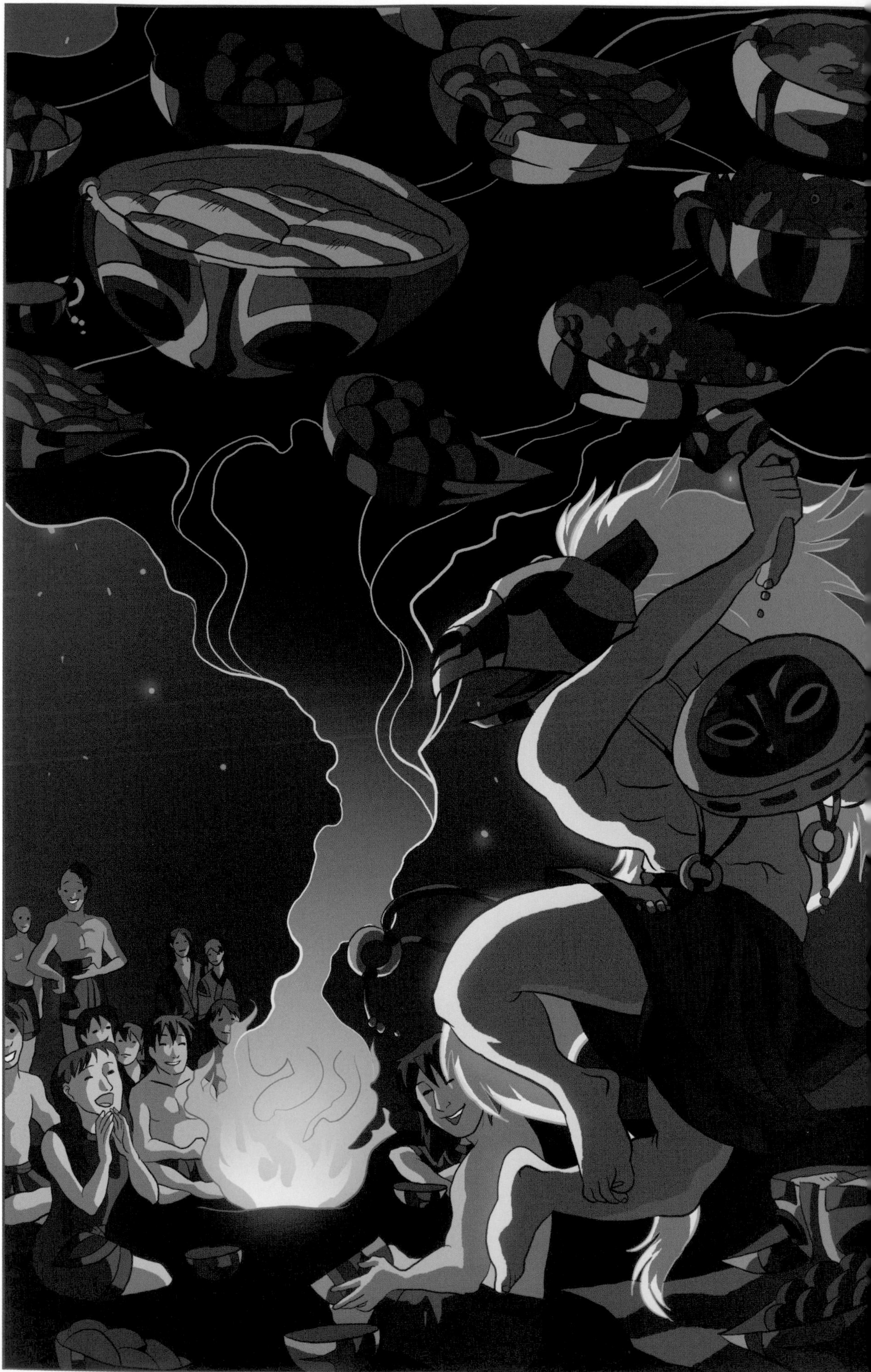

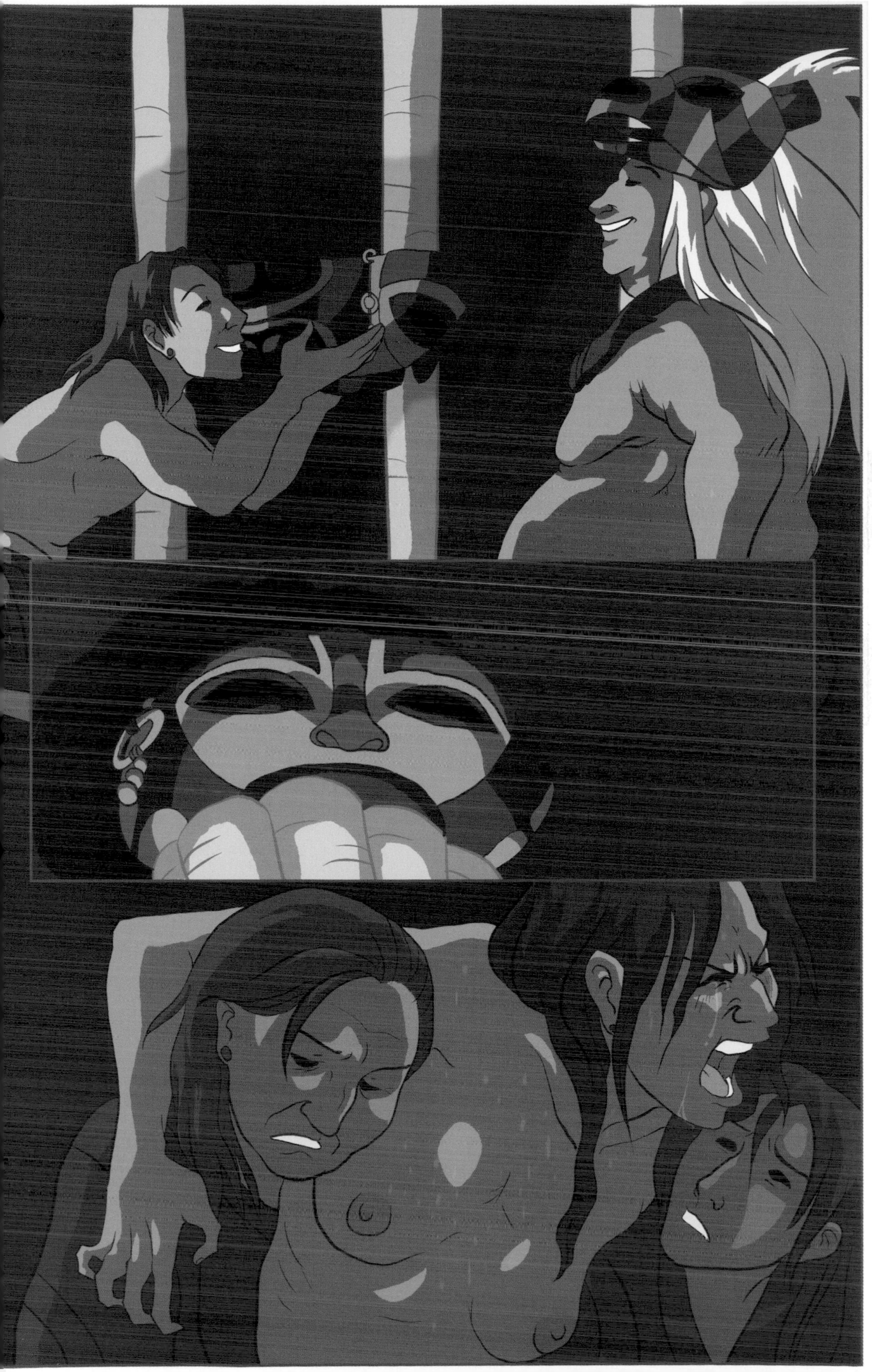

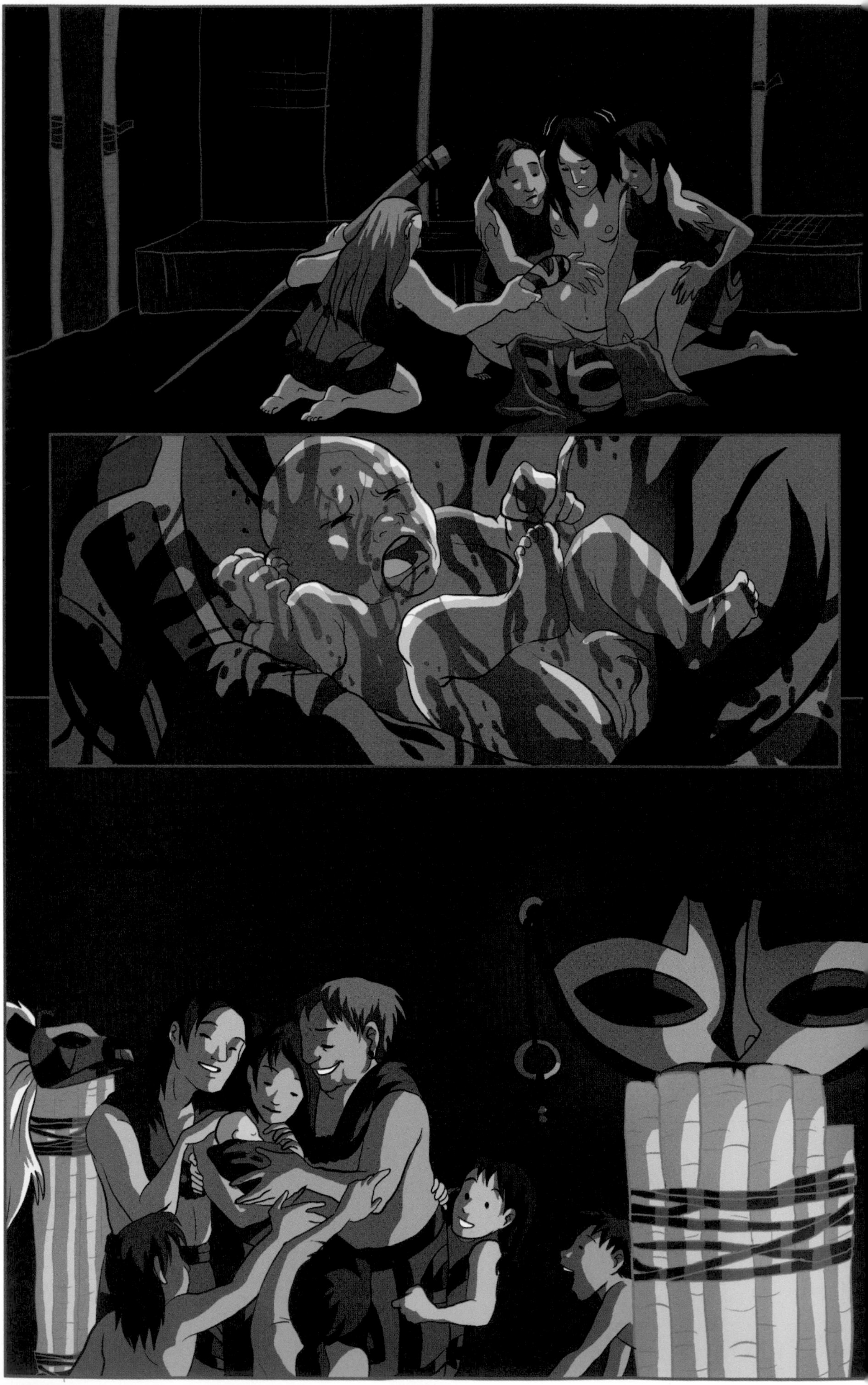

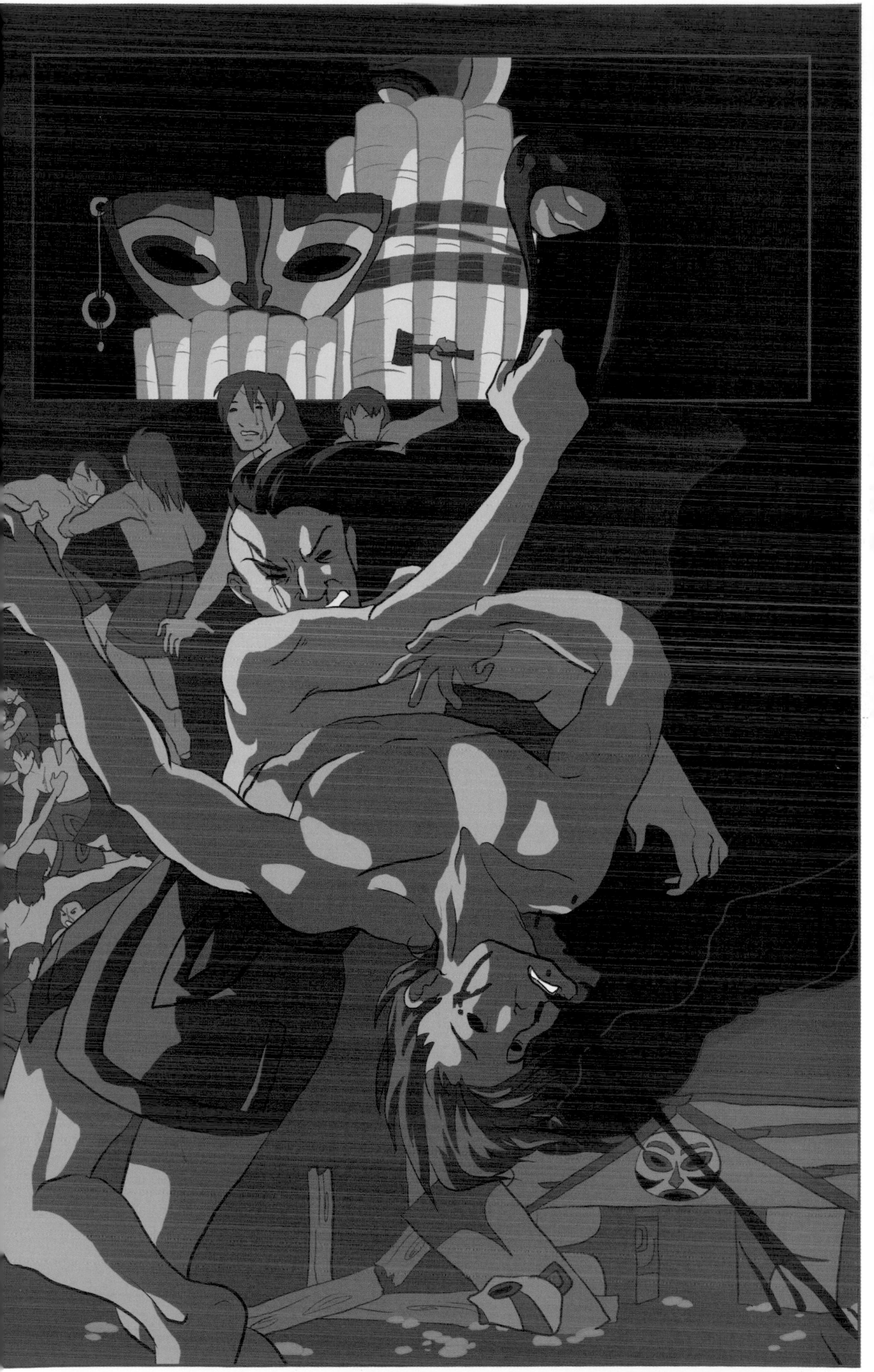

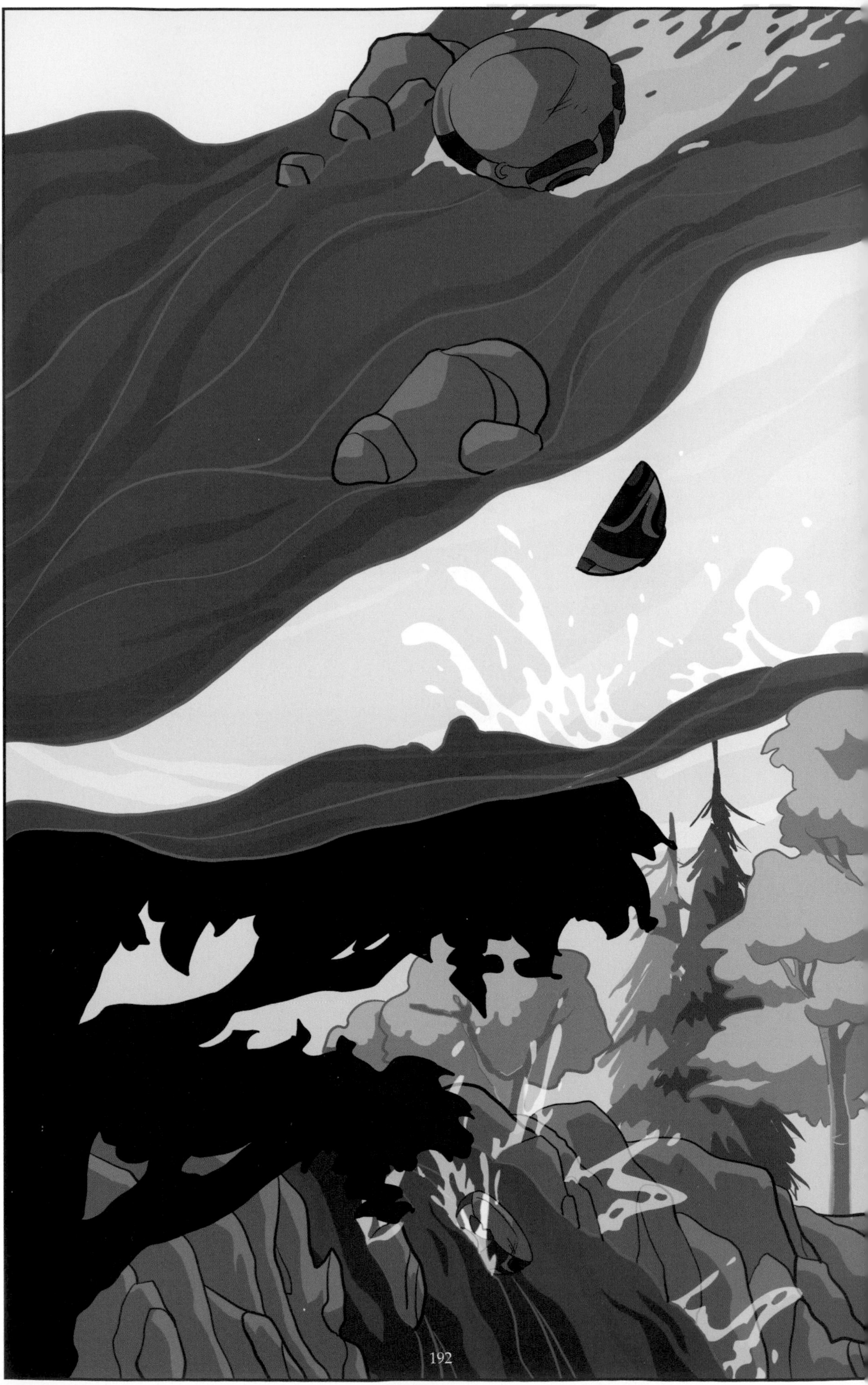

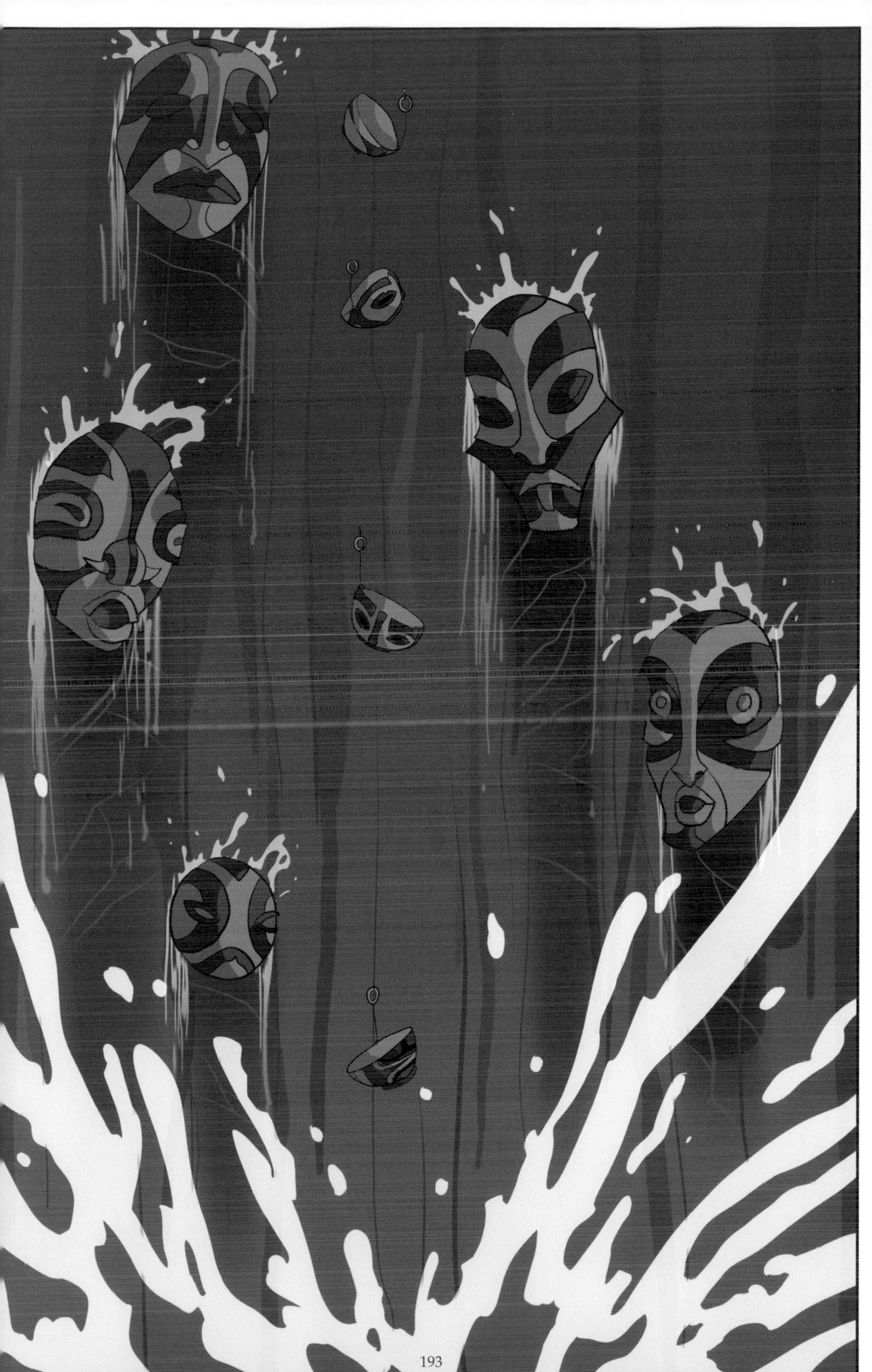

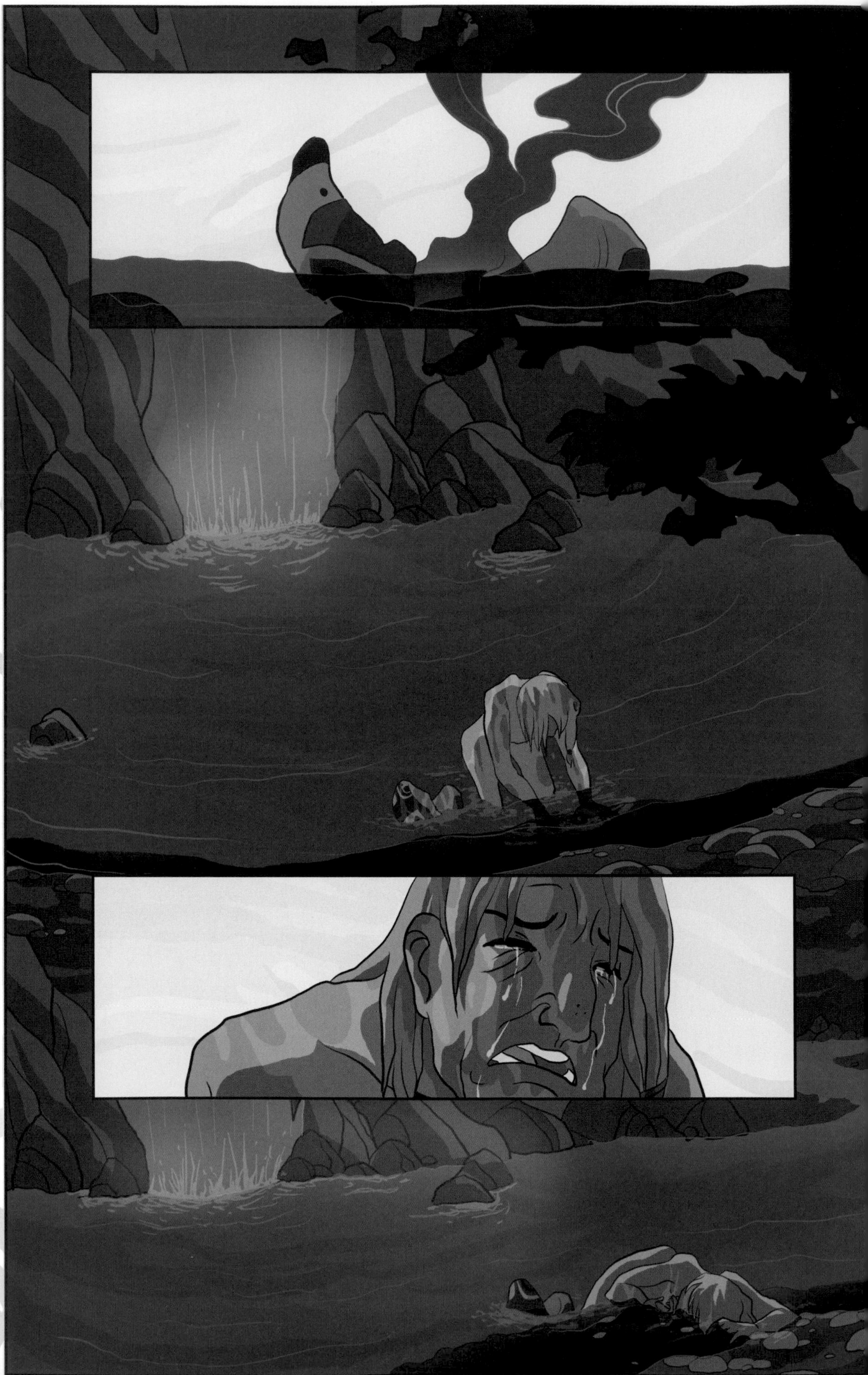

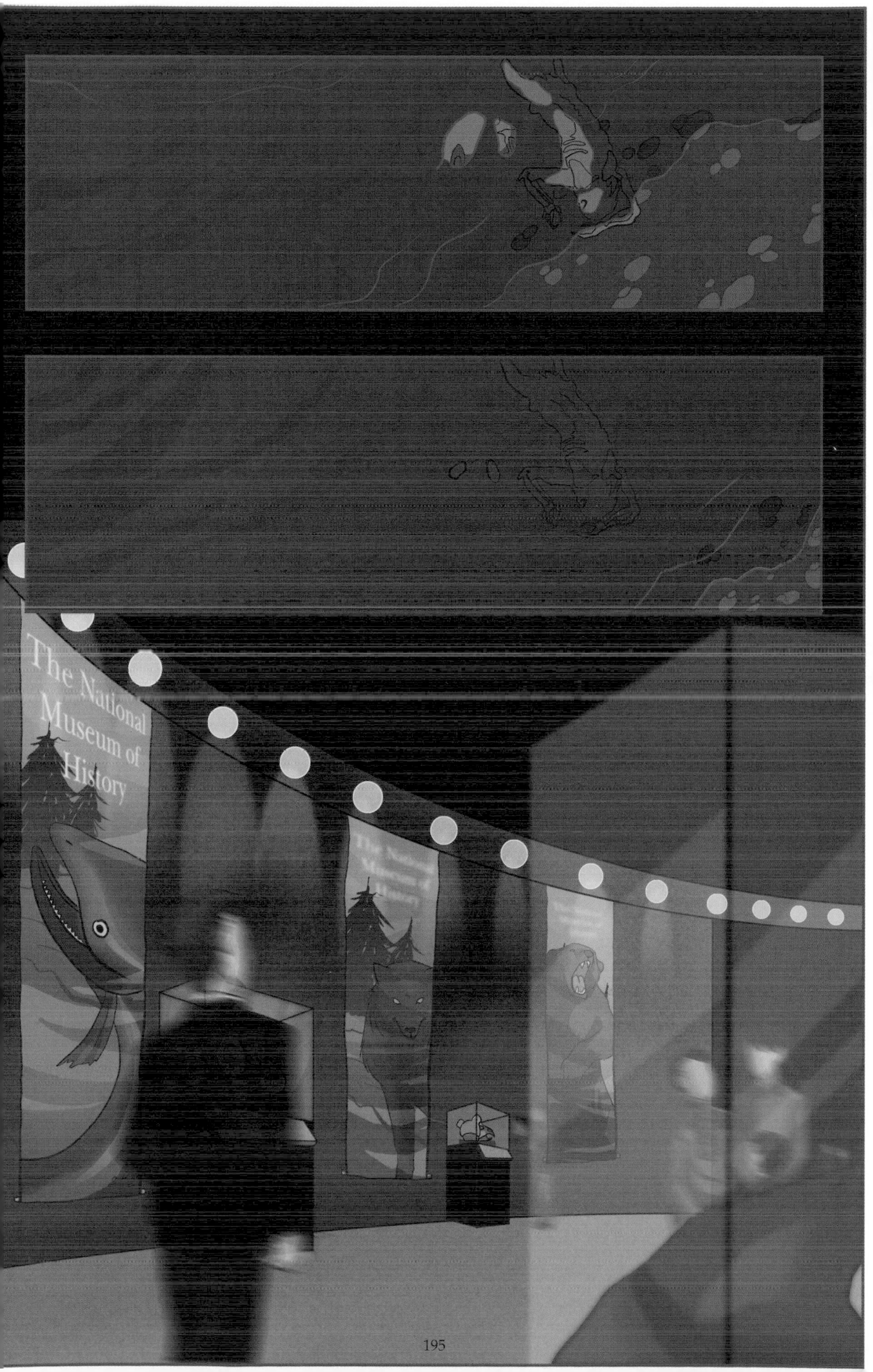
The National Museum of History

The National Museum of History

Bowl
c. 1840

Durnsmith Collection

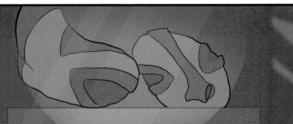

Funding for the extraction of this bowl was generously donated by the Wayne and Mary Durnsmith Association.

Pronounced scratches and calcium residue on the surface and interior of this abnormally large bowl have led researchers to believe that it was used to clean and handle shellfish, and was owned by an elderly man whose body was found alongside the artefact.

Clio Chiang

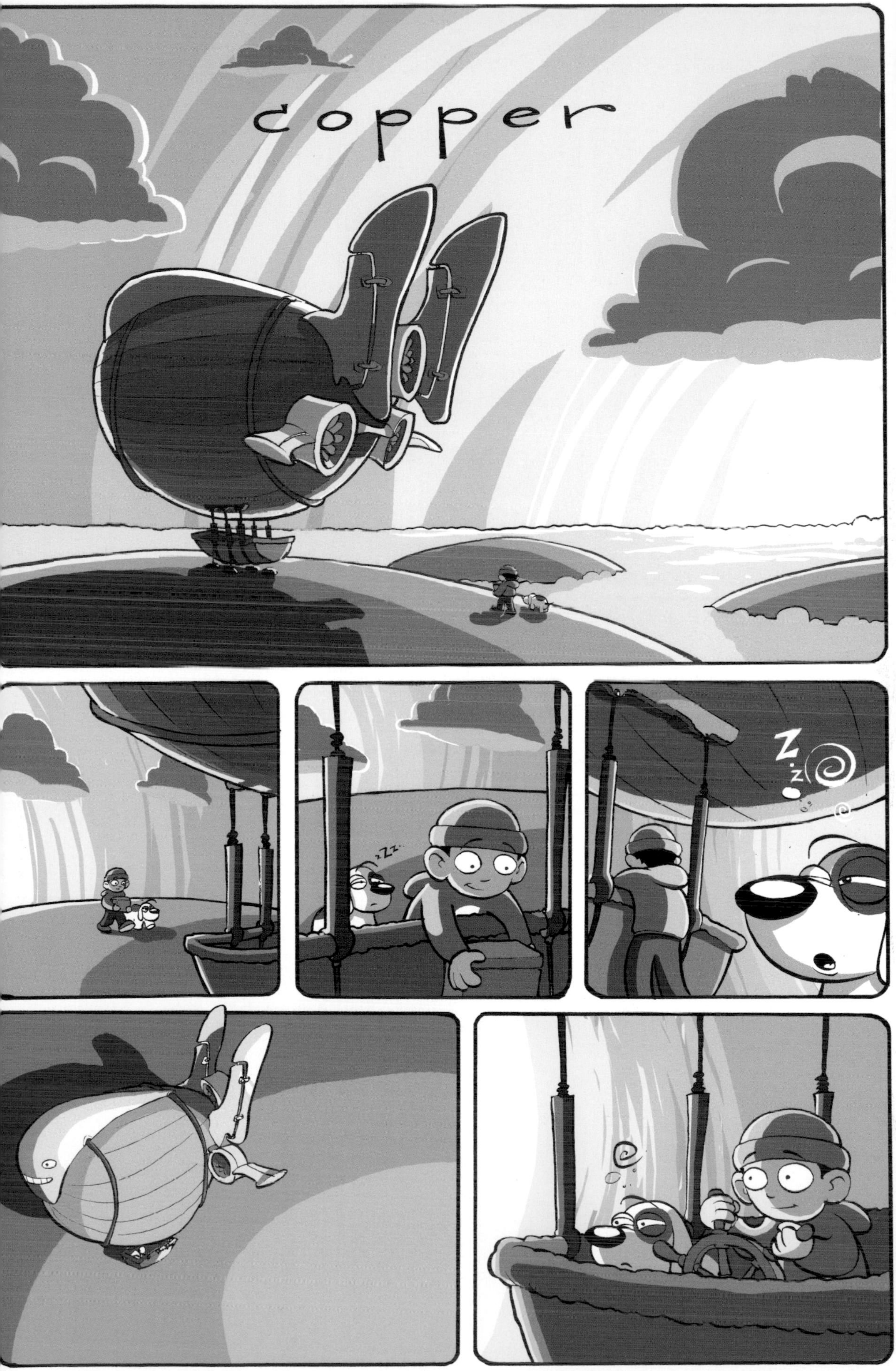
copper
Z z

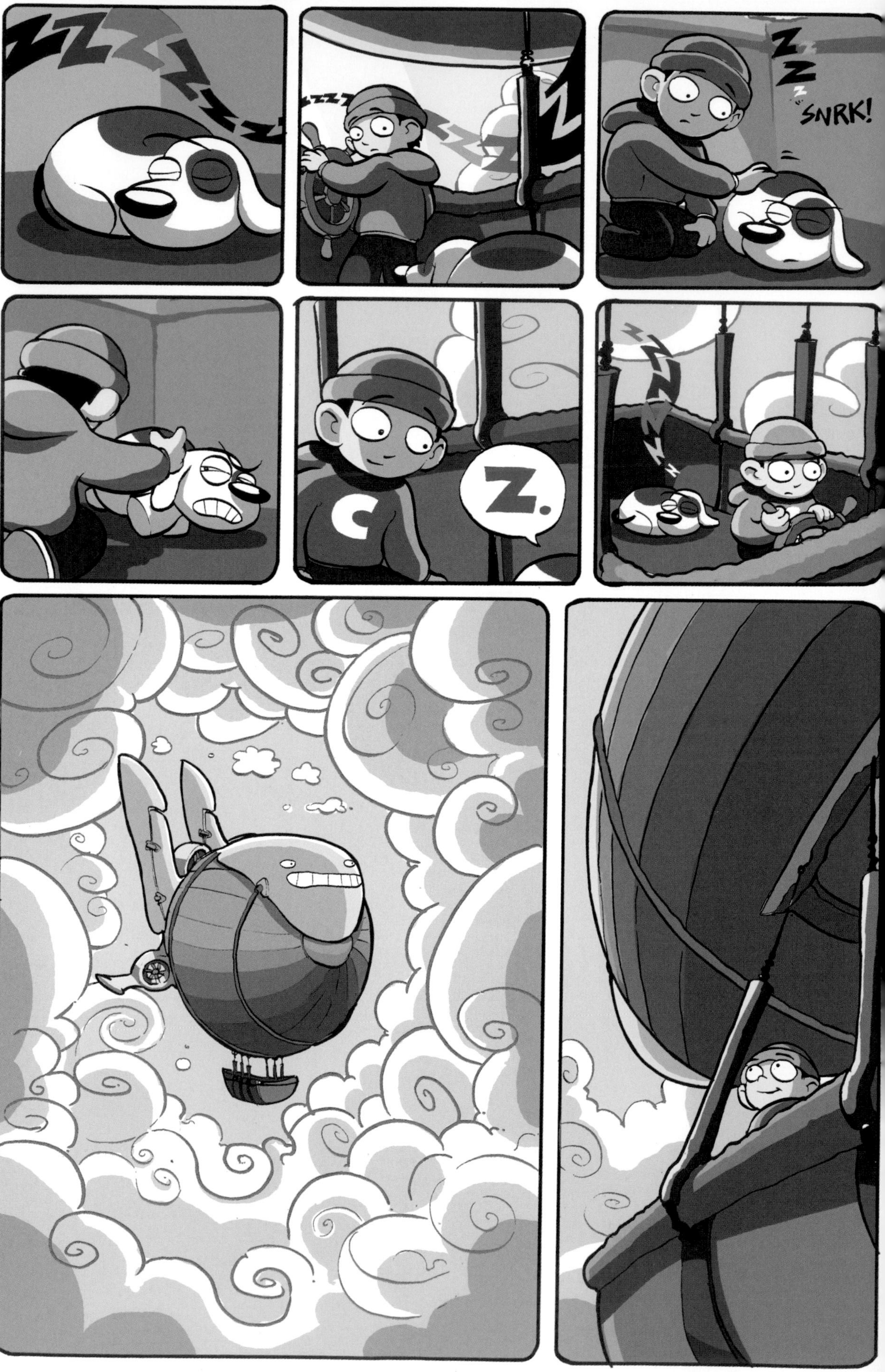
SNRK!
Z.

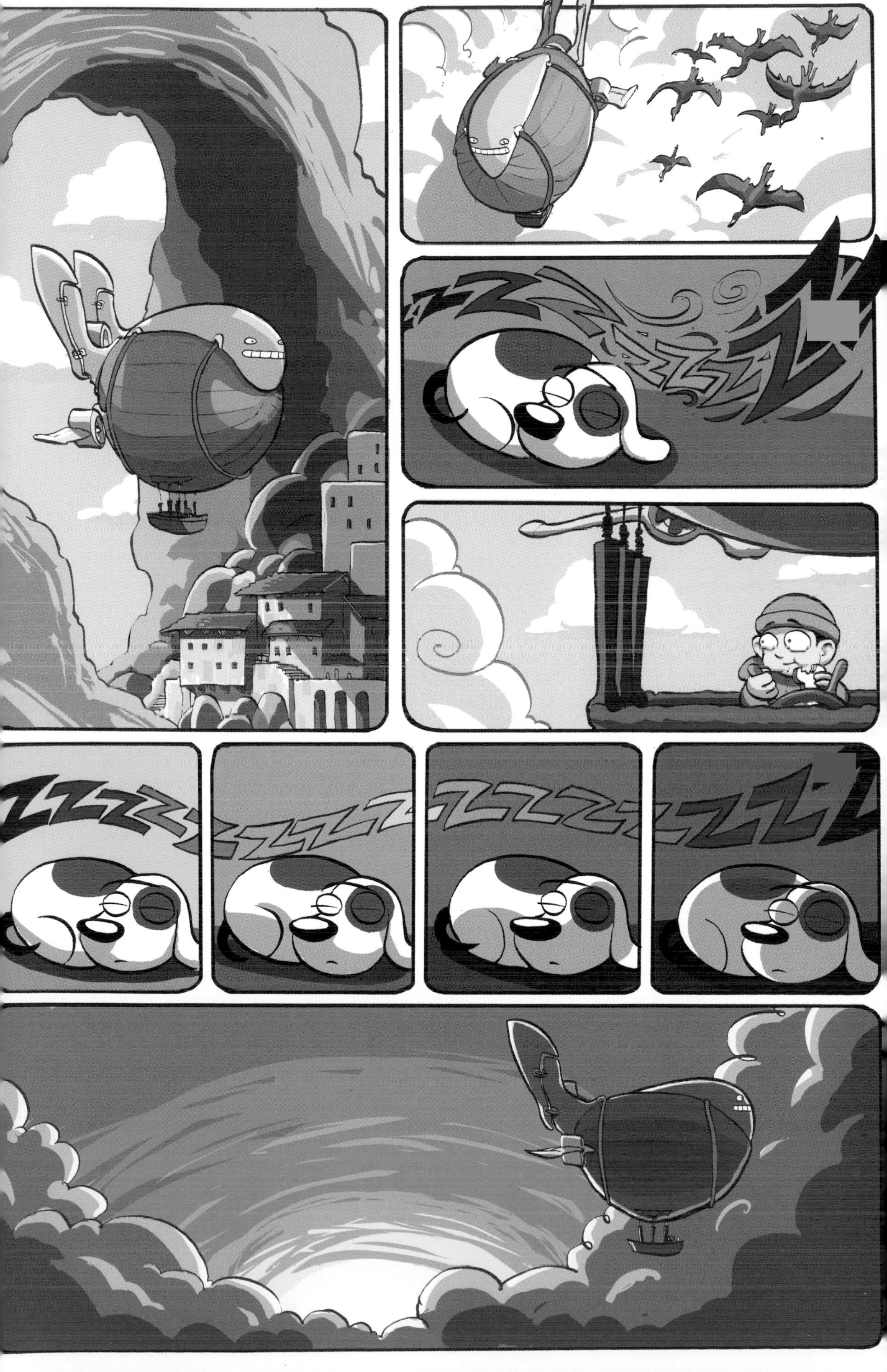

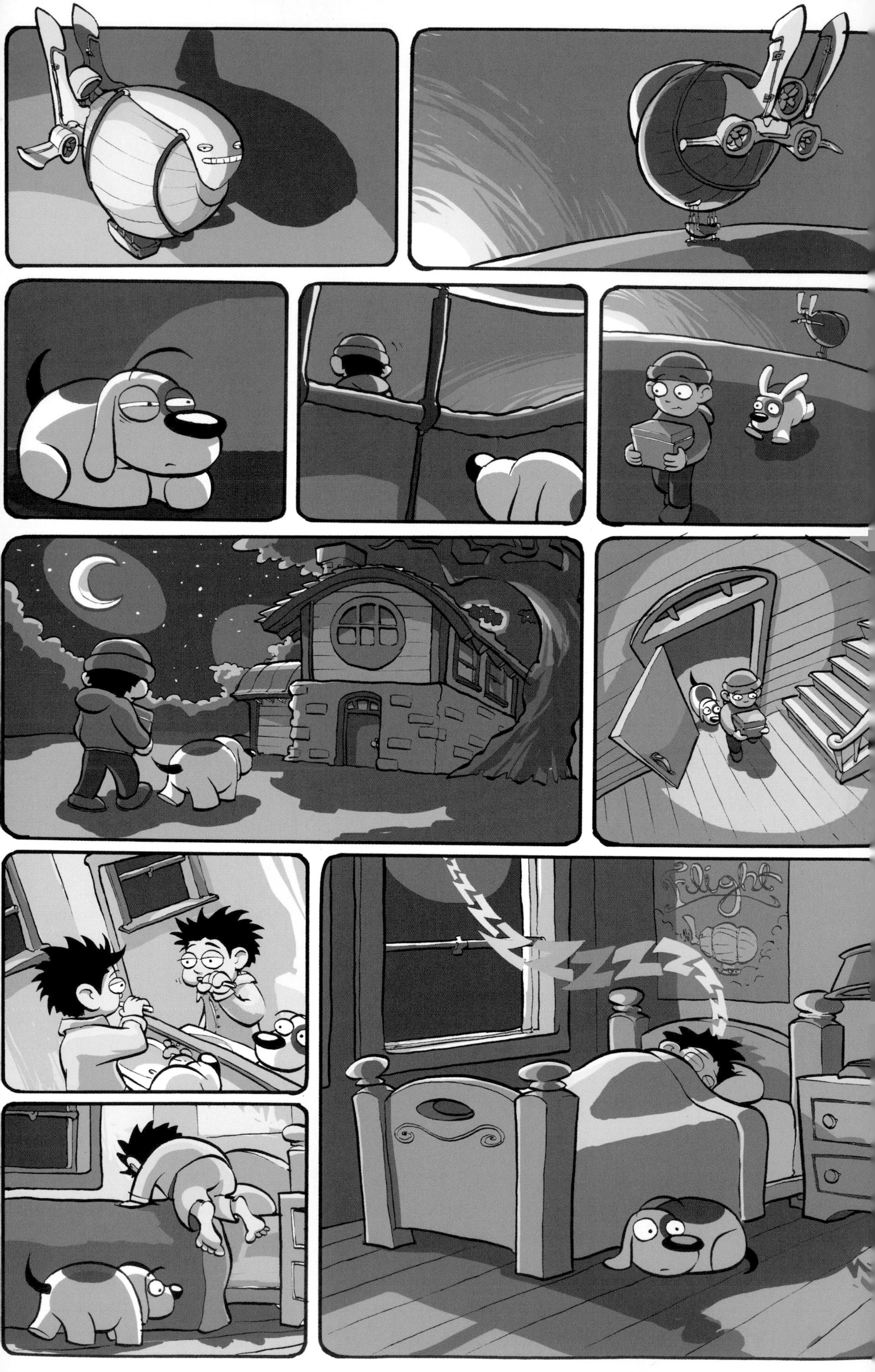
ZZZZZ
Flight

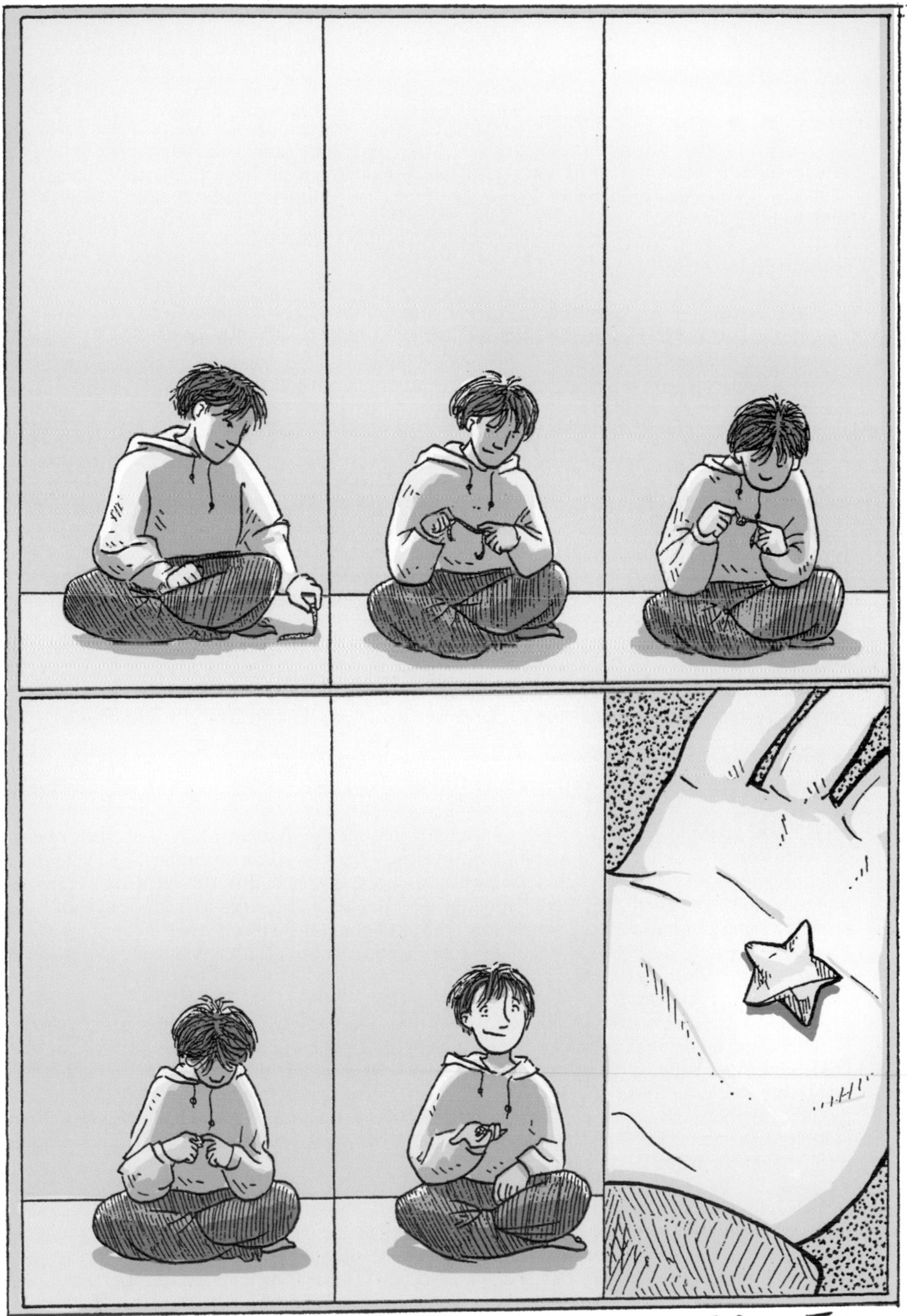

CREATE

THE YEAR THAT COMICS TOOK FLIGHT

By Scott McCloud

Ah, 2004. I remember it well.

Today, fifty years later and with the benefit of hindsight, it's easy to see the historical significance of the *Flight* anthology first published in that year. Many of its contributors would become giants of the comics industry not long after its release, and three would eventually become household names, yet in its day it was seen as just one of several such books, noted for its high quality, but unremarkable in most other respects.

Little did they know.

In 2004, the American comic book industry was barely an industry at all. Just one in a thousand Americans read the comics magazines from their native land. Comics on the Web were beginning to proliferate and the graphic novel was gaining slightly in stature, but many of the best sequential artists, whether in print or online, tended to create comics more for the love of it than as a viable career.

Much has been made of the Comics Renaissance of the twenties (more properly 2017–26), when comics first took their modern shape in the media landscape we know today. But in 2004, that generation was still in grade school, crowding into the manga sections of oversized turn-of-the-century book palaces decorated with giant portraits of dead poets and stocked with snacks and coffee costing a king's ransom. The young adult cartoonists of 2004 were fewer in number, gathering around their flickering primordial screens for the fellowship of one anothers' text diaries ("blogs," as they were known then), and gathering just once or twice a year at small comics conferences to break bread, converse, and exchange quaint gifts such as hand drawings on napkins and homemade knitted articles of clothing.

Yet, few in number though they were, the generation emerging in 2004 managed in a single book to embody four of the most crucial turning points in early twenty-first-century comics culture.

Turning Point #1: The Web Strikes Back

Most of the contributors to *Flight* met one another through the Internet. Many made their reputations through their online work. And for most readers, *Flight* was their first printed encounter with these talented young cartoonists. Yet the barricades between print and Web comics that seemed so important to "Generation Zero" cartoonists like me made little difference to them. They didn't see print as a step up or step down; they didn't try print as the fulfillment of a lifelong dream; they didn't try it as a desperate compromise. Print was simply another way to connect with their readers and to express themselves in a new venue.

That said, it was an astonishing thing for us old-timers to see the way the project came together. Without a second thought, these twenty-two young artists had barreled ahead, completing two hundred color pages before a publisher had even been found, secure in the laughably naive notion that good work would somehow find its level—which, of course, is exactly what happened. Conditioned by their experiences on the Web, none of them waited for permission to create these gems. Their attitude was simple. Step One: Draw the comic. Step Two: See what happens. It's an attitude we take for granted here in 2054, but to printed comics veterans in 2004, it was downright bizarre.

Most laughable of all was their attitude toward color. Color printing was still prohibitively expensive in the early twenty-first-century—and a hellishly complicated challenge to achieve the right effect in the finished product. Yet along comes the *Flight* team, accustomed to having color whenever they damn well pleased and—boom! It's in color. Although it scared the crap out of many a prospective publisher, and certain contributors famously wept when they discovered print's sad inability to represent their beloved screen colors, it was nevertheless the right decision; great care has been taken in this fiftieth anniversary commemorative reprint to faithfully reproduce that original book's colors as they were first seen those many years ago (along with the original editor's foreword by Dr. Kibuishi).

Turning Point #2: The Tribal Shift

In the decade prior to *Flight,* most of the progressive wing of comics was dominated by the Iconoclast and Formalist Tribes. Walking through the turn-of-the-century expositions devoted to "small press" comics, visitors were greeted on one side of the aisle by roughly drawn "zines" about disaffected white youths with bad jobs, failed relationships, and genital warts, and on the other by strange, multidirectional experiments and oddly-shaped cardboard constructions with day-glow silkscreen covers. I loved both types of comics (and make no apologies for my alleged complicity in the latter) but by 2004, a change was clearly in the air.

The return of the other two tribes to independent comics found its focus in *Flight.* The Animists' love of pure transparent storytelling and the Classicists' attention to craft and enduringly beautiful settings was evident on many of the anthology's pages. While so many of the previous generation's revolutionaries had put raw honesty and innovation over straightforward plots and surface gloss, the *Flight* contributors tried to have it all—and in several cases succeeded. *Flight* gave readers something to read and something beautiful to look at again and again. For all the innovations of the rebel tribes, it was this kind of appeal to a broader readership that comics desperately needed in 2004. These artists delivered.

Turning Point #3: The Metabolization of Manga

Although manga and anime would have their strongest and most lasting effect on the generation that followed *Flight,* the artists in this historic anthology were among the first to have taken an early appreciation for Japanese storytelling and transcended it through their own fully realized personal styles. As the great Japanese artist Hayao Miyazaki had gobbled up and fully metabolized the European world-building aesthetic of artists such as Moebius, so too did the *Flight* contributors gobble up and metabolize Miyazaki and his ilk. The result was markedly American in some cases, but also profoundly international in spirit-the beginnings of a trend that has continued to this day.

No big-eyed schoolgirls or sword-wielding samurais were in attendance when these stories were conceived. No parodies. No slavish imitations of favorite styles. A few influences float to the surface here and there, but for the most part these are young artists who've learned from their heroes and moved on.

Turning Point #4: The Changing Face of Comics

After an entire century of male-domination in the print comics field, the Web cartoonist community was in the process of an astonishingly rapid correction in 2004, and this was their first foray into the boys' club of print. Although not quite half of the contributors to *Flight* were women, the roster included several of the very artists who would quietly lead an army of their sisters onto the field just a few short years later (resulting in the male underrepresentation crisis of the late twenties, I might add . . . but let's not open that old can of worms).

The face of comics was changing in other ways, too. In 2004 the comics field was ruled by the concepts of "mainstream" and "alternative" comics ("mainstream" at the time meaning a rather stagnant collection of companies specializing only in superhero comics, perversely enough), but *Flight* turned the idea on its side, creating a work clearly designed to appeal to a broad audience, without merely aping the status quo of its day. It wasn't the first time such a thing had been tried, but it had been never done so well. It was at this point in comics' development that a tipping point was reached and the explosion in diversity of genre that followed not long after may well have found its fuse in this book.

Four turning points of comics history in a single publication. Not bad, considering the casual spirit in which it was created five decades ago! But we have the advantage of hindsight, don't we? Fifty years of after-the-fact reasons to admire the book. Did it seem like a big event at the time? No. Not to most. Not at first. But it was to the contributors themselves. And it was to me, because I had an inkling of the revolutions it might trigger.

Ah, but I'd be lying if I said that aesthetics was the only reason that *Flight* was an important publication to me. Because unlike many of you, I had the privilege of meeting many of the contributors around this time, and now I remember them not just as industry figures and artistic demigods. I remember them as people.

I can see their faces even now: Dr. Kibuishi—still just "Kazu" to his friends—before all the Claire Danes stories threatened to eclipse his many accomplishments (and no, whatever you may have read, he did not lead her on in the least and the restraining order against Ms. Danes was entirely justified). Professor Meconis, still just an undergrad, but already writing up a storm, hand in a brace like everybody else that season, her great American graphic novel just some scribbled notes in a drawer. And the Legendary Mudron. Fresh-faced and cheerful; long before the Barcelona incident . . .

The world knows them as the grand old men and women of comics. Yet when this anthology was published in 2004, the average age of the contributors was just twenty-four—their whole careers still ahead of them. And that's how they're frozen forever in my mind. Laughing around a dinner table, karate chopping the air for passing cameras; or relaxing under a billowing white canopy beside a grand tentieth-century convention hall on a long summer afternoon.

Fifty years ago, and it seems like only yesterday.

Scott McCloud's Brain
Sri Lanka, 2054

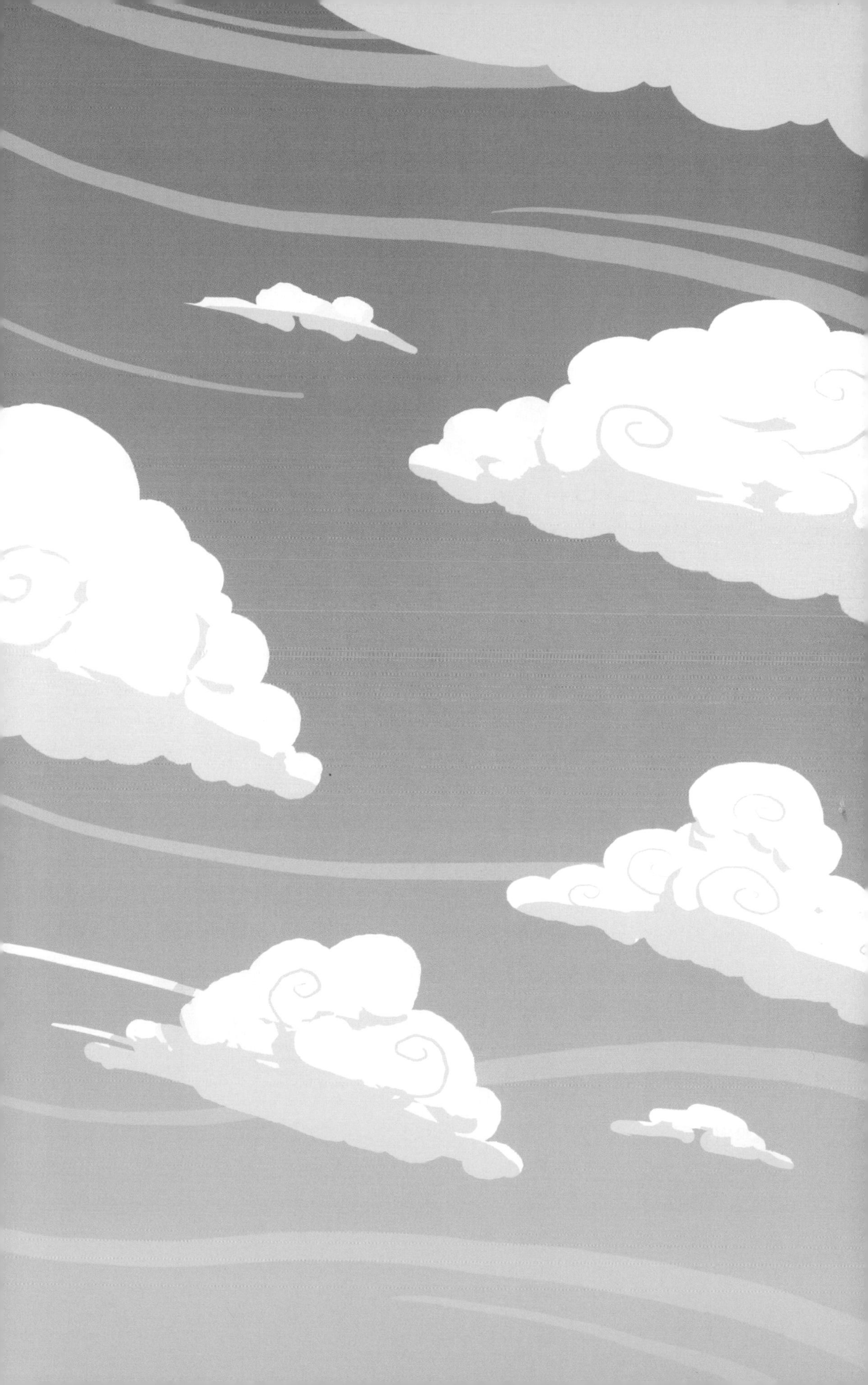

FLIGHT: VOLUME ONE CONTRIBUTORS

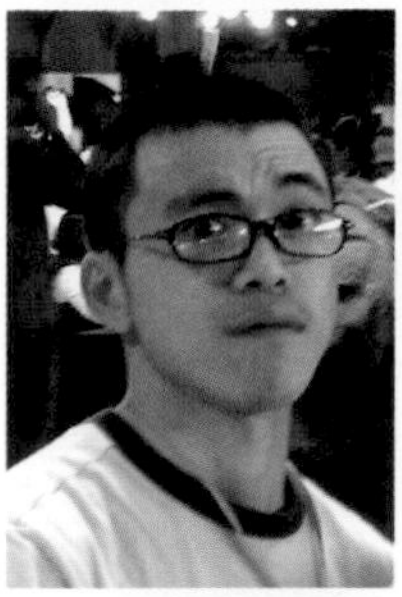
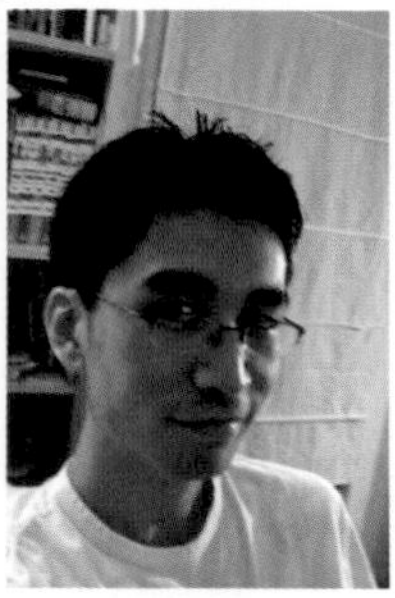
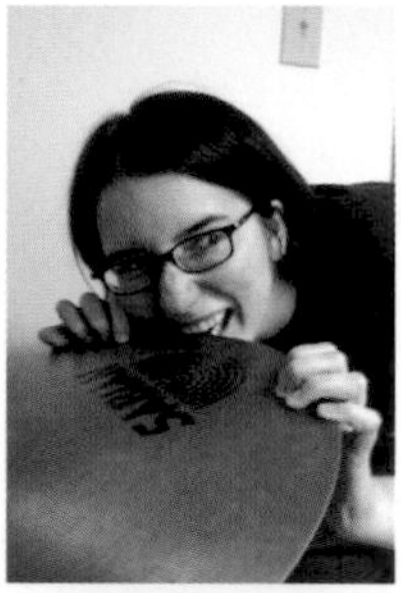
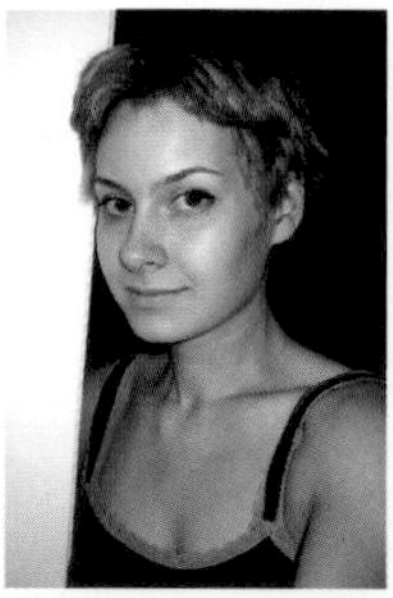
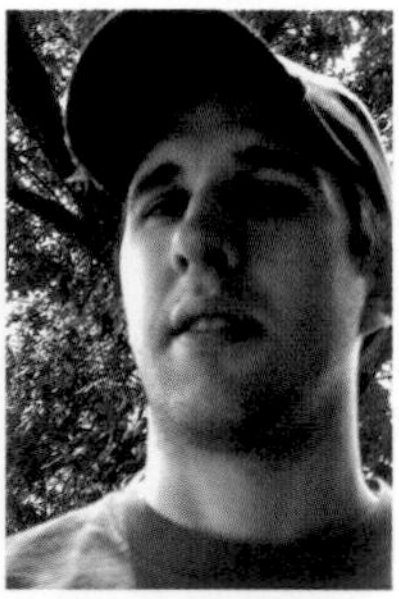
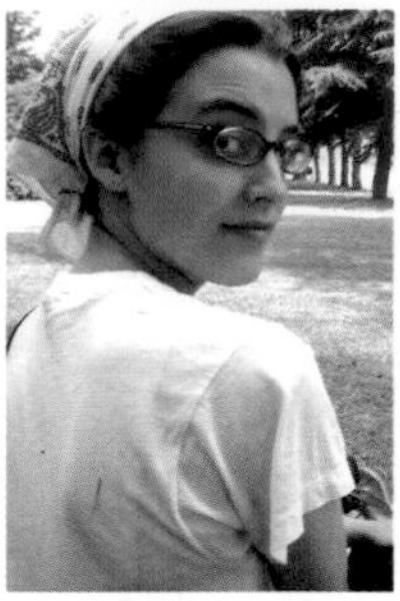
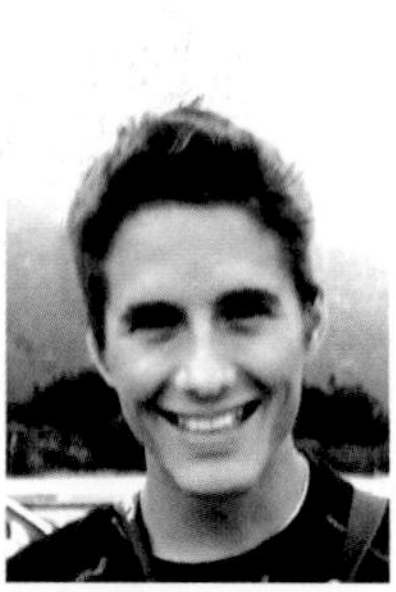
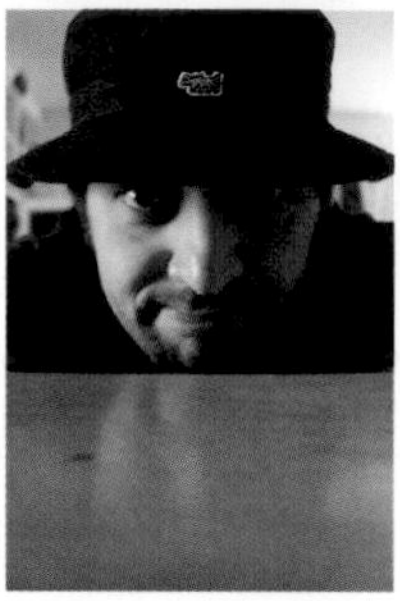
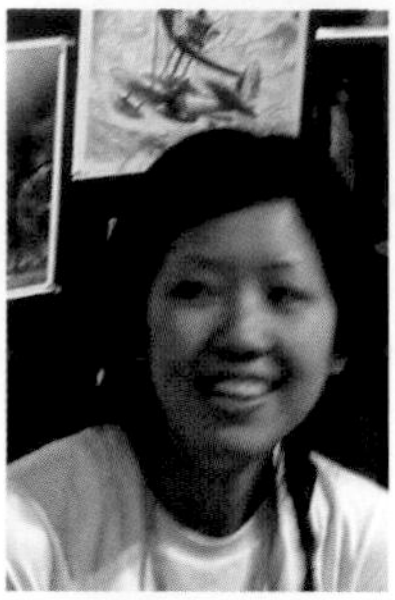
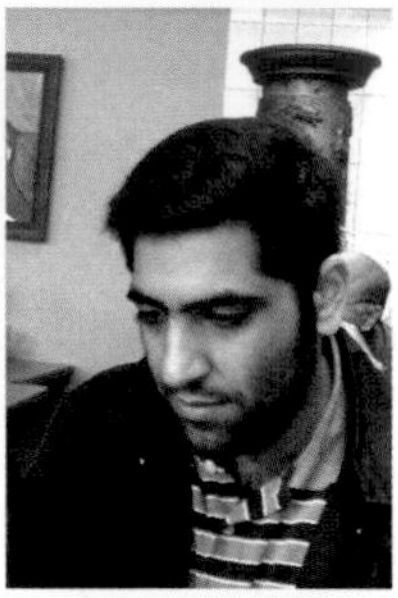
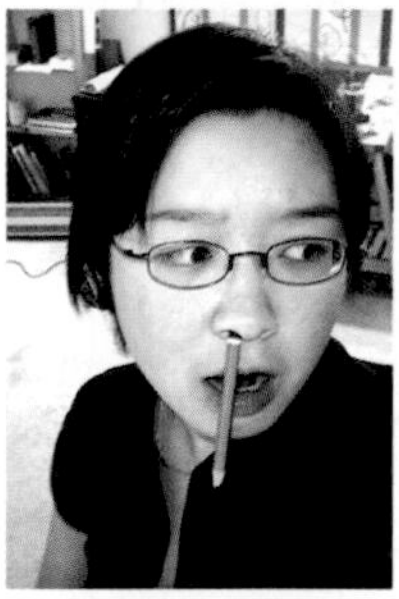
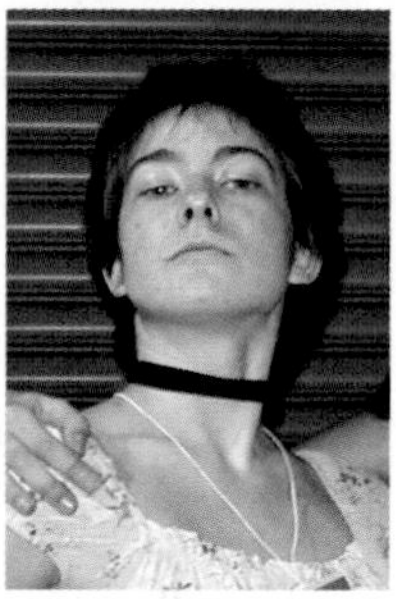
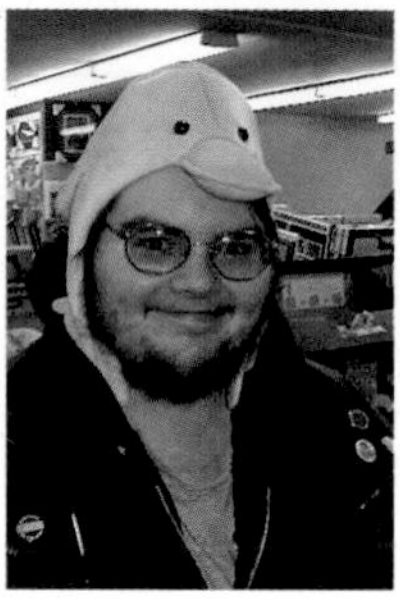
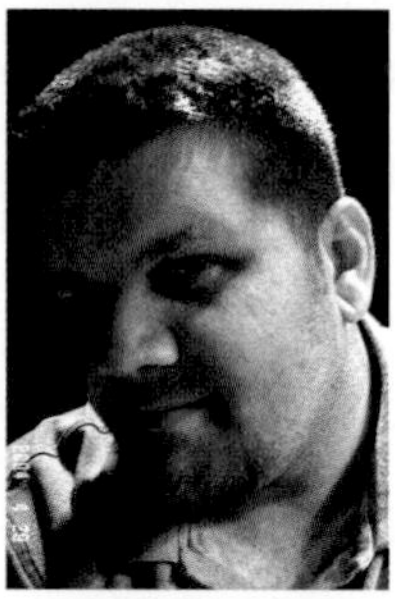
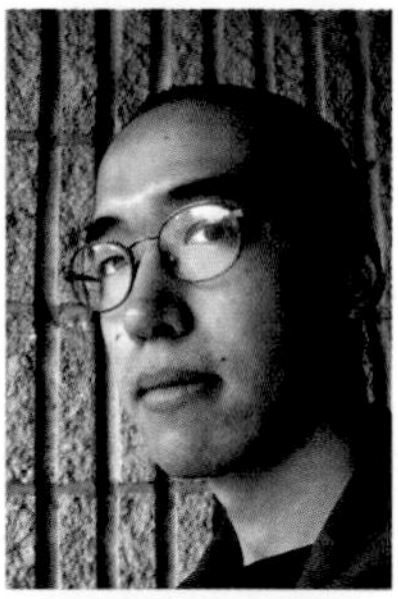
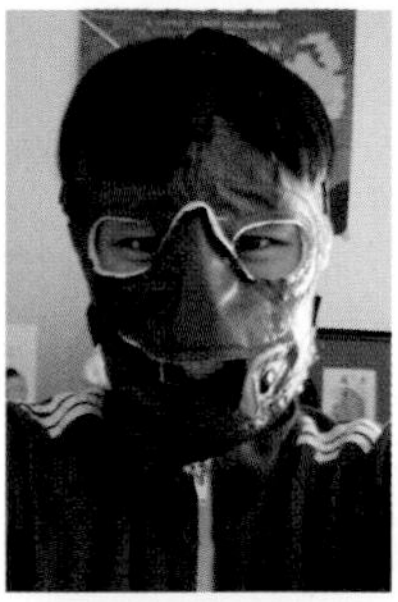
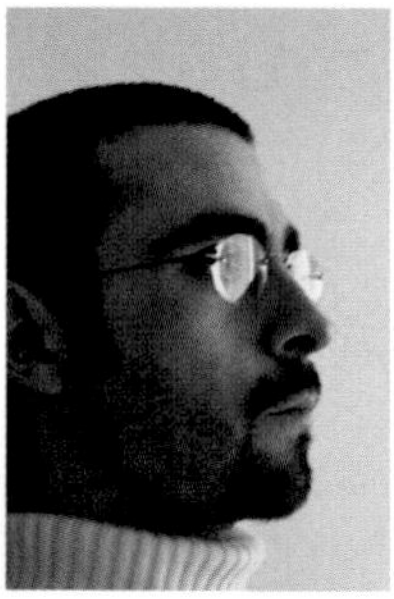
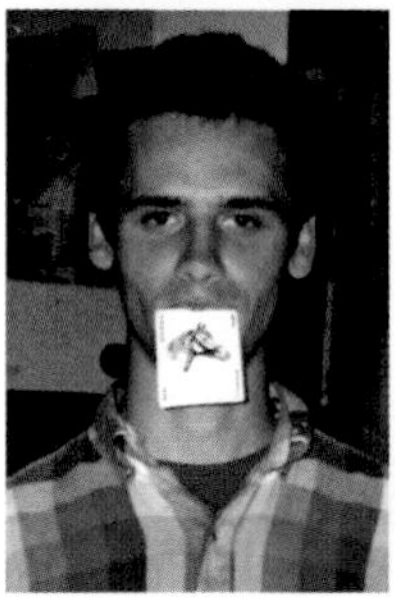
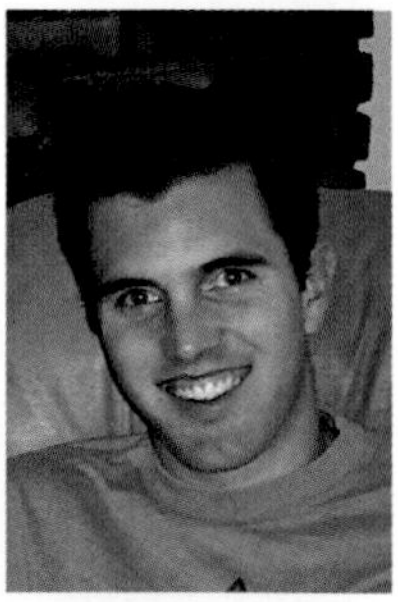
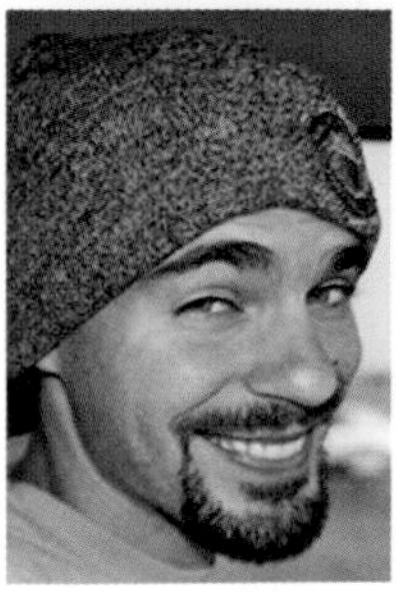

From left to right:

Top Row: Khang Le, Kazu Kibuishi, Vera Brosgol, Hope Larson, and Jake Parker. **2nd Row:** Dylan Meconis, Chris Appelhans, Enrico Casarosa, Catia Chien, and Neil Babra. **3rd Row:** Clio Chang, Erika Moen, Bill Mudron, Joel Carroll, and Kean Soo. **4th Row:** Derek Kirk Kim, Bengal, Jacob Magraw-Mickelson, and Rad Sechrist. **Bottom Row:** Phil Craven and Jen Wang

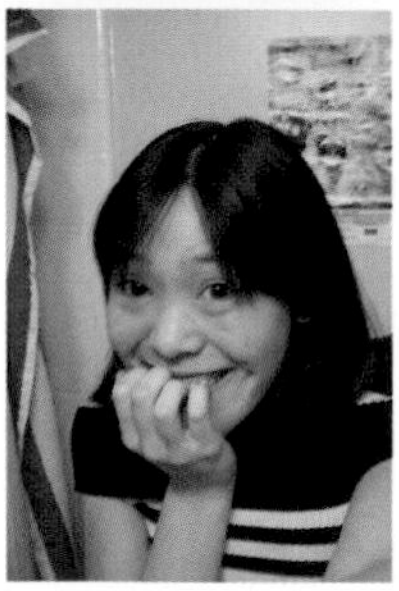

Bengal, a French comicker, designer, and illustrator, is twenty-seven years old and lives in Paris. His first graphic novel, *meka,* was recently released in France. He is currently working on several new projects.
www.cafesale.net/bengal

Bill Mudron is just a man, with a man's courage. He knows nothing but a man, but he can never fail. He's also twenty-eight years old, hails from Pittsburgh, Pennsylvania, and eats babies.
www.excelsiorstudios.net

Catia Chien was born and raised in Brazil and read comics ever since she was a wee little girl. She remembers making up stories and getting in trouble for drawing on walls. As she joins the line of starving artists to become one herself, she feels lucky to be pursuing a career doing something she truly loves.
www.catiachien.com

Clio Chiang is twenty-two, a grad of UBC in fine arts, and is currently learning traditional animation. She lives in Vancouver, B.C., with two cannibalistic koi.
www.verunne.net

Chris Appelhans survived teenage stardom and a career as a male dancer to become a well-fed writer/illustrator/ musician in Pasadena, California.
www.froghatstudios.com

Derek Kirk Kim pukes comics at lowbright.com. When he was in sixth grade he went a whole week without taking a dump.

Dylan Meconis is a rare species of dolphin found only in the Pacific Northwest region. Nevertheless, she has been known to colonize as far as Wesleyan University in Connecticut, where she is nourished on raw kelp, hapless tuna, and the pages of comic books thrown into the sea by careless sailors. projectkooky.com/dylan/

Enrico Casarosa lives in San Francisco, making a living as a storyboard artist at Pixar Animation studios. He no longer lives off pasta and Japanese cartoons as he used to back in Italy. Sadly, while he still watches the occasional anime, he developed a wheat allergy. He does, however, love his new hat. www.enricocasarosa.com

By the time this book is published, **Erika Moen** will have turned twenty-one years old; both events shall be heavily celebrated with cheap booze, running around in circles, and gratuitus lapdances from Mudron. While she may be something of an idiot, she is nonetheless an enchanting lotus blossom of femininity who enjoys biting her nails. www.projectkooky.com/erika/

Hope Larson, twenty-one, is a recent graduate from the School of the Art Institute of Chicago. She promises a story of her own next time around.
http://thingwithfeathers.com

Jake Parker was born in 1977. Despite showing signs of great promise from an early age, he became an artist. He lives comfortably in Texas with his classy wife and two above average children. He is still trying to prove that you can indeed make a living as an artist.
www.agent44.com

Jacob Magraw-Mickelson lives in the Pacific Northwest and currently attends Art Center College of Design.

Jen Wang is twenty, but was nineteen when the comic was completed. She lives in San Francisco where owning ferrets is illegal, but Korean music video countdown is on every weekend, so that's okay.
http://www.stringsoffate.com/art

Joel Carroll, thirty-one, is a five-year veteran of video game development, and now tries his hands at creating comics, caught in the debilitating and unemployment-inducing "Flight Effect." He thanks his beloved Mamy for years of support.
www.joelcarroll.com

Kazu Kibuishi is a twenty-six-year-old writer and illustrator of comics and films. He is the editor and art director of *Flight:* Volume One, the creator of Copper, and the writer/illustrator of the upcoming *Daisy Kutter* four-issue miniseries. Kazu lives and works in Pasadena, California. He also makes the *Flight* artists write their own bios, because he's lazy.
www.boltcity.com

Born in the United Kingdom, **Kean Soo** grew up in the urban jungle of Hong Kong and currently calls Toronto home. With a degree in electrical engineering, he spends his time listening to an unhealthy amount of music and finds it extremely difficult to take anyone who talks in the third person seriously.
www.keaner.net/

Khang Le grew up in the jungles of Saigon, Vietnam. He failed to pass his SATs, so he's pursuing an illustration career instead. He will eventually graduate from the Art Center College of Design in Pasadena and plans to open his own restaurant, Pho Khang Good.

Neil Babra is a twenty-five-year-old grad student escaping from Pittsburgh, Pennsylvania, where he lives all by himself. Making art and telling stories is an essential avocation for him these days.
http://neilcomics.com and http://serializer.net

Phil Craven earned an MFA in sequential art from Savannah College of Art and Design in his home state of Georgia. He now lives on the West Coast, making comics and drawing storyboards for animation.
www.bluepillow.net

Rad Sechrist is a twenty-three-year-old graduating mechanical engineer, who is leaving engineering behind to pursue a career in cartooning. In addition to *Flight,* he is also contributing a short story to the *Daisy Kutter* miniseries created by his friend Kazu.
www.radsechrist.com

Vera Brosgol is nineteen and studying classical animation in Oakville, Ontario. She is currently rocking out on a disposable income, but comics should soon change that.
http://art.lunistice.com

Let Your Imagination Take Flight!

Now available from Villard Books:
every volume of this groundbreaking anthology.

Savor the work of today's top illustrators—
complete your FLIGHT library today.

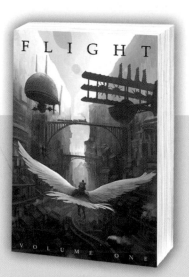

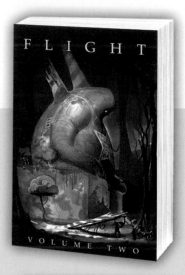